61641

GN
485
.S5
1970

Simmons, Leo William, 1897-
    The role of the aged in primitive
society, by Leo W. Simmons. [Ham-
den, Conn.] Archon Books, 1970
[c1945]
    vi, 317 p. map. 23 cm.

    Bibliography: p. [293]-308.

    1. Old age. 2. Society, Primi-
tive. I. Title.

GN485.S5 1970   301.43'5
ISBN 0-208-00824-1
                                            74-103998
                                            MARC
Library of Congress
0 3422   o   827789   B   © THE BAKER & TAYLOR CO.   6304

THE
ROLE OF THE AGED
IN
PRIMITIVE SOCIETY

BY
LEO W. SIMMONS

ARCHON BOOKS
1970

SBN: 208 00824 1
Library of Congress Catalog Card Number: 74-103998
Printed in the United States of America

To
EUGEN KAHN

PREFACE

THIS is a report on the status and treatment of the aged within a world-wide selection of primitive societies. The chief question is: What in old age are the possible adjustments to different environments, both physical and social, and what uniformities or general trends may be observed in such a broad cross-cultural analysis? More specifically, what securities for long life may be provided by the various social milieus and what may the aged do as individuals to safeguard their interests?

The twofold aspect of the problem is well expressed in the word *role*, and especially with Linton's connotations of ascribed and achieved status.[1] The purpose is to study the ways in which various primitive societies have ascribed positions of security and prestige to the aged, and in what ways old people have been able to achieve such stakes through personal initiative. So stated, the question implies that in the general process of adjustment there is an interplay of impersonal, automatic forces on the one hand, and very personal, conscious efforts on the other. Attention is focused upon this interplay.

In the selection of peoples and cultures the range of variables on what appears to be the impersonal side of adjustment is exceedingly wide and complex. But in the midst of all this diversity the main problems remain rather constant, and the broad general patterns prove to be simple and relatively uniform—indeed, they seem quite predictable and all but inevitable in an over-all view.

Or when the problem is examined from the side of personal variations and adaptations, it appears that almost every possible expedient has been tried out by different individuals in attempts to safeguard their interests. But even here there is a noticeable degree of uniformity in what persons may or may not do to gain advantage under certain conditions. This is especially true within a given social setting, but it also holds to a large degree for a broad and more variable cultural background.

Perhaps the main value of such a study as this lies in the fact that an over-all comparative analysis tends to reveal and to test apparent uniformities that cut across and underlie the separate

1. Linton (176), pp. 113–131.

cultural unities. Special emphasis will be placed upon such general trends and their implications for old-age security.

For any scientific merits which this treatise may possess, gratitude should be expressed to four persons in particular: to Albert G. Keller, the most stimulating teacher I have known; to Maurice R. Davie, an ever-constant guide and support; to Dr. Eugen Kahn, a good friend and counselor; and to Raymond Kennedy, a valuable colleague whose editorial pen has touched and improved almost every page.

L. W. S.

September 20, 1945

CONTENTS

TABLES

RESEARCH PROCEDURE

THIS study began with a random selection of ethnographic and historical data on the status and treatment of the aged in widely different societies. A preliminary analysis of the material revealed significant contrasts on the basis of sex alone. In addition to this, marked differences appeared which seemed to be correlated with the particular characteristics of various groups; such, for example, as geographic factors, climate, the degree of permanence in residence, type of economic organization, form of kinship system, and possibly the degree of religious development.

A plan was thus devised to go rather fully into the natural and cultural backgrounds of every group of people selected for intensive study and to make a statistical test of a wide range of possible correlations. One hundred and nine physical and cultural characteristics (called traits for convenience) were eventually selected and listed roughly in three groups: (a) habitat, maintenance, and economy; (b) political and social organization; (c) religious and miscellaneous beliefs and practices. The plan was to test correlations between these, any one with another, in order to discover general trends, and then to draw correlations between them and the various characteristics found to be associated with the status and treatment of the aged. It should be stated that these general background traits were selected in something of a hit-and-miss manner, for there were no comparable studies of this type on old age which might serve as a guide (see Table I, pp. 2–3).*

The next step was to list the special characteristics which were found to be related to the status and treatment of the aged. This selection of traits was made on a more empirical basis, since a large amount of general data on old age had been assembled and analyzed.

* See John Koty, *Die Behandlung der Alten und Kranken bei den Naturvölkern.* Stuttgart, 1933.

TABLE I

Trait List

A. *Habitat, Maintenance, and Economy*

1. Permanency of residence
2. Group life in contrast to atomism
3. Durability of dwellings
4. Communal houses
5. Separate men's house
6. Collection
7. Hunting
8. Fishing
9. Herding
10. Agriculture
11. Use of grain for food
12. Constancy of food supply
13. Domesticated animals (other than herded)
14. Mining and smelting of metals
15. Metals secured from outside
16. Pottery
17. Basketry
18. Weaving
19. Manufacture of bark cloth
20. Use of bow and arrow
21. Use of spear-thrower
22. Use of blowgun
23. Slavery
24. Debt-relations
25. Trade
26. Money, or a standard medium of exchange
27. Communal ownership of land
28. Private property in objects other than land
29. Private property in land
30. Communal sharing of food

B. *Political and Social Organization*

31. Power vested in the chief
32. Government by general assembly
33. Government by restricted council
34. Influence of women in government
35. Secret societies
36. Prevalence of warfare
37. Practice of blood-revenge
38. Codified laws
39. Group responsibility for crimes
40. Authority of judges
41. Fines paid to judges
42. Matrilocal residence
43. Patrilocal residence
44. Matrilineal descent
45. Patrilineal descent
46. Matrilineal inheritance
47. Patrilineal inheritance
48. Matrilineal succession
49. Patrilineal succession
50. Matripotestal family authority
51. Patripotestal family authority
52. Avunculate
53. Ownership of dwelling by wife
54. Age-grades
55. Hereditary castes and classes
56. Plutocracy
57. Exogamy with reference to kin-group
58. Exogamy with reference to local group
59. Group-marriage
60. Polyandry
61. Polygyny
62. Monogamy
63. Betrothal of infants and children

64. Marriage by consent of parents, ruler, uncle (lack of freedom of choice in marriage for either sex)
65. Marriage by capture
66. Marriage by purchase or bride-price
67. Dowry (payment made by bride's people to groom or his family)
68. Wife-lending or wife-exchange
69. Remarriage of widow
70. Levirate
71. Funeral suttee
72. Difficulty of divorce for women
73. Difficulty of divorce for men
74. Subjection or inferiority of women
75. Uncleanness of women
76. Post-marital sex restriction on women
77. Mother-in-law avoidance
78. Primogeniture
79. Scalps and heads sought as trophies
80. Property rights in women

C. *Religious and Miscellaneous Beliefs and Practices*

81. Organized priesthood (true priests)
82. Prevalence of shamanism
83. Ancestor worship
84. Elaboration of ceremony and ritual
85. Legendary heroes
86. Legendary heroines
87. Human sacrifice (other than grave escort)
88. Totemism
89. Fetishism
90. Cannibalism
91. Reincarnation
92. Intensity of ghost-fear
93. Exposure of the dying
94. Abandonment of house of the dead
95. Grave escort other than widows
96. Mortuary sacrifice of property
97. Elaboration of mortuary ceremonies
98. Attractiveness of future life
99. Belief in natural death
100. Circumcision
101. Infanticide
102. Picture writing
103. Written language
104. Couvade
105. Transmigration
106. Phallicism
107. Preference for male children
108. Preference for female children
109. Preferred status of first wife

One hundred and twelve such items were selected which were related to the status and treatment of the aged as revealed in the material already on hand. In the listing of these items a sex differentiation was made in every case by assigning odd numbers for aged men and even numbers for women. Two divisions were made of these characteristics; namely, the participation of the aged in their social milieu and the treatment which they received (see Table II, p. 4–6).

TABLE II

Trait List

A. *Participation of the Aged*

(Odd numbers apply to aged men and even numbers to aged women)

121. Chiefs
122.
123. Membership in councils of elders
124.
125. Judges and disciplinarians
126.
127. Property rights including slaves
128.
129. Traders
130.
131. Officials in secret societies, clubs, and fraternities
132.
133. Family rights including seniority rights
134.
135. Marriage to young mates
136.
137. Aids to conception, abortion, and determination of sex
138.
139. Childbirth and infant services
140.
141. Education and care of the young
142.
143. Initiators of the young
144.
145. Marriage, preliminary and wedding services
146.
147. Funeral services
148.
149. Priestly services, ritualism, ceremonialism, and guardians of the sacred
150.
151. Religious retreat in prayer, asceticism, meditation, and pious hope
152.
153. Shamanistic practices
154.
155. Initiators of important and hazardous enterprises, including the breaking of taboos
156.

157. Magic power of personal exuviae
158.
159. Treatment of diseases (practical remedies, nursing, etc.)
160.
161. Professional decorators
162.
163. Auxiliary maintenance aids pertaining to agriculture
164.
165. Auxiliary maintenance aids pertaining to hunting and fishing
166.
167. Auxiliary maintenance aids pertaining to herding
168.
169. Auxiliary maintenance aids pertaining to collection
170.
171. Household auxiliary maintenance aids
172.
173. Makers of toys, implements, and utensils
174.
175. Expert craftsmanship advice and supervision
176.
177. Information, instruction, and entertainment pertaining to morals, legends, fables, proverbs, history, and genealogies
178.
179. Suicide (willingness to die)
180.
181. Leaders in festivals, songs, dances, games, etc.
182.
183. Defenders of the status quo
184.
185. Personal ornamentation and ostentation
186.
187. Demonstration of physical powers
188.

B. *Treatment of the Aged*

191. Respected or feared
192.
193. Community support
194.
195. General family support
196.
197. Son-in-law support
198.
199. Fees for various services
200.

201. Distinguished and aided because of past achievements
202.
203. Senility food-taboo privileges
204.
205. Senility social privileges
206.
207. Glorified as daimons
208.
209. Glorified and favored in legends, stories, and proverbs as powerful heroes and magicians
210.
211. Glorified in legends and stories as the special friends of children
212.
213. Derided in traditions, stories, jokes, and inferences
214.
215. Persecuted as witches and sorcerers
216.
217. Abandoned or exposed to the natural elements
218.
219. Physically assaulted and killed
220.
221. Sacrificed
222.
223. Kindness or glory associated with violent death
224.
225. Near-death favors
226.
227. Memorials and taboos to aged dead
228.
229. Attractiveness of future life for the aged
230.
231. Cannibalistic use of the aged
232.
233. Loss of heads, scalps, etc., as trophies
234.

When all items for investigation were listed and clearly defined, a selection of tribes was made for the intensive study. The plan was to limit these to the so-called primitive peoples, or those of antiquity, to try to make the selection world wide, and to cover as many significant variables as possible with respect to natural conditions, racial differences, cultural areas, manner of subsistence, social organization, and other general characteristics.

Seventy-one separate peoples were chosen. Sixteen of these are in North America, 10 in Central and South America, 14 in

Africa, 3 in Europe, 16 in Asia, and 12 in Oceania and Australia.
Thirty-one tribes are within the torrid zone, 35 within the temperate, and 5 within the frigid zone. (For list of tribes in alphabetical order and with geographic and climatic distribution, see Tables III, IV, V, and accompanying maps, pp. 8–12.)

TABLE III

List and Numerical Identification of Tribes

1. Abipone		37. Kazak
2. Ainu		38. Kiwai
3. Akamba		39. Kutenai
4. Albanians		40. Kwakiutl
5. Andamanese		41. Lango
6. Araucanians		42. Lapp
7. Arawak		43. Lengua
8. Arunta		44. Mafulu
9. Ashanti		45. Maori
10. Aztec		46. Mangbetu
11. Bakongo		47. Menomini
12. Banks Islanders		48. Mongols
13. Berber		49. Munda
14. Bontoc Igorot		50. Navaho
15. Bushmen		51. Norsemen
16. Chin		52. Omaha
17. Chippewa		53. Palaung
18. Chukchi		54. Pomo
19. Creek		55. Rwala
20. Crow		56. Samoans
21. Dahomeans		57. Semang
22. Dieri		58. Sema Naga
23. Eskimo, Lab.		59. Seri
24. Eskimo, Pt. B.		60. Shilluk
25. Eskimo, Polar		61. Tasmanians
26. Euahlayi		62. Toda
27. Fan		63. Trobrianders
28. Haida		64. Tuareg
29. Hebrew		65. Vai
30. Hopi		66. Vedda
31. Hottentot		67. Witoto
32. Iban		68. Yahgans
33. Inca		69. Yakut
34. Iroquois		70. Yuchi
35. Jivaro		71. Yukaghir
36. Xosa		

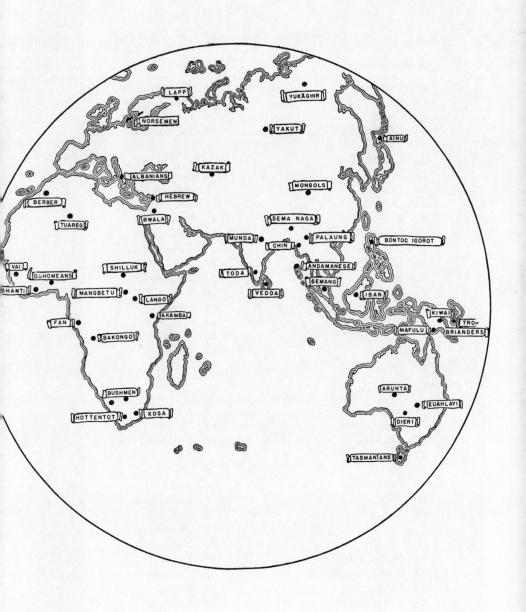

TABLE IV

Geographic Distribution of the Tribes

North America

17. Chippewa
19. Creek
20. Crow
23. Eskimo, Lab.
24. Eskimo, Pt. B.
25. Eskimo, Polar
28. Haida
30. Hopi
34. Iroquois
39. Kutenai
40. Kwakiutl
47. Menomini
50. Navaho
52. Omaha
54. Pomo
70. Yuchi

Central America

10. Aztec
59. Seri

South America

1. Abipone
6. Araucanians
7. Arawak
33. Inca
35. Jivaro
43. Lengua
67. Witoto
68. Yahgans

Oceania

12. Banks Islanders
14. Bontoc Igorot
32. Iban
38. Kiwai
44. Mafulu
45. Maori
56. Samoans
63. Trobrianders

Australia

8. Arunta
22. Dieri
26. Euahlayi
61. Tasmanians

Africa

3. Akamba
9. Ashanti
11. Bakongo
13. Berber
15. Bushmen
21. Dahomeans
27. Fan
31. Hottentot
36. Xosa
41. Lango
46. Mangbetu
60. Shilluk
64. Tuareg
65. Vai

Europe

4. Albanians
42. Lapp
51. Norsemen

Asia

2. Ainu
5. Andamanese
16. Chin
18. Chukchi
29. Hebrew
37. Kazak
48. Mongols
49. Munda
53. Palaung
55. Rwala
57. Semang
58. Sema Naga
62. Toda
66. Vedda
69. Yakut
71. Yukaghir

TABLE V

Climatic Conditions of Tribes
(Listed in correlations as 0)

Severe

(Cold with long winters)

18. Chukchi
23. Eskimo, Lab.
24. Eskimo, Pt. B.
25. Eskimo, Polar
37. Kazak
39. Kutenai
42. Lapp
48. Mongols
51. Norsemen
69. Yakut
71. Yukaghir

Temperate

(About equal summer and winter)

2. Ainu
3. Akamba
4. Albanians
6. Araucanians
13. Berber
16. Chin
17. Chippewa
20. Crow
28. Haida
29. Hebrew
30. Hopi
34. Iroquois
40. Kwakiutl
45. Maori
47. Menomini
49. Munda
50. Navaho
52. Omaha
54. Pomo
58. Sema Naga
61. Tasmanians
62. Toda
64. Tuareg
68. Yahgans

Warm

(Little winter and much summer)

1. Abipone
5. Andamanese
7. Arawak
8. Arunta
9. Ashanti
10. Aztec
11. Bakongo
12. Banks Islanders
14. Bontoc Igorot
15. Bushmen
19. Creek
21. Dahomeans
22. Dieri
26. Euahlayi
27. Fan
31. Hottentot
32. Iban
33. Inca
35. Jivaro
36. Xosa
38. Kiwai
41. Lango
43. Lengua
44. Mafulu
46. Mangbetu
53. Palaung
55. Rwala
56. Samoans
57. Semang
59. Seri
60. Shilluk
63. Trobrianders
65. Vai
66. Vedda
67. Witoto
70. Yuchi

Droughts

(Danger of famine)

3. Akamba
7. Arawak
8. Arunta
15. Bushmen
22. Dieri
26. Euahlayi
29. Hebrew

30. Hopi
37. Kazak
41. Lango
43. Lengua
45. Maori
48. Mongols
59. Seri
66. Vedda

The total culture of each tribe was investigated as a unit and all the statistical data were kept within the natural context so that the related facts on a given group could be reviewed together. Special efforts were made to secure classifiable information on as many as possible of the 221 subjects of specific inquiry. Some personal field work was possible within two tribes, the Hopi and the Navaho.

The data obtained for each of the categories, or traits, in each of the 71 tribes, are presented by means of symbols on two master charts (Tables VI, VII). It seemed insufficient to show merely the presence or absence of a trait or social practice, since this would give no indication of its relative importance in the culture. To give the same rating for hunting, for example, to two tribes, one of which relies upon hunting for its food supply while the other depends principally upon herding or agriculture and hunts only incidentally or occasionally, would be to present a distorted account and one of little value for correlative purposes. Likewise, merely to say that the aged are abandoned in two tribes, in one of which this occurs very seldom while in the other it is a regular practice, would be equally misleading. In the combing of selected sources, an attempt was made, therefore, to form a judgment as to the relative importance of the trait or practice in the culture at the time represented by the general descriptive data. These judgments are expressed in the master chart by the following symbols:

+ Dominance, marked elaboration, or strong social importance of the trait in the particular tribe under investigation

= presence without dominance, moderate elaboration, or intermediate importance of the trait

− incipient presence, slight elaboration, or cultural unimportance of the trait

0 absence or nonappearance of the trait, when definitely indicated in the sources

☐ Lack of information on the subject in the sources (indicated by a blank space)

On the original work sheets full bibliographical references were recorded for every piece of information with indications as to whether the judgment was implied rather than specifically expressed; but it has proved too cumbersome to publish all these sources. Therefore, in the text specific references are only given for direct quotations. Thus the actual bibliography of sources is much longer than listed. (For all tabulated data, see Tables VI, VII.)

Although considerable care has been exercised in weighing the evidence of different authorities, the extent to which scientific objectivity is jeopardized by imperfect information, conflicting reports, lack of preciseness in the sources, oversimplified and perhaps arbitrary classifications, and inescapable subjective judgments is, at this point, woefully apparent. All that can be claimed for the study, therefore, is that it represents a more reliable approximation to objective analysis than earlier and less well-controlled procedures. Moreover, full account is taken of all negative data and the defects of subjectivity and partial information are, we believe, less serious and best allowed for when they intrude in the initial stages of investigation and classification, before the facts are lifted from their cultural setting, than when they enter in at the end of the study in the summation of materials removed from their context.

The master charts (Tables VI, VII) list by name the tribes studied, and by number, across the top, the traits as enumerated in Tables I and II. The symbols, when read from left to right, reveal the presence, absence, or cultural importance of the various traits in the particular tribe, and thus preserve in some measure the cultural context of each. When read from top to bottom, they show the tribes in which a particular trait does or does not occur, and its relative importance. Therefore, the general prevalence of any listed trait can be checked by glancing down the appropriate line of symbols.

The method of statistical correlation employed is the coefficient of association (Yule). By way of example, a correlation is here drawn between the prevalence of private property rights to land (trait 29) and agriculture as a means of maintenance (trait 10). The number of tribes representing a dominant or fairly regular tendency to private property in land (29+=), and which also show a tendency to dominance in agriculture (10+=), is placed in the upper left-hand corner of a box. The number of tribes with little or no evidence of agriculture (10—0), but nevertheless possessing private property rights to land in a strong or fairly strong degree (20+=), is placed in the upper right-hand corner. Those with a fair amount of agricultural activity and little or no private property in land are placed in the lower left-hand corner; and those with little or no agriculture or private property in land, in the lower right-hand corner.

		Agriculture (Trait 10)	
Private property in land (trait 29)		Dominance	Absence
		+ =	— 0
Tendency to dominance	+ =	19	3
Tendency to absence	— 0	16	16

If the sections of the box are labeled $\begin{array}{c} ab \\ cd \end{array}$, and the coefficient calculated by the formula $\dfrac{ad-bc}{ad+bc}$, the resultant figure will be .72, which indicates a strong positive correlation of the two traits. The highest possible positive coefficient by this formula, of course, is 1.00, absence of any association being indicated by 0, the maximum negative association by —1.00. Whenever any corner of the correlational box contains a 0, one unit is added all around, and the coefficient is calculated in the usual manner, but an asterisk is placed after the coefficient to indicate that this has been done.

The above assemblage of sampled and tabulated facts relating to specific cultures and to the position and treatment of the aged within them, when subjected to a standard statistical method of analysis, establishes a controlled basis for testing and checking generalizations pertaining to the social and cultural implications of old age.

In Appendix A (pp. 245–284) appears a complete numerical list of all the correlations made in the study (1,146) in the order in which they are cited in the text. It should be noted that more information is given in these tables than the resulting coefficient. After identifying correlation numbers, the first column lists the trait numbers of the items correlated as identified in the master charts (Tables VI, VII), and names the trait item to be correlated. In the first column under "ratio" is given the total number of tribes possessing the first trait listed, in the degree of "dominance" or "intermediate" strength (+=), and the number of the same tribes which possess the correlative trait to a like extent (+=). Under the second "ratio" column is given the total number of tribes which do not possess the first-named trait or possess it to only a very slight degree (−0), and the number of these same tribes which possess the second or correlative trait to a dominant or intermediate degree (+=). Thus it is easy to see the general presence or absence of the traits under consideration and the simple numerical shift in correlative incidence. For example, in the first correlation listed in Appendix A, traits 30 and 193, communal sharing of food is correlated with communal support of aged men, and it is seen from a count of the tribes that 32 are reported as practicing communal sharing of food and that 19 of these are also reported as providing communal support of the aged. In the next column it is indicated that the practice of communal sharing of food is absent or very slight in 13 tribes and that in only 1 of these is communal support of aged men dominant or intermediate. In the last column, under "coefficient," the coefficient of association is given as +.92, which indicates that where communal sharing of food is practiced it is strongly correlated with communal support of the aged. In a careful reading of the text it is highly instructive, therefore, to follow the correlational data in detail. It will inspire much greater confidence in the generalizations. In Appendix B all the statistical correlations have been conveniently indexed for ready reference. This makes the tables useful for other purposes than the study of the aged.

A word should be said about what constitutes old age. Even for modern societies with reliable records of births there are no clear-cut biological tests or other generally accepted standards to establish just when old age begins or senescence is actually reached; and those which are cited are often too crude, variable, and irrelevant for practical use, except with qualifications and for a particular social milieu, or even a special occupational group. But in most preliterate societies chronological age is of even less use, since accurate birth records are rarely if ever available.

In such a study as this the only reliable criterion for the onset of old age seemed to be the social and cultural one. The simplest and safest rule to follow was to consider a person as "old" whenever he was so regarded and treated by his contemporaries. All the general statements about old age in the ethnographic sources had to be interpreted in a similar manner.

It was also impossible to be very exact in estimates of the extent of old age among primitive peoples. Few enumerations were found in the present study, and they indicated a relatively small percentage of persons who lived to be very old. For example, a census of the Bontoc Igorot in the Philippines, secured from a Spanish manuscript in 1894, indicated that 4.5 per cent of the men and 5.9 per cent of the women were above 50.[1] Rivers made a careful census of the Toda, published in 1906, which reported 4.7 per cent of the men and 5.3 per cent of the women above 50;[2] and a census of the Omaha in America, for 1884, showed 7.2 per cent of the men and 8.2 per cent of the women above 55.[3] But even these reports are based in part upon very rough estimates of age.

Scattered fragments of data indicate, however, that a few individuals even in very primitive societies live to about as great age as in modern civilization. Samples culled from the sources of the present study include references to men among the Abipone in South America who lived "almost a hundred years," [4] and certain Araucanians are said to "span a century." [5] In North America there are recorded cases of Chippewa of 95,[6] of Hopi men and women nearly 100,[7] and of Iroquois men of 103.[8] The Chin in Burma are reputed to reach great age,[9] and the Toda in India are called centenarians.[10] A chief among the Kazak in South Russia is reported to have lived to 111.[11] Tregear mentions Maori in New Zealand who were over 100 and reports one man who saw his descendants of the sixth generation.[12]

While such noteworthy examples of longevity are found in

1. Jenks (153), p. 42.
2. Rivers (247), p. 469.
3. Fletcher and La Flesche (103), p. 34.
4. Dobrizhoffer (75), II, 39, 145, 222.
5. Smith (282), p. 252.
6. Densmore (73), p. 54.
7. Field notes of author.
8. Seaver (267), pp. 150–151.
9. Carey and Tuck (48), p. 185.
10. Thurston (310), p. 151.
11. Hedin (126), pp. 287–288.
12. Tregear (313), p. 10.

primitive societies, and can be duplicated almost anywhere, they may be regarded as exceptions to the general rule of a relatively limited span of life and perhaps a rather early onset of old age. General statements are abundant to support this conclusion. For example, Portman states that length of life for the Andamanese, west of Burma, rarely ever exceeds 60 years.[13] Im Thurn writes that the Arawak in British Guiana seldom attain more than 50 years. "Between the thirtieth and the fortieth years, in case of men, and even earlier in the case of women, the rest of the body, except the stomach, shrinks, the fat disappears and the skin hangs in hideous folds . . . ."[14] Some Arunta women in Australia are regarded as fortunate if they reach 50, displaying a "stage of ugliness that baffles description."[15] Among the Bontoc Igorot in the Philippines a woman reaches "her prime" at 23, while at 30 she is "getting old," before 45 she "is old"; and by 50, if she is so fortunate as to live that long, she is a "mass of wrinkles from foot to forehead." Jenks also says of these people: "By forty-five most men are fast 'getting old.' Their faces are seamed, their muscles losing form, their carriage less erect, and their step slower. By fifty-five all are old and most are bent and thin. Probably not over one or two in a hundred live to be seventy . . . ."[16]

Among the Bushmen of South Africa, Bleek reports that really old people are rare. "The women die off at about fifty or sixty; the men wear better . . . . Almost every Bushman presented to me as being exceptionally old proved on investigation to be twenty or thirty years younger than supposed."[17] Alberti relates of the Xosa of South Africa that their length of life appears to be about 50 or 60 years. "It is extremely rare to find any who have attained the age of 70."[18] The Creek of North America are said to be lucky to see the gray hairs of their children before they die.[19] According to Musil, few Rwala of North Arabia reach very old age.[20] Howorth says that Mongol women in Mongolia are middle-aged at 30, and old and wrinkled at 40.[21]

13. Portman (225), p. 370.
14. Im Thurn (151), pp. 190–191.
15. Spencer and Gillen (289), p. 32.
16. Jenks (153), pp. 42–45.
17. Bleek (24), p. 13.
18. Alberti (2), p. 83.
19. Adair (1), p. 229.
20. Musil (212), p. 666.
21. Howorth (146), pp. 42–43.

Both sexes of Labrador Eskimo are described as "worn out" before 70; and a great grandmother is a rarity.[22] Seventy or 80 is a rare but possible age for the Chukchi in Siberia,[23] and 65 is very old for the Polar Eskimo.[24] Murdock writes of the Eskimo of Point Barrow: "It is exceedingly difficult to form any estimate of the age to which these people live, though it is natural to suppose that the arduous and often precarious existence which they lead must prevent any great longevity. Men and women who appear to be sixty or over are rare." [25] Ray adds that "they very rarely attain a great age, and the majority by far die under the age of forty years, and a man at sixty becomes very decrepit." [26]

It would appear that while statistical data are inadequate for a definite statement of the proportion of the aged in primitive societies, most general estimates would indicate that the number of persons reaching 65, for instance, is quite low and perhaps rarely ever exceeds 3 per cent.

The general plan of this report is to divide the material into eight chapters which deal with the following broad themes: the assurance of food, chiefly by communal sharing; property rights which may be utilized by the aged; the safeguarding of their prestige; routine activities of the aged which are related chiefly to economic functions and personal services; civil and political functions of the aged; their reactions to knowledge, magic, and religion; their adjustments to family life; and their treatment with respect to death.

When a problem is defined, such as any one of the above, a liberal selection of concrete "cases" or examples is presented from the particular tribes under investigation, but no effort is made to cover every tribe or to include all the available sources. This material is used solely to demonstrate the range of adaptation, to point up the issues more concretely, and to illustrate them amply.

The generalizations are based entirely upon the statistical analyses which are formulated at the end of the chapters, or in some instances at the end of divisions in chapters. By this method, all the information of a negative as well as a positive nature can be properly noted and assessed, thus applying a brake to over-zealous generalizations. For the author such a procedure has

22. Hutton (149), pp. 284–285.
23. Bogoras (28), pp. 544–546.
24. Steensby (293), p. 390.
25. Murdock (210), p. 39.
26. Ray (241), p. 45.

proved extremely useful in the integration of masses of data into mosaics of apparent order and sense, and especially in the determination of probable trends.

The actual results, however, are still tentative. In addition to the defects already pointed out (e.g., the intrusion of subjective judgments and the use of a possibly arbitrary system of classification), the study suffers from insufficient data. In the first place, ethnographers have been none too careful in reporting all relevant information on the status and treatment of the aged, or in placing it in convenient categories. The whole subject has been, in fact, much neglected, and it is hoped that this study will inspire a change in practice. Every grain of available information had to be culled from scattered sources, and even then the picture was often very incomplete for a given tribe. Furthermore, 71 tribes are too few to justify placing overmuch reliance upon any single statistical coefficient. Much greater confidence, however, may be placed in the general trend of large numbers of coefficients bearing upon a major hypothesis. In this respect the data and findings are often very impressive, certainly sufficient to tip the scales on the side of strong probability.

I

THE ASSURANCE OF FOOD

A DOMINANT interest in old age is to live long, perhaps as long as possible. Therefore, food becomes a matter of increasing concern. Its provision in suitable form, on regular schedule, and in proper amounts depends more and more upon the efforts of others who are in a position to provide or withhold it. And, as life goes on, the problem of supplying and feeding the aged eventually reaches a stage at which they require the choicest morsels and the gentlest care.

Among animals in their native habitat old age never reaches such an extreme state of dependence; and with man in his most primitive conditions it was probably rare. But some established customs of food sharing have existed in the simplest known societies in forms varying from a more or less free-for-all, in which the aged were at a disadvantage, to detailed regulation of food distribution, stringent rules of hospitality, elaborate requirements of gift-exchange, and some well-regulated systems of old-age assistance. As far back as we can go, the hands of the aged have reached out for a little food when they could do nothing more—and they have not been entirely ignored, nor always filled. The evidence would indicate that cases of general sharing have included the aged, but sharing with the aged may not always imply that the same privilege extends to others. What has happened has depended upon the customs of the group.

Examples of food-sharing customs in varying forms are reported from widely dispersed areas. The Labrador Eskimo shared with those in misfortune, and families or individuals in need were often fed by the whole village. Although orphans and widows are reported to have had a rather hard time of it "there is always someone to give them a little food or an old garment, so that they manage to get along." [1] Similar practices of group aid to dependents have been observed among the Point Barrow[2] and Polar Eskimo.[3] The Lapp are also described as very "hospitable."

1. Hawkes (124), pp. 91, 117.
2. Murdock (210), p. 64.
3. Rasmussen (233), pp. 44, 54.

"They freely received and entertained poor people in their huts, sometimes for the whole, sometimes for a half year . . . and afterwards conducted them with their reindeer to another place. They were very ready to assist the poor . . . ." [4] Leem says, "It is much to the praise of the Lapland nation that strolling beggars are very seldom seen there." [5] The Norsemen cared for their poor and aged under customary rules of hospitality. "While chatting at one of the houses, an old man entered dressed in a suit of new clothes and wearing a high hat, and was bidden to take a seat; when, upon inquiry, it was whispered in my ear that he was a pauper. I could hardly believe it . . . . Each person who has to be supported has to prove beforehand before the board of elders that he is too old and infirm to work, then he goes and remains six days on every farm. I was surprised to see how kindly they were treated—in many cases like visitors—having better food than the daily use for the family, and a good bed; so they go from one farm to another. They are well cared for, for it would be a great disgrace if the report should spread that Farmer So-and-So was hard-hearted to the poor." [6]

The Yukaghir in Siberia shared shelter and food with dependents,[7] and among the Chukchi persons without relatives were provided for, at least meagerly, in the camps of the more fortunate herders.[8] It has been said of the Yakut: "Care for the poor and unfortunate has always been regarded as an obligation of the sib." And they "would not believe the author when he told them that in this country, there were rich and populous cities in which people sometimes died of starvation. They asked why anyone should die when he could go and eat with his neighbors." [9]

Food sharing has been found among many tribes in the United States. It was a rule with the Omaha that those elected to be chiefs should be generous men, giving freely and remembering the poor and aged.[10] Among the Crow it has been said that "Men and women, old and young, are constantly passing from lodge to lodge for a word or a smoke, and food is always placed before them. Sometimes one man killed as many as fifteen buffalo in a run. He would then cry, 'I do not take the arrows back, nor the

4. Scheffer (263), pp. 35–36.
5. Leem (173), I, 382.
6. Du Chaillu (83), I, 173.
7. Jochelson (154), pp. 43, 119, 124.
8. Bogoras (28), pp. 624–625, 635.
9. Sieroshevski (272), pp. 68–69.
10. Dorsey (78), p. 358.

skin'; it was then known that all but a few, which he kept for himself, were for the use of the poor old people who had come hurrying out from the camp when the butchering began . . . . After a hunt a broad level stretch of land was dotted with dead buffalo, men butchering, old men hurrying to and fro receiving a piece of meat from this one and that . . . ." "Iron Bull always had a number of poor old men eating day by day in his lodge . . . for he was a great hunter." [11] According to Lowie: "The most impressive thing in the Hot Dance performance to an outsider is the extraordinary generosity with which property of all kinds is given away to the aged poor of the tribe, as well as to the visitors from other tribes. Women can be seen staggering away under loads of blankets presented to them and their husbands. Horses are ridden directly into the dance house and presented to the old people." After one of their famous Sun-dance ceremonies: "The old people then came and stayed outside the lodge, where the meat was distributed among them. They feasted there and sang and enjoyed themselves and finally went home with whatever meat was left." [12]

The Kwakiutl engaged in elaborate ceremonial distributions of food and property in which the aged shared,[13] and Chippewa chiefs made it a practice to see that widows and orphans received proper care.[14] Among the Iroquois there was great hospitality in food sharing. "Upon the operation of such a simple and universal law of hospitality, hunger and destitution were entirely unknown among them." [15]

Every Creek belonged to a particular clan with village groups scattered over a wide area. In any of these and among individuals who were total strangers to him, he had the right of food and lodging as long as he chose to stay. Aged men often spent their last days moving from house to house among members of their clan. Bossu observed: "I have often noted that when they returned from the chase the chiefs took great care, before dividing the food, to set aside the share for the old men." [16]

It was reported of the Seri that "every member of the clan is entitled to necessary food and raiment, and it is the duty of every other person to see that the need is supplied. The stress of this

11. Curtis (62), pp. 6, 13, 51.
12. Lowie (183), p. 205; *ibid.* (184), p. 29.
13. Curtis (63), p. 141; Ford (104), p. 21.
14. Densmore (73), p. 21.
15. Morgan (207), I, 319.
16. Swanton (303), pp. 79, 445.

duty is graded partly by proximity but chiefly by standing and responsibility in the group, whereby it becomes the business of the first at the feast to see that enough is left to supply all below him; and this duty passes down the line in such wise as to protect the interests of the helpless infant, and even the tribal good-for-naught or hanger-on, who may gather the crumbs and lick the bones within limits fixed by the tribal consensus." [17]

The Navaho have been "hospitable" in sharing food with guests, even strangers; and among the Hopi no aged person needed to fear starvation as long as his many relatives had food to spare and he was able to go to their houses to eat. But the very old and decrepit who could no longer feed themselves were some-times neglected and died alone.[18]

In South America, Latcham writes that a redeeming trait of the Araucanians was their hospitality. "An inhospitable person is generally condemned by public opinion as sordid and mean. Not a beggar or an indigent person is to be found throughout the whole Araucanian territory. Even the most infirm and most in-capable of subsisting themselves are decently clothed. This be-nevolence is not confined only to their countrymen; they conduct themselves with great hospitality toward all strangers of what-ever nation, and a trader may live in any part of their country without the least expense." [19]

Among the Lengua the aged were kept at the expense of the community, as also the sick or disabled; but Grubb has further commented: "The old are often neglected, not so much from in-tention, as on account of the extreme poverty into which the peo-ple have fallen, and of the selfishness of many who insist upon sharing the food instead of exerting themselves to increase the supply." [20] But communal maintenance of the aged among the Witoto has been described as less secure. Whiffen reports that the old and feeble were left to forage for themselves. "The Indians judge it by their standards of common sense; why live a life that has ceased to be worth living when there is no bug-bear of a hell to make one cling to the most miserable existence?" [21]

It has been more difficult to find references to communal shar-ing of food or even of hospitality customs in Africa;[22] but it is

17. McGee (188), p. 273.
18. Field notes of author.
19. Latcham (172), p. 354; Spencer (290), No. V, Div. I, Pt. 4A, p. 132.
20. Grubb (119), p. 191.
21. Whiffen (331), pp. 156–157.
22. See Table VI, t. 30, p. 14 f.

reported of the Lango that strangers were invited to the feasts and "even a beggar . . . is greeted . . . with 'Go and glean the grain fields'; and then given a hearty meal with the family." [23] After a hunt among the Fan, it is said that the brains, lungs, and soft parts of the animals slain were given to the old men.[24]

Westermarck writes that among the Xosa, when a person advanced in years became sick or helpless, it was customary for everyone to appear eager to render assistance.[25] Kidd's description of an unfortunate old woman is not so favorable, however. She was "literally bent with age, . . . her body being supported by her hands, which clutched her thighs as if they were the angle-bit of a bracket. Her nose was eaten away with disease, and she was blind and deaf . . . her scraggy and pendant breasts were like empty bags of dirty skin hanging from a wrinkled, shrunken body. It was long since she had a tooth in her head, and handsful of skin could have been taken up at any part of her body . . . . She piteously begged for a little salt." [26]

The ancient Hebrew had certain provisions for the unfortunate in their code of laws. "Thou shalt not pervert the judgment of the stranger nor of the fatherless; nor take a widow's raiment to pledge. When thou cuttest down thine harvest in thy fields, and hast forgot a sheaf in the field, thou shalt not go again to fetch it; it shall be for the stranger, for the fatherless, and for the widow; that the Lord thy God may bless thee in the work of thine hands. When thou beatest thine olive tree, thou shalt not go over the boughs again; it shall be for the stranger, for the fatherless and for the widow. When thou gatherest the grapes of the vineyard, thou shalt not glean it afterwards; it shall be for the stranger, for the fatherless and the widow." [27]

A prominent feature of the social intercourse of the Kiwai Papuans in New Guinea was the distribution of food. Although the natives acknowledged individual ownership in property, the use of the proceeds of any kind of work bore witness to certain communal practices. The distribution of game, for example, was compulsory and there were instances of men being punished for keeping secret the killing of a pig in order to retain the flesh for their own exclusive use. A large catch of game was divided among

23. Driberg (82), p. 69.
24. Trilles (314), p. 73.
25. Westermarck (329), I, 546.
26. Kidd (161), p. 23.
27. Deut. 24:17.

the people in an ostentatious way. "Besides food, all sorts of other presents are exchanged between people, particularly if they are close friends or kinsfolk of a certain lineage. If a man gives a boy presents, the latter, when grown up, is bound to bring him presents in return, not only once, but repeatedly for an indefinite period, notwithstanding the length of time which may have elapsed since he received the gifts." [28]

Among the Samoans it has been reported that "the sick, the aged, the blind, the lame, and even the vagrant, has a house and a home with food and raiment as far as he considers he needs it. A stranger may at first sight think a Samoan one of the poorest of the poor, and yet he may live ten years with that Samoan and not be able to make him understand what poverty really is in the European sense of the word. 'How is it?' he will always say, 'No food! Has he no friends? No home to live in! Where did he grow? Are there no houses belonging to his friends? Have the people there no love for each other?' " [29]

Among the higher civilizations reported in this study are the Inca and the Aztec. Aged Incas were supplied with food and clothing from the public storehouse. "There was no such thing as poverty or destitution, for the infirm or incapable were cared for by their neighbors according to the law, a regular order in tilling the soil being observed. First the land assigned to the Sun was cultivated (for religious purposes); second, those of widows, orphans, sick or aged, or persons otherwise unable to work, as also the land of absent soldiers. After the land of the poor and distressed had been attended to—and only then—the people worked their own lots, neighbors assisting each other. The people also paid another sort of tribute, which was to make clothes, shoes, and arms for the soldiers and the poor who could not work for themselves owing to age or infirmity." [30] Their laws decreed that those who were called poor, the blind, lame, aged and infirm, who could not till their own lands so as to clothe and feed themselves, should receive sustenance from the public stores.[31]

Aztec dependents were provided for at public expense. When their leader, Athuitzotl, about 1500 A.D. received tribute sent by the provinces, he was in the habit of calling the people together and distributing clothes and provisions among those in need. Motleuczoma II established an asylum for citizens who, having

28. Landtman (171), pp. 199–200.
29. Turner (315), p. 161.
30. Markham (195), II, 18, 205–206.
31. Enock (95), pp. 20–21.

served the country either in public office or in the army, might be
of limited means. He gave them the city of Calhuacan, where
they were lodged, clothed, and fed at the expense of the state. A
portion of the numerous contributions, augmented by the spoils
of war, and by presents from governors of provinces and from
feudatories, went "to help widows, orphans, invalids, and old
men; classes of people for whom the Aztecs always felt great com-
passion." [32] A counselor in the coronation address advised a new
ruler in the following terms: "Look to what you do: take into
account the conditions of the orphans, the widows, the old men
and women who can no longer work, because they are the plum-
age, eye-brows, the eye-lashes of the former ruler . . . ." [33]

The above cases, which could be multiplied with material from
other societies, demonstrate that not infrequently and in widely
distributed areas of the world the aged, along with other dependents, have found some reliable assurance of support through customs of food sharing, through social requirements of hospitality,
obligations imposed upon relatives, customs of communal responsibility, and in the most advanced societies—such as the Inca
or Aztec—through organized systems of old-age assistance. Further generalizations based upon statistical analysis are made at
the end of the chapter.

A social expedient of particular advantage to the aged has
been the custom of food taboos. A very common means of court-
ing disaster was by indiscriminate eating, and in many societies
protective food taboos developed which proved a godsend to the
old people. Long lists of delicate morsels, "pregnant with danger," were strictly forbidden to children, young and middle-aged
men, and childbearing women. But old men, and frequently
women, were exempt on grounds of immunity acquired through
age. While it cannot be demonstrated that these oldsters invented
such social expedients in behalf of their own palates, many of the
tabooed foods were regarded as quite tasty, and frequently the
aged have been observed manipulating such taboos to their personal advantage—and it is rather remarkable that the choicest
bits were so often tabooed to younger people.

Many examples of food taboos are available. Among the Polar
Eskimo, eggs, entrails, hearts, lungs, livers, and such small animals as young seals, hares, and ptarmigan grouse, are said to

32. Biart (22), pp. 83, 96, 194.
33. Saville (261), p. 26; Biart (22), p. 55.

have gone to the old men—who might share them with certain others who had captured at least one of every animal that is hunted, and with women who had given birth to more than five children.[34]

Aged Omaha advised the young to leave alone the choice morsels that were customarily returned in borrowed kettles: "If you eat what is brought home in the kettle your arrows will twist when you shoot . . . . The youth who thinks first of himself and forgets the old will never prosper, nothing will go straight for him." The *washna*, or tender part of the intestine of the buffalo, was considered harmful to youths, and thus became the portion of the aged. "You must not eat the *washna*, for if you do, and go with a war party for spoils, the dogs will bark at you." Young people who unjointed bones to secure the marrow were warned by the old men, "You must not do that, if you do, you will sprain your ankle." Neither could a young man drink the broth: "If he does, his ankles will rattle and his joints become loose." When the marrowfat was tried out and the youth desired some of it with his meat, the old men would say, "If you eat of the marrowfat you will become quick tempered, your heart will become soft, and you will turn your back on your enemy." A native reports, "In my day young men were forbidden to smoke, for smoking, we were told, would make young men short winded and when they went into battle they would be quickly overcome." If a lad wanted to eat a turkey's head, he was told, "If you eat that, tears will come into your eyes when you hunt, you will have watery eyes." A hunter was even warned against eating the marrow from the bones of game which he had killed. "Once when I had killed an elk," reports an informant, "I wanted to eat the marrow in the bone; so I roasted it, but when I was ready to eat it some old men saw me, and they said, 'If you, a young man, eat that, your leg bone will become sore.' "[35]

The Crow turned over the entrails and the marrow bones to the aged.[36] Larks, among the Pomo, were said to be eaten only by the old people. Loeb adds that the young were not allowed to partake of worms and caterpillars, but that they might sip the water in which the worms were stewed.[37] Privileges of eating and drinking

34. Rasmussen (233), pp. 121–122.
35. Fletcher and La Flesche (103), pp. 331–333.
36. Lowie (184), p. 28.
37. Loeb (180), p. 164.

among the Seri were rated according to seniority.[38] It has been said of the Witoto that only the aged could eat the flesh of enemies slain in battle.[39]

Old Aztec men were permitted to drink stimulants, prohibited to others, in order to "warm the cooling blood of their age." [40] The Codex Mendoza, which describes in native hieroglyphic writing the daily life of the Aztec, depicts the heavy penalties for drunkenness, which was regarded as a capital offense. "From this punishment only men and women over seventy years of age were exempt. Drinking, except in the worship of the gods, was the prerogative of age." [41]

Among the Lango in Africa the larger animals were believed to possess a *Tipo*, or a shadow, which was very dangerous. When one was killed the slayer had to return to his village and consult a shaman, who advised the sacrifice of a black ram. The carcass of the ram was dragged whole into the bush and left near a river where only old men might go and eat of it. Driberg indicates that there were many such food taboos which favored the aged. Old people claimed the heads in the ceremonial slaying of goats after a battle. Women were not allowed to eat chickens or the flesh of goats until after the birth of a third child, and only those too old to bear could eat mutton. Tobacco could be smoked only by old men, since it was held to be injurious to women, hunters, warriors, and suitors in lovemaking.[42] Younger men among the Fan never ate tortoise, being told that it would impair their vigor and fleetness of foot. "But the old men eat tortoise freely, because having already lost the power of running they can take no harm from the flesh of the slow-footed animal." The brains, the lungs, and the soft parts of other animals also went to them.[43]

Bleek writes of the Bushmen of South Africa that the paauw meat and ostrich eggs were eaten chiefly by old men. It was also claimed that children and women who had not become mothers would fail to reach maturity if they ate steenbock.[44] For the Hottentot, a sheep struck down by lightning was very dangerous, and none but the aged could safely touch it.[45] Among the Xosa only

38. McGee (188), p. 272.
39. Farabee (97), p. 146.
40. Macleod (189), p. 30.
41. Bunzel (41), p. 362.
42. Driberg (82), pp. 106, 110–111, 192–204, 230.
43. Frazer (107), p. 495; Trilles (314), p. 73.
44. Bleek (24), p. 7.
45. Hoernlé (132), p. 69.

the very young and the very old could eat certain ducks, domestic fowls, birds' eggs, and porcupines, or drink fresh milk. Kidney meat made men sterile. Therefore, the "only men who would eat the kidney are the very old men, and so the phrase 'kidney-eater' signifies an old man." [46] At the feast of an Akamba ceremony for circumcision only the elders could crack bones and get out the marrow, and it was an exclusive right of the oldest men to drink honey-beer.[47]

The Iban of northwest Borneo forbade their young men and warriors to eat venison because it would make them as timid as the deer—but the old men consumed it with relish.[48] Among the Trobrianders: "Certain fish were eaten only by the old men. It was believed that if unmarried or only recently married men ate these they would become unpleasant to the opposite sex who would not then permit them free access." [49] And at the feast of the wild pig among the Kiwai Papuans the oldest people ate the meat. A young man would die if he took any except a small bite administered to him as "medicine." [50]

The Chukchi of Siberia claimed that the milk of the reindeer caused impotence in men and flabby breasts in women. It was therefore tabooed to the young of both sexes, but the aged could drink it.[51] Hutton writes of the Sema Naga: "Besides prohibited flesh, food ordinarily good may become prohibited for some special reason. Thus if the spoon breaks with which the cooked rice is being taken from the pot, males may not eat of the rice (except the very old and practically bed-ridden). If this prohibition were not observed and the eater were at any time to run, he would get a pain of violent and appalling severity as though a piece of broken bamboo spoon were piercing his vitals." He further states: "In regard to the latter class of food *gennas* (taboos) among the Semas, it is to be noticed that the ill consequences which are held to follow the use of certain animals and birds as food more often attend the offspring of the eater than the eaters themselves, and these foods can therefore be eaten only by old or childless men who have no prospect of bringing more children into the world." [52]

Food taboos which could be disregarded by the aged and child-

46. Shooter (270), pp. 28, 215; Kidd (161), p. 142.
47. Lindblom (174), p. 60; Dundas (85), pp. 488, 494.
48. St. John (255), pp. 186, 206.
49. Seligmann (268), p. 681.
50. Landtman (171), p. 361.
51. Bogoras (28), p. 196.
52. Hutton (148), pp. 90, 95–96.

less persons among the Sema Naga include flying squirrels, because the eaters would be liable to beget idiotic children; the
huluk ape, lest the eater bear children who cry "hualu, hualu,
hualu" like the ape; the otter, since hair on the head would become hard, dry, and difficult to shave; the muskrat, to avoid a
horrible smell; and the fork-tails who defecate as they fly away
when disturbed, and thus induce a timid and fearful disposition.
The hornbill was believed to cause coughing and choking, the
dung-crow turned the hair white, the house martin or swallow
caused dysentery, and goats' meat made younger women too
passionate.[53]

Old men among the Euahlayi in Australia were said to "have
great influence over the females and young men as to regulations
of their food, preventing them from eating such food as emu and
their eggs, wild turkey and their eggs." "Should a boy or girl eat
plain turkey or bustard eggs while they were yet . . . taboo, he
or she would lose his or her sight. Should they eat the eggs or
flesh of kangaroo or *piggie billah*, their skins would break out in
sores and their limbs wither." Honey was also taboo except to
the very old or very young.[54]

It was reported that among the Arunta of Australia, "The
idea throughout is evidently that which obtains so largely in savage tribes; of reserving the best things for the use of the elders,
and more especially the elder men." A list of forbidden foods
among these people includes the following, with consequent penalties:

Wild turkey and its eggs: premature age.
Female bandicoot: probable bleeding to death at circumcision.
Emu fat: abnormal development of the penis.
Parrots and cockatoos: development of a hollow on top of the
    head and a hole in the chin.
Quail and its eggs: general stoppage of growth and no beard.
Eagle-hawk, except the legs: premature age and leanness.
Wild-cat: painful and foul-smelling eruption on head and
    neck. Applies until very old age is reached.
Pogargus and its eggs: an ugly enlargement of the mouth.

The following additional food restrictions apply to girls and
young women until they have had a child or until their breasts
begin to be pendant:

53. *Ibid.* pp. 90–95.
54. Howitt (143), p. 769; Parker (218), pp. 23, 25.

Female bandicoot: continued flow of menses.
Large lizards: abnormal craving for the opposite sex.
Large quail and its eggs: no development of the breasts.
Kangaroo tail: premature age and baldness.
Brown-hawk: absence of milk from the breasts, but a swelling
that will cause them to burst.[55]

An interesting example of economic security in old age through
a culturally conditioned system of both communal food sharing
and food taboos is provided by the Pukapukans who have occupied three islets about forty miles northwest of Nassau. The
population of approximately six hundred was divided into rather
sharply defined age grades with the old gray-haired men (*tupele*)
constituting a governing body. They were promoted to the office
on the basis of age, relieved of physical labor, provided with food
from the common stock, and placed in control of the distribution
of food. Consequently the choicest diet was often reserved for
them, such as the belly fats and internal organs of turtles. In fact,
these delicacies were tabooed to younger people on the grounds
that they caused sickness and gray hair. In former times crabs
could be caught only on stated occasions and were then divided by
the old men who reserved ample portions for themselves. At feasts
the old men were the official food distributors and culled choice
pickings for themselves. For the Pukapukans, according to the
Beagleholes: "Old age does not bring fear of economic insecurity.
Old people are cared for by their children and relatives, and no
one ever suffers from lack of food and shelter." [56]

While examples of culturally patterned food-sharing and food-
taboo privileges favorable to the aged have been used freely for
the purpose of illustration, any generalizations, even tentative
ones, will be more reliable if based upon statistical analysis which
take into account negative as well as positive evidence. A statistical summary of data on the 71 tribes which were selected for
detailed study shows that no definite information was obtained
on 38 tribes for aged men and on 41 for aged women, and a negative report was listed for both men and women from only one
tribe. The fact that in only one tribe were negative data reported
is, of course, much more significant than the absence of either
affirmative or negative information in many. The custom of food

55. Spencer and Gillen (289), I, 490, 492–494.
56. Beaglehole (13). Summary from many pages. This case is given only as an
illustration since the tribe was not included for the statistical analysis.

sharing is also listed as very slightly evident in 7 tribes for both sexes. The practice is reported to be fairly common for aged men in 13 tribes, and for women in 12, and pronounced for men in 12, and for women in 8. Therefore in 25 tribes for men and 22 for women, out of a total of 71, or 33 for both sexes in which information could be tabulated, it is reported to be a customary practice for the aged to receive shares of food from communal sources other than the immediate family.

The statistical record of the prevalence of a custom or trait is far more pertinent for general conclusions than is the copious citation of random cases; and it is on this basis that one may determine best whether the distribution of the trait is subject to reliable generalization, and possibly some degree of prediction, or must be regarded as due to chance, accident, or unknown factors. Statistical correlations on the distribution of the custom of communal food sharing show an impressive degree of order and consistency under varying environmental and cultural conditions.

The first important generalization to be observed, and one with very strong statistical support, is that the aged among primitive peoples had greater opportunity for securing provisions from a common store in societies where group sharing of food was an established practice irrespective of age considerations than in societies where this was not the case. In statistical correlations there are here very high coefficients of association, e.g., +.92 (trait 30 correlated with traits 193 and 194. See Cor. 1–2).[57] It would seem, therefore, that the general sharing of food was not in any sense a special provision for the aged, but developed as a common safeguard against hunger and destitution for all members of a given group.

A second generalization which can be drawn from the statistical data, though not as strongly supported, is that in primitive societies there has been a pronounced tendency toward communal sharing of food, irrespective of age (trait 30),[58] in areas where the climate is severely cold or serious droughts are common (Cor. 3).[59] It would seem, indeed, that in very difficult physical environ-

57. For all statistical correlations of trends in primitive societies, see Appendix A, p. 245. The reader who wishes to follow the supporting evidence for these and other generalizations should carefully examine this section and check each correlational reference with the statistical tables. The manifold consistencies in the coefficients of association justify the effort of following them. All traits are listed in Tables I, II, VI, and VII, pp. 2, 4, 14 f.

58. See Tables I, VI, pp. 2, 14 f.

59. All coefficients of association are listed in Appendix A.

ments communal sharing of food has tended to be a necessity to survival. The hazards of hunger and privation might be so threatening that the group could not afford to permit any individual or subgroup to monopolize the food supply. Communalism thus appears to have developed more readily under hard and difficult circumstances which jeopardized group security and even existence than in environments characterized by comfort and plenty. It would appear to be an adjustment to scarcity rather than to plenty. Perhaps it is no surprise to find a similarly strong statistical trend toward communal sharing of food with the aged in very cold or parched regions, and negative tendencies in milder climates with adequate rainfall (Cor. 4–5). Where life has been hardest general food sharing with the aged has been most prevalent.

A third generalization concerns the chief forms of maintenance in primitive societies—collection, hunting, fishing, herding, and agriculture. Here it is found statistically that, again irrespective of age (trait 30), there has been greater access to communal food stores among collectors and fishers and relatively less among hunters, while pronounced negative trends appear among herding and agricultural peoples (Cor. 6–10). Communal sharing of food with the aged seems to have followed almost identical trends. This suggests that, in addition to environmental conditions, varying forms of maintenance activities have also influenced the custom of communal food sharing. Among collectors and fishermen the tendency has been for the aged to participate in communal food sharing; among hunters and herders the statistical balance becomes nearly neutral; while a decidedly negative trend appears again among cultivators of the soil (Cor. 11–20). With development of the techniques and complexities of maintenance, communal food sharing with the aged, or with anyone, seems to have declined as an essential part of the cultural complex in primitive societies.

A fourth generalization is that a strong negative trend in communal sharing of food is correlated with many cultural traits usually associated with more highly developed societies. Specifically, quite negative coefficients of association are found with community support of the aged and permanency of residence, constancy of the food supply, the use of grain for food, private property in land or in objects other than land, trade, use of money as a means of exchange, debt-relations, and slavery, all of which generally imply a more complex level of economy and social organization (Cor. 21–38). It would seem, then, that with more complex cultural developments society has tended to rely less upon communal food sharing both in general and with the aged, and has regulated its distribution on the basis of other factors than need.

A fifth and final generalization is that in customs of food sharing with the aged there has been no significant difference in the treatment accorded to aged men and women. This can be demonstrated more simply by listing in parallel lines all the above coefficients of association.*

The custom of food-taboo privileges which favored aged men (trait 203) was found to be very pronounced in 10 tribes, common in 13, very slight in 5, and negative in 1, out of the 71 surveyed. The same custom (trait 204) was found less frequently with respect to aged women. Food taboos which favored the aged women were reported as pronounced in 2 tribes, common in 8, very slight in 5, and negative in 1. No information was obtained on similar customs in other tribes. These figures indicate that aged men have been more often favored by food taboos than have aged women. Some coefficients of association were worked out, but the incompleteness of the data and the irregularity of the statistical trends are such that it was difficult to draw any trustworthy generalizations (Cor. 39–52).

In summary, then, individuals everywhere seem to have become progressively dependent upon others for their food with the onset

* Positive coefficients

	No	1, 2	4, 5	11, 12	13, 14
	Traits	30	0	6	8
Aged men	193	+.92	+.53	+.64	+.54
Aged women	194	+.92	+.50	+.60	+.67

Negative coefficients

	No	15, 16	17, 18	19, 20	21, 22	23, 24	25, 26	27, 28	29, 30	31, 32	33, 34	35, 36	37, 38
	Traits	7	9	10	1	12	11	29	28	25	26	24	23
Aged men	193	−.07	−.06	−.78	−.33	−.08	−.71	−.25	−.52	−.62	−.62	−.20	−.31
Aged women	194	−.06	−.02	−.79	−.33	−.17	−.66	−.25	−.55	−.62	−.50	−.26	−.38

of old age. The assurance of food from a group or communal source has not been entirely lacking in the simplest known societies. In fact, it appears that customs of sharing food with the aged have been strongest in very harsh and difficult environments, when the food supply has been less constant, and where types of maintenance have been less well developed, as among collectors, fishers, and hunters. With advance to herding and agriculture, and the development of cultural traits characteristic of "higher" civilization, such as grain supplies, property, trade, debt-relations, and slavery, support of the aged through communal sharing of food appears to have declined in importance or to have taken on features more characteristic of "organized charity." In the analysis of food-taboo privileges favorable to the aged, trends could not be clearly traced, but it would appear that in the evolution of society these privileges have also occurred as adaptations within a limited phase of societal development, and that they too have eventually given way to other and more adequate forms of social security in old age.

II

PROPERTY RIGHTS

PROPERTY rights have been lifesavers for the aged. Wherever such prerogatives are firmly entrenched in a culture they have supplemented, and often supplanted, communal forms of food sharing and support. They have enabled the individuals to store up reserves, or credits, against the hard days ahead. Property rights have proven very flexible, quite impersonal, and extremely effective in securing the services of one's associates irrespective of kinship ties or other social bonds. Moreover, the enforcement of property rights has depended very little upon the physical stamina of their individual possessor and very greatly upon the mores and authorized agents of society who compel observance by means of sanctions. There has probably always been a marked difference in growing old with and without property; for nearly everywhere the requests and commands of the aged who possessed such rights have been more promptly observed than the "petitions of the decrepit and poor." Vested interests in the goods of the world provided, even in feeble hands and in primitive societies, very effective means of getting wants satisfied, and such power has been appreciated by the aged. The person who controlled property was able to get more out of life and to get it much longer. Indeed, the importance of property for old-age security can hardly be overrated.

Perhaps the simplest and most universal form of property rights shared by the aged has been the exchange of gifts and the receipt of fees for services rendered or in the fulfillment of obligations. Such transactions, in one form or another, have been found practically everywhere and have tended to increase in importance with the development of property rights. They require only brief illustration here.

Aged women among the Labrador Eskimo received food for the care of men's boots and other services.[1] Chippewa men purchased the knowledge of medical herbs from the old "doctors."[2] The young Crow surrendered their marital rights to older men

1. Turner (316), p. 206.
2. Densmore (73), p. 328.

in exchange for "medicine," and a feast was the popular way of rewarding the aged storyteller.[3] Navaho natives bartered with old men for knowledge of magic songs, charms, names, etc.; and young men trained in magic were required to give their aged teachers large gifts, sometimes equal to half their earnings. Certain old men could make a good living by the performance of healing rites.[4] Aged Pomo medicine men exacted heavy fees for their services, and a bear doctor received half the spoils gathered in by his pupil.[5]

Aged Hopi men received substantial "gifts" for treating diseases, and for almost any other service they could render; and they held on to their property rights into very great age, exchanging them bit by bit for care and support in their "helpless stage." Old women owned the houses in which they lived, household equipment, objects they had made with their own hands, and, not infrequently, fruit trees, garden patches, and small herds. Where the aged had property they got better care in their old age and even in death, for relatives who buried them received extra shares of the personal possessions.[6]

The Creek rain-maker received rewards in food. One old native who expressed doubt in the efficacy of his own charms asserted, nevertheless, that it was "very reasonable" for his people to continue this custom; "especially as it was both profitable in supporting many of their helpless old beloved men, and very productive of virtue by awing their young people from violating the ancient law." [7] Old Lengua medicine men asked for a handful of beads after their service;[8] and the aged Bontoc Igorot demanded as much as two-fifths of a laborer's daily wage for a professional call.[9] Many of the Iban priests were blind and maimed for life, but by following their profession they earned a livelihood. "Whether the patient live or die the *Manang* is rewarded for his trouble. If a cure be effected, he receives a present in addition to his regular fee." [10]

Old Kiwai men and women received gifts for conducting various rites. "Charms are made by the older men and sold to the

3. Lowie (185), p. 63; *ibid.* (186), p. 13.
4. Reichard (242), pp. 90–91; Matthews (203), p. 3.
5. Kroeber (166), p. 265; Barrett (10), pp. 452–453.
6. Field notes of author.
7. Swanton (302), pp. 630–631.
8. Grubb (119), p. 153.
9. Jenks (153), p. 199.
10. St. John (255), p. 63; Gomes (117), p. 165.

younger for food. There are house charms, canoe charms, and plantation charms." Aged women for a fee taught the girls to dance, and an old man engaged to drum was paid in bananas, yams, taro, and sugar cane.[11] Samoan midwives were compensated for their services and priests received fees.[12] The Semang midwife was also well paid.[13] Albanian medicine men expected fees for the treatment of diseases.[14] The better part of a fat animal went to the aged midwife among the Yakut; and shamans were rewarded according to the success of their undertakings.[15]

There was a complex system of fees among the Akamba for all promotions into age-graded groups and for the necessary information which must be acquired. "The whole learning of the elders of Ukuu is a matter of great secrecy, and may be imparted bit by bit to those who have the necessary qualifications and who pay the fees." [16] The traditional fee for midwifery among the Ashanti was paid in gold dust.[17] Old Xosa men were rewarded for information, and aged women worked magic for pay. "Mbona was a great rain-maker who died long ago, and an old woman acts as his prophetess. She tours the country . . . with two old men who are the only persons that are allowed to see her. As the people hear she is coming they hide in their houses and she collects the offerings left outside the huts." [18]

The receipt of gifts or fees by the aged for services rendered, or in payment of obligations, appears almost to be taken for granted by ethnographers. They practically always provide confirming evidence by implication, are as likely as not to ignore the question specifically, and in no case in the survey was definite negative information observed (traits 199 and 200). It can be assumed, then, as a general rule, that aged persons have attained some security almost universally by the receipt of gifts or fees, but specific information seems too meager and vague for useful statistical treatment. The more pertinent question, however, is the extent of property rights shared by the aged in various social systems, and for this problem there is an abundance of data. Even in the simpler social systems, and where collection, hunting, and

11. Landtman (171), pp. 353–356; Chalmers (50), p. 199; Riley (245), p. 37.
12. Turner (315), pp. 31, 80.
13. Schebesta (262), p. 233.
14. Durham (88), p. 266.
15. Czaplicka (66), p. 143; Sieroshevski (272), p. 102.
16. Hobley (131), p. 150; Dundas (85), pp. 539–541.
17. Rattray (238), pp. 56–58.
18. Kidd (161), pp. 102, 158–159, Alberti (2), p. 96.

fishing were the chief means of maintenance, some important property rights were always in evidence.

The following illustrations are selected from societies with such forms of maintenance. An African Bushman's ornaments and wearing apparel were his own possessions in late old age.[19] Trinkets, weapons, and private claims upon certain women were recognized property rights of the aged Dieri.[20] An elderly Vedda was observed to possess "one axe, bow and arrows, three pots, a deerskin, a flint and steel, and supply of tinder, a gourd for carrying water, a betel pouch containing betel cutters, and some form of vessel or small box . . . for holding lime." Most of the Vedda owned some cloth besides that actually worn by them. Seligmann states that the aged sometimes held property rights to land which they exchanged for food and clothing, or passed on to their children. Near relatives of dying men were especially considerate—expecting gifts.[21]

Aged Ainu men controlled heirlooms and family treasures.[22] The elders among the Haida, both men and women, owned blankets, cloth, ornaments, and other wares, and these frequently represented quite extensive investments.[23] The same was true of the Kwakiutl.[24] Chippewa rights in hunting territories were often controlled by old men;[25] and a proverbial remark among the Crow was: "How can a man be poor when he has plenty of horses and many sons to look after him when he is old?"[26]

The aged Pomo possessed bows, arrows, deer heads, hunters' songs, and charms. A fisherman could trade or bequeath harpoons, nets, charms, bags, fishing and love songs, and bows and arrows. Other articles owned by the aged consisted of food, blankets, baskets, and wampum. The ground about the house and certain trees was claimed by the oldest woman, although used by members of the family.[27] Aged matrons among the Seri appear to have controlled the little property carried along in their constant wanderings.[28]

Among the Yukaghir of Siberia it has been reported: "What-

19. Bleek (24), p. 10.
20. Howitt (142), p. 58.
21. Seligmann (269), pp. 114–115, 117.
22. Batchelor (12), pp. 19–21.
23. Harrison (123), pp. 64–65.
24. Ford (104), pp. 10–12, 17–23.
25. Speck (285), pp. 5, 70.
26. Curtis (62), p. 57.
27. Loeb (180), pp. 158, 197–199, 239.
28. McGee (188), p. 276.

ever is procured through hunting or fishing is turned over by the
hunters and fishermen to the women, the oldest of whom looks
after its distribution. The furs of animals killed by the hunters
are in the hands of the oldest man in the family who pays the
tribute or other debts, and barters them for products imported
by merchants. According to the ancient custom the son-in-law and
all the products of his work are in the power and at the disposal
of the father-in-law and he is not permitted to speak to the old
man in case of conflict of interests . . . . After the death of both
parents, the control of the property is transferred to the oldest
member of the family." [29]

Among herders property rights were generally much more pronounced and the amount of capital was usually greatly increased.
Aged Navaho generally owned horses, sheep, cattle, and goats.
There was much wealth in such intangible property as songs,
dances, medicine bundles, prayer sticks, formulas for increasing
flocks, and knowledge of magic. If a man "built up" a good name,
it could be traded for wealth. Old men often required payment for
information. One aged man possessed at the time of his death
three thousand head of cattle, sheep, and horses, and vast wealth
in medicine lore, sacred names, legends, songs, and "power." It
was believed that his "knowledge wealth" was more valuable than
his material effects, and even after his death the entire family
were meticulously careful to carry out all his wishes. Reichard
also states: "The mother of the family plays a large role in the
social and economic life. She possesses a number of sheep and
goats—oft times more than her husband—and has charge of
them . . . ." [30]

Leem reports that it was the custom of the Laplanders to bury
their wealth, especially "money," so cautiously that their heirs
could not recover it. If, at the hour of death, the father did not
choose to reveal the secret hiding place, the heirs simply lost it.
Keane has supported this by stating: "Their foresight is carried
even beyond the grave, and it is no uncommon practice to bury or
hide away money and other treasures for use, not only in this, but
also in after life." [31] Norse legends also imply that both men and
women stored up wealth as safeguards against the hazards of old
age.[32]

29. Jochelson (154), pp. 108–109.
30. Reichard (242), pp. 53, 95.
31. Keane (also quoting Leem) (159), p. 229.
32. Williams (333), p. 171.

Old men among the Chukchi received great consideration, especially in the reindeer-breeding section of the tribe, because the herd belonged to the father as long as he lived. "In many camps in various parts of the territory of the Chukchee," writes Bogoras, "I have met very old men, perhaps of seventy or even eighty . . . . Some of these old men were almost in their dotage; still they had retained possession of the herd and the general direction of life in their camps. For instance, in a camp on the Oloi River, a man named Kauno, who had great-grandnephews ten years old, owned two large herds and decided himself the most important question of the seasonal migration of the Chukchee, that of choosing the place of abode for the summer time. Though enfeebled by age, he still made the April trip to the Wolverene River every spring for barter with the Maritime traders from the Arctic villages, who came there at that time, bringing maritime products and American wares. Kauno's own housemates told me that the old man had grown childish and often purchased things of little use in their life. Instead of sugar he took bottled molasses, because it was red and pleased his eye; he bought table knives instead of hunting knives, because they were brighter, etc. This was told, however, with broad grins and without any visible signs of protest. 'Foolish One,' they added quite good-humoredly, 'What is to be done? He is an old man.' And I am quite sure that Kauno kept the direction of his house till his natural end." [33]

Another Chukchi of sixty had a dislocated hip and could move about only with the aid of crutches. "He continued to be the master of his herd and the head of his family. . . . Every year he would go to the Ainu fair for barter, carrying along peltries and reindeerskins. He was very fond of strong liquor, bought it every time, and drank most of it himself, giving to each of the other members of his family only a few drops." "I remember one old man with whom I was staying over night," continues Bogoras. "The night was dark and windy, and the wolves succeeded in making an assault upon the herd, driving away several animals. The next morning, when the old man left the sleeping room and came outside, he found two of the herdsmen of the camp who told him the unpleasant story. Immediately he grew very angry, caught up a lasso, and began chastizing them both. They were of large bulk and tall of stature; and he was a small, half-decrepit fellow, who, to make his blows more effective, skipped around and

33. Bogoras (28), pp. 544–546.

tried to strike them upon the face with the iron ring of the lasso. They did not show any resistance. From the Chukchee point of view, the old man was in the right, and they in the wrong." It is also stated that among their Maritime neighbors the owners of property, "though ever so old, continue to hold it, and their position in life does not become lower with increasing age." [34]

Aged Yakut women had few private possessions, but the old men were usually heads of households and exercised considerable property rights.[35] Elsewhere it is stated: "In well-to-do families, where there is a great quantity of cattle or where the right to large advantages from land, or the possession of well established trade . . . the rule of the father is strengthened and maintained for a long time, namely, to the moment when the old people become decrepit and lose the capacity to comprehend the simplest things. Generally they die before that time." [36] Sieroshevski stated, however: "Sometimes, of course, very old people make out in the courts official donative notes to their sons and even to strangers, in which they enumerate how much property they give and on what conditions, in detail. Conditions usually consist of 'maintenance, guidance and respect for life and a decent burial after death.' Sometimes it is enumerated in detail how much and of what the persons endowed must furnish the donors, per year or month. These conditions often lead to quarrels, and in the end the interests of the old people always suffer." [37]

Property rights were pronounced among the ancient Hebrew. Abraham in his old age was described as very rich in cattle, silver, and gold, and his trusted servant is quoted thus: "The Lord has blessed my master greatly; and he has become great: He hath given him flocks and herds and silver, and gold, and men servants and maid servants, and camels and asses." The same picture of age entrenched in wealth is neatly drawn in the legend of Job: "And the Lord turned the captivity of Job, when he prayed for his friends; also the Lord gave Job twice as much as he had before. . . . So the Lord blessed the later end of Job more than his beginning; for he had fourteen thousand sheep, and six thousand camels, and a thousand yoke of oxen, and a thousand she asses." [38]

Mongol patriarchs have also appeared to possess substantial

34. *Ibid.* (28), pp. 544–546, 619.
35. Sieroshevski (272), p. 76.
36. Bogoras (28), p. 78.
37. Sieroshevski (271), pp. 522–523.
38. Gen. 24:35; Job 42: 10–17.

property rights. In one instance a man above fifty owned horses and exercised considerable authority, even though both legs were cut off at the knees.[39] A Toda's wealth consisted of herds of buffalo which safeguarded his security in old age.[40] The aged Tuareg were rich in herds and their old women enjoyed property rights perhaps even more than the men. "As they grow older, the women of good family and wealth become fat . . . for fatness is a sign of affluence, since it implies a sufficiency of the good things of life, like slaves and food, to obviate having to do much manual work . . . nearly all the old women look typical aristocrats and conscious of their breeding." [41]

Property rights were very much in evidence among Kazak herders. Atkinson writes: "I counted one hundred and six camels, including their young; there were more than two thousand horses, one thousand oxen and cows, and six thousand sheep and goats. Even these, large as the number may appear, were far short of the total amount of animals belonging to the patriarchal chief (an old man)." [42] Esteemed elders acted as judges and accepted presents from both sides, thus accumulating much property. Huntington has drawn a vivid picture of an aged patriarch in the glory of his wealth as he moved with party and herd to fresh grazing grounds. "In front of them an old graybeard with a black hat and a waddle gown rode proudly on a spirited horse. His gloved right hand rested in the wood crotch at the upper end of a short stick which stood in a little stirrup, and on his wrist perched a hunting eagle with a leather hood over his eyes." [43]

Property rights in the hands of the aged have been no less common in Africa, where herding and agriculture are often found together. Old Lango men controlled much wealth and disposed of it in the form of presents for various services.[44] The same was true of the Shilluk.[45] It was also reported of the Akamba: "To the old man belongs all the cattle and the goats; none of his sons possess anything; even their wives are bought with his property. All the dowries paid for daughters of the village and blood-money for members of the family who have been killed go to increase his stocks." [46] Hobley thus described a typi-

39. Howorth (146), pp. 194–195.
40. Thurston (310), p. 117; Rivers (247), p. 563.
41. Rodd (249), p. 173.
42. Atkinson (4), p 228; Spencer (290), p. 16.
43. Huntington (147), p. 117.
44. Driberg (82), p. 248.
45. Westermann (328), p. xxvii.
46. Dundas (85), pp. 493–494.

cal deathbed scene for an aged man: "If the head of the family feels that he is nearing his end he will assemble his sons, and to the eldest he will probably say, 'The goats belonging to such a hut shall be yours, and if any of you break these wishes, he shall surely die.' Sometimes, too, a man when he is very old will entrust a son with charge of his live stock, and the son may abuse the trust and let the flocks and herds melt away. Cases have been known where the old patriarch when dying has put a curse upon his son, to the effect that he can neither grow rich nor have wives, but to the end of his life he shall be condemned to perpetual poverty." [47]

Old Xosa men were rich from the labors of their women and the sale of their children. Kidd writes: "I once asked an old chief who had selected the site of his kraal amidst the most beautiful scenery whether he admired the view. The old man did not want to be rude, but knew not how to conceal his merriment. He went off into a hearty chuckle . . . and said he chose it only that he might be able to feast his eyes on his cattle feeding and his corn ripening in the valley beneath." [48] Shooter has added: "We can imagine the pride with which the old man goes from kraal to kraal, advising here, commanding or reproving there, respected and obeyed everywhere; or with what complacency he looks around him from the hill on which his own habitation stands and viewing those of his children says inly, 'They are mine.' " [49]

Firmly entrenched property rights which enhanced the powers of the aged have also been very common among all cultivators of the soil. Jenks reports for the Bontoc Igorot that even old men without relatives usually had at least a little property with which to secure the ready service of their fellows. [50] Venerable men among the Vai of southwest Africa were usually of high standing and wealth, possessing farms, slaves, servants, and several wives. [51] Rights to wealth were no less pronounced among the Ashanti, and the aged head of a family on becoming conscious of approaching death, "summons his relatives to his death-bed, and instructs them as to the disposition of his property; being careful to recount the names of his pawns and slaves, the amounts from which he holds the former, and the sums due to him from his debtors." [52]

47. Hobley (130), pp. 427–428.
48. Kidd (161), p. 53.
49. Shooter (270), p. 91.
50. Jenks (153), pp. 70–71.
51. Ellis (92), pp. 40, 59–60.
52. *Ibid.* (90), p. 237.

Weeks reported: "A woman among the Bakongo is the best gilt-edge security in which a man can invest his surplus wealth. Pigs, goats, and fowls may die, slaves run away, speculations in trade expeditions may prove a failure, and thus he loses his money; but he rarely if ever loses the money he has invested in a wife. Should she die, he takes a calabash of palm wine and going to her family, i.e., to her maternal uncle's family, he informs them of the death, and demands another wife in place of the deceased. If the family has not another woman free for this purpose then the marriage money must be returned in full." [53]

Overbergh affirms that the father of a Mangbetu family was also the sole possessor of wealth.[54] Aged Mafulu men controlled their property until death.[55] If a Banks Islander with children died while his parents were still alive, the children could not claim the land until they had bought off the rights of the grandparents with money and pigs. It was also "a common thing for a man to hide a portion of his wealth, and only reveal it to his son, if the latter perform his filial duties satisfactorily when old age creeps on." [56]

A Kiwai Papuan woman could not own real estate in a strict sense, but a man's most valuable possession was his land, and in former times its transfer from one owner to another was practically unknown except by inheritance. "As the sons in a family grow up, they are given land by their father, who keeps the rest of it for himself, definite partitions of the inheritance taking place at his death or sometimes later still. If the father becomes too old to work his gardens himself, the whole of the plantations are taken over by the sons who then support him till his death." A son is said to have had the right to use his father's personal property—for instance, to take coconuts from trees planted by his father. It is reported to have been different, however, with fruit from the trees inherited by the father from his father. "When I die," the father is reported to have said, "he belongs to you—this time he belongs to me—you no can take him." In many cases old men were glad to make over their gardens to persons willing to serve them in their senility.[57]

An aged Iban also owned property in land, precious jars,

53. Weeks (327), p. 147.
54. Overbergh (216), p. 138.
55. Williamson (334), p. 119.
56. Codrington (54), pp. 64–65; Rivers (248), pp. 36–37; Coombe (55), p. 63.
57. Landtman (171), pp. 197, 199, 245.

gongs, brass ware, weapons, war-coats, boats, beads, cloth, bird-nest caves, bee trees, and slaves. Enfeebled parents, by a special bequest of valuables, could induce sons or daughters to remain in the house and look after them until their death.[58] Old men among the Trobrianders held on tenaciously to their landed interests, and nephews could gain access to them only by degrees and by making substantial payments.[59] According to Malinowski, every village or community "belonged to" or was "owned by" a subclan, and the oldest male was the headman. The formal title in the communal territory was nominally vested in the head of the subclan which was under the direction of the oldest male of the oldest lineage.[60] Maori youths were carefully instructed in land boundaries by their fathers and grandfathers, and a dying man's wishes regarding his property were viewed much as people now look upon a signed will.[61] A Sema Naga nearing the end of life held on to his property rights and from his death bed passed them on to dutiful descendants.[62]

During the lifetime of a Munda father, his sons and their wives usually lived under the paternal roof, joined hands in cultivating the family fields, and brought their separate earnings to the common family fund. The father, even in his old age, could expel a disobedient son without giving him any movable property or share in the lands, and he was regarded as having almost absolute control over the family wealth.[63]

The above cases, only samples of the mass which could be gathered, clearly imply that property rights, even in primitive societies, have played a significant role in providing security for individuals facing old age. A firm hold on the strings of a fat purse was one effective compensation for declining physical powers. While the enfeebled individual could in no sense defend such rights by the strength of his might, they were guarded and maintained for him by the prevailing mores. The point of interest for our investigation is now to determine, if possible, just what types of societies have insured the greatest degree of property rights to men and women hampered by age.

The participation of aged men in the exercise of property rights was found to be pronounced in 38 tribes, average in 8, and

58. Hose and McDougall (140), I, pp. 83–84.
59. Silas (273), pp. 102–103.
60. Malinowski (193), I, 30–31, 345–346.
61. Best (20), I, 394; II, 52.
62. Hutton (148), p. 159.
63. Sarat (257), pp. 427–429.

slight in 7. For aged women the practice was reported as pronounced in 7, average in 8, and slight in 13. It is important to note that in no case was it stated that aged men did not participate in property rights, but in 4 tribes such control was not customary for aged women (traits 127, 128). The evidence is similar for the participation of aged men and women in trade, but not as complete (traits 129, 130).

Two outstanding generalizations can be drawn from a statistical analysis of the material. First, sex differences have been striking; aged men and women have not shared alike in opportunities to acquire control of property, and apparently the same societal factors have not always operated uniformly to favor both. Second, the opportunities to acquire and exercise property rights by either sex in old age have been quite variable and highly conditioned by both environmental and cultural factors. How much security an aged man or woman might achieve through property rights has been determined largely by circumstances beyond personal control, and these factors seem to show an orderly development when viewed upon a broad cultural background.

Aged women have acquired important property rights in much fewer primitive societies than have old men, but severity of climate and inconstancy of the food supply have appeared equally detrimental to the success of both (Cor. 53–56). Apart from these factors, the tendencies for aged men and women to acquire property have differed a great deal in terms of positive and negative coefficients of association, and have not infrequently followed opposite trends. Old women have shown a relative advantage over men in the control of property rights among collectors (Cor. 57–58), hunters (Cor. 59–60), and fishers (Cor. 61–62), although the sex difference grows less in the latter. But among farmers, and especially herders, aged men have apparently been at great advantage over women (Cor. 63–66). Communal food-sharing customs and communal ownership of land showed negative coefficients of association when correlated with property rights possessed by old men, and positive coefficients with property rights of aged women (Cor. 67–70). Aged men have far outranked women in the tendency to control property wherever such rights are well established in objects other than land (Cor. 71–72); in land (Cor. 73–74); where industrial techniques for mining and smelting metals have developed (Cor. 75–76); where slavery exists (Cor. 77–78); where there is money or a standard medium of exchange (Cor. 79–80); where debt-relations are established procedures (Cor. 81–82); and where trade is in common practice (Cor. 83–84). In other words, with general cultural advance, men have gained advantage over women in the possession of property.

Significantly different trends are reflected in the ownership of property by aged men and women when correlations are drawn with respect to family organization. Matrilocal residence (Cor. 85–86) and matrilineal descent (Cor. 87–88), inheritance (Cor. 89–90), and succession (Cor. 91–92) have uniformly accompanied tendencies unfavorable to the acquirement of property by aged men in contrast to aged women. The same trends are strongly indicated where the dwelling is owned by the wife (Cor. 93–94); where matripotestal authority is recognized (Cor. 95–96); and where the avunculate is pronounced (Cor. 97–98). It should be noted, however, that the coefficients of association are much more strongly positive for the control of property by aged women than they are negative for aged men, which indicates that aged men were likely to possess property even under these conditions. In other words, property rights of aged women show greater variations and seem to be more strongly influenced by the prevailing type of social organization. The prerogatives of women are the significant cues in a study of sex status in terms of property rights.

Under the patriarchal system of family organization, reverse tendencies appear. Aged women were at considerable disadvantage in the possession of property rights under patrilocal residence (Cor. 99–100) and patrilineal descent (Cor. 101–102), inheritance (Cor. 103–104), and succession (Cor. 105–106); while aged men under such conditions found great advantage. In societies where patripotestal authority is pronounced (Cor. 107–108), where bride-price is paid (Cor. 109–110), where rights to property in women are recognized (Cor. 111–112), where there is an organized priesthood (Cor. 113–114), and where ancestor worship is well established (Cor. 115–116), the same trends were intensified, with disadvantage to aged women and substantial gains to men.

It is obvious, however, that such findings merely show trends and do not indicate that the possession of property by anyone has been determined entirely by any single or small number of cultural factors. Innumerable social forces, closely interrelated and interdependent, always worked together. "In their adjustments the mores move forward in rank, not in file, though that rank may not be without its irregularities." "Property, law, rights, government, classes, marriage, religion—are all born together and linked together." "They all march together for the sake of expediency and under the strain of consistency." [64]

The most impressive statistical finding is that so many coefficients of association (Cor. 53–116) have consistently agreed and together supported the basic generalization that the exercise of property rights by the aged in primitive societies has undergone a process of change and evolution in conformity with certain identifiable cultural factors. More specifically, aged women, in contrast with men, have tended to acquire property rights more readily in simple societies characterized by collection, hunting, and fishing, and also within the matrilineal type of family organization; while aged men have gained their greatest advantage in the control of property among farmers, and especially herders, as well as within the patriarchal system of family organization and amid social traits characteristic of more advanced cultures.

This is not to imply, of course, that aged women have not sometimes fared better in herding or agricultural societies than among hunters or fishers. Indeed, when farming and herding societies have been characterized by the mother-family system, aged women have even had the advantage over men. But in more complex societies, especially where a pronounced patriarchal family system has prevailed, aged men have generally surpassed women in opportunities for the possession of property. In conclusion, then, to "get capital" would have been an apt slogan for old-age security almost anywhere, anytime, and for everyone. In the simpler beginnings aged women seem to have had a more nearly equal chance to acquire property, but with the development of society their mates and brothers have found it possible to get and to control more property, and the women have had to rely mainly upon other forms of old-age security.

64. Sumner and Keller (299), I, 260, 502; II, 1997.

III

PRESTIGE

RESPECT for old age has resulted from social discipline. In primitive societies there are no signs of a deep-seated "instinct" to guarantee to elders either homage or pity from their offspring. Whatever prestige they received was not a boon of nature; it was a product of social developments, it rested primarily upon rights, and it stemmed from the force a custom or the fear of consequences. Underlying any high regard for old age was some enforcing power, real or imaginary, to safeguard it. Opportunities for social status in senescence, as in the sharing of food and the possession of property, were thus conditioned by social and cultural factors. In brief, the evidence indicates that when conditions called for respect to the aged they got it; when these conditions changed they might lose it.

Prestige in old age is a complex subject, involving many aspects of culture, and this has made it difficult to formulate any clear-cut plan of analysis. The problem is further complicated by the fact that much personal treatment of the aged may be considered as either a mark of esteem and sympathy or as a sign of neglect and abuse, depending upon social interpretations and customary standards of propriety. There are cases, for instance, where the killing of the aged is regarded as a special tribute, an "honor" which is anticipated or actually requested by the aged themselves; but in other cases it can be regarded as nothing short of redhanded murder. In any study of homage and sympathy for the aged, therefore, careful consideration must be paid to the customary meaning of given experiences for particular cultures and for the parties involved.

For the sake of order in the presentation of the illustrative material, the subject has been divided into four categories: general respect for the aged; social taboos favorable to old age; glorification of the aged in legends and stories; and deification of them in religion.

Most primitive societies have insured some respect for the aged —often remarkable deference, in fact—at least until they have become so "overaged" that they are obviously powerless and in-

competent. But under close analysis, respect for old age has, as
a rule, been accorded to persons on the basis of some particular
asset which they possessed. They might be respected for their extensive knowledge, seasoned experience, expert skill, power to work
magic, exercise of priestly functions, control of property rights,
or manipulation of family prerogatives. They might be highly
regarded for their skill in games, dances, songs, and storytelling.
They might even receive consideration for their faithful performance of camp or household chores. It is important to note
both the extent of general respect accorded to them in old age
and the range of avenues which afford "access to homage." Some
social systems have provided many ways by which the aged could
attain prestige, while in others the opportunities were all too
meager. The purpose here is to try to learn which cultural factors
are conducive, and which are detrimental, to the achievement of
prestige by aged men and women.

In presenting illustrative cases of general respect for the aged,
the so-called simpler cultures of tribes characterized chiefly as
collectors (with subsidizing hunting or fishing) are examined
first; these are followed by true hunting and fishing groups; and
these by herding and agricultural societies.

Among the Yahgans, regarded as a very primitive group,
"nearly every old man was a wizard," and occasionally aged
women practiced the evil art and inspired enough fear and respect
to be well treated. In families and small groups it is said that the
words of the elderly men were accepted as law.[1] It has been reported of the Arawak that "powerless old age meets with no respect." [2] The Semang honored and respected their aged, who, it
is claimed, were rarely ever contradicted. Even when they were
incapable of working, their children provided for them, frequently carrying them on their backs in moving camp; and one
very popular old man was called "Grandfather of the Community." [3] Care and respect were accorded to aged Andamanese.
Certain ones were honored as medicine men, some as officials at
weddings, and others as counselors of the people. "Respect for
seniority is kept alive partly by traditions and partly by the fact
that the older men have had greater experience . . . ." Children
were taught to respect their elders.[4] The Vedda of Ceylon used

1. Cooper (56), pp. 160, 170; Garson (112), p. 144.
2. Im Thurn (151), p. 224.
3. Murdock (208), p. 100; Skeat and Blagden (277), II, 171.
4. Mann (194), p. 14; Brown (40), pp. 44, 69, 73–74, 79.

special terms of respect in addressing their aged. Sarasin described the chief as an "intelligent old man," and reported an aged woman who exercised great authority over her group, both young and old.[5] Bonwick has reported that among the Tasmanians, generally assumed to be of very low cultural attainment, the old men and women got the best food and received respect until they became decrepit, after which they were often neglected.[6]

The aged received great homage in Australia. Among the Arunta, special titles were given to those learned in tribal lore, and many were feared because of their power to bring sickness. It has been emphasized by ethnographers that the main objective of the very drastic initiation ceremonies was "to bring the young men under the control of the old men, whose commands they have to obey explicitly . . . ."[7] However, it is also stated: "Everything does not depend upon age . . . some of the oldest men were of little account; but on the other hand, others who were not so old as they were, but more learned in ancient lore or more skilled in matters of magic, were looked up to by the others, and they settle everything."[8] Seniority was no less rewarded among the Dieri, where old men dominated practically everything. Howitt has remarked upon the great respect and even reverence shown to very aged men, and cites an instance: "Some of the old men came to visit me, and asked me to go with them to see the *Pinnapinnaru* (The Great-Great-One) who could not come to see me. I went with them and found, sitting in one of the huts, the oldest black fellow I had ever seen. The other Pinnarus were mostly grey-headed and bald, but he was so old as to be almost childish and was covered with a grizzly felt of hair from head to foot. The respect with which he was greeted by the other old men was as marked in them as the respect which they received from the younger men. They told me that he was so old that he could not walk, and that when they traveled some of the younger men carried him."[9] Howitt further explained: "In the Dieri tribe, as in all others of those kindred to it, the oldest man of a totem is its *Pinnaru*, or head . . . . But it does not follow that the head of a totem or of a local division has necessarily much, or even any, influence outside his totem or division. I remember such an instance

5. Seligmann (269), p. 70; Sarasin (256), pp. 468, 486–487.
6. Bonwick (30), pp. 64, 80.
7. Spencer and Gillen (289), I, 39, 161, 223, 248, 398.
8. *Ibid.* (289), I, 12.
9. Howitt (142), p. 65; Briffault (38), I, 744–745; Howitt (143), p. 300.

at Lake Hope where the *Pinnaru* was, by reason of his great age, the head of the eagle-hawk totem, but he had otherwise little personal influence, for he was neither a fighting man, a medicine-man, nor an orator." [10] In the Dieri circumcision ceremony, the directors and instructors were always elderly people "so that their teaching shall be respected." [11] Gason observed that "as a rule old, but not senile men made all important decisions." [12] Horne and Aiston wrote of the Wokonguru, a group related to the Dieri and having essentially the same culture: "Seniority runs through the whole aboriginal system. It is maintained by the old men, who always retain some rite or ceremony which is not made known to the juniors. Of course upon this rite the utmost stress is laid, and its import (often most trifling) is kept among the fewest possible number . . . . Age in itself, quite apart from fitness, seems to give a right to authority." [13]

In tribes of hunters the aged are also reported to have received considerable respect. The Polar Eskimo were very considerate of old men and women on account of their wisdom and power. A native said, in speaking of aged magicians: "We do not all understand the hidden things, but we believe the people who say they do. We believe our *Angakut*, our magicians, . . . because we wish to live long, and because we do not wish to expose ourselves to the danger of famine and starvation . . . . If we did not follow their advice, we should fall ill and die." [14]

The Labrador Eskimo treated the aged with great deference and regarded their words as final, because it was believed that in them was embodied the wisdom of their ancestors. Old women were respected for their ability to interpret dreams, aged men were renowned as healers of disease, and both were sought out for their legends and stories. According to Turner, "disrespect to parents is unknown." [15]

Among the Eskimo of Point Barrow, "Respect for the opinion of the elders is so great that the people may be said to be practically under what is called 'simple elder rule.' " An "old, feeble, tottering man, very deaf, and almost blind," was honored as "Chief" and treated accordingly. Old people were always in de-

10. Howitt (143), p. 297.
11. *Ibid.*, p. 657.
12. Gason (113), p. 262.
13. Horne and Aiston (138), p. 12.
14. Rasmussen (233), pp. 16–22, 123; Ross (250), p. 134.
15. Hawkes (124), p. 117; Turner (316), pp. 190, 200, 260–261, 269; Hutton (149), p. 290.

mand for their tales, legends, and general information. Those too feeble to hunt whales were still honored for their power to cure the sick and to "talk up" east winds which could drive the ice off shore so that the whales would come in. Children spoke of their parents with the highest respect, even after death. "In each village there is a number of old women who are treated with the greatest consideration by all, they being credited with wonderful powers of divination, and are consulted on all important affairs." [16]

Homage to the aged was a stern precept of the ancient Iroquois. "It is the will of the Great Spirit that you reverence the aged, even though they be as helpless as infants." They associated long life with wisdom. A common prayer was: "Preserve our old men among us . . . ." [17] For a son to be rebellious to his aged mother was considered the most horrible crime. Aged women had important political power and commanded respect. It was said that they could stop a war with which they were not in full sympathy; and they boasted: "We own the land." [18]

Concerning the Chippewa, Jones has written: "Some have supposed that age is not respected . . . but this is a great mistake . . . . The advice of the 'long dweller upon the earth' is generally listened to with great attention . . . where there is no literature it cannot be otherwise than that they should think much of those who impart to them all the knowledge they most prize, and who are supposed, from the length of time they have lived, to have gained great experience. These remarks refer particularly to the males, as the aged females are not in general looked up with the same degree of reverence." [19] The elderly men held the central positions in council gatherings where the young were expected to sit in silence. Fathers instructed their children to be kind to the poor and the aged, and the young feared very much to bring themselves under their reproach. [20]

The oldest Omaha men were highly regarded and held such honored positions as the chieftainship and "Keeper of the Sacred Pole," as well as being leaders at ceremonies and public gatherings. Parents taught their children to respect the elders and never interrupt them in conversation. "When a man of distinction

16. Murdock (210), p. 427; Ray (241), pp. 39, 43–45, 47.
17. Morgan (207), pp. 165, 188; Loskiel (181), I, 15.
18. Beauchamp (14), pp. 86–88; Briffault (38), I, 148.
19. Jones (156), p. 69.
20. Kohl (163), p. 273; Densmore (73), p. 122; Jones (156), p. 78.

was spoken to, etiquette demanded that he be addressed as *isha'ge*,
'aged one.' The term was one of respect and implied his position
of wisdom, dignity, and position." The titles of "grandfather"
and "old man" were terms of veneration used in addressing the
gods.[21]

Pomo youths were constantly admonished to give place to the
elders and be kind to them, "for these are the people who know
most about poisoning." Aged "bear-doctors," both men and
women, were greatly feared. Aged matrons were in possession of
the houses and many of the fruit-bearing trees, and thus enjoyed
high regard. Big chiefs were almost always past the prime of life;
and aged men were highly respected in council affairs.[22]

Among fishers, as well as collectors and hunters, the aged were
often highly respected. The Ainu of Japan, described as both
hunters and fishers, showed great deference to their old men.[23]
The men among the Yukaghir enjoyed a guarded and respected
old age. "This is one of the reasons the Yukaghir love their children so much. The advantage of having children extends even beyond the grave; for young people are believed to live in the other
world in the same family group in which they lived on earth. The
old parents will enjoy in the other world, after their children's
death, the same respectful position as heads of families; while
during their children's lives they will receive offerings from
them." The son paid such homage to his father that he seldom
undertook anything without the old man's approval.[24]

The Kwakiutl honored their old men, made them masters of
ceremonies at public gatherings, and at all meetings strictly observed their rank. "*Watsiti*" was a title of regard commonly· applied to the eldest member of the family.[25] The Haida also respected their elders, whose advice in most matters had great
weight. Old women attained considerable influence as soothsayers
and "because of their venerable appearance." Chiefs who grew
old turned their duties over to more energetic men, but they retained their rank and titles until death. Honored places were reserved for aged men at weddings and other public festivities.[26]

21. Fletcher and La Flesche (103), pp. 50, 329, 335, 370; Dorsey (78), p. 217;
ibid. (79), p. 368.
22. Loeb (80), pp. 198, 237–241, 271; Barrett (10), pp. 444, 452.
23. Batchelor (11), p. 109.
24. Jochelson (154), pp. 107–109.
25. Curtis (63), pp. 139, 217; Boas (27), pp. 440–443.
26. Niblack (213), p. 240; Harrison (123), pp. 64–65, 115–116, Swanton (301),
p. 51.

The aged among the Menomini Indians were popular for their folk tales and interpretations of life told about the camp fires during the long winter nights.[27]

Respect for the aged has been no less common among herders. Ostermann has said of the Navaho: "Gray hair is rare and is as a rule treated with deference and respect." [28] Reichard indicates that aged women were custodians of much property and held in high regard in both family and public life. "My father" was a term of respect accorded a man one generation removed. Aged men rich in herds and magic lore were shown special consideration.[29] Aged Lango men were maintained by the family when they had passed the stage of active participation in village life, and were respected for their wisdom. Old men held the leading roles in practically all ceremonies, some of which were in their honor.[30] Aged Tuareg women were especially honored as the repositories of the learning and traditions of their tribe, as well as for the fact of their motherhood.[31] Among the Toda young men were taught, as an act of homage to the old, to place their heads ceremonially beneath the feet of certain elders.[32] To the Berber of Morocco, the term *baraka* denoted a mysterious wonder-working force, a sort of "holiness" acquired through long life, but in women it was believed to have the power of a curse. Therefore old men were highly and truly esteemed, but aged women were honored and greatly feared.[33]

Among the Hottentot a report states that "respect for the aged is inculcated in every possible way," and that it was reflected in the whole social organization of the people. "In the family, deference must always be paid to the elders. Thus of a number of brothers the oldest always has the honored place and the first voice in any debate." According to Hoernle, there "is evidence that in the early days the older people in the tribe did have an exceedingly strong and important position, and this notwithstanding the well known fact that old people were exposed [to die] by the Hottentots. Even nowadays [1918], I observe that an old person keeps his power as long as he keeps his vigor and his judg-

27. Hoffman (135), p. 210.
28. Ostermann (215), p. 806.
29. Reichard (242), pp. 52, 56, 95.
30. Driberg (82), pp. 52–73, 243.
31. Campbell (46), pp. 94, 224, 233.
32. Rivers (247), pp. 35, 356.
33. Westermarck (329), I, 46, 420.

ment, though he is likely to have a sad life if times be hard and he is rather a burden than a help to the family." [34]

In Akamba society elderly men held prominent positions as heads of families, public officials, and directors of ceremonies, even maintaining their exclusive clubs.[35] Xosa patriarchs in control of property received great homage and were regarded as very wise on account of their years and success.[36] Kidd added: "Natives show extraordinary respect to old men," but "old women are excluded from such attention, so that their lot is sad indeed." Natives would say of them: "Their use is over; they are cast off things." [37]

Seniority received great consideration among the Chukchi, especially where property and family rights were involved. Cases are cited where sturdy young men would stand meekly and suffer floggings from enfeebled old fathers.[38]

In Yakut society, a patriarch, with entrenched property rights, was strictly honored. "Inside the house he is treated with almost slavish respect and consideration. His presence puts an end to cheerfulness, the excuse for which is that he must maintain respect." According to tradition, *sesen*, "white-haired, honored, much-experienced old men . . . who know everything," played major roles in the assemblies and settled all important questions. But "not every old man was considered *sesen*, since for that a special 'prophetic' gift was needed: in other words, a recognized wisdom, experience and knowledge . . . ." [39] Sauer stated: "I have never seen an old man contradicted or opposed, but always implicitly obeyed as father of a family. A young man even gives his opinion with the greatest respect and caution; and even when asked, he submits his ideas to the judgment of the old." [40] And Sieroshevski reported that once he saw "a weak old man of seventy beat with a stick his forty year old son, who was in good health, rich and a completely independent householder, who had just been elected to an office in the sib. The son stood quietly and did not dare even to evade the blows." "But," the author ex-

---

34. Hoernle (133), pp. 21–22; also (132), p. 68.
35. Dundas (85), pp. 493–494; Hobley (131), pp. 54, 276, Vanden-Bergh (321), p. 67.
36. Shooter (270), p. 92; Alberti (2), p. 118.
37. Kidd (161), pp. 22–23, 29.
38. Bogoras (28), pp. 544–546, 551, 619.
39. Sieroshevski (272), p. 78.
40. Sauer (259), p. 124.

plained, "the old man still had an important amount of property at his disposition and he ruled the family by the fear that he could deprive any recalcitrant one of a share in the inheritance." It is important to note that Sieroshevski also found contrary cases: "The Yakut treat their old relatives, who have grown stupid, very badly. Usually they try to take from them the remains of their property, if they have any; then constantly, in measure as they become unprotected, they treat them worse and worse. Even in houses relatively self-sufficient, I found such living skeletons . . . wrinkled, half-naked, or even entirely naked, hiding in the corners, from where they creep out only when no strangers are present, to get warm by the fire, to pick up together with children bits of food thrown away, or to quarrel with them over the licking of the dish emptied of food." [41]

According to ancient Hebrew precepts: "The hoary head is a crown of glory . . . ." [42] "The glory of young men is their strength; and the beauty of old men is the hoary head." [43] "A wise son heareth his father's instruction." [44] "Hearken unto thy father that begat thee, and despise not thy mother when she is old." [45] "Thou shalt rise up before the hoary head, and honor the face of the old man . . . ." [46] "Honor thy father and thy mother, that thy days may be long upon the land which Jehovah thy God giveth thee." [47] "And he that smiteth his father, or his mother, shall be surely put to death." [48] In the literary dialogue between Elihu and Job the former remarks: "I am young and ye are old. Wherefore I was afraid and durst not show you my opinion. I said days shall speak and a multitude of years shall teach wisdom." [49]

Finally, among cultivators of the soil there are many peoples who have respected the aged, at least until they became incapacitated. Among the Creek, the words for "Grandfather" and "Grandmother" were honorary terms used in addressing old people. Funerals and mourning rites were much more elaborate for them. It was reported that in the good old days the young people were orderly and obeyed their elders: "Formerly they always went at once and did as they were told . . . when we tell them to do anything now, they seem to stop and think about it." [50]

The Hopi say: "A long, long time ago we were good to our old

41. Sieroshevski (271), pp. 465, 510–513.
42. Prov. 16:3.   43. *Ibid.* 20:29.   44. *Ibid.* 13:1.   45. *Ibid.* 23:22.
46. Lev. 19:32.   47. Ex. 20:12.   48. *Ibid.* 21:15.   49. Job 32:7.
50. Swanton (302), pp. 80, 367; Bushnell (44), p. 100.

people, realizing that our lives depended upon them. Children were taught that if they did not respect old age they would die young. Now we are not well cared for when we get old." [51] The aged are still respected as long as they can keep control of property rights, are active as special officers in the ceremonies, or hold the confidence or fear of the people as powerful medicine men. But the feebler and more useless they become, the more relatives grab what they have, neglect them, and sometimes harshly scold them, even permitting children to play rude jokes on them. Hopi women have not infrequently remarked to their very aged mothers: "You are old, you can do nothing, you are no good for anything any more"; [52] or a young man might say to his aged parent: "You have had your day, you are going to die pretty soon." [53] Aged Hopi have been heard to remark: "We looked forward to the old-age sleep, yet we have such a hard time when we are old." A missionary who had lived with them twenty years summed up the matter thus: "When the aged get so they are of no more use the people are done with them, that's all there is to it." [54]

Old Bontoc Igorot were said to "represent the knowledge and wisdom of the people." They were highly regarded for their wise judgments, and were accorded special funerals when they died. [55] Old men in the Banks Islands who held property rights over their maternal nephews received special homage; and it was not uncommon for them to hide portions of their wealth, to be revealed only on condition that their nephews remained in their good graces. In earlier times they gained prestige and deference through monopolizing the more desirable young women. [56]

The aged received considerable respect among the Iban of Borneo on account of power attributed to them in the interpretation of signs and the working of magic. The young people thus heeded their counsel and treated them with consideration long after they were too feeble to work. [57] Kiwai Papuans also showed great regard for their aged and stood in awe of their mysterious powers. Children appeared devoted to their parents, showed them honor and obedience, and cared for them in their weakness. Prac-

---

51. Field notes of author.
52. Field notes of author in 1938.
53. Kennard (160), p. 494.
54. Field notes of author in 1938.
55. Jenks (153), pp. 39, 74–79, 168
56. Rivers (248), I, 36–37.
57. Roth (252), I, 195, II, 227; Gomes (117), p. 62.

tically every old man in a village was called *baba* (father), and most old men were active in political affairs.[58]

The *Moguru* ceremonies associated with puberty rites were under the direction of old men greatly esteemed for their previous sacrifices and contributions of "Big Life." "When the ceremony is over, the people bring the old men and women who conducted the rites all kinds of presents . . . . They owe the prosperity of the sago palms to the old folks . . . . The people's appreciation has also a deeper meaning, for the old leaders of the ceremony are expected to die not long afterwards . . . ."[59]

In Samoa old men of wisdom were accorded great respect.[60] Aged Maori were also highly regarded and were believed to possess powerful magic. They were honored as directors of weddings, funerals, and political affairs.[61] The Munda were also noted for their deference to age and authority.[62] Patriarchs were no less highly regarded among the Sema Naga.[63]

Aged Ashanti women were respected and exercised considerable political influence. The children were taught to honor parents and grandparents and to keep silent in their presence.[64] Among the Vai, secret societies were used to prepare the young for the duties of adult life and to train them in respect for their elders. Ellis states that at one time children were killed by their parents for disobedience and disrespect.[65] Respect for elders was inculcated in Bakongo children and youths. They had a saying: "He who forgets what his mother did for him when a child is not worth calling a son." A general complaint was sometimes made that "The elders wear the cloth first and then the boy gets the rags." "Grandfather" was a term of respect.[66] Among the Lango old men were honored for the wisdom which they were supposed to have acquired in their long lives.[67]

Among the Dahomeans it is reported: "In old age both men and women are greatly respected, for with age comes considered judgment, but more important, with age comes a closer affinity to the

58. Landtman (171), pp. 175, 236; *ibid.* (170), p. 7.
59. *Ibid.* (171), p. 353–356.
60. Williamson (335), II, 367.
61. Firth (100), p. 317; Ratzel (240), I, 620; Best (20), I, 470; Donne (76), p. 72; Tregear (313), p. 391.
62. Sarat (257), p. 426.
63. Hutton (148), p. 97.
64. Rattray (237), p. 81; *ibid.* (239), p. 13.
65. Ellis (92), pp. 59, 126–127, 137.
66. Claridge (53), p. 151; Weeks (327), pp. 81, 104.
67. Driberg (82), p. 67.

ancestral dead, and it is injudicious to act rashly with one who may any day have the opportunity to carry a grievance to the world of the dead." [68] A popular proverb was: "Respect the elders, for they are our fathers." [69] "This deference to the old, or to those of superior position in the family, is fundamental to Dahomean usage and is reflected in all types of behavior as, for example, when a mature man of position will sit on the floor instead of on a stool when in the presence of his father or of an elder brother who has inherited the headship of his family." [70]

Probably nowhere has age received greater homage than among the Palaung of North Burma, who attributed long life to virtue in a previous existence. "Old people have happy lives among the Palaungs." No one dared to step upon their shadow lest harm befall him. The stool of a father was periodically anointed after his death, and the dutiful son often prayed: "Thou art gone, my father, but I still respect these things that belong to thee. Give me long life and health, O my father." It was such a privilege and honor to be old among the Palaung that as soon as a girl married she was eager to appear older than her age. "The older a person becomes, the greater is the respect that is paid to her. The young women are expected to do a great deal of hard work along with the girls, such as bringing wood and water to the village before any festival; so married women are a little inclined to make out that they are older than they really are, in order that they may evade the extra work." [71]

The Witoto, when along in years, usually became medicine men, and were feared because of their magical powers. Hardenberg states that they had high regard for the aged in general; but others infer that they might be abandoned "unless they possess great wisdom and experience." [72] Withered old women with shamanistic skill were quite highly regarded.[73]

It is also reported that among the Inca the aged were treated with very great consideration.[74]

When the Aztec youth was taken from the school of the priests

68. Herskovits (127), I, 351.
69. Duncan (84), II, 10; Ellis (91), pp. 258–278.
70. Herskovits (127), I, 73n.
71. Milne (205), pp. 51, 189, 205, 314–315
72. Hardenberg (122), p. 16; Whiffen (331), pp. 170, 183.
73. Dobrizhoffer (75), II, 72–73; Briffault (38), II, 523–524; Frazer (107), pp. 254–255.
74. Markham (195), I, 305; Sarmiento d Gamboa (258), p. 100; Locke (178), p. 42; Westermarck (329), I, 607.

to be married, he was formerly adjured to be courageous in battle, to honor and obey his parents, and to "show respect to his
seniors and all aged persons." Bancroft states that modesty and
esteem for one's elders were a child's first lesson.[75] The following
is a sample of a father's admonition:

My son, . . . Revere and salute thy elders, and never show them
any sign of contempt. Be not silent to the poor and the unfortunate;
but make haste to console them with kind words. Honor every one,
but especially thy father and mother, to whom thou owest obedience,
fear and service. Take care not to imitate the example of those bad
sons, who, like brutes devoid of reason, do not respect those who have
given them life; who do not listen to their advice, and do not wish
to submit to the punishment their elders judge necessary. He who
follows the path of these evil-doers will come to a bad end; he will
die in despair, thrown into the abyss, torn by the claws of wild
beasts. Never mock at old men my son, nor at deformed people. . . .
Never pass before the elders unless forced by necessity, or unless
they order thee to do so. When thou takest thy meal in their company, drink not before they do, and offer them what they need in
order to gain their good will. . . .

Biart concludes: "A young Aztec was brought up with such a
profound respect for his parents that even a long time after his
marriage, he scarcely dared speak in their presence."[76]

An important generalization from the illustrative cases is that
deference for the aged has been very common in primitive societies, even as reported by white travelers, traders, missionaries,
and ethnographers, who, it may be assumed, tend to be more or
less prejudiced by standards of treatment in "civilized societies."
Respect, or even reverence for the aged may be accorded to very
senile persons in some instances, but in cases recorded with ample
details deference appears very clearly to decline when individuals
become physically and mentally incompetent and socially useless
in actual or imaginary terms. Dr. John P. Gillin, an astute ob-
server, has summed up the matter so well for the Barama Carib
in British Guiana that it deserves quoting (although the Carib
are not included in the present study); it could apply as a generalization for many other, but not all, tribes:

75. Bancroft (5), II, 240, 253.
76. Biart (22), pp. 214–219.

Old people, of whom there are relatively few in this society, are treated with respect, but not exaggerated deference. In fact in many respects they are considered less than complete members of society, inasmuch as they are unable to carry out many of the functions required of more vigorous members of the group. The respect for old age varies with the intelligence of the aged individuals. For instance, David at Sawari is deferred to on account of his lore and skill in religious techniques; his mind is still functioning actively, and thereby he maintains his social position despite his uselessness as a hunter and laborer. He is the only aged person in Sawari, and he is by no means completely decrepit. Two very infirm old women observed by me, one at Kurasani, the other at Baramita, were unable to move from their hammocks. They were fed and treated well, but ignored in regard to the decisive actions of their respective communities. Several old men, still more or less active physically, whom I observed at various places in the area, occupied positions no better and no worse than their personalities, physical exploits, and intelligence won for them. There is no pattern of implicitly obeying old age, of consulting it with reverence, simply because of age.[77]

There have been many social taboos imposed upon children, childbearing women, and men in their prime which did not apply to the aged, thus permitting old people some favors and greater freedom, as well as setting them apart as "privileged characters." It is sometimes apparent that these privileges have resulted from general respect for the aged which stemmed, in turn, from other rights. And often, especially for women, these generally tabooed privileges have been associated with declining sexual or reproductive powers and have come into force soon after the menopause, or for men when they were no longer regarded as potential fathers. The grounds for such privileges have varied, but are not infrequently based on beliefs that the "change of life," or a long life, builds up protective virtue or immunizes one against dangerous objects or practices, as in the case of eating tabooed foods. Some have implied that through greater wisdom, experience, or favor with the gods certain aged persons are able to do things that would prove much too hazardous for younger people. Other tabooed privileges have appeared to arise out of the assumption that an aged person can afford to take more risks since his life is nearly over anyway; or, perhaps, that he has become so unim-

77. Gillin (114), p. 137.

portant that his conduct no longer matters. But in many instances it has been obvious that the tabooed privilege was a rewarding experience anticipated by all and cherished by the aged
as their special prerogative.

A limited number of cases of social taboos favorable to the aged
are presented as illustrations. Women past childbearing among
the Labrador Eskimo enjoyed wide freedom both in conversation
and conduct.[78] Haida matrons past the menopause were no longer
barred from the company of shamans at their work.[79] Such women
among the Kwakiutl could enter secret societies;[80] and among
the Chippewa they might attend the Mide feast which was forbidden to others.[81] Aged Crow were excused from certain unpleasant tasks and at the Sun dance ceremonies they might come and
go at will.[82] Aged Omaha were no longer obliged to scarify themselves on the occasion of a death.[83] Young women and girls were
required to sit in a certain modest and dignified manner; but the
old women could sit with their feet stretched out in front—for
"that was the privilege of age." [84] Elderly Pomo women could
smoke with the men and sometimes they even went into the men's
sweat-houses.[85] Among the Seri, eating and drinking followed
order of seniority.[86] A Creek soldier wounded in battle was attended in isolation only by an old woman "past the age of sinning
with men," and no female except a half dozen "beloved old
women" were allowed in the square during the first four days of
the busk ceremony.[87] At the Aztec public festivals those who were
seventy could become intoxicated with impunity, and the oldest
people were in the front ranks at the feasts and festivities.[88]

It has been reported of aged Arawak dames that they "adorn
themselves no more," and, likewise, that they no longer worry
"even about covering their shame," going around "naked with
long pendant breasts swaying in front of their bodies." [89]

When the Akamba women rebelled against the domination of

78. Hutton (149), p. 116.
79. Curtis (64), p. 137.
80. Boas (26), p. 419; Curtis (63), p. 164.
81. Densmore (73), p. 123.
82. Lowie (184), pp. 20, 30.
83. La Flesche (167), p. 6.
84. Fletcher and La Flesche (103), p. 329.
85. Loeb (180), pp. 160, 188.
86. McGee (188), p. 272.
87. Swanton (302), pp. 592, 625; Adair (1), p. 125.
88. Featherman (98), p. 78; Markham (195), II, 20; *ibid.* (196), p. 162.
89. Roth (254), p. 639,

their men and chased them with clubs, they showed enough respect for "grandfathers" not to molest them. Beer drinking was formerly an exclusive right of these old men. The wood from a certain "spirit tree" could be used only by a senior elder or a very old woman. And the old people were "supposed to be immune from the operation of most curses." [90]

In Ashanti only women past the menopause might go near the sacred stools of the ancestors.[91] Berber grandmothers had the special privilege of going to markets with the men.[92] Clay pipes were used only by aged men among the Lango.[93] Old Xosa women could go into places forbidden to those of childbearing age, and were often called "men" because of their special privileges.[94]

Among the Dahomeans, indigo was gathered from the wild plant only by "women who had passed the menopause, since Dahomean custom holds that when a man finds a woman gathering indigo, and he desires to have connections with her, she may not refuse him." A widow who had attained old age when her husband died might return to her own family instead of being inherited by her husband's sons or brothers, and she could then become "one of the *akovi* or women who officiate at the rites of the ancestral cult and who enjoy the greatest respect of all the members of their relationship group." [95]

Aged Ainu men and women, particularly very old persons "with one foot in the invisible world which is inhabited by their ancestors," were regarded as the safest mediators between the living and the dead, and in some villages the old people also had the exclusive privilege of conversing with foreigners.[96]

Old Kiwai Papuans permitted beards to grow under the chin, a mark of distinction not allowed to others; and old women might go into the men's houses.[97] Trobrianders never allowed the beard to grow except in the case of old men "who do not wish to have anything to do with women"; but it is not clear how much distinction was involved in the privilege.[98] Samoans of advanced age could "sit in the sun and talk without regard to sex." "Conform-

90. Dundas (85), pp. 494–495; Hobley (131), pp. 32–33; Lindblom (174), p. 97.
91. Rattray (237), pp. 95–96.
92. Ubach and Rachow (318), p. 7.
93. Driberg (82), p. 88.
94. Kidd (162), p. 113; *ibid.* (161), p. 239.
95. Herskovits (127), pp. 124, 350.
96. Pilsudski (223), p. xiii; *ibid.* (224), p. 72.
97. Landtman (171), pp. 8, 168.
98. Malinowski (192), p. 299.

ance to brother and sister taboo begins when the younger of two
children feel 'ashame' at the other's touch and continues until old
age, when the decrepit, toothless pair of old siblings may again sit
on the same mat and not feel 'ashame.' " [99]

Certain very old women shared the secrets of Arunta ceremonies; [100] and among the Dieri there was a special circlet or coro-
net of emu feathers worn only by aged men. [101] Of the Andamanese
it is reported that only very old men were permitted to eat with
any other women than those of their own households. [102] The aged
Palaung were offered the chief seats of honor both in households
and at festivals and received the greatest deference on the
grounds of age alone, which was regarded as proof of virtue acquired in a previous existence. [103] Old men among the Toda were
accorded special privileges in the "catching of buffalos" at the
funeral services. [104] In one very important ceremony the leading
role could be filled only by a woman past childbearing age. [105] It
was tabooed for young men among the Sema Naga to keep a calendar. Only "the old men who know" might do so; and utensils
left by women who died in childbirth might be touched only by the
aged. [106] Of the Yakut it has been reported: "Only old, ugly
women enjoy any freedom in the home." [107] And among the
Chukchi: "Women eat only after men have finished . . . . Only
an elderly woman, the mother of a family of grown-up daughters,
or some other woman under her rule, goes into the inner room
with the men and eats with them." [108]

Any prestige accorded to old age has tended to be reflected in
the current legends and myths, and it seems significant that in so
many of these accounts the star performers have been portrayed
as old, wise, and very important persons. This is to be expected,
perhaps, since it was chiefly the aged who related the stories, had
the longest memories, and were the final authorities concerning
past events. Probably no one would presume that the old people
invented such patriarchal heroes and heroines in order to enhance
or glorify their own position, for such legendary characters were

99. Mead (204), pp. 44, 194.
100. Spencer and Gillen (288), p. 134.
101. Woods (336), p. 289.
102. Mann (194), p. 134.
103. Milne (205), pp. 186–187, 214.
104. Emaneau (94), pp. 109–110.
105. Rivers (247), p. 156.
106. Hutton (148), pp. 234, 260.
107. Sieroshevski (271), p. 577.
108. Bogoras (28), p. 548.

the products of long existing traditions. But such leading roles
could be potential assets to the aged storytellers who were thus
able to embellish their tales with qualities and inferences which
built up their own prestige; and the smart old narrators have
often appeared to turn legends and traditions very cleverly to
their own advantage whether for entertainment, instruction, or
the inculcation of moral precepts. And whenever they related
their own personal exploits they seem often to have exaggerated
them. Examples of the glorification of old age in legends and
stories are easily found in almost any primitive society.

The Polar Eskimo maintained that all their powerful magic
formulae were dreamed by the old men long ago, and many of
their charms were attributed to their great-grandmothers. For instance, if a man were endangered by a falling stone he might save
himself by saying, "My great-grandmother and grandmother
bade me come." The danger of drinking from a strange pool
could be overcome, it was held, by declaring, "My great-grandmother and my grandmother said that I might drink freely and
now I drink." [109] They had legends of how old women trained
bears to bring food to them. There was a tale of an old man who
could, with a simple word, turn women into stone. Another story
related how war had its origin in the conflict of two old men over
their grandsons. Still another tradition described the first man
who ever died, and how when he was buried he kept sticking his
head up out of the ground until a smart old woman pushed it
down and commanded it to stay down.[110]

The Labrador Eskimo had legends of how certain wise old men
could secure food when the rest of the village died of starvation.
The Haida have told of grandmothers able to watch the soul of
a baby pass in and out of its body; and of an old man who could
strip off his skin and lend it to anyone wishing to practice magic.
Another old man could remove bones from anyone and replace
them with stones.[111]

The Kwakiutl had legends of an old man who possessed such
power that his aged successors preserved and wore his skin when
they wanted to see things invisible. It was also held that a very
old woman first discovered and taught dancing.[112] The Chippewa

109. Rasmussen (233), p. 144.
110. *Ibid.* (233), pp. 61, 101, 180; *ibid.* (234), pp. 41–43; (235), p. 55.
111. Turner (316), pp. 34–50; Swanton (300), pp. 119, 136–137, 168–169, 170–171.
112. Curtis (63), p. 264; Boas (26), pp. 397–400.

boasted of an old patriarch who could charm food out of an enemy camp; of another who was able by song to restore an estranged wife to her husband; and of still another who made medicine bags which, when worn around the neck, would supply all one's wants. To one old man the gods were said to have revealed all the songs of the Medicine Society. There was also a very powerful old medicine man who could let men cast themselves from high cliffs, where they were dashed asunder, and then, collecting the pieces, restore their lives. A certain old legendary hero could change a person's character by means of charms and songs.[113] The following is a sample of Chippewa stories which glorified old age: "Once an old man said, 'I am going to make a doll resembling a man.' So he started out to look for a bulrush, and when he had found it he started to transform this bulrush into a doll. Then when it was finished he took some medicine and blew upon it and told his friends to come and see the doll he had made. 'Now I am going to make it dance.' So the people came over. Then the man sang and shook a rattle and the doll danced. The Indians were afraid of this old man. Then he took his medicine bag and sang and shook his rattle, and the medicine bag ran over to where the people were watching everything. Then he took off his moccasins and blew medicine upon his feet and hands. Then he sang and started to dance toward the fire; when he got there he grabbed some red-hot coals and bit off pieces and yet did not get burnt. The people who watched him were very much afraid of him." [114]

The Menomini Indians explained in their legends that all their rites and magical power originated with the "grandfathers." There was a fable of an old woman who possessed a dried snake-skin which, whenever she threw it upon the ground, came to life and chased any person whom she did not like. Fire was first possessed by an old fellow who dwelt in the center of a great lake.[115] The Iroquois believed that in former times their old men could change themselves into animals at will.[116] They had a story of a very feeble old gentleman who had been refused hospitality in several lodges, and it turned out that he was extremely wise and possessed knowledge of all healing herbs useful in curing diseases. A cyclone was personified as an old man who in a contest was able to control spring and summer. Out of a collection of ninety Sen-

113. Densmore (71), pp. 22, 27, 97, 101–102, 105.
114. Radin (231), p. 499.
115. Skinner (279), pp. 48–83; Hoffman (135), pp. 40, 105.
116. Smith (281), p. 73.

eca myths and legends, two-thirds mentioned old men or women in heroic roles.[117]

The Crow cherished legends of old "cunning men" who could "kill the heart of a woman" for a strange man and turn it back to her husband. Fire-drilling was regarded as the invention of an old man, as was also the origin of the famous Tobacco Society. "Once an old man was fasting on a mountain top. The stars came down and taught him to sing songs and gave him tobacco." [118] A certain old "Big-Iron" was clever enough to change himself into a young man at will. An old woman possessed a bucket which was able to draw anything into it, no matter how far away. There were many legends about "Old-Man-Coyote" and his remarkable exploits. The following is a sample tale with a moral: Three men once decided to see which one could live longest. The first gave presents to the sun and became a chief but died early. The second built sweat lodges but was killed when he was only fairly old. The third, who gave presents to his father's clansman, lived to be very old. "Since then we have given food to our clan fathers. We never pass in front of them unless we have previously given them a present." [119]

To the Creek knowledge of the healing art was first made known through mysterious animals who revealed it to the old men. It was claimed that the "busk medicines" were brought from heaven by two old graybeards. "As soon as the old men had delivered them they disappeared, returning to the sky." In one legend, told by an elder, the hero gave this advice to a rash young companion: "We have always been counseled not to undertake to do anything unusual without the advice or consent of persons older than we and of greater experience." [120]

The Omaha related how certain old men were the originators of the very sacred pipes. There was also a legend of how one of them discovered the charmed tree which provided the "sacred pole." Another first learned how to pray to the gods. A very old woman was the first to have the menopause; and was later able to call forth wild animals in periods of famine.[121] Navaho myths attributed great power to the aged. Certain old men won in all con-

117. Beauchamp (15), pp. 157–158; Curtin (60), pp. 53–61, also entire volume.
118. Lowie (186), pp. 256–258; *ibid.* (185), p. 215; *ibid.* (185), pp. 185–187; *ibid.* (186), p. 331.
119. *Ibid.* (186), pp. 30, 61, 292; *ibid.* (185), p. 56.
120. Swanton (302), 71, 547, 647.
121. Dorsey (78), pp. 223–224, 267; Fletcher and La Flesche (103), pp. 128, 148–149, 217–218.

tests for the love of fair women, and could renew their youth by smoking a charmed pipe. Another aged hero was honored as the first discoverer of the healing arts. An old man and woman were the first on the scene at the creation of the world, and they discovered how to worship and what would please the gods.[122] To one mythical patriarch was accorded such powerful magic that with his breath he could blow a hole under a rock large enough for a house. An old woman could become young again at will, simply by passing through a certain door of her house.[123] A hero on one of his journeys came upon the "Cold Woman" who controlled the climates. "She was a wrinkled old woman sitting nearly naked on a bed of snow. She had neither food, nor fire, nor shelter, her eyes streamed tears, she shivered constantly, and her teeth chattered so that she could scarcely talk. She said to the warrior, 'You may kill me if you will, but man will be worse off when I am dead than he is now. For when I die, it will always be hot, and the land will dry up, and the spring will cease to flow, and men will die of heat and thirst. You will do better to let me live.' "[124] In another account an old "Spider Woman" had a house in the underworld reached by twelve ladders, and she often gave people magic feathers to assist and speed them on their journeys.[125]

Among the Hopi there are many accounts of the amazing powers and exploits of the aged. One old gentleman kept the skins of dogs hanging on the walls of his house and could compel them to come down and dance at his pleasure. Other old men were once overtaken by a mighty flood, but they simply changed themselves into turkeys and buzzards and flew over the waters.[126] Certain old men could mold piñon gum into giant-like figures and endow them with life by singing and breathing upon them. One oldster could, by whistling, summon the Star and Cloud deity to appear in person and defend his cause. Or he could spit upon his hands and attract *skeleton* flies who would feed upon his saliva and then sting and slay his enemies. There were also plenty of evil-minded old people to be feared for their magical powers. They could bring evil winds, droughts, disease, and famine. They could shoot

122. Curtis (61), pp. 106–111; Reichard (242), p. 130; Stevenson (296), pp. 284–285.

123. Matthews (202), pp. 400–401; Buxton (45), p. 302.

124. Matthews (201), p. 848.

125. Curtis (61), p. 100.

126. *Ibid.* (65), pp. 82, 89–93, 165; Hough (141), pp. 187–188; Lockett (179), pp. 69–70; Titiev (312), p. 555.

poison arrows into people, killing them either suddenly or by slow
degrees. They could change themselves into animals at will, pil-
lage and rob the graves of dead women, restore these corpses to
life, and rape them. In fact it was difficult to imagine anything
beyond the powers of these old people.[127] And examples could be
cited in which lack of respect for them resulted in premature
death to young upstarts.[128]

The Arawak had a legend in which their ancestors were jour-
neying in a large boat under the leadership of an old man who
guided them safely over dangerous waters; and all went well so
long as they listened to his advice. He warned them not to shoot
a fish because he recognized in it a human being. But, alas, one
man did not heed his counsel and lost his life. When they came to
land, he gave directions for a hunt which was followed by all but
one man who went his own way and, as a consequence, failed to
catch anything and suffered the jibes of all his companions. The
old guide warned each of them to build a house and sleep in it
overnight as protection from the bats. One careless man ignored
the instructions and hung his hammock in a tree. All that was left
of him next morning was "a few bones." Again the old man cautioned them to avoid certain beautiful canoes. All took his advice
but one, who slipped into a canoe while the rest slept and was carried out to sea and lost. It is a long story with a series of disasters
all detailing the baneful consequences of ignoring the old man's
counsel.[129]

The Tuareg related how some very wicked people were able to
atone for all their sins by building a city of refuge for the aged
and the poor.[130] The Ashanti told how a woman in her old age was
able to infatuate a god and finally win his love and special favors.[131] The Xosa told of very old men who were powerful magicians. A fairy is said to have appeared once to the king's son in
the form of a very old woman, showing him a magic stone and
teaching him "power" songs. In another legend a prince lost in
the woods met an old hag, very deaf and dumb, who saved his life
by means of a magic wand with which she could also produce food
at will. There was another tale of a clever old woman who could
take off her kilt of black oxskin, hang it on the handle of her pick,

127. Simmons (275), pp. 46, 51, 428–429; additional field notes of author.
128. Curtis (65), p. 80.
129. Roth (253), pp. 220–222.
130. Campbell (46), p. 188.
131. Rattray (237), p. 56.

and command it to go on working while she rested or returned to her house.[132]

A Kiwai legend described how an old woman discovered the first bull-roarer. While she was chopping firewood, a large splinter whirled up into the air with a whizzing noise and fell sticking into the ground; and the use of the bull-roarer spread thence all over the world.[133] The Semang had legends of "invulnerable old men." [134] A Maori tradition related that land was first hauled up out of the sea and given to an old woman. "The Maori folklore contains many simple tales. The name of the old woman, Ruruhi-kerepo, appears in a number of tales, in several variant forms, all of which denote a blind old woman. In some cases she appears as a veritable ogress . . . ." [135]

The Arunta had many legends indicating the manner in which aged grandparents punished young men for not providing them with food; and there were other tales in which loyal and praiseworthy youths heroically nourished the older generation on their own blood. An old man was described who could pluck boils out of the body and change them into stones. Once he was torn to pieces by dogs, but his skin crawled over the scattered flesh and bones with ease, and he went on his way as though nothing had happened.[136] It was said to be an old woman who first discovered how to circumcise boys with a stone knife.[137] Old Dieri men of long ago were believed to have been able to make plants bear bitter or sweet fruits by the power of their songs.[138] The Toda possessed legends of an old woman who was the mother of the race;[139] and the Chukchi had many tales of aged wonder-workers.[140]

Respect for the powers of the aged Ainu were taught by such legends as the following:

At the head of Japan there was a very hard pine tree. Now the ancients, both noble and ignoble, came together and broke and bent their swords upon that tree. Then there came a very old man and a very old woman upon the scene. The old man had a useless old axe in his girdle, and the old woman a useless old reaping-hook. So they

132. Bourhill and Drake (31), I, 18–27, 58–59, 237–238.
133. Landtman (171), p. 82.
134. Skeat and Blagden (277), II, 345.
135. Tregear (313), p. 530; Best (20), I, 212.
136. Spencer and Gillen (289), pp. 313–336, 385; *ibid.* (288), pp. 197–198.
137. *Ibid.* (289), p. 319.
138. Howitt and Seibert (144), pp. 103–104.
139. Rivers (247), pp. 195–196.
140. Bogoras (28), pp. 300, 330–331.

caused the ancients to laugh at them (at the idea of their being of any assistance). Even the ancients were unable to cut down the tree; so they said, 'Old man and old woman, what have you come hither to do?' The old man replied, 'We have only come that we may see.' As the old man said this he drew his useless old axe, and, striking the metal pine tree, cut a little way into it. And the old woman, drawing her useless old reaping-hook, struck the tree and cut it through. There was a mighty crash and the earth trembled with the fall! . . . Therefore the Ainu say, 'Let not the younger laugh at the elder, for even very old people can teach their juniors a great deal, even in so simple a matter as felling a tree.' [141]

Yukaghir myths and legends portrayed the aged as very cunning and mysterious. Jochelson stated: "In some tales the Mythical-Old-People are so tall that they carry killed elks tied to the strings of their coats . . . . Out of the earlier series of twenty-seven tales, ten deal with the Mythical-Old-People." [142] A sample is presented:

Many people lived in one place. Among them was a young hunter, married with a child. There was also an old man and an old woman without children. They had no one to hunt for them. The hunter gave the old people part of his produce. Thus, when he killed an elk, he would give them one leg. But the old man was not satisfied with this. Once when the sun was setting, the old man lifted the edge of the tent and said to the sun: 'Sun, rise a little, I have something to tell you.' The sun rose. The old man said, 'Sun, you know how the hunter offends me. Cause him to eat what his child eats.' The old man was making his request in the form of a riddle. The following day the hunter went out to the chase, and met an elk. He drove it past his tent and stopped to call his wife to bring him water. She brought out some water but he did not take it. He became crazy, seized her by the breast, cut off the nipple, swallowed it, and ran on after the elk, but soon he fell down and died.[143]

It is evident that the above sampling of legends and stories current in primitive societies have portrayed old people in "starring" roles. It was the very aged hero or heroine who controlled the weather, drove away the famine, changed stones into bread, invented warfare, sang the first songs, formulated the sacred

141. Batchelor (11), pp. 113–114.
142. Jochelson (154), pp. 303, 307.
143. *Ibid.* (154), p. 143.

rites, and produced fire from the midst of the sea. It was an old man or woman who developed the rhythm of dancing, discovered the efficacy of prayer, exercised the art of healing, and practiced rejuvenation. It was also the aged who communed with demons and gods, charmed beasts, men and women, and blew great caves into stone cliffs for their dwelling places. Their legendary attributes were wisdom, magic, ingenuity, and invulnerability. In their counsel was safety, in their service success; but woe to the knave of the plot who turned away his face and heeded not the voice of experience and age.

Old age was not only glorified in legends and tales; its attributes were even deified in mythological accounts of demons and gods. And it is perhaps noteworthy that although the gods might appear either "noble" or "base" in deportment, they were almost always described as worldly wise and very powerful—and, although aged, never stupid or senile. They acquired the coveted attributes of age without its baneful liabilities. They grew old but not too old, and indeed some followed cycles of ageing and rejuvenation. It would almost appear that the aged have "created gods in their own image," or that mythologies have accommodated themselves significantly to the aspirations and coveted roles of the aged.

A few selected samples follow: The Polar Eskimo believed that the goddess *Nerivik* was a very old woman who lived beneath the waters, with the spirits of the dead, and that sometimes she refused to prosper the seal hunters until shamans visited her and combed her tangled hair.[144] In another myth an old man changed himself into a luminous body and shot up to the sky where he now sits as a "great star." "We see it in the west when the light begins to return after the long dark." [145]

The Labrador Eskimo related how the ocean tides were governed by an old, old woman who lived below the waters and who also controlled all creatures of the sea. Whenever worship of her was neglected, she sent sharks to break up the fishermen's nets.[146] They also believed that inland there lived an aged goddess who controlled all land animals, especially the reindeer, and was surrounded by the spirits of Eskimo who had died and now spent their time hunting.[147] The clouds were believed to be large bags of

144. Kroeber (165), p. 317.
145. Rasmussen (233), pp. 166–167.
146. Hutton (149), pp. 42–43.
147. Hawkes (124), pp. 124–125.

water which two old women would draw to and fro across the sky. Flashes of lightning were their torches and the thunder was the murmuring of their voices.[148]

The Kwakiutl explained that an old woman controls the winds, and they prayed to her: "Do not be rough, Old Grandmother West Wind, when you pull aside the clouds." [149] The Thunder-God was called "Grandfather" by the Iroquois.[150] The Crow saw an old woman in the moon and saluted the sun as "Old-Man-Coyote." This "Old-Man" formed human beings out of mud, breathed life into them, and admonished them to multiply and replenish the earth.[151]

According to the Hopi, two aged goddesses (Harung Wuhtis) lived in the distant oceans to the east and west and sometimes visited each other over the rainbow. They created all living things and still answer Hopi prayers. An old Spider Woman (who is also the Salt Woman) was said to have invented most of the arts and crafts, still lived in a shrine near each village, and was able to help or hinder people as she saw fit. She could protect or curse the village, cause the sickness and death of a child, draw people to her underground home and entangle their souls in her web. In order to keep her pacified the people sacrificed prayer-feathers to her annually, left firewood on her shrine whenever they passed nearby, and made sacrifices to her to insure success in pottery making and salt expeditions.[152]

The Navaho addressed *Yebitsa* as "grandfather" and worshiped a goddess who grew old and became young again in a never-ending cycle.[153] The Omaha addressed the thunder-god as "Grandfather," and believed that at the forks of the path of the dead (the Milky Way) there sat an old man wrapped in a buffalo robe who turned the steps of good and peaceable travelers toward the short path which led directly to the abode of their relatives, but allowed the wicked to take the long road over which they wearily wandered.[154] The Creek addressed the fire as "Grandfather";[155] and the Yuchi worshiped "Old-Men" and

148. Turner (316), p. 267.
149. Boas (26), p. 507; Curtis (63), p. 50.
150. Smith (281), p. 56.
151. Lowie (186), pp. 320–321; *ibid.* (186), pp. 7, 14, 16; Curtis (62), pp. 19, 69.
152. Simmons (275), pp. 17–18, 224–257; Fewkes (99), p. 592; Goddard (116), p. 124.
153. Matthews (203), p. 9; Briffault (38), II, 729.
154. Fletcher and La Flesche (103), pp. 124, 590.
155. Swanton (303), p. 484.

"Old-Women." Their abode for the spirits of the dead was in the sky, reached by a path over the rainbow. There departing spirits came under the supervision of an "Old Woman." [156]

The Witoto worshiped *Hosinimui,* an old bald-headed man with a long beard who wore the sun as his crown. When the sun set, it meant simply that the old man had gone to bed and put out the light—laid aside his crown.[157]

The Aztec "God of Dawn," *Quetzalcoatl,* was regarded as an old man. Other legends related how gods in the form of very old men appeared in revelations to certain leaders.[158] The Inca addressed the sun by "Our Father." [159] The Abipone saluted an evil spirit with the title "Grandfather," and the Pleiades were also addressed as an aged grandparent. Whenever that constellation disappeared from the sky, the "Grandfather" was said to be "sick," and the people were thus under a yearly apprehension; but as soon as these stars were visible again they welcomed the deity back to health with joyful shouts and festive music on pipes and trumpets.[160]

When an Ashanti farmer planted his crop he took a fowl to the plot of ground, wrung its neck, let the blood drop upon the ground, and prayed: "Grandfather So-and-So, you once came and hoed here and then you left it to me. You also Earth, Ya, on whose soil I am going to hoe; the yearly cycle has come round and I am going to cultivate; when I work let a fruitful year come upon me, do not let a snake bite me." [161] A local deity, resembling an old woman and addressed as "Grandmother," was believed to remain in the town as protectress of the women when the men went to war.[162]

The Bushmen believed the moon was an "Old-Man";[163] and the Hottentot worshiped a deity called *Toosib,* the "Old Man of the Waters." Before drinking at a certain stream one should throw in some little offering saying: "O Grandfather, give me food, give me flesh of rhinoceros, of antelope of zebra, and all that I desire." [164]

156. Speck (286), pp. 102, 108.
157. Farabee (97), p. 146.
158. Spence (287), p. 80; Biart (22), p. 121.
159. Markham (195), I, 66.
160. Dobrizhoffer (75), II, 65.
161. Rattray (237), pp. 215–216.
162. Ellis (90), pp. 53–54.
163. Bleek (24), p. 27.
164. Quatrefages (230), pp. 213, 220.

The Iban had a deity whom they called "Grandfather of Paddy," and claimed that he first taught them to plant crops and to observe the rites. Their legends told of the "great god of the world," who was an old man. The tears and the gifts of bereaved mourners were thought to be received by an old goddess who lived in Hades. "Old Grandmother holds the key that unlocks the door to the lower world." [165] Two of the gods of the Maori were the Sky Father and the Earth Mother.[166] A Kiwai Papuan folk-tale related how a man paddled his canoe to the rising moon. It appeared to him as a small boy, a young man, and finally as a gray-haired old man, and on each occasion invited him to come ashore. "It was only when he appeared as a very old man and walked with the help of a stick that the stranger trusted him and went ashore." [167]

The Semang believed that "Old Granny Lanyutis" had charge of the underworld. They made blood-sacrifices and offered prayers to her. Another old woman, living below, built her house with the bones of the dead and kept horned dragons for pets.[168] The Samoans worshiped "Old Grandfather Tangaloa of the Heavens." [169] Legends of the Euahlayi describe a deity who had charge of the storms. When clouds gathered, they exclaimed, "See the old man with the net on his back; he is going to drop some hailstones." It was said that within the Milky Way there was an "Old One" who was such a great rain-maker that he could cause it to rain merely by turning around. Venus was "a rude old man, that laughing star." *Byanbee* was the Great Spirit and the "All Father" widely worshiped as lawgiver and supreme power.[170] Among the Vedda *Maha Yakino* were the spirits of old women who were said to kidnap children and spread diseases, and were therefore propitiated.[171] Palaung myths held that certain old female deities would feed wandering shades of the dead with fruit plucked from a mango-like tree by the trail of weeping spirits.[172]

Laplanders feared to call the bear by his true name lest he ravish their herds, so they worshiped him as "the old man with the

165. Hose (139), p. 198; Gomes (117), pp. 141, 301–314; Roth (252), II, 182.
166. Best (20), I, 115, 408.
167. Landtman (171), pp. 52–53.
168. Skeat and Blagden (277), I, 243; Schebesta (262), p. 253; Evans (96), p. 210.
169. Turner (315), p. 11.
170. Parker (218), pp. 5, 95, 99.
171. Seligmann (269), p. 162.
172. Milne (205), p. 339.

coat of skin." [173] The thunder-god was their "Great Father" with power of life and death, sickness and health. The rainbow was the bow of this great and powerful old man, and from it he shot the arrows of lightning.[174] The Yukaghir had a deity called "Father Fire" who lived in the sky. In the lower regions lived an old man known as "Grandfather with the pointed head," who was believed to be the chief of all evil spirits, and the most terrible. An aged woman was gatekeeper at the kingdom of shades. The Yukaghir were very much afraid of smallpox, brought in by the whites, and made propitiations to the "Big Grandmother" of this disease.[175]

Both Chukchi and Russianized natives, whenever they moved to a new place for a protracted stay, offered a sacrifice to the mythical "Old Man" who was master of the place. One incantation for improving bad weather was, "Old Woman, scrape the sky all over with your little copper butchering-knife." Another supernatural being mentioned in prayers was the "Old-Woman-of-the-Time-of-the-First-Creation." [176]

The Yakut held that the divine spirit, the essence of fire, was a gray-haired and fussy old man. "He is never entirely at rest and is a very garrulous fellow. The cracking, snarling, jumping, and hissing of the fire are his remarks and whisperings. The old man knows what the people are saying and doing about him in the house, so all must be careful not to hurt his feelings, which would be very dangerous. Rubbish may not be cast into the fire, and one must take care that no leaves or dirt be scraped off the feet near it. A good housewife always takes care that the old man is satisfied with her, and casts into the fire a small portion of everything which is prepared for food." [177] The great evil spirit, "Under-Ground-Old-Man," was said to live in the far north.[178]

Among the Ainu the goddess of fire was an old woman called "grandmother," and married to a great "Governor of the House." "Any visitor to the Ainu is sure to find set up behind the lacquer-ware tubs and heirlooms in the northeastern corner of such huts as he may be pleased to enter, a big fetish made with clustered willow shavings depending from the top of a thick stem. This is called by several names, 'The Ancestral Governor of the House,' 'Divine Householder'; and is invested with mighty magic powers.

173. Frazer (105), II, 398.
174. Keane (159), p. 230; Scheffer (263), pp. 93–94.
175. Jochelson (154), pp. 140–141, 152–153, 157.
176. Bogoras (28), pp. 288, 476, 498.
177. Sieroshevski (272), pp. 180–182.
178. Czaplicka (66), p. 279.

It is of the male gender and is the most important one the men make. He is sometimes called the 'Divine Husband' of the fire upon the hearth. This fetish and his wife, the fire, are supposed to look after the welfare of the family and rule over them." He is often addressed as "Old Man." [179] To the Rwala, the sun was a jealous old woman who never had any children and therefore took her spite out on others by sending droughts.[180] And it is well known that the Ancient Hebrew addressed the Almighty as "Our Father" and made allusions to his great age: "For a thousand years in thy sight are but as yesterday . . . ." [181]

Perhaps the most striking fact about respect for old age is its widespread occurrence. Some degree of prestige for the aged seems to have been practically universal in all known societies. This is so general, in fact, that it cuts across many cultural factors that have appeared to determine trends in other topics related to age. This is not to imply, however, that all the aged have been honored everywhere, or that honor has increased in proportion to age alone. There have usually been extenuating circumstances, qualifying conditions, and an opportune period—a "prime of life" in old age—when prestige has been attained; and other circumstances under which it has been denied or has practically disappeared.

Under statistical analysis, extremes of climate, such as severe cold and aridity, appear to have exercised a reducing influence on homage accorded to both aged men and women (Cor. 117–118); and impermanency of residence has seemed even more adverse, for both sexes (Cor. 119–120). In societies characterized by collecting, hunting, fishing, there are no very significant variables in the coefficients of association; but aged women have seemed more likely to be held in high regard than old men, especially among fishers (Cor. 121–126). Aged women appear definitely to have suffered a diminution in prestige among herders but have gained status among farmers; while the old men seem to have fared relatively well in both instances (Cor. 127–130). Aged men have been much more likely to enjoy prestige as the constancy of the food supply increased, but such prerogatives have not been equally shared by aged women; indeed with them the coefficients of association were very significantly negative (Cor. 131–132). Debt-relations, trade, the use of money, and

179. Batchelor (12), pp. 175–176.
180. Musil (212), pp. 1–2.
181. Matt. 6:9; Ps. 90:4.

private property in objects other than land have tended in general to favor opportunities for prestige among aged men and to a much less degree among aged women. (Cor. 133–142). Wherever important property rights have been controlled by aged men or women they have enjoyed prestige (Cor. 143–144).

Respect for the aged has also been influenced by factors of government. Where there have been codified laws, where political power has been centered in restricted councils, and especially where old men have sat in council and served as judges, their opportunities for prestige have been great; and aged women have tended to gain also from these conditions, especially where they have had some authority in government (Cor. 145–154). When aged men have controlled secret societies for the initiation of the young their prestige has appeared to increase and to be shared by aged women (Cor. 155–156).

The social organization of the family has been reflected in the prestige accorded to the aged and has seemed to be one of the determining factors in the care of old women. They have been assured of far greater respect where residence has been matrilocal and descent, inheritance, succession, and authority matrilineal; where the avunculate has prevailed; and where ownership of the dwelling has been in their control (Cor. 157–163). A pronounced contrast appears in the relative loss in prestige suffered by aged women where residence has been patrilocal and descent, inheritance, succession, and authority patrilineal (Cor. 164–168). Contrariwise, aged men have been at some disadvantage in prestige where residence has been matrilocal and descent, inheritance, and succession matrilineal; where the dwelling has been owned by the wife; and where the avunculate has prevailed (Cor. 169–174). It is apparent, however, that aged men have been favored in prestige where residence has been patrilocal, and descent, inheritance, succession, and authority patrilineal (Cor. 175–179).

Aged men also have scored prestige points in societies where polygyny has been practiced, where property rights in women have been common; and where aged men have controlled property, married young women, and exercised important prerogatives in family life (Cor. 180–186).

The statistical data are too meager and scattered to provide reliable correlational trends in the analysis of information on social-taboo privileges of the aged and their glorification or deification in legends and mythologies.

In summary, then, it may be concluded that considerable prestige has been accorded to the aged in primitive societies, but only under culturally determined circumstances and for a limited age period which rarely extended into decrepitude. Sexual differences have been significant. The more favorable cultural milieu for aged men has been found to be within a patriarchal type of family organization; where herding or agriculture has been the chief means of maintenance; where there have been more or less permanent residence, a constant food supply, and a well-regulated political system; and where property rights in land, crops, herds, goods, and even women have been deeply entrenched. Aged women seem to have gained relatively more prestige in simpler societies characterized by collection, hunting, and fishing; and particularly in matriarchal forms of family organization. Their position also seems to have been better among farmers than herders. Aged men have been able to achieve considerable prestige even under circumstances normally conducive to elevating the rights of women; but old women have often been at very great disadvantage where cultural factors have been weighted in favor of aged men. Wherever aged women have been respected, old men have rarely been without honor; but prestige for aged men has offered no assurance of the same status for women. If either sex has lost respect in old age, it has been more likely to be the women than the men.

IV

GENERAL ACTIVITIES

IT HAS been observed that in primitive societies certain forms of security for the aged—such as food sharing, property rights, and social prestige—have arisen as by-products of impersonal environmental and social forces which vary from culture to culture. The factors of personal initiative and individual adjustment have thus far been touched upon only incidentally. But the activities of the aged themselves have exercised an important influence upon their security. Their roles have hardly ever been passive. Their security has been more often an achievement than an endowment—an achievement in which favorable opportunities have been matched with active personal accomplishments. Evidence of this is found in the fact that individual achievements in security have varied immensely under similar social and cultural conditions, and even within the same society. The adaptive activities of the aged, therefore, are important for an adequate understanding of their status in any society.

In primitive groups all able-bodied persons have generally participated directly in the tasks of subsistence. They have collected and prepared food, and fished, hunted, or herded. They have cultivated plants, manufactured or wielded weapons, made and operated tools or rudimentary machines, and practiced useful arts and skills. But as old age or physical ailments have overtaken them, they have generally stepped aside, relinquishing the tasks of maintenance and defense to others. Their work has then become supervisory or auxiliary, and the paths to their goals no longer direct but through the interests and activities of others. Their security has come to depend less and less upon the manipulation of things and more and more upon the adjustment to and manipulation of people. Their further accomplishment and security have usually involved the pressure or enticement of others into their service. This has made it necessary for them to cooperate more actively with others and to direct or assist them in order to insure support and deference in return.

Perhaps the simplest and most effective means of eliciting the support of others has been to render essential—if possible, indispensable—services to them; a common adjustment of the weak who would gain the support of the strong. It has been no secret that the aged or otherwise handicapped person who lent a helping hand or a useful idea after he had become too feeble to forage for himself stood a better chance of sharing in the fleshpots of the strong. The case is neatly presented in a report by James Moffat, quoting an old Hottentot woman whom he found abandoned in a desert place: "Yes, my own children, three sons and two daughters, are gone to yonder blue mountain and have left me to die. . . . I am very old, you see, and am not able to serve them. When they kill game, I am too feeble to help in carrying home the flesh. I am not able to gather wood and make a fire, and I cannot carry their children on my back as I used to." [1]

Opportunities for maintaining security through auxiliary services to others, although available everywhere to some degree, have varied from place to place, and have been conditioned by such factors as climate, permanency of residence, constancy of food supply, and especially by the maintenance activities of the particular group. A general survey of the cases, which are illustrated below, would seem to indicate that such opportunities have been less available in the simpler societies characterized by collection and hunting, and perhaps fishing.

The Polar Eskimo continued to fish until very old and feeble. Rasmussen mentioned the "oldest man in the tribe," with white hair and tottering steps, who was still fishing; and he described another, "old and somewhat bowed with rheumatism," who still hunted, fished, and insisted that he would never stop, for he would die sometime and keep on hunting and fishing in the happy hunting grounds. Old couples, the infirm, and cripples went every summer to the cliffs to help cache the winter's reserve of bird meat. Old women too feeble to travel stayed indoors, attended household chores, repaired garments, tanned leather—chewing it to make it soft—and shredded with their very worn teeth the sinew of dried caribou and narwhal.[2] It was said that among the Point Barrow Eskimo old people were rarely idle, for while aged men were busy making seal spears and nets, the old women worked on clothing, boots, and the dressing of skins. The camps were in a constant state of bustle during the hunting and fishing season. "Daily the old men . . . meet at the seashore and talk for an east wind so the ice will be driven off shore and whales may come

1. Dowd, quoting Moffat (81), p. 56.
2. Rasmussen (233), pp. 10, 23–24, 46; Ekblaw (89), pp. 173–174, 191.

in." [3] Enfeebled Labrador Eskimo women eked out a meager existence at indoor jobs such as plaiting straw hats and baskets, caring for wearing apparel, and attending to the family boots. "When a pair of boots has been worn for some time, during a few hours in warm weather they absorb moisture and become nearly half an inch thick on the soles. When taken off they must be turned inside out and dried, then chewed and scraped by some old woman who is only too glad to have the work for the two or three biscuits she may receive as pay." [4]

The aged Yukaghir helped with hunting as long as possible, and then they would "sit in the house doing nothing . . . ." [5] For the Maritime Chukchi life was reported to be hard. "Each morsel of food has to be obtained by great exertion, danger, and hardships; therefore an old man unable to get his store . . . becomes a charge on other people . . . . The experience of an old hunter does not count for much when he remains at home, and in times of privation he is one too many to feed." [6] The Ainu went to their old men for carved pegs and skewers. [7]

In Kwakiutl fishing parties an old man went along to steer the boat, while the aged women stayed at home and spun fish lines. [8] Crow grandmothers were considered essential elements in the household, engaged in domestic chores, and relieved the childbearing mothers of petty worries and heavy burdens. Following a successful hunt the "old women were seen everywhere slicing the meat and hanging it on long poles to dry . . . ." [9] Old Chippewa women winnowed rice, made fish nets, tanned hides, and supervised the storing of fish and the work of the young girls. [10] While the Chippewa family slept with their feet toward the coals an old man kept watch, smoked, and fed fuel to the fire. During the day he carved ladles and pipe stems. [11] Old Iroquois men sat in the sun and whittled out wooden ladles and bark bowls. [12] Aged women among the Creek gathered wood and busied themselves about camp. [13] Old Seri women are reported to have made poison

3. Ray (241), pp. 45, 49.
4. Hutton (150), p. 48; Turner (316), p. 206.
5. Jochelson (154), p. 107.
6. Bogoras (28), pp. 544–546.
7. Batchelor (12), p. 170.
8. Curtis (63), pp. 62–63; Boas (27), pp. 485–486.
9. Marquis (197), p. 37; Curtis (62), p. 113.
10. Densmore (74), p. 316; *ibid.* (73), p. 122.
11. Densmore (73), p. 138.
12. Barbeau (9), pp. 22–23.
13. Swanton (302), pp. 385–386.

for arrows.[14] Powers said of the Pomo: "When an Indian becomes too infirm to serve any longer as a warrior or hunter, he is henceforth condemned to the life of a menial and scullion. He is compelled to assist the squaws in all their labors in the picking of acorns and berries, in threshing out seed and wild oats, making bread, drying salmon, etc. These superannuated warriors are under the women's control as much as children and are obliged to obey their commands implicitly." [15]

In South America Jivaro matrons far past their prime were said to sit around a wooden trough, chew yucca roots, and spit the contents into an earthen jar where they were left to ferment and later used as a beverage.[16] Among the Abipone of the Gran Chaco it is reported that only the eldest woman was qualified to fetch water from a certain spring.[17] Aged Arawak women kept the fires going, cooked, and labored at household chores; and an aged warrior who was obliged to cook was called "an old woman." [18] Lengua graybeards would sit out in the sun, cross-legged, and make string puzzles or miniature bows and arrows for the entertainment of small boys.[19]

Old Negrito Semangs in Malaya were famed for making blow-guns.[20] Aged Andamanese supervised the moving of camps, and both old men and women made baskets and cared for children and the sick while stronger persons searched for food. They also supervised the young men in canoemaking.[21] The aged Dieri fashioned tools and weapons while the younger people foraged for food.[22]

While some customary economic activities have, doubtless, engaged the aged in all societies, opportunities for regular work have tended to be much more plentiful and varied among herders, and especially among cultivators of the soil. These two groups are illustrated together.

Old men among the Hopi tended their flocks until feeble and nearly blind. When they could no longer follow the herd, they worked on in their fields and orchards, frequently lying down on

14. McGee (188), p. 87.
15. Powers (226), p. 160.
16. Orton (214), p. 167.
17. Briffault (38), II, 638.
18. Martius (199), p. 699; Im Thurn (151), p. 256; Schmidt (264), p. 8.
19. Grubb (120), p. 187.
20. Schebesta (262), p. 63.
21. Brown (40), pp. 42, 44, 218.
22. Horne and Aiston (138), p. 105.

the ground to rest. They also made shorter and shorter trips to gather herbs, roots, and fuel. When unable to go to the fields any longer they sat in the house or kiva and spun, knitted, carded wool, or made sandals. Some continued to spin when they were blind and unable to walk, and it was often said that "an old man can spin to the end of his life." Corn shelling was woman's work but men would do it, especially in their dotage. Old women would cultivate their garden patches until very feeble and "carried wood and water as long as they were able to move their legs." They prepared milling stones, wove baskets and plaques out of rabbit weed, made pots and bowls from clay, ground corn, darned old clothes, cared for children, and guarded the house; and when there was nothing else to do, they would sit and watch the fruit drying in the sun. The old frequently expressed the desire to keep on working until they died.[23] Dennis wrote of them, "Retirement is impossible at any age. One cannot, in Hopi society, pile up credits which will support one, nor can one save materials on which to live long. Some of the 'rich' may have enough corn to last for four or five years, but that is always to be treated as a reserve store, never as something which in the future will provide leisure. The aged who have sons and daughters who could provide for them continue to work as long as they are able to do anything whatsoever." [24]

According to Inca laws, elderly persons unfit for work should still serve as scarecrows to frighten birds and rodents from the fields.[25] "Occupation was found for all from the child four years old to the aged matron not too infirm to hold a distaff. No one, at least none but the decrepit and sick, was allowed to eat the bread of idleness . . . ." [26] Those who were unable to do ordinary work were employed in collecting leaves and straw, and in delousing themselves and bringing the lice to the decurions, places for the disposal of vermin. Even the blind were given jobs picking seeds out of cotton and husking maize.[27]

In Africa aged Xosa tended gardens and old women frightened off the birds. Old women in want were received into a kraal and set to work at small chores. As long as they could stagger under a burden of firewood or carry a vessel of water, they were fed; but

23. Field notes of the author
24. Dennis (70), p. 16.
25. Sumner (298), p. 653.
26. Prescott (227), I, 31.
27. Markham (196), II, 40.

upon becoming imbecile and useless they were liable to be turned
out to starve.[28] Dundas wrote of the Akamba: "There seems to be
no age at which the women are excused from work. I have seen
some who must have been well over seventy years of age working
in the fields. . . . Often a woman lives alone with her son, a sturdy
young loafer . . . she is the one who keeps the wolf from the
door." [29] Aged Ashanti women picked cotton and spun it into
thread.[30] In Bakongo villages old women were often seen shelling
peanuts or cracking pumpkin seeds between their teeth as they
peddled gossip culled from the market place.[31] Some aged Shilluk
were good blacksmiths, thatchmakers, and plaiters.[32]

Old Rwala women could work in the men's tents.[33] Among the
Sema Naga, men and women who were too old to work stayed in
the village and dried paddy in the sun, keeping off pigs and fowls.
If they had no paddy of their own to dry, they worked for others
and received a little salt, rice, or chilis.[34] Aged Chin widows
worked in the households of their sons.[35] Old Kazak women supervised moving, setting up tents, and the making of felt covers.[36]

The Bontoc Igorot expected work from their elders. Besides
guarding the fields, they fetched water, prepared and cooked
food, and spun materials for clothing; and even blind women
shared in these labors.[37] In Samoa: "It is the general custom for
women, becoming aged, to settle down to performing skilled tasks
in the household, to weaving and the making of bark cloth." A
Samoan girl's description of her grandmother was: "Oh, she is
an old woman, very old, she's my father's mother. She is a widow
with one eye. She is too old to go inland but sits in the house all
day and makes bark cloth." Large quantities of cinet used for
twine were plaited by the old men, who sat in their houses and
twisted on it continuously, or even took it with them to political
assemblies and worked on it during palavers.[38] They also spun
the coconut fiber and braided it into native cord for fish lines,

28. Shooter (270), pp. 81, 95; Kidd (162), p. 191.
29. Dundas (85), p. 485.
30. Rattray (238), p. 221.
31. Weeks (327), pp. 105–106.
32. Westermann (328), pp. xxx–xxxii.
33. Musil (212), p. 235.
34. Hutton (148), pp. 71, 117.
35. Carey and Tuck (48), pp. 208–209.
36. Vámbéry (320), pp. 77–78.
37. Jenks (153), p. 136.
38. Turner (315), p. 170.

nets, sewing canoe parts, and binding in housebuilding. Mead added: "Old men sit apart unceasingly twisting palm husks on their bare thighs and muttering old tales . . . ." [39]

Aged men among the Maori were rarely idle; they watched the fields at night, tinkling mussel shells on lines to frighten rats from the crops. They also planted tubers, plaited baskets, carved wood, made nets, ground and fitted stone implements, and rubbed down green-stone to adzes and ornaments. It was a common sight to see them laboring over these objects or sitting on the ground digging in their gardens. [40]

In the above cases opportunities to keep on working at essential but lighter and less direct tasks of maintenance have been obvious assets to old-age security, at least under the existing circumstances. But such privilege, or necessity, of working on into late senescence may offer little more than mere subsistence. Menial and humdrum tasks imposed upon powerless old people may be no more than last resorts in survival and may become quite barren of social status and personal satisfactions. Indeed, for ageing individuals, release and retirement from such physically exhausting and monotonous daily duties have often been much more rewarding than repeated demotions in types of drudgery. Compromise jobs, while lighter than normal labor may involve a threat to personal prestige, as in the case of dignified old warriors consigned to "women's work." Subsistence work alone has provided no more than a toe hold on social security in old age.

There have been certain jobs, however, in which the aged could participate to much greater advantage. One enviable role has been the direction of the activities of others through the exercise of property rights, as described above. Others have included the control of people through political power, or family prerogatives, which will be discussed later. In addition to these, the aged have often acquired job rights through the accumulation of experience and familiarity with special skills. In most primitive societies, in fact, the aged have commonly possessed certain professional or semiprofessional skills which have enabled them to become leaders, if not monopolists, in these expert services. Not infrequently have they been skilled in arts and crafts such as pottery, basketry, housebuilding, metal work, and the manufacture of clothing, tools, weapons, and other implements. Furthermore, they have often been in great demand as initiators in complicated tech-

39. Mead (204), pp. 16, 48, 126, 192–193.
40. Firth (100), pp. 201, 221.

niques; and quite generally they have filled the roles of magicians,
healers, shamans, and priests—activities which will be discussed
later on.

A rather surprising specialization often open to the aged has
been that of "beauty experts." In many instances they have been
responsible for operations performed on the human body in order
to enhance personal charm, to signify adult status, or to protect
against evil spirits.

Among the Abipone, for example, the barber was an old woman
who sat on the ground by a fire, held the head of a man in her lap,
rubbed his face with hot ashes, and plucked out his beard and
whiskers with horn tweezers. And it is reported: "As soon as a
woman is of age to be married she is ordered to be marked according to custom. She reclines with her head on the lap of an old
woman, and is pricked in order to be beautiful. Thorns are used
for a pencil, and ashes and blood for paint. The ingeniously cruel
old woman, sticking the point of the thorn deep into the flesh,
describes various figures till the whole face streams with blood." [41]

Albanians went to old women to be tattooed, "for it is they who
know the patterns." [42] Among the Arunta an old man knocked
out the front teeth of younger men to make them more acceptable
to the women.[43] In the Dieri tribe, nose boring was performed by
the old men. "This operation is inflicted on the boy or girl at the
age of from five to ten years. The father generally proposes to
the other denizens of the camp to have his child's nose pierced,
and one old man is selected to perform the ceremony." [44] Aged
Bushmen tattooed successful hunters and received gifts of game.
An old woman generally acted as the barber. "She sat on the
ground, with his [the patron's] head in her lap, and shaved him
with a scrap of tin about an inch long, which she kept stropped on
her hard old hand." Young women were tattooed on the face,
thighs, and buttocks. An old woman was the operator. "She cuts
them at any convenient time during their childhood or girlhood
and receives a present for doing so. I asked an old woman why
they had themselves tattooed? 'That the men may see us pretty,'
was her reply." [45]

Young Tasmanians went to old women to be cut with stones on
the thighs, shoulders, and breasts, raising cicatrices for ornamen-

41. Dobrizhoffer (75), II, 14, 20–21.
42. Durham (88), p. 103.
43. Spencer and Gillen (289), p. 457.
44. Woods (336), p. 266.
45. Bleek (24), pp. 10–12.

tation.[46] Furness mentioned an old woman as the tattooer in a Sema Naga village.[47] Among the Toda aged women did the tattooing.[48] It was also reported that when a young Labrador girl arrived at puberty she was taken to a secluded place and there tattooed by an old woman.[49] Among the Crow the job of painting the females for the various ceremonies was the business of an old woman whose monopoly was so complete that anybody else who did it had to pay her a fee.[50]

In a later chapter detailed accounts are given of the activities of the aged in the initiation of the young into secret societies or into the status of adulthood. It is sufficient here, therefore, to note that this has been one other way in which aged men and women have found opportunities for performance of specialized roles.

Midwifery has been a professional or semiprofessional activity very widely associated with old women. Although aged men have generally treated sick women and prescribed remedies for pregnant ones, even "turning the child to come out," they have less frequently assisted in actual childbirth, except perhaps in difficult cases. They have functioned more often, however, in the naming of children and in the performance of rituals believed to safe-guard their welfare. When a Labrador Eskimo mother's time drew near, for example, an old woman arrived, ordered the patient to kneel on the floor, and tied a cord around her waist. Taking her position back of the patient, she embraced her around the abdomen and exerted strong downward pressure. When the babe was born, "The old woman picks it up, blows into its mouth, and shakes it gently to make it cry, and as soon as a wail breaks forth, begins a song intended to make it a strong and powerful hunter, if a boy, or an industrious, fruitful woman, if a girl." [51]

Curtis has given elaborate accounts of similar techniques of midwifery practiced by aged women among the Kwakiutl—techniques sufficiently involved to require "experts." After a birth the old men also played important roles, and one native has described the activities of those who came to see his new child. They asked the father, "What do you want your son to become? You are a great hunter and you had better make him one." Then he related how on the fourth day when the navel cord came off, the old people

46. Smyth (283), II, 386.
47. Furness (110), p. 456.
48. Thurston (309), p. 382.
49. Turner (316), p. 208.
50. Lowie (185), p. 149.
51. Hawkes (124), p. 111.

came again and wrapped it tightly in a bit of cloth bag which contained four shavings of a bear-claw, four of a mink-claw, and others from whatever claws they had been able to obtain. "They doubled the bag, placed the ends of a stout string of sea-lion intestine between the two folds, and wrapped another cord about it so that the gut string was held firmly. They hung this about my neck and brought the spear from my canoe. With soft cedar-back they wiped the baby's face and right hand, and after removing the wrappings from the socket of the spear-point they placed the bit of bark fibre in the base. They replaced the wrappings and said, 'Now tonight, if the weather is clear, go spearing.' That evening I used the spear on two hair-seals, and the old men exclaimed, 'Good luck, he will be a great spearsman.' I wore the bag until the boy, old enough to hunt for himself, put it on his own neck . . . . Frequently when he comes home with a good load of game, the people say, 'Well it is no wonder.' " [52]

Kutenai deliveries were expedited by several old women who seized upon the patient and shook her. Afterwards relatives gathered around, and a prominent old man named the child.[53]

Aged Omaha men predicted when births would occur, and "turned the child" for easy delivery. When the occasion arrived two or three old women attended the patient, but the baby was named by the father or grandfather.[54] When the child began to walk, it was taken to the tent of an aged man, who cut its hair and shod its feet with the first pair of moccasins. "The old man then lifts the little one by the arms and turns it around, following the sun, letting its feet touch the ground at the four points of the compass, and when the East is reached, the child is urged forward and bade to 'walk forth on the path of life.' " [55]

Aged women, and sometimes men, rendered parturition services among the Hopi,[56] and in the consecration of the babe to the sun an old grandmother, or the oldest woman of the paternal clan, was the chief officiant.[57] Navaho mothers were assisted by aged midwives while medicine men sang to ease the pain.[58] Among the Creek, "the old women are natural midwives." [59]

52. Curtis (63), pp. 95, 309–310.
53. Chamberlain (51), p. 557; Boas (25), p. 842.
54. Dorsey (78), p. 263; Fletcher (102), p. 115; Fletcher and La Flesche (103), pp. 44–45.
55. Fletcher (102), pp. 115–116.
56. Curtis (65), p. 59; Voth (323), pp. 54–55, 67–68.
57. Simmons (275), pp. 25–34.
58. Reichard (242), p. 134.
59. Swanton (302), pp. 614–615.

Aged matrons were in demand for midwifery among the Pomo,[60] Chippewa,[61] Yuchi,[62] Jivari,[63] Lengua,[64] Witoto,[65] Bontoc Igorot,[66] Banks Islanders,[67] Samoans,[68] Trobrianders,[69] Arunta,[70] and Dieri.[71] Kiwai women engaged in midwifery and were experts in matters of abortion. "They warn the younger ones not to dabble in such affairs because of risk to their lives." [72]

Euahlayi women had their own devices for inducing children to come forth. Old grandames stood about a mother in labor and decanted on the glories and attractions of the world. "First, perhaps, they will say, 'Come now, here is your auntie waiting to see you. Here is your sister. Here is your father's sister'; and so on through the whole list. Then, as the relatives and friends do not draw; 'Make haste. The bumble fruit is ripe. The guiebet flowers are blooming. The grass is waving high, the birds are talking. And it is a beautiful place, hurry up and see for yourself.' But it generally happens that the baby is too cute to be tempted, and an old woman has to procure what she calls a clever-stick which she waves over the expectant mother, crooning a charm which brings forth the baby." [73]

Maori traditions related that in olden times the grandfather was in attendance at childbirth, playing upon a flute fashioned from the thigh of an ancestor in order to call back forebears from the spirit world, whose assistance was needed in the delivery of their heir.[74]

Among the Chukchi of Siberia all the males had to leave the hut when a mother was in travail, and an old woman had charge of operations.[75] Aged Yakut women would take a newborn babe before the blazing fire, wash it, sprinkle it with water, smear it

60. Loeb (180), p. 250.
61. Radin (231), p. 659.
62. Speck (286), p. 91.
63. Simson (276), p. 388.
64. Grubb (119), p. 143.
65. Whiffen (331), pp. 148–149.
66. Jenks (153), p. 59.
67. Codrington (54), p. 229.
68. Mead (204), p. 133.
69. Malinowski (192), I, 229–230.
70. Spencer and Gillen (289), I, 106, 488.
71. Gason (113), p. 168.
72. Landtman (171), p. 229.
73. Parker (218), p. 40.
74. Best (20), II, 25.
75. Bogoras (28), pp. 37, 509.

with fresh cream, and make a sacrifice of fats to the god of the fire.[76] Almost any old woman might act as a midwife among the Toda. She rolled a rag the size of a small wick, dipped it in oil, lighted it, and branded the pregnant woman in four places—and if the baby was not wanted, she smothered it.[77] For some reason, and as a very unusual exception, Palaung mothers are reported to have feared to have the aged with them in their confinement and required the services of very young women. A pregnant woman rarely ever went to the house of an old lady, fearing that she might become afflicted with some serious illness when the child was born.[78]

In Africa the aged are professional midwives. Old Berber women supervised births and named the babies.[79] Tuareg women of long experience attended mothers in travail and massaged their bodies with hands steeped in butter or fat.[80] Old Lango midwives were on hand for supervision and chanted luck songs to expedite deliveries.[81] Fan women with child were left to the care of matrons skilled in such matters.[82] Bleek said of the Bushmen: "Birth takes place in the open as often as in the huts. A little soft grass is collected wherever the event may befall, and any old woman or women present give their assistance." When a second babe came before the former was weaned, the mother slipped off with an old woman to a lonely spot in the woods where they tried to force the birth and leave the child buried in the bushes.[83] It has been reported that "in every Hottentot kraal there is a midwife who holds her office for life, receiving occasional presents for a fee." [84] Old women were in demand for Akamba births.[85] Lindblom states that there were no special midwives, but that any old woman with experience in such matters might help. "The husband may not be present. The woman usually stands upright in front of the hearth. . . . She holds on to two of the roof supports and stands in a straddling position. Some of the women take a

---

76. Sieroshevski (272), p. 80; Czaplicka (66), p. 143.
77. Marshall (198), p. 69; Thurston (309), p. 398; Rivers (247), p. 479; Thurston (311), p. 210.
78. Milne (205), pp. 277–279.
79. Ubach and Rachow (318), p. 45.
80. Rodd (249), p. 179.
81. Driberg (82), pp. 140–143.
82. Martrou (200), p. 755.
83. Bleek (24), pp. 30–31.
84. Spencer (290), IV, Div. I, Pt. 2A, p. 16.
85. Dundas (85), p. 519.

firm grip on her legs, two hold on to her shoulders, and another receives the child. They talk and laugh if all goes well." Offerings were then made by old women who were past childbearing.[86]

In a Xosa hut where a new baby was born the father was led in by an elderly woman and asked to admit its paternity. "Having thus publicly acknowledged that the baby is his own, he is allowed to go into his wife's hut as much as he pleases, and she is allowed to cook for him." When only one of twins is wanted, an old woman, generally the grandmother, killed the second child by holding her hand over its mouth.[87]

Expert skill and practice in activities associated with childbirth have doubtless provided aged women, and sometimes men, with points of advantage in social security. For it would seem that, as a general rule, persons who have got control over the major crises in the lives of others and have influenced the question of life and death for them have tended to profit out of the situation, however unselfish their own motives.

The knowledge and experience of the aged has also often qualified them to be leaders in games, songs, dances, and various other forms of entertainment. Rules for the games have been stored in their memories, the songs have come first to their lips, and the dances have not infrequently been led by their steps. Above all, they have functioned as leaders of festivals and ceremonies where ritual has been important. Illustrations of such activities on their part are copious.

Turner writes that among the Labrador Eskimo every one from tottering youngsters to aged and bent old women played "football." The only musical instrument that he discovered was a crude violin, possessed by an old woman who boasted of her ability to play the traditional airs.[88] Aged Kwakiutl men and women were reported to be great dancers. In ceremonies recorded by Boas, the old men would beat time and sing the songs which recounted their traditions, old ghost dancers performed their ceremonies, and grandmothers danced in accompaniment to songs.[89]

Old Iroquois women led "thieving parties" of young people to collect gifts of food and knickknacks for parties.[90] Aged Chippewa men were masters of ceremonies, led songs, and joined in the

86. Lindblom (174), pp. 31–33.
87. Kidd (162), pp. 21, 45.
88. Turner (316), pp. 255, 259.
89. Boas (26), pp. 553, 598, 601; Curtis (63), p. 217.
90. Morgan (207), I, 204.

dancing.[91] In the victory celebrations of the Crow, the aged led songs of praise to heroes, and danced in the Tobacco Societies. Lowie also wrote: "At about four o'clock an old woman called out a song to the musicians. Then she and a middle aged man knelt at the foot of the altar, each holding a rattle in one hand and a fan in the other. Finally they beat the ground with their rattles, at the same time shaking their fans . . . . At about five o'clock an old woman wearing a head-band and holding a fan in one hand stood up alone to dance to the drummer's final song." [92] In certain Navaho ceremonies old men sang all night and did much of the dancing. Crane states that on one such occasion, "The most astonishing thing of all was the endurance of that aged vocalist, the old medicine man." [93]

Among the Hopi old men were leaders of songs, rituals, and ceremonies as long as they were able to attend assemblies, and were often carried into the kivas to perform after they had become blind and very decrepit. They were also sought out for instruction in the ancient songs and ceremonies until their memories failed them. The aged Yokeoma is quoted as saying, "I am an old man and of little use, and my chief work is the ceremonies." Leaders in the ceremonies held office until they were so old and infirm that they could no longer stand the strain. Voth wrote of the Powamu ceremony: "It is extremely interesting to watch the two moving circles with their constantly varying combinations of the couples as they meet and join hands at the apex of the line. In some instances the two are young and handsome figures; in others the male dancer is an old decrepit man, the mana a child; still in others the male is a youth, the mana an old crone . . . ." [94] Bourke, commenting on the skill of the old men in handling poisonous reptiles in the Snake ceremony, remarked: "These old men, from the respect they inspire, must have been of great consequence among the people." [95] Crow Wing, a native at Walpi, described how in a certain ceremony an aged man made a rawhide ball, stuffed it with seeds, and taught the boys to play. "The old man said the game had to be played four days, because they had to tear the ball and let the seeds come out, so it will be well and they will have good crops in the summer. If the ball does not tear

91. Densmore (73), p. 90; *ibid.* (73), p. 201
92. Curtis (62), p. 110; Lowie (185), pp. 131, 154, 156.
93. Reichard (242), pp. 120–121; Crane (59), p. 71.
94. Voth (322), p. 122.
95. Bourke (32), p. 17.

in four days then, they say, it is not well. This time it was very good. This game is not played for money or anything, but for the crops. And so when the game was all over everybody said thanks for it." [96]

Before the Yuchi began certain games, an address of encouragement and instruction was given by an elderly man of the Warrior society who supervised the event. Games were arranged by old men for small boys in order to give them practice.[97] Jivaro dances were conducted by elderly women.[98] At the "debut" of a Lengua girl, when she was gaily decorated for the first time and adopted a longer skirt: "The women dance by themselves, each holding a long cane, with a bunch of deer's hoofs tied at the top. These they strike on the ground, producing a loud jangling sound. An old woman in the center rattles her cane and keeps the same step as the others, chanting with them but in a louder tone. She goes through many strange contortions of the body, at times pretending to tear out her own hair." [99]

Old men and women participated in the dancing festivals of the Iban. "After this [ceremony] three of the elders clothed in long white cabayas or robes commenced dancing a slow, stately, almost comical measure, the arms extended, and the feet keeping time to the slow strains of the music, the toes being turned inwards and outwards without ceasing." Roth quotes an early traveler: "Having finished my meal . . . the dancing was commenced by the old men of the tribe, who were tottering under all the fine clothes the village could produce. This uninteresting performance consisted in placing and sustaining their bodies in the most contorted positions, and moving up and down the verandah with the slow shuffling step and shrill scream of the Sea Dyak dances, which, excepting in the exhibition of heads, this performance much resembled." Roth cites many other instances in which old people do the dancing; and quotes Grant that "the principal dancers seemed to be the old ladies, whose beauty, if they ever possessed any, had long since faded. . . ." [100]

Best has reported of the Maori: "It is interesting to note how old folks enter into youthful pastimes and other pleasures. I have seen old grey-headed men rise and join the ranks of posture dancing persons . . . . Kite flying was indulged in by men advanced in

96. Parsons (219), pp. 41–43.
97. Speck (286), pp. 87, 123.
98. Karsten (158), p. 67.
99. Grubb (119), pp. 177–178.
100. Roth (252), I, 245–255; II, 172.

years." Old women were prominent in war-dances. "Few uglier
sights could be imagined than these old hags when leading a *haka*
or war-dance." Cowan adds that ceremonial dances were led by
"uncomely tattooed old dames." [101]

Old people were great dancers among the Samoans, and were
popular for chanting the legends.[102] Aged Semang engaged in
dancing,[103] old Trobrianders led in the ceremonies,[104] and old
Arunta men sang the songs.[105] On the return of the Arunta vengeance party, the group came marching and prancing up and was
met by an old woman bedaubed from head to foot with white pipe-
clay. As they reached the camp, she, with a fighting club in her
hand, went through a series of grotesque dancing movements in
front of them. Every one stood in perfect silence until her performance was over.[106]

A favorite game of the old men among the Euahlayi was skipping the rope. "After skipping in an ordinary way for a few sec-
onds, he [the aged skipper] begins toe variations, which consist,
amongst other things, of his taking thorns out of his feet, digging
up larvae of ants, digging yams, grinding grass-seed, jumping
like a frog, doing a sort of cobbler's dance, striking an attitude
as if looking for something in the distance, running out, snatch-
ing a child and skipping with it in his arms, or lying flat on the
ground, measuring his full length in that position, rising and letting the rope slip under him; the rope going all the time, of
course, never varying in pace nor pausing for any of the variations. The one who can most successfully vary the performance
is the victor. Old men over seventy seem best at skipping. There
are many other games in which they claim to excel." [107]

Among the Ainu, it was said that "the old women show themselves the more vigorous and wildest dancers." [108] Broughton
wrote of the Albanians: "In order to give additional force to their
vocal music, it is not unusual for two or three old men of the party
to sit in the middle of the ring, and set the words of the song at
the beginning of each verse at the same time with the leader . . .
and one of them has often a flute to accompany their voices." [109]

101. Best (20), II, 115; *ibid.* (20), 134; Cowan (58), p. 345.
102. Mead (204), p. 115; Spencer (290), III, 70.
103. Schebesta (262), p. 90.
104. Malinowski (190), p. 374.
105. Spencer and Gillen (289), I, 185–242.
106. *Ibid.* (289), pp. 451–453.
107. Parker (218), p. 125.
108. Hitchcock (128), pp. 478–480.
109. Broughton (39), I, 144.

At the Palaung festivals there were paid dancers. The more they could contort and bend the body, the more they were admired. "The old men sit watching them with critical eyes. Now and then a grandfather rises, steps out on the level ground, waves his arms with the proper gestures, and makes a few dancing steps. The other men look on with sympathetic interest, saying to each other, 'How well he danced when he was young.' Even the children look on with serious faces, and not a smile of derision crosses the faces of anyone as the old man dances with tottering steps. A lad helps him to return to his seat and says, 'O Grandfather, how well thou must have danced when thou didst court the ladies!' and the old man replies, 'It is true, it is true,' and squats down again in the shade." [110]

The Yukaghir of both sexes and all ages danced together, old men and children, healthy and ill, and especially old women. Jochelson reports: "I once saw a sick old woman, who could not get up, become so excited at the sight of the dancing of young people, that she got up and began to imitate all the movements of the dancers, until finally she fell down exhausted." [111]

Old Akamba women had a dance of their own which consisted of drumming by one while the others competed grotesquely in writhing and twisting about. "I have noticed that the older the women are, the more vigorously they take part in this, and as the main object is to compete until one of them is tired out, I presume that their object is to show 'that there is life in the old dog yet.' " Dundas also mentions old women who sang together for hours at a time, the lone phrase of their song being, "The bowl is full." [112]

It has appeared not uncommon in many societies for the aged, who might well be conserving their strength, to exert themselves strenuously in leadership, games, and entertainment. This has been done at great effort and perhaps to compensate for their declining strength. Their use of humor may have been a further form of compensation. The point of significance with respect to their security is that in some societies these performances have been highly rewarded—the aged becoming the star performers.

Another popular and very common activity of the aged has been storytelling, a pastime which has served the threefold function of entertainment, instruction, and moral admonition. One who enjoys modern facilities for entertainment can hardly ap-

110. Milne (205), p. 215.
111. Jochelson (154), pp. 34–35.
112. Dundas (85), pp. 508–509.

preciate the enviable position held by the aged man or woman of primitive societies who has accumulated an ample supply of interesting tales and legends.

The aged were the great storytellers among the Polar Eskimo. Almost every question was answered and every problem explained by a tale. One old native reported: "Our tales are men's experiences . . . to the words of the newly born none give much credence, but the experience of the older generations contains truth. When I narrate legends, it is not I who speak, it is the wisdom of our forefathers . . . ." [113] Rasmussen explained that the fables and legends were told in the houses on long winter evenings as the people sat about heavy and tired after great banquets of raw, frozen meat. "Then it is the task of the story-teller to talk his hearers to sleep. The best story-tellers boast of never having told any story to the end." It is the grandmother's business to teach the legends to the children. [114]

Rasmussen has given an interesting case of adjustment similar to that of the aged on the part of one Polar Eskimo who was an invalid. "When anything unusual happened and you wished to hear of the matter from various points of view, you had only to go down to Tateraq. He was the animated newspaper of the place . . . . He was a palsied man, who lay out on his sledge, day and night, all through the summer; nothing that happened as far as the eyes could reach escaped his vigilance, and when he called out, as he occasionally did, you were quite certain to see the whole place bestir itself; everybody knew that the helpless man on the sledge had nothing to do but wait for something to happen. And should there be a paucity of happenings now and again, he would take refuge in his dreams, which often augured remarkable things; and in this way he succeeded in keeping the interest of the public in himself alive." [115]

Turner wrote of the Labrador Eskimo: "They are exceedingly fond of storytelling. Sitting in the hut engaged in the evening work, the old men tell what they have seen and heard. The old women relate the history of the people of former days, depending entirely on memory, often interspersed with recitations apparently foreign to the thread of the legend. The younger members sit with staring eyes and countenances which show their wandering interest in the narration. Far into the night the droning tone

113. Rasmussen (233), p. 97.
114. *Ibid.* (233), p. 161.
115. *Ibid.* (233), p. 60.

of her voice continues reciting the events of the past until one by one the listeners drowsily drop to sleep in the position they last assumed." [116]

Folk tales were recited by the old Menomini Indians during the long winter nights.[117] Aged Chippewa narrated stories of the creation and of deeds of bravery to inspire in the children a desire to grow up like their fathers. "The winter was the time for story-telling, and many old women were expert in this art. One old woman used to act out her stories, running around the fire and acting while she talked." [118] Kohl reported, "I have often heard it stated that men are the only story-tellers, and that men and boys are alone permitted to listen to them. I know not if this be the case, though it may be so with some sorts of stories, but it is a fact that I found many old women equally eloquent and inventive." [119]

Lowie writes of the Crow: "Stories were told on winter nights when the people were sitting by the fire or had stretched out before falling asleep. Old people with a reputation as raconteurs were invit*r*d for a feast and then expected to narrate their tales. The audience was expected to answer, 'Yes' after every sentence or two. When no one replied it was a sign that all had fallen asleep and the story-teller broke off his narrative, possibly to resume it the following night." [120]

Hopi elders told stories of the "wondrous past" when all the animals talked like human beings, and aged men and women were begged to tell their tales again and again.[121] Storytelling was the delight of the Omaha during the long winter nights. "It was then that the old folk drew on their store of memories, myths, fables, and adventures of pygmies and the little people who play about the woods and prairies and lead people astray. All these and also actual occurrences were recited with varying intonations and illustrative gesture, sometimes interspersed with song, which added to the effect and heightened the spell of the story or myth as the listeners clustered about the blazing fire." [122] A common introduction to the Yuchi myth was "The old people tell it . . . ." [123]

116. Turner (316), pp. 260–261.
117. Hoffman (135), p. 209.
118. Densmore (73), p. 97; Copway (57), p. 56; Densmore (73), p. 29.
119. Kohl (163), pp. 88, 91.
120. Lowie (186) p. 13.
121. James (152) p. 39.
122. Fletcher and La Flesche (103), p. 370.
123. Speck (286), p. 101.

It has been said of the Arawak that "as they lie in their hammocks, or squat around the fire with knees drawn up to the chin, they listen to the endless tales, told sometimes by the shaman, sometimes by a headman of the settlement, sometimes by the old women—who in this are great tradition-mongers." [124] Old Inca related the ancient traditions of their ancestors, and the most aged usually recounted stories to the family.[125] Aged Bontoc Igorot were great storytellers.[126] Feeble old Kiwai Papuans would spend three hours on a single legend.[127] Malinowski reported of the Trobrianders that the experiences of the past generations are repeated by the aged around village fires.[128] Best said of the Maori: "How many times has the writer, over a space of five decades, listened to these puerile folk tales, as told by merry children and grey-headed old bushmen, told in rough huts, in the darkening solitude of the old, old, forests, by the rushing waters of many streams . . . . Fancy a tattered old bush fighter . . . relating the myths of Uenuka the Rainbow God and the Mist Maid, or such puerile folk tales as that of the woman who ate her child's heart." [129]

Gason wrote of the Dieri: "At times an old man, when in good humor, will relate some wild tales to the younger folk, i.e., how he killed some wild black fellow when he was a young man, and how he was speared through the body, and left no wounds visible. These childish stories are listened to with the greatest interest and wonder, and believed." [130] Andrews has noted the aged storyteller among the Berber,[131] and Rattray mentioned an old Ashanti "full of traditions, stories, and proverbs." [132] Westermann was of the opinion that among the Shilluk "for stories, riddles, etc., old women are the best source." [133] Little Xosa children sat around the fire at night and listened to tales from their aged grandmothers. Theal said of them that "the best narrators of traditional tales are almost invariably ancient dames, and the time chosen for the story is always in the evening." [134] Bakongo stories

124. Im Thurn (151), p. 371.
125. Markham (195), I, 62; II, 421.
126. Jenks (153), p. 225.
127. Riley (245), p. 27.
128. Malinowski (191), p. 219.
129. Best (20), I, 213.
130. Gason (113), p. 176.
131. Andrews (3), p. 36.
132. Rattray (237), pp. 124–125.
133. Westermann (328), p. xxviii.
134. Bourhill and Drake (31), p. v; Theal (307), p. vl; Kidd (162), p. 138.

were told around the fire on nights that were too dark for dancing. They were "told with dramatic power and forceful eloquence,
the narrator acting the parts and imitating the sounds of the different animals . . . . A father correcting his children will tell
them a story to enforce his teaching . . . ." [135]

"Songs around the fire finished off the [Sema Naga] day, and
on such days, too, the old men tell stories—many of them of un-
printable import—to any who care to listen . . . ." [136] Aged
Palaung engaged in gossip, riddles, and storytelling after supper
in the evenings. Milne wrote: "Each day I spent also some hours
writing down Palaung stories and rhymes dictated to me in their
own homes by old men too infirm to work, to whom story-telling
was quite a pleasant occupation." [137]

The very limited number of cases cited here should not be considered indicative of the full extent to which the aged have managed to utilize their powers in entertainment. They are presented
merely as illustrations of a type of adjustment on the part of the
aged that is found practically everywhere. Storytelling has been
one of the universal opportunities afforded them for holding
their place in the social life of the group.

Although concrete cases portray the activities of the aged in
sharp relief, they should be subjected, wherever possible, to more
careful statistical checks. But in this chapter it is difficult, for the
classifiable facts are often too meager for reliable statistical usage. It appears, however, that opportunities for the aged to continue active participation in the primary maintenance activities
have been relatively slight among collectors, have increased somewhat with hunters and fishers, and have been more common among
herders and especially cultivators of the soil (Cor. 187–195). Opportunities for the aged to manufacture tools and implements
seem to have been more general, irrespective of the stage of maintenance (Cor. 196–203). Household chores have been more commonly reported for aged women, especially in agricultural
groups; but again there are no observable trends when correlated
with the basic maintenance activities (Cor. 204–211).

Statistical data are not much better on the professional and
semiprofessional activities of the aged, and on the subject of personal ornamentation they are entirely inadequate for correlational use. The activities of the aged at childbirth are better re-

135. Weeks (326), pp. 271–272.
136. Hutton (148), p. 117.
137. Milne (205), pp. 7, 197.

ported, however, and three generalizations may be stated with some confidence: First, midwifery has been much more frequently the work of aged women than of aged men, and has been practiced by them nearly everywhere, irrespective of cultural determinants (Cor. 212–223). Second, aged men have tended to be more active in the birthchamber and in early infant services wherever residence has been relatively permanent and in agricultural societies, but very rarely in herding societies (Cor. 218–223). Third, aged men have seemed less likely to perform services in childbirth and in early infant care under the patriarchal type of family organization than in societies where the matriarchal form of family has existed. This trend is indicated when services by aged men in childbirth and infant care are correlated with matrilocal residence, matrilineal descent, inheritance, and succession, matripotestal authority, and the avunculate, all of which show consistently high coefficients of association (Cor. 224–229). On the other hand, the same correlations with patriarchal traits, or with aged women as participants in either form of family organization, show neither high coefficients of association nor the same consistency (Cor. 230–245). It would appear, therefore, that aged women with initiative and suitable qualifications have almost universally participated in midwifery in primitive societies, while there are some limitations on the same activities by aged men. There is a temptation to hypothecate that the men's relative insecurity with respect to their own children in the matriarchal system has provided greater incentive for them to associate themselves with activities in childbirth and infant care, but this is a psychological problem which cannot be adequately handled with the present data.

Opportunities for the aged to function as leaders in games, songs, dances, ceremonies, and festivities have been present in all societies, and in no references from the literature were statements found to the effect that the aged have not participated in these activities. (Table VII, traits 181, 182.) In fact, these appear to have been so nearly universal roles of the aged whenever they have been competent to perform them that there is no point in making statistical correlations. The same generalization applies to the activities of the aged in providing information, instruction, and entertainment by means of storytelling; and also in the repeating of legends, proverbs, genealogies, and traditions. Here again, no references were found in which it is stated that the aged have not participated in such activities. The information is much more complete for aged men (Table VII, traits 177, 178), but the practice is so nearly universal that statistical correlations show no dominant trends.

In summary, therefore, it may be stated that, although documented data are scanty, an important means of security for the aged, when they have become too feeble to forage for themselves, has been active association and assistance in the interests and enterprises of others. They might engage in secondary economic roles and make themselves as useful as possible in field, camp, shop, and household. They might concentrate on the lighter tasks and, wherever possible, utilize their long experience and greater knowledge in the more complicated skills, rituals, and ceremonies of daily life. They have also been able to ally themselves with others competent to support them through professional and semi-professional services. In general, opportunities for such adjustments have been dependent upon both individual initiative and contemporary social and cultural factors. Roughly stated, opportunities for the aged to participate actively in the daily affairs of life have been shown to be conditioned to a great degree by climate, permanency of residence, the basic maintenance activities, and the form of family organization. Although these opportunities might differ for men and women, they have been basic adjustments in social security for both in their old age.

V

POLITICAL AND CIVIL ACTIVITIES

THE point has been stressed that the aged must depend largely upon others for security. The treatment which they receive at the hands of younger people, and the deference and support which the latter are persuaded or impelled to give them, are crucial to their well-being and comfort. Without such a sustaining relationship the aged cannot even survive for long. A partial survey of the activities of the aged has shown that some security has been attainable through the performance of lighter tasks useful to others, but the sweat and toil of the old in lowly labors have rarely been as rewarding as the exercise of wisdom, skill, and tact in social relations. In fact, security for the aged has depended far more upon their wits than their works: and a fruitful field for such talent has been found in political, civil, and judicial affairs.

The office of chieftainship and membership in official councils, regulative organizations, clubs, and secret societies have afforded the aged positions of usefulness in which well-established prerogatives, ripe experience, and special knowledge could often more than compensate for physical handicaps and waning vitality. Not infrequently age itself has been regarded as a qualification for such offices; but more often those who have shown exceptional ability or who have achieved positions of importance and power through long and active lives have managed to hold on to them into late old age. The extent to which aged individuals have attained and held such positions has depended upon both personal initiative and impersonal cultural factors.

A statistical analysis of correlative data indicates that peoples who have settled down to more or less permanent habitation have developed more centralized and authoritative forms of political organization with greater administrative powers vested in a chief executive, than is the case among nomadic groups. While chieftainship has been found to be almost universal, the authority exercised by the chief has tended to be minimal among collectors and hunters, greater among fishers and herders, and most effective among cultivators of the soil (Cor. 246–251). It would seem also that prevalence of warfare has tended to increase the authority of the chief, and we find an exceptionally strong correlation between government by restricted councils and augmented authority of the chief (Cor. 252–253). Briefly, development of a powerful chieftainship, organized participation in warfare, restricted councils, group responsibility for crimes, existence of codified laws, and judicial powers are all interrelated and appear to have arisen together, each supporting the others and gradually increasing in importance upon the scale from collection, hunting, and fishing, to herding and finally agriculture. In agricultural groups with more or less permanent residence they all tend to reach their greatest strength (Cor. 246–283). These numerous correlations, and many others,[1] indicate that the basic institutions and agencies of political regulation and social control have appeared in rather rudimentary form in simple cultures, and have gradually developed with advancing economic organizations, reaching their greatest strength among herders and tillers of the soil. From this it seems proper to conclude that among herders and farmers the aged men have been able to derive greatest advantage through adjustments of a civil and political character.

The chieftainship has been a key position existing almost universally in primitive societies, and it has not infrequently been occupied by aged persons. Indeed, old men have functioned as chiefs in the simplest as well as the most complex social organizations. Among the Polar Eskimo, for example, while there was no organized political power, aged magicians were recognized as headmen and leaders.[2] The Point Barrow Eskimo also had little formal organization; nevertheless, an "old, feeble, tottering . . . and very deaf" man was pointed out as the "so-called chief." [3] Among the Haida, "it sometimes happened that when a chief grew old and poor he was virtually succeeded in authority by a younger, wealthier, and more energetic man, but he always retained the honorable title of chief, when once elected, until he died." [4] "Besides the principal chief, there are others, who are the heads of the other principal clan totems or households of the village. Their rank or claim to distinction and respect is relative to that of the chief in the degree of their wealth, age, superiority of natural understanding, and general good fortune . . . ." [5] Many references are made to aged chiefs among the Kwakiutl,[6] the

1. Simmons (274), pp. 499–517.   2. Rasmussen (233), pp. 126–127.
3. Murdock (210), p. 39.   4. Harrison (123), pp. 41, 64–65.
5. Niblack (213), p. 250.   6. Curtis (63), p. 56; Boas (26), pp. 564, 581.

Chippewa,[7] and the Crow;[8] while Dorsey states that aged Omaha headmen were never deposed but continued in their office until death or resignation.[9]

According to Loeb, the Pomo chief was usually past his prime and rarely ever participated in active enterprises requiring much physical exertion. A native offered an instructive account of the place aged men held in the political life of the Pomo: "My uncle (mother's brother) Jose was a chief; my grandfather was also a chief . . . over eighty years of age; I was nineteen . . . it never entered my mind that they had decided to resign their post and make me chief . . . . Well, one time my grandfather told me to stay in the next Sunday . . . . He said that he would need me . . . . I began to get uneasy . . . I noticed my uncle going in and out and talking to the people outside, so I guessed that they were preparing a feast . . . . Then my grandfather told my uncle, 'All right, go and tell the people to get ready.' Then he said to me, 'Son, I am getting old. I have taken care of our people for a long time; I have always tried to do good and to do what is right; I have kept away from quarrels and I have made peace . . . . I have gone around among our people and told them good words . . . . Now I am an old man, and your uncle also is old.' I was sitting between the two men and each of them took by hand. Then my grandfather continued, 'We have decided to give you our post. Now you are the chief of our people and from now on you must take care of them as we have.' When he said that I began to feel dizzy, and I started to tremble; I was afraid, and things began to swim around my head and I couldn't see clearly. Then my grandfather undid his shirt, and putting his hand inside his bosom he fumbled around in there; he was a very old man and his hand trembled; then he began to pull out a string of wampum; and it came and it came, more and more of it, yards and yards of it. I have never seen so much wampum. Then my uncle went to the corner of the room and he brought out his wampum and there was also a lot of this. Then my grandfather tied together the ends of both strings, so that it made now only one string. After this he started to coil it on his arms slowly, coil after coil, coil after coil, and when he was through he could hardly lift it; he was a very old man; but he lifted it and put it around my neck and then he said, 'Son this is the wampum of our people; with it we have taken care of our people for all these years; now you must take care of it and care for our people as we have. Now

7. Kohl (163), p. 73.   8. Curtis (62), p. 7.   9. Dorsey (78), p. 362.

we will go and tell the people.' " Such aged Pomo leaders might
resign but they were never deposed; they always chose their successors, and remained very influential.[10]

At the head of the Hopi village was a chief whose office required
years of training and lasted for life—or until the incumbent chose
to resign. "Old Man" was an honorable title for him.[11] Yuchi
tribal chiefs were chosen for life and so were the heads of the
Creek towns. When one wanted an assistant, because of age, infirmity, or any other reason, he selected a man approved by the
council.[12] Itzacoatl, the Aztec king, served his country for thirty
years and died at "a very advanced age";[13] and Sarmiento states
that the Inca rulers held office until late in life and selected their
successors.[14]

One of the most powerful Araucanian chiefs was a "corpulent,
thick-set old gentleman, with a big head and a pleasant good-
natured face"; and another chief "between ninety and a hundred
years of age" had eight wives, much property, and was called
"The Grass-of-Heaven." The aged Araucanian rulers appointed
their successors.[15] An old chief among the Arawak was described
as "infirm" but influential.[16] Grubb depicted Short-Neck of the
Lengua tribe as an old man, but a most important chief of the
community.[17] It is said that Jivaro who qualified for the office of
chief should be "elderly and experienced" men; and a chief was
called the "old one" because he was nearly always aged. Up de
Graff spoke of one leader of a Jivaro party as a "smooth tongued
old scoundrel." [18]

In Africa the Bakongo obeyed leaders who were too old and
infirm to attempt travel, and mention was made of one who assumed office in late middle age and ruled for thirty-two years.[19]
Very aged chiefs were reported among the Akamba;[20] and Kidd
stated that a headman among the Xosa might be seventy and the
possessor of twenty or thirty wives.[21] Ricards added that "age

10. Loeb (180), pp. 237, 239, 240–241.
11. Goddard (116), p. 109; Crane (59), p. 95.
12. Speck (286), p. 113; *ibid.* (284), p. 113; Hawkins (125), p. 70.
13. Biart (22), p. 75.
14. Sarmiento d Gamboa (258), pp. 123–153.
15. Smith (282), pp. 190, 252; Featherman (98), p. 476.
16. Brett (35), p. 121.
17. Grubb (118), p. 129.
18. Karsten (158), pp. 8, 20; Up de Graff (319), p. 269.
19. Weeks (327), p. 42.
20. Tate (305), p. 136.
21. Kidd (161), pp. 29, 212.

gives great weight to the authority of the chief." But there are other reports that sometimes a chief was killed after he reached a certain state of senility.[22] Old chiefs with long beards were also common among the Dahomeans and one is described as "old and venerable, his age being estimated as . . . ninety years." [23] The Ashanti obeyed old men as their leaders, some of whom were described as "perfectly charming old gentlemen," while others were so aged and infirm that they were confined to their homes.[24] The Hottentot also had superannuated chiefs; and one Berber leader was reported to be a "fat and infirm old man." [25]

Among the ancient Hebrew Moses was said to have held the leadership of Israel into very great age and until his death.[26] Joshua complained while yet in command: "I am old and well stricken in years," and he is reported to have died at one hundred and ten.[27] David ruled until his death at seventy.[28] "Now David was old and stricken with years; and they covered him with clothes, but he got no heat." [29] Bathsheba petitioned him: "And thou, my lord, O king, the eyes of all Israel are upon thee, that thou shouldest tell them who shall sit on the throne of my lord the king after him." [30] "Now David was so old and full of days; and he made Solomon his son king over Israel." [31]

Jochelson believes that among the Yukaghir of Russia the clan as well as the family was based on the principle of the supremacy of the eldest male. When the Russian conquerors, in search of responsible persons to collect the imposed tribute, asked them to name their leaders, they pointed to the old men. "The old man was the elder of the clan . . . . He administered war, and hunting expeditions. He selected the fishing districts, and assigned to each family their proper place." [32]

Bogoras related how on his early visits to the camps of the Chukchi, those who came to meet him would say: "Let us take you to the oldest man. First talk to him." [33] Aged chiefs were also

22. Ricards (244), p. 21.
23. Duncan (84), pp. 5, 244.
24. Bowdich (33), pp. 17, 56, 277; Rattray (237), p. 175; Becham (17), p. 21.
25. Andrews (3), p. 168.
26. Numbers, Chap. 27.
27. Joshua, Chaps. 23, 24.
28. II Sam. 5:4.
29. I Kings 1:1.
30. *Ibid.* 1:20.
31. I Chron. 23:1.
32. Jochelson (154), pp. 115, 119.
33. Bogoras (28), pp. 544–546.

found among the Kazak and Mongols;[34] and of the latter it is reported that the oldest man in the hamlet exercised general control over the group.[35]

Mutevan, headman of a Toda group, was "a very old man probably about eighty . . . ."[36] In the Vedda tribe it was said that "Poromala is one of the oldest men of the community and is its leader as far as a leader can be said to exist." Seligmann described another village headman as "an extremely old man."[37] Westermarck also wrote: "Among the Veddas of Ceylon the oldest man is regarded with a sort of patriarchal respect."[38] The Palaung chiefs often lived and reigned to a great age, after which their bodies were cremated as a special honor.[39] The dwarf Semang of the Malay Peninsula recognized the civil authority of the aged. "Crippled old Juke . . . was regarded as a sort of chief who settled disputes, and if necessary admonished." The Kenta group of Semang required of their chief that he must be, if not the oldest, at any rate an elderly man, distinguished by judgment and clemency, and in a position to settle disputes. The only functionaries of the Sakai Semang were the *Penghulus*, of whom there was one in each village who held office for life. An old headman was called the Grandfather of the community, and there were legends of famous chiefs who were "invulnerable old men."[40]

In Australia wherever the Arunta were gathered: "One or two of the old men are at once seen to wield a special influence over the others." Age and magic combined were said to be far more effective than sheer physical prowess.[41] In the Dieri tribe the oldest man of the totem was its head. "Formerly the old man by virtue of his age was the ruler . . . . Seniority runs through the whole of the aboriginal system. It is maintained by the old men who always retain some rite or ceremony which is not made known to the juniors. Of course upon this rite the utmost stress is laid, and its import is kept among the fewest possible number. Age in itself, quite apart from fitness, seems to give a right to authority . . . . In matters affecting the natives the old men's influence and wishes are still paramount."[42]

34. Atkinson (4), 224; Carruthers (49), II, 326.
35. Howorth (145), IV, 76–77.
36. Rivers (247), p. 556.   37. Seligmann (269), pp. 49, 194.
38. Westermarck (329), I, 603.   39. Milne (205), 309–311.
40. Schebesta (262), pp. 210, 234–235; Skeat and Blagden (277), I, 500; II, 171, 345.
41. Spencer and Gillen (288), p. 12; *ibid.* (289), I, 466.
42. Horne and Aiston (138), pp. 12–23; Howitt (143), p. 297.

A typical chief among the Ainu of Japan was an old man with a very long beard.[43] The control of Bontoc Igorot villages was often in the hands of aged headmen.[44] Among the Mafulu the office of chief was hereditary and passed on to the eldest son;[45] and in the Banks Islands a man remained in authority although his powers diminished with age.[46] Each Dyak or Iban village long-house had its headman, who was called the "Old Man of the House." He settled all disputes, decided the amount of fine to be paid by guilty parties, and maintained general order.[47]

Leaders among the Trobrianders ruled on into senility and they even wondered whether old age could ever be the cause of death, especially the death of an important person. "When I asked about M'tabaly, a very old and decrepit man, the chief of Kasana'i, whether he was going to die soon, I was told that, if no evil spell were thrown on him, there was no reason why he should not go on living." Every Trobriand village community was "owned" by a sub-clan, and the eldest male was a headman of the town. When the sub-clan was of the highest rank, its eldest male was not only headman of his own village, but exercised paramount rule over the whole district.[48]

Aged chiefs also ruled in Samoa, and a native of twenty-seven complained of his awkward position: "I have been a chief only four years, and look, my hair is grey, although Samoan grey hair comes very slowly, not in youth as it comes to a white man. But always, I must act as if I were old. I must walk gravely and with a measured step. I may not dance except on solemn occasions, neither may I play games with the young men. Old men of sixty are my companions, and watch my every word, lest I make a mistake. Thirty-one people live in my households. For them I must plan, I must find them food and clothing and settle their disputes, arrange their marriages. There is no one in my whole family who dares to scold me or even address me familiarly by my first name. And the old men shake their heads and agree that it is unseemly for one to be a chief so young." [49]

These sample cases clearly indicate that aged men have been commonly found in the office of headman or chieftain, and that

43. Batchelor (12), pp. 23, 36–37, 65–66; Landor (168), p. 7.
44. Jenks (153), pp. 32–33.
45. Williamson (334), p. 94.
46. Codrington (54), p. 53.
47. Gomes (117), p. 88.
48. Malinowski (190), p. 360; *ibid.* (192), I, 30.
49. Mead (204), p. 37.

although in very late life some of their authority and duties might be delegated to others—in some cases they could be relieved of them altogether—they were rarely ever deposed. They often continued to exercise authority in very late age and not infrequently had the right to select their successors. Out of 71 tribes aged men were reported as chiefs in 56; in 8 more it was implied that they could hold office; while in no tribe was it stated that chiefs were regularly deposed on account of their age. The record is quite different for aged women, however. In only 2 tribes did they hold positions equivalent to chiefs; in 7 it was implied that they might hold such offices; while in 22 information was definitely negative. (Table VII, traits 121, 122.)

The tendency for old men to continue in the chieftainship appeared clearly in a statistical analysis relating the existence of the office of chief and the percentage of tribes in which aged men or women held such offices.* Thus we may conclude that in primitive societies the recognition of certain old men as chiefs or headmen has been as widespread as the office of chieftain itself. Indeed, the percentage may be higher, suggesting that the office grew in part out of the leadership and domination of old men who were regarded as "chiefs" even before there was a formalized office.

This conclusion is further supported by the fact that while there is a negative coefficient of association for the existence of the office of chief among tribes classified as collectors, the acceptance of elders as leaders in such groups shows a strong positive coefficient (Cor. 284–285). The same is true for hunting tribes (Cor. 286 cf. 248), and even more for fishing peoples (Cor. 287 cf. 249); while a partially reverse trend is indicated for herders (Cor. 288 cf. 250). Among cultivators of the soil both the office of chief and its occupancy by old men show strong positive coefficients of association (Cor. 289 cf. 251). Correlations on perma-

*

Traits	Office 31	Aged men 121	Aged women 122
a. +	35.2%	46.4%	00.0%
b. + =	71.8%	78.8%	2.8%
c. + = −	95.7%	90.1%	12.3%

The first column represents the percentage of tribes in which the office of chief is reported, the second lists the percentage of tribes in which aged men are reported as "chiefs," and the third does the same for aged women.

nency of residence also support these trends (Cor. 290 cf. 246).
Such statistical evidence thus indicates that generally it is among
agricultural tribes that chiefs have had the very best chance of
retaining office into late senescence.

It would seem that the prevalence of warfare has also tended
to increase the authority of the chief or leader (Cor. 291), as
there is a positive relationship between the extent of warfare and
aged chiefs. The fact, however, that this correlation is not so pronounced (Cor. 292) as the ones mentioned above may indicate
that chiefs have tended to retire earlier in more warlike tribes.

Where government has been administered by restricted councils and where considerable authority has been vested in the chief,
aged men have tended to stay in office (Cor. 293–294). Apparently the influence of women in government has had no serious
effect upon the retention of office by old chiefs (Cor. 295); but
the presence of secret societies, group responsibility for crimes,
codified laws, and recognized authority of judges all show substantial positive coefficients of association with the occupancy of
the chieftainship by old men (Cor. 296–299). Age-grades, hereditary castes and classes, and matriarchal or patriarchal forms
of family organization do not seem to have greatly influenced the
tenure of office of old chiefs. At least there appears to be no consistency in the slightly fluctuating statistical trends (Cor. 300–
313). Private property rights in general, however, and especially
property rights of aged men, are strongly correlated with long
tenure of office by chiefs (Cor. 214–215).

If tenure of office had involved chiefs and headmen only, the
subject would not be very significant in a study of old age. But
usually there has been associated with rulers certain aged councilmen and advisors who have exercised considerable influence in
government and over the office of chieftainship. The fact that the
use of the term "elder" has so commonly implied leader, headman,
or councilman suggests the important role of the aged in government. Indeed, there have been societies in which age alone has
qualified men for membership in government councils, but active
participation has usually depended upon other personal qualifications than mere age. The office of councilman or advisor to a
more energetic and active administrator has been an especially
suitable role for individuals of broad practical experience and
wisdom who had become physically incapacitated by age but were
still mentally alert and keenly concerned with public affairs. It
has provided opportunities for active participation which were

sufficiently rewarding to attract the interest of aged persons in nearly all societies. A more or less random selection of cases amply illustrates this fact.

Murdock has reported of the Point Barrow Eskimo: "Respect for the opinion of the elders is so great that the people may be said to be practically under what is called 'simple elder rule.' " [50] Those who sat in Chippewa councils did so according to their age and wisdom, the youngest generally remaining silent.[51] One native reports: "The old people, in our meetings at La Pointe, always sat in the center of the circle, close to the place where the American agents have their tables, and where the speakers stand. Some of them, who were very old, were allowed chairs to sit on. The other old men sat together in the grass near them. Further out the young fellows lay about in groups. Among them were men of twenty and twenty-five years, but they never interfered in the discussions, save now and then uttering a loud 'Ho Ho,' or some other cry of applause. The opinions of the Indians as to the long-lasting minority of the young men are very strict, and if the latter do not act in accordance with their views, they are very roughly reminded of their position. Once, I was told, a very old and celebrated speaker was interrupted by a young imprudent fellow in a most improper manner. The old warrior was so incensed at it, that he drew his tomahawk, split the young man's skull open, and then quietly continued his harangue as if nothing had happened." [52]

Curtis states that if an enemy made an attack on a party of moving Crow and killed some of them, the chief regarded it as a sign that he had for the time lost his power with the spirits. Then he cried out to the old men: "My people, choose someone to take my place for a time for my day is bad." [53] All questions of movement were decided by a council of elders, and it was said to be the daily habit of Chief Red Bear "to call his old men and let them talk as much as they would. From their conversation he took the good things and made them his own." [54]

Among the Iroquois a native has reported: "We pay special attention to the old men, inasmuch as they are the ones who determine and decide all matters, and everything is ordered by their

50. Murdock (210), p. 427.
51. Copway (57), p. 141.
52. Kohl (163), p. 273.
53. Curtis (62), p. 9.
54. *Ibid.* (62), p. 11.

advice." [55] Creek chiefs consulted old men in councils and at their meetings the oldest men spoke up while the young were very circumspect.[56]

The minister of finance among the Aztec was "an old and faithful servant of the government." Their clan government was administered by a council of old men, and when the new king Moteuczoma was crowned he gave the "government of the provinces to the oldest and bravest officers of the army." A council consisting of a number of old men formed the highest authority of the *calpulli*, which exercised criminal as well as civil jurisdiction and attended to all grave questions affecting the kingship. Six aged lords attended the royal person and shared his meals with him as a mark of favor. At the coronation of a new king the main address was delivered by an aged nobleman of state or the high priest, presumably an old man.[57]

In Africa old men were active in council assemblies. They were very influential in the village councils of the Vai, for example.[58] Shilluk chiefs were surrounded by aged counselors who advised and admonished them;[59] and the Mangbetu government was described as "absolutism modified by a council of elders." [60] Every aged Hottentot man was said to have a place in the council, and Hoernle states that the "whole conduct of affairs in the Nama tribe was, and is, the concern of the older men . . . ." [61] The government of the Akamba was in the hands of elders who had passed many degrees in accordance with their age and their payment of fees. They were mostly old men, and to them were known all the customs of the people, so that a correct decision often required their advice.[62]

During the minority of an Ashanti king, or in the earliest part of his reign, the oldest counselors visited him every morning and repeated, in turn, all the great deeds of his ancestors. "The greatest deference seemed to be paid to aged experience or wisdom." [63] The chief assistant to the Dahomey king was at one time "an old,

55. Stites (297), p. 105.
56. Swanton (302), pp. 311, 319.
57. Bancroft (7), I, 112: Priestly (228), p. 25; Biart (22), p. 89; Bandelier (8), p. 633; Featherman (98), p. 110.
58. Delafosse (69), p. 135.
59. Westermann (328), p. xlviii.
60. Dowd (81), II, 105–106.
61. Hoernle (133), p. 15.
62. Dundas (85), pp. 539–541.
63. Bowdich (33), p. 296.

old man with hollow cheeks and toothless gums which made his mouth appear lipless . . . he easily forgets, appears to be half asleep; and is manifestly becoming childish. The king has occasionally hinted at his retirement, but the decrepit senior clamors to be kept on, declaring, perhaps truly, that do-nothingness would kill him." [64]

Kidd related how an old Xosa chief, seated by a cattle kraal and surrounded by aged counselors, tried court cases and settled disputes. "Such a chief, dying in his old age, leaves a minor, often a mere child, to succeed him. What then is the position of the young chief? He finds himself surrounded by a number of grey-headed, veteran associates of his father who are strong in the possession of long-continued popular influence and insolent from their consciousness of possessing it. If he will yield himself to their sway his course is smoothened for him . . . and they will sometimes hint that they can unmake as well as make chiefs." [65]

The Hebrew were no exception to the rule of authority of the elders. "And He said unto Moses, 'Come up to Jehovah, thou and Aaron, Nadab, and Abihu, and seventy of the elders of Israel . . . .' " [66] Years later, "King Rehoboam consulted with the old men, that stood before Solomon his father while he yet lived and said, 'How do you advise that I may answer the people?' " And Scripture records it as a grave folly that he ignored their counsel.[67]

Although Bogoras has stated that the Chukchi had no such thing as a council of elders, he also reported: "I was told that in olden times when some awkward case happened within the limits of a family-group, the old men and the young men would hold a council. The old men would sit down and talk about the case. The young men stood behind and listened." Likewise, when any trouble arose between two different family groups, men from both sides would assemble. The old of each side would elect one or two speakers, who had to speak in turn, one side after the other. The old men spoke and the young men had to obey their decision. "If, however, an agreement could not be reached, or the parties particularly interested in the case refused to listen to reason, the old men would say, 'let them play.' Then the interested parties, armed with spears, would have an encounter." [68]

64. Burton (42), I, 223.
65. Kidd (161), p. 37; Holden (136), p. 326.
66. Ex. 24:1.
67. I Kings, chap. 12.
68. Bogoras (28), pp. 574, 662.

Of the Kazak it was said that the authority of seniors and of the council was strictly preserved in the clans.[69] Among the Yakut, mass meetings, or popular assemblies, were held in the open air, the oldest and most influential men sitting in the first rank. In the second sat or knelt the independent but less wealthy heads of households, and in the third were the youths, children, poor men, and often women, for the most part standing. In general it was the first row which settled all issues; the second row might offer remarks and amendments, but no more. The third row only listened.[70]

In Toda councils the influence of the old men predominated.[71] Sema Naga elders were prominent in politics,[72] and old men were the leaders in Palaung society.[73] Among the Andamanese questions of popular interest, such as migrations, were settled by a leader and the elders. Brown stated: "There is no organized government in an Andamanese village. The affairs of the community are regulated entirely by the older men and women. The younger members of the community are brought up to pay respect to their elders and to submit to them in many ways." [74]

Among the Vedda it was the elders of the district who gave permission for strangers to cross land boundaries.[75] Albanian "governing councils consisted of elders—old men. The idea of the administration of law had been so closely connected with old age that 'to arbitrate' was *me plechnue*, which meant both seniority and arbitration." [76]

Unless the assembled elders assented to the decisions of an Ainu chief his judgments were void.[77] Rivers believed that in early times the Banks Islanders were under a complete gerontocracy.[78] The Bontoc Igorot are said to have had no clan organization, but each *ato* (section of a village) was governed by a group of old men. The council was democratic in the sense that it was composed of all the old men of the *ato*, "no matter how wise or foolish, rich or poor—no matter what the man's social standing may be." Again it was democratic—the simplest kind of democ-

69. Czaplicka (66), p. 55.
70. Sieroshevski (272), p. 73.
71. Rivers (247), pp. 550–552.
72. Hutton (148), p. 150.
73. Milne (205), p. 291.
74. Brown (40), p. 44.
75. Seligmann (269), pp. 107–108.
76. Durham (88), p. 63.
77. Batchelor (12), p. 36.
78. Rivers (248), II, 68.

racy—in the sense that there were no elective organization, no headman, and no superiors or inferiors whose status was determined by the members of the group. "The feature of self-perpetuation displays itself in that it decides when the various men of the *ato* became 'old,' and therefore members of the *intugtukan*." "In other words the pueblo is a federation made up of seventeen geographical and political units, in each of which the members recognize that their sanest, ripest wisdom dwells with the men who have had the longest experience in life; and the group of old men—sometimes only one man and sometimes a dozen—is known as *intugtukan*, and its wisdom is respected to the degree that it is regularly sought and is accepted as final judgment, being seldom ignored or dishonored." [79]

Probably in no place on earth have aged men exercised greater authority than in Australia. The Dieri offer a good example of what was called "The Great Council." Their general assembly consisted of all fully initiated men, but within it was a Great Council composed of all men of advanced age or those eminent because of some physical or mental superiority combined with their years. It included, therefore, the extremely old men, the heads of totems, the principal warriors, the great orators, and the powerful wizards; and the most eminent man of all became the head of the group. "The younger men look forward for years to the time when having been presented at the great Mindari ceremony, they will be permitted to appear, and ultimately to speak, at the council of men." [80] Howitt writes of the Dieri: "I have constantly observed in these tribes with which I have had personal acquaintance, the old men met at some place apart from the camp and discussed matters of importance, such as arrangements to be made for hunting game, for festive or ceremonial meetings, or indeed any important matter. Having made up their minds, one of them would announce the matter at another meeting at which all the men would be present, sitting or standing around; the younger the man the less he would have to say. Indeed, I never knew a young man who had been only lately admitted to the rights of manhood presume to say anything or to take any part in the discussion." [81] The domination of aged men was also common in other Australian tribes. Euahlayi natives claimed that one of the three deadly sins was "lying to the

79. Jenks (153), pp. 167–168.
80. Sumner and Keller (299), I, 512; Howitt (143), pp. 320–321.
81. *Ibid.* (143), p. 320.

elders";[82] and Spencer and Gillen said that among the Arunta the only possible chance for a change of custom was by the consent of the old men.[83]

In brief statistical summary, occupancy of the office of "council elder" by aged men was found to be very widespread. In contrast, aged women seldom held such positions. Old men were reported to be prominent in such roles in 38 tribes, fairly prominent in 16, and slightly so in 2; with doubtful information on the others. In contrast, aged women were reported to have participated importantly in public assemblies in 1 tribe, fairly so in 5 tribes, slightly in 2, but not at all in 15; while no definite information was found on the subject in 48 (Table VII, traits 123, 124).

The office of council membership for the aged reflects the same line of development as has been established in the case of the chieftainship, namely a gradual increase in opportunity for the fulfillment of such roles accompanying an advance toward permanent residence, agricultural economy, constancy of food supply, and accumulation of property rights, especially by old men (Cor. 316–324). Although a positive correlation exists between extent of warfare and employment of aged men as counselors, it is not very pronounced (Cor. 325). The greater the degree of government by restricted council and the more important the authority of the chief, the more likely have aged men been to occupy positions of political importance (Cor. 326–327). Positive coefficients of association for aged men as council elders appear where women have exercised some influence in government (Cor. 328); where secret societies have prevailed (Cor. 329); where group responsibility for crimes (Cor. 330), codified laws (Cor. 331), and judicial authority has been recognized (Cor. 332); and where age-grades have existed (Cor. 333). An important positive correlation emerges with respect to hereditary castes and classes (Cor. 334); but no significant trends can be noted in the functioning of aged men as councilmen as correlated with matriarchal and patriarchal forms of family organization. Old men seem to have had about an equal chance in either case (Cor. 335–340). The opportunities for old men to participate in public affairs have therefore followed the same lines of development as tenure of office for aged chiefs, with optimum advantages in stable agricultural societies having well organized government facilities, almost irrespective of the system of family organization.

82. Parker (218), p. 78.
83. Spencer and Gillen (289), I, 9–12.

Closely associated with eldership and council influence have been arbitration of disputes and administration of justice. Indeed, very often the office of ruler and judge, the authority of scepter and bench, could not be distinguished; for in many instances the political councils of elders have also constituted the tribunals of judges for civil and criminal cases. The role of the aged in the maintenance of order and the settling of disputes—as guardians of the status quo—has been so prevalent, indeed, that only a few cases need be cited for the purpose of illustration. Already, incidentally, many examples have been given of the regulation of food taboos by the old.[84]

Among the Polar Eskimo the aged women, as well as men, helped to keep order and decorum, explaining: "We observe our old customs in order to hold the world up, for the powers must not be offended." [85]

Martrou has pointed out that among the Fan in Africa "the oldest of the village, the leaders, the keepers of the traditions, have an influence, moral at least, on the affairs of the small clan. They point out the way to follow in the rules of the pending action or trial, the work to do at the present season, and scold those who seem not to work to the good name and to the wealth of the village." [86] "To go to law is one of the most exquisite enjoyments in existence for a Kamba negro, and in what a number of actions every old man has been a party!" According to Dundas, the meeting usually took place in the open air and crowds flocked to it. "After the disputing parties have been heard and the case debated, the oldest and most experienced *atumai* (judges) withdraw to decide on a verdict." [87] If their judgment should be ignored, they had an effective instrument for forcing offenders into submission. "They assemble at one of their meeting places and there mass together beating their staves on the ground in unison, calling out, 'We curse you on the *mithegi;* the person who disobeys the order of *kiama* shall be cursed.' " *Mithegi* was the name of the staves always carried by the old men as symbols of authority. Although the accused had been absent, it was believed that the curse began to operate immediately. To remove it the offender had to pay an extra fine and give public evidence of repentance.[88]

84. See pp. 26–30, 34.
85. Rasmussen (233), p. 124.
86. Martrou (200), p. 754.
87. Lindblom (174), pp. 143–144; Dundas (85), p. 517.
88. Hobley (130), pp. 416–417.

Dundas explained that the senior elders or judges were of necessity old men and never withdrew their legislative functions, though sometimes they might practically retire by reason of extreme senility.[89]

Johnston, describing a Bakongo market, remarked: "Although the strife of tongue is great, few real quarrels occur. There is in most cases a chief of the market, perhaps an old fetish man, who regulates all disputes, and who so heavily fines both litigants that all are chary of provoking his arbitration." [90]

Wherever a serious crime was committed among the Dieri, a council of all the old men of the tribe was called, judgment was passed, and a delegation of young men was assigned to execute immediate justice, sometimes by taking the life of the offender.[91] Old Arunta men made most of the judicial decisions. "Shortly before arriving at their destination, the men who formed a party halted, and the old man who was acting leader, sitting in front of the others, scraped two long shallow holes in the ground. One represented the man whom it was intended to kill and the other a woman. The leader asked who wanted the woman. Two men said, 'I do.' The leader after a short pause, during which he made up his mind, took a hand full of earth out of the hole and gave it to the man to whom he decided to allot the woman. His decision was not contested." When there were grievances between the Arunta tribe and the Iliaura, the Arunta approached the enemy and parlance was held between the old men of the two groups. If it was agreed that men of the Iliaura tribe should die, old men engaged them in conversation while appointed parties stole up and speared them.[92]

If a member of the Ainu was selfish and offered no food and drink to departed ancestors, the old people warned him: "O stupid and wicked person, thou art a fool, and thou dost not understand, thou shall die a hard death." All their trials took place in public, and unless the assembled elders assented to the decision of the chief his judgment was void.[93]

Old Bontoc Igorot men determined when the sacred days should be observed, and punished those who ignored them with heavy fines in firewood, rice, or chickens. One of their tests for determin-

89. Dundas (87), p. 220; *ibid.* (86), p. 241.
90. Johnston (157), p. 119.
91. Woods (336), p. 263; Howitt (143), p. 182–183.
92. Spencer and Gillen (289), I, 444–445, 466.
93. Batchelor (12), p. 16; *ibid.* (11), p. 8.

ing the guilty was to make all the suspects chew a mouthful of rice which when thoroughly masticated was ejected into a dish and examined. The person with the driest rice was considered guilty, it being believed that his nervousness during the trial checked the flow of saliva. Jenks adds: "I was once present at an Igorot trial when the question to be decided was whether a certain man or woman had lied. The old men examined and cross questioned both parties for fully a quarter of an hour, at which time they announced that the woman was the liar. Then they brought a test to bear evidence in binding their decision. They killed a chicken and cut it open. The gall was found to be almost entirely exposed on the liver—clearly the woman had lied. She looked at the all-knowing gall and nodded her acceptance of the verdict." [94]

Among the Iban punishment was usually by means of a fine imposed by the old men.[95] In Trobriand villages the elders kept watch to see that certain laws were not broken.[96]

Toda elders decided marriage and divorce questions. "At some distance a conclave of Toda men . . . was squatted in a circle, among whom were many venerable white-turbaned elders of the tribe, protected from the scorching sun by palm-leaf umbrellas. Amid much joking and speech making by the veterans, it was decided that as the eldest son of the deceased woman was dead leaving a widow, this daughter-in-law should be united to the second son, and that they should live together as man and wife. On the announcement of the decision the bridegroom elected saluted the principal Toda present by placing his hands on their feet." [97]

Milne has described a Palaung trial. "Twelve elders were present and it was a solemn affair, the elders sitting on the ground in a row, and in front and facing them were the accused men. At a little distance was a crowd of onlookers, who were ordered to keep silence. The proceedings began by each man swearing that he was not guilty. Then each took off his jacket baring his body to the waist, and raised his jacket on a line with his forehead, when he again swore by the Buddha and the spirits that he was innocent. The elders addressed each man in turn with these words, 'If thou art guilty may thy back show that it is so.' The jackets were next laid on the ground in a row, between the elders and the accused, each in front of its owner. Then one of the elders, a worthy

94. Jenks (153), pp. 169, 202.
95. Roth (252), II, 228.
96. Malinowski (192), I, 115.
97. Rivers (247), p. 524; Thurston (310), p. 154.

and learned man . . . took in his hand the 'oath stick,' a small rattan cane which was kept in the house of the headman and was used for no other purpose. All the elders prayed to the spirits to come down and to point out the guilty man. The stick was blown upon four times, and the jackets were struck with it five times. The accused then put on their jackets. Their backs were examined, and those of the guilty displayed red blotches. I have been assured by many old men that they have seen those red marks appear. They said that they were quite visible but that they faded very quickly." The aged judges had many other clever devices for either detecting the criminal or supporting their own decisions.[98]

While the above examples, selected more or less at random, cannot provide proof of the extent to which aged men and women have participated in administrative and judicial affairs in primitive societies, they do indicate a widespread practice of such activities, which have naturally provided a useful means of social adjustment for those with waning physical powers but possessing an accumulation of wisdom and experience. These old arbiters of justice and order have doubtless rendered a distinct social service —perhaps indispensable to the welfare of the group—and by it they have been enabled to enhance their own prestige and security.

As judges and formal disciplinarians aged men have far outnumbered old women. Their judicial functions were reported as extensive in 29 tribes, common in 12, slight in 2, and negative in only 1; while such activities by aged women were described as important in none, common in 3, slight in 2 and negative in 8; in all the rest they are not even mentioned. As in the case of chieftainship and council membership, opportunities for aged men to function as judges have tended to be more frequent where there have been permanency of residence; and among fishers, herders, and especially farmers (Cor. 341–346). The same trend accompanies increasing constancy of food supply, firm entrenchment of property rights, and especially vested rights to property among the aged (Cor. 347–349). The influence of women in government does not appear to be significant (Cor. 350); but there are positive coefficients of association between judicial prominence of aged men and extent of warfare, government by restricted council, authority of the chief, secret societies, group responsibility for crimes, and codified laws (Cor. 351–356). Wherever there have been well-established hereditary castes, classes, or age-

98. Milne (205), pp. 240–241.

grades, and wherever considerable authority has been given to judges, aged men have tended to possess judiciary powers (Cor. 357–359). No statistically observable trends are found to be associated with matriarchal or patriarchal forms of family organization (Cor. 360–365); but wherever aged men have been leaders of secret societies, priests, or ceremonial leaders, they have also shown a tendency to officiate as judges (Cor. 366–367).

The aged, especially men, have frequently been associated with secret societies, and have thereby been able to increase their authority through the instrumentality of well-guarded secrets and elaborate, sometimes very severe, initiatory rites. Although only limited data on secret societies have been secured in the present study, the indications are clear that wherever such organizations have existed they have tended to come under the control of old men who could use them to advantage in the domination of youths and even adults. Indeed, initiatory devices have been so effective as disciplinary measures that they have been widely used, often even where organized secret societies have not existed, as in *rites de passage* marking the attainment of puberty and adulthood. The manipulative facility of these rituals and the opportunities which they have afforded aged persons to control the conduct of others can hardly be appreciated without firsthand experience with some of the cases.

Horne and Aiston explained that the aged Dieri of Australia maintained their authority and exceptional prerogatives by withholding the knowledge of certain rites and ceremonies from young men and women and by making them appear very mysterious and powerful. During certain rites, for example, all the women and uninitiated youths would be driven hurriedly from the village by an old man who twirled the dreaded bull-roarer.[99] When hair appeared on a youth's face the old men would take him in hand, bore the septum of his nose, circumcise him with crude implements, and soon after anoint his body with their own blood, making deep incisions on his neck and shoulders. When the hair on the face of the young man was long enough to permit tying the ends of the beard, a council of old men assembled and planned the *koolpie* ceremony. On the appointed day the unsuspecting young man was invited out for a usual hunt and at a given signal he was seized, bound hand and foot, and one of the party, provided with a sharp flint, seized the youth's penis and made an incision under-

99. Horne and Aiston (138), pp. 12–13, 112.

neath into its passage, from the foreskin to its base. This done, a piece of bark was placed over the wound and tied so as to prevent its closing up. It goes beyond saying that such initiates were not likely to treat lightly the authority of the old men.[100]

Spencer and Gillen claimed that among the Arunta the main purpose of the fire ceremony was: "first, to bring the young under the control of the old men, whose commands they have to obey explicitly; secondly, to teach them habits of self-restraint and hardihood; and thirdly, to show the younger men who have arrived at mature age, the secrets of the tribe." Describing the effects of another rite, they stated: "It also helps to impress him [the young man] strongly with a feeling of the deep importance of compliance with tribal rules, and further still, with a strong sense of superiority of the older men who know and are familiar with all the rites." Arunta youths were circumcised and subincised by elderly people. One old man directed, a second operated, and a third chanted, while two old women rendered "first aid." During the Engwura ceremony the young men had to separate themselves completely from the women and were entirely under the control of the old men whom they had to obey explicitly.[101]

In another Arunta ceremony the youth was taken by the old men to a distant place in the bush and showed certain stone and wooden fetishes *(churinga)*. He was then held tightly and one old man pushed an opossum tooth under each of his thumb nails, tearing them off, and cut eight deep wavy lines across his forehead. Then the lad was shown a sacred stone, was told to rub it on his forehead and then received his secret churinga name; thus being duly impressed, as the author implies, with the superiority of the old men.[102]

Euahlayi girls were initiated into womanhood by undergoing certain ordeals under the control of aged women. The old men would bind youths in graveyards and leave them overnight to dream and see visions.[103]

In Africa the Beri and Sande societies of the Vai had severe rites for preparing youth for the duties of adulthood and to "train them to respect their parents and elders." [104] Although the Akamba were not noted for secret societies, each village had a sort

100. Woods (336), pp. 266–270, 273.
101. Spencer and Gillen (289), pp. 191–206, 223, 234, 283.
102. *Ibid.* (289), I, 116, 183, 233.
103. Parker (218), pp. 25–28, 56–58.
104. Ellis (92), pp. 126–127.

of exclusive club for old men, and should a woman happen to stray into this place she was beaten and driven out like a dog.[105] Dundas explained that every adult male belonged to one degree or another, into which he was admitted on payment of certain fees; that the highest order was composed principally of the oldest men; and that it was they who controlled the government of the country.[106] In the puberty initiation of Akamba girls the *Preputium clitoridis* was cut away by an old woman, usually the wife of the male circumcisor.[107]

Secret societies were found in most Ashanti villages, and initiates were controlled by a local patriarch who was head of the organization and had charge of the magic. Eligible youths were placed in his authority and he kept them secluded for several months, instructing them in the proprieties of adult life. They were given new names and warned that even to mention the old name was to suffer sickness and death.[108]

In the Death and Resurrection Society of the Bakongo: "Obedience is the primary duty of every candidate, and extreme discipline is exercised to enforce it. The first lesson is made as nauseating as possible. The oldest men in the lodge, with the worst decayed teeth, are chosen to masticate some food. When they have chewed it well it is put out of the mouth onto the head of a drum with a liberal quantity of salivary dressing. Every novitiate must kneel with hands behind, and eat it all up without scruple and without diffidence." [109]

Bushmen boys were initiated by old men who took them to the bush where they spent a month of hardships. "Treatment is very hard and the weaklings die." [110] In the Hottentot rites of "passing the crisis of life" none but old men and women qualified for the ministrations. A boy remained with the women until about eighteen years of age, when the men decided to call him into their society. He was placed in the midst of a group of elders and informed that he must take an eternal farewell of his mother and enter into manhood. "The youth having daubed himself with fat and soot, the old man urines [sic] him, which the initiate receives with joy, rubbing in the briny fluid with a quickness of action

105. Vanden-Bergh (321), p. 67.
106. Dundas (85), pp. 539–541.
107. Lindblom (174), p. 40.
108. Cardinall (47), p. 237.
109. Claridge (53), p. 191.
110. Bleek (24), pp. 23–24.

expressive of satisfaction of the honor done him. The sage then gives him his benediction. 'Good fortune attend thee, live to old age. Increase and multiply. May thy beard grow soon.' " The youth was then solemnly proclaimed a man.[111]

At the time of puberty the Witoto girls of South America were segregated in the depths of the forest under the protection of an old and wise woman of the tribe who instructed them in their new duties.[112] In order that an Arawak girl might become a woman, strong and willing to work, some old woman whose character was known to be strong and good, and herself a willing worker, was chosen to place an ant frame on the young girl's forehead, hands, and feet. The ants were attached at the middle in the interstices of the plaited strands forming a framework, the frame itself being applied on the side from which all the little heads were projecting to bite the girl. In this ordeal the young woman learned discipline and endurance under the control of the aged.[113]

When an Abipone woman was of age to be married she was, as we have seen, tattooed by an old woman. If she groaned or drew her face away, she was loaded with reproaches, taunts, and abuses: "No more such cowardice! You are a disgrace to your nation, since a little tickling with thorns is so intolerable to you. Do you not know that you are descended from those who glory and delight in wounds? For shame on yourself, you faint-hearted creature! You seem to be softer than cotton. You will die single, be assured. Which of our heroes would think so cowardly a girl worthy to be his wife?" [114]

In the Yahgan initiation rites the oldest and wisest men of the group had full charge; one was master of ceremonies, another 'official instructor,' and still others 'policemen' whose duty was to assemble the candidates in the lodge—by force if necessary—and to see that they were submissive at all times. They were made to fast for the first three days, during which time they received instructions in the arts of making a living and rearing children. At night the candidates were forced to bathe in ice water, and after the first bath boys were tattooed on the chest. In one ceremony the candidate spent much time in solitude, was instructed in tribal lore, terrified by masked men representing spirits, and

111. Hoernlé (132), pp. 67–68; Kolben (164), p. 37.
112. Whiffen (331), p. 157.
113. Roth (253), p. 309.
114. Dobrizhoffer (75), II, 20–21.

had wooden splinters thrust in his arms and lighted—to burn themselves out against his flesh. Then the true nature of the spirits was revealed and the initiates were sworn to secrecy.[115]

When Kiwai lads had been shown the secret effigies, firebrands were showered over them by the old men, and they were warned against revealing anything said or done, under penalty of being murdered, poisoned, or afflicted with a fearful disease from which they could never be cured. When elderly men would swing the bull-roarers all the women and children fled from the village, running into the bush. It was said that part of the initiation of a Kiwai girl was for the old man to inform her on sexual matters and forcibly perform the act of defloration.[116] In the puberty ceremony for youths there was an ordeal of fire controlled by the old men. In order to become a strong and successful harpooner of dugong, a boy had to crawl along a dead dugong's back and between the legs of an old man, while his mother put in his mouth some powerful concoction and the old man chewed and spat quantities of "medicine" over his body. Riley stated that during the period of general initiation the youths and maidens might be placed in an enclosure and guarded by some of the old men who inflicted upon them various physical and mental tortures with a view to making them submissive to authority. Harmless snakes were thrown into their midst and they were threatened with death by clubs and arrows. "So great was their terror that before 4:00 P.M. the enclosure became like a cesspool." [117]

When a girl arrived at puberty among the Hudson Bay Eskimo she was taken to a secluded locality by an old woman and stripped of her clothes. A small quantity of half-charred lamp wick or moss was mixed with oil from the lamp. With a needle her skin was pricked and the pasty substance smeared over the wound. The blood was mixed with the paste to make dark bluish spots on the skin. The operation continued for four days, after which the girl returned to the tent, and it was made known that she had become a woman.[118]

Omaha youths were sent alone into the forest where they fasted four days and were then instructed by worthy old men.[119] Pomo girls were initiated by their grandmothers at puberty.[120] Aged

115. Lothrop (182), pp. 165–171.
116. Chalmers (50), p. 119; Haddon (121), p. 104; Landtman (171), p. 354.
117. Beaver (16), p. 186; Landtman (171), p. 140; Riley (245), p. 39.
118. Turner (316), p. 208.
119. Fletcher and La Flesche (103), p. 31.
120. Loeb (180), p. 274.

Chippewa men were leaders in initiation rites and had most to do with the instruction and discipline of youth. A native described how his grandfather led him deep into the forest, selected a lofty red pine, and had the lad spend a long period in the tree top without food or drink, while he waited for a vision.[121]

A modern Hopi native's report of his initiation into the Katcina society at nine and into "manhood" at twenty-one vividly portrayed the role of the aged in control of the young. "I thought of the flogging and the initiation as an important turning point in my life, and I felt ready at last to listen to my elders and to live right." And later: "I could not put off initiation into the Wowochim. My father, my grandfather and two great uncles urged me to forget about school and become a man. My ceremonial father, clan father, mother, godmother, clan mother, and other relatives encouraged me; and they implied that any boy who did not seek membership in the Wowochim proved himself to be either incompetent or Kahopi [not Hopi]. They said that only hopeless cripples . . . or young men who had been spoiled by Christianity failed to take this important step into manhood." After a long and strenuous sixteen-day initiation in which he received the instructions and discipline of a secret society dominated by aged men, he says: "I had learned a great lesson and now knew that the ceremonies handed down by our fathers mean life and security, both now and hereafter. I regretted that I had ever joined the Y.M.C.A. and decided to set myself against Christianity once and for all. I could see that the old people were right when they insisted that Jesus Christ might do for modern Whites in a good climate, but that the Hopi gods had brought success to us in the desert ever since the world began." Later when he successfully participated in an important ceremony he states: "The old people praised my work and said that when this ceremony was not performed correctly famines occurred. They also cautioned that people who perform their parts carelessly often either die soon after or lose a relative. I resolved never to neglect the ceremony or to fail in its proper performance." [122]

Although data on the activities of the aged in secret societies and in the performance of initiatory rites are too sketchy for reliable statistical treatment, they have indicated that such agencies and roles have provided rather strategic opportunities for the old people to keep control over important mysteries and

121. Densmore (71), p. 25; Radin (232), p. 660; Kohl (163), p. 235.
122. Simmons (275), pp. 87, 157, 197.

rites, and to use them for disciplinary purposes. Aged women have not been in such a favorable position with respect to secret societies (Table VII, traits 131, 132); but the performance of initiatory rites in connection with puberty or social recognition of adulthood provided many opportunities for them to participate. In fact, the aged of both sexes have been very frequently found occupying dominant roles in such activities and they have been able thereby to realize for themselves a great deal of authority and prestige. Monopoly on the secrets and manipulation of the initiatory rites have provided very convenient and effective instrumentalities for the instruction, coercion, and domination of youths.

In summary, then, political, judicial, and civil preferment has provided a major field for effective social participation of aged people, particularly those who had already attained positions of prominence and responsibility in the prime of their lives. The title, and often the office, of chieftainship has tended to be life-long. Councilmen and elders have also not infrequently fulfilled their functions into very late old age. Old men, moreover, might serve long and well as law makers, judges, and administrators of justice. Finally as leaders of secret societies and initiatory rites, the aged have quite generally received deference, for they have, more often than not, been the ones who have controlled the "rites of passage" from immaturity and subordination to adulthood, status, and privilege.

But such positions of influence and power in primitive societies have been largely dependent upon three factors: individual ability and initiative; sex; and a favorable combination of social and cultural conditions. In relatively rare cases has age alone qualified one for civil positions of responsibility, and in most instances a state of senescence would eventually be reached when the incumbent of office had to cease active participation, and retaining little more than symbolic powers. Old men have been overwhelmingly favored over old women in important political and civil offices in most societies; although aged women have often performed prominent functions in initiatory rites. Finally, with advancing economy, greater complexity and integration of social organization, and with general improvement in societal stability the aged have tended to enjoy a steadily rising enhancement of status in civil and political affairs.

VI

THE USE OF KNOWLEDGE, MAGIC, AND RELIGION

K NOWLEDGE, wisdom, and experience are social assets which normally accumulate with age and outlast physical stamina. Some of the advantages which they have afforded to the aged—through the performance of professional and semiprofessional services, through participation in governmental, civil, and judicial affairs—we have already discussed. In addition, however, the possessors of knowledge, wisdom, and experience have always been in great demand for imparting general information, interpreting puzzling and mysterious phenomena, preaching ethical standards and ideals, diagnosing and treating diseases, and providing comfort and guidance to the distraught and bereaved. Seers, magicians, medicine men, and priests have frequently been aged persons, who have served as mediators between man and the great unknown—the imaginary environment—peopled with unfriendly spirits and devils as well as benevolent beings and gods. Faced with common perplexities, distressing anxieties, and personal crises of every kind, people have turned for help and counsel to the "old wise ones"; and the aging individual with enough experience, insight, and skill to suggest or do something, or even to make it appear that something could be done in the hour of human need has generally reaped a reward.

Among preliterate peoples memories have been the only repositories of knowledge, skills, and rituals. Where writing and records have been unknown—where all that was worth knowing had to be carried in the head—a lucid mind, a good memory, and a seasoned judgment, even when housed in a feeble frame, have been indispensable and treasured assets to the group. Those endowed with the art of writing and surrounded by printed documents can scarcely appreciate the inestimable value of an aged person possessing more knowledge than any other source within reach. There are unlimited examples of the role of the aged as custodians of folk wisdom.

Rasmussen has reported of the Polar Eskimo: "The myths which are handed down . . . by the eldest to the youngest within

the community are looked upon as the saga of the Inuit people."
An intelligent old native described the situation thus: "Our tales
are the narratives of human experience . . . . The word of the
new-born is not to be trusted, but the experience of the ancients
contains truth. Therefore, when we tell our myths we do not speak
for ourselves; it is the wisdom of the fathers which speaks through
us." [1] Others explained: "Men used to have stronger sap than
now . . . . Then things were done that we do not understand
now, and the eye saw things which are hidden from us. But the
tongue has carried down the experiences of the old men to us,
whose vital sap is more limited." "Our forefathers talked much of
the making of the world and of men . . . . They did not understand how to hide words in strokes [write] . . . . They only told
things by word of mouth . . . they told of many things which we
have heard repeated time after time, ever since we were children.
Old women do not fling their words about without meaning, and we
believe them. There are no lies with age." It was believed that the
magic formulas essential to a successful life were first discovered
by old men in their dreams; and the aged who were able to pass
on this information regarded themselves as "givers of great
gifts"; and they were usually ready with an explanation and a
formula for every situation.[2]

It was reported of the Labrador Eskimo: "The aged are
treated with great respect, and the word of the old man and
woman is final." The Eskimo would say that the old have lived a
long time and understood things in general better than the young.
They also felt that in the aged was "embodied the wisdom of their
ancestors." [3] The Haida turned to their old men for explanations
of sickness and death.[4] It was said that in the memories of the
aged Menomini "repose the rituals and ceremonies of their
people." [5] Hoffman wrote of the Chippewa: "In the bosoms of
these old men are locked up the original secrets of their most
sacred beliefs." [6] It was also thought that the Chippewa elders
alone knew the best remedies for sickness and that their advice was
necessary for a long life. They handed down the ancestral traditions and explained the origin of the world and of life. In their
keeping were the formalities of religion, such as fasts, feasts,

1. Rasmussen (235), p. 27.
2. *Ibid.* (233), pp. 101–102, 144, 158.
3. Hawkes (124), pp. 71, 117.
4. Swanton (301), p. 14.
5. Skinner (280), p. 27.
6. Hoffman (134), p. 162.

offerings, songs, dances, and ceremonies. Jones stated that no people reverenced old age more than these Indians: "The advice of the 'long dwellers upon the earth' is generally listened to with great attention, as it is from them that the youth receive their instructions respecting pow-wowism, medicines, and the traditions of their forefathers. Where there is no literature it cannot be otherwise than that they would think much of those who impart to them all the knowledge they most prize, and who are supposed, from the length of time they have lived, to have gained great experience." [7]

Aged Omaha taught others the meaning of their music and their ritual, "for only the old men knew the songs perfectly." Fletcher states: "The aged were the historians, so to speak, they were the ones who treasured up the memory of the tribal incidents and passed them on to the younger generations." It was also their function to give comfort and counsel to the discouraged and bereaved. A sample admonition from an old man to a young one who had lost his wife is the following: "My grandson, it is hard to lose one's mother, to see one's children die, but the sorest trial that can come to a man is to see his wife lie dead. My grandson, before she came to you no one was more willing to bring water for you; now that she is gone you will miss her care. If you have ever spoken harshly to her the words will come back to you and bring you tears. The old men have taught us that no one is so near, no one can ever be so dear, as a wife; when she dies her husband's joy dies with her. I am old; I have felt these things; I know the truth of what I say." [8]

The aged among the Hopi were the repositories of countless legends, traditions, migratory accounts, and stories of exploits in hunting and warfare. Often they alone knew the old land boundaries, the sites of distant shrines, and the complicated rituals associated with hunting and salt expeditions. Aged women were the best technicians in pottery and basketry, and old men were skilled instructors in weaving and the tanning of hides. Old men watched the sun, kept the calendar, and supervised dates for crop-planting, katcina dances, rain-making ceremonies, and harvest regulations. In their minds were stored the rituals and songs of the elaborate sixteen-day ceremonies, such as the Snake dance and the winter solstice rites. The young men's very complicated initiation ceremony was under their supervision. Most of the

7. Densmore (74), p. 323; *ibid.* (73), pp. 8, 62, 97; Jones (156), pp. 69, 164–165.
8. Fletcher and La Flesche (103), pp. 30, 287, 327, 479, 595.

ceremonial knowledge was well guarded in secret societies, and not infrequently an aged leader refused to share the most important information with anyone until shortly before his death, and then only to his successor. Knowledge of remedies for the treatment of accidents, disease, and conjuration were kept in control of a relatively few aged persons who were usually organized into secret societies for the promulgation of their specialties. The aged were sought out for dream interpretations, were special advisors in sickness, misfortune, and sorrow, and were in constant demand in large and small gatherings as storytellers, song leaders, instructors in games and dancing, participants in prayer-smoking ceremonies, and public narrators of past events. A common admonition to the young was that "old people are important. They know a lot and don't lie. Listen to them . . . ." [9] Hough remarked: "When men grow old, they become, as if realizing their passing years, willing or even anxious to transfer to younger minds what they have learned . . . . So when an old man dies there is a feeling of regret . . . for who knows whether the pictures of his brain are impressed upon the minds of the new generation or whether they are lost forever." [10]

A few pen sketches of aged Hopi personalities illustrate their roles as custodians of knowledge and instructors of the people. Of one a native reports: "He was nearly blind now but an important old man, and whenever he talked everyone listened closely. He knew most of the ceremonies, and people came to him to check the songs in their memories." The same informant described a relative thus: "Before very long my old . . . uncle died. He had outlived three wives and was said to be a hundred years old. His first serious weakness of age had come in 1919 when I took over his herding. For eleven years longer he had been able to farm a little, bring wood on his back, look after his peach orchard, and weave blankets. Finally he gave up these jobs in the order named and spent most of his time weaving . . . . Although he was somewhat deaf, he was still an important man in the Soyal [ceremony], knew hundreds of stories about Hopi history, and could compose almost any kind of Katcina song. Whenever he talked we paid close attention, for he was a Special Officer. Most of his history stories were too long and the people grew tired and sleepy. But he had some first-rate stories on love-making, and the record of his

9. Simmons (275), p. 51.
10. Hough (141), p. 201.

life was proof of his right to speak on the subject." One native informant hesitated to set any limits on the knowledge of another blind old healer: "He is a very important man and is supposed to know everything that his old uncle knew before him. He knows everything that is going to happen in the future. He knows what medicine to use for pain and he can cure bone complaints, stomach troubles, and heart ailments." [11]

Hough described a Hopi woman in these words: "Saalako is an old, wise woman. The mystery which hangs around her is born of her connection with the fearful rites of the snake cult and her store of knowledge which has been passed down from time immemorial 'by living words from lips long dust.' This connection carries her to distant pueblos to mix 'medicine' for the ceremonies, no one in the whole province being better versed in herbs and spells than she . . . . It is difficult to measure, especially in a limited time and short acquaintance, the respect and honor given by the Walpi people to Saalako . . . ." [12]

Reichard, speaking of the Navaho, was quite emphatic with respect to the property rights possessed by aged persons in knowledge, wisdom, songs, chants, charms, and prayer formulas. Aged men charged high prices for sharing such information, and one old man's store of medicine lore, sacred names, legends, secrets, and songs was said to be worth more than his herd of three thousand animals—sheep, cattle, and horses.[13] The Iroquois affirmed that "long life and wisdom are always connected together," and they often spoke of "the oldest and wisest" as though the terms were synonymous.[14] It is remembered that among the Crow it was the daily habit of a chief to "call his old men and let them talk as much as they would." [15] When Creek made statements implying great knowledge and wisdom, they supported them with: "So the old people say." [16]

Among the ancient Aztec the advice of certain wise old people was sought after and received as the word of oracles, even by the monarchs. At the installation of a new king he was addressed by an aged counselor of state and advised with respect to his duties. Aged Aztec matrons were accustomed to say to a young woman:

11. Simmons (275), pp. 306, 312; additional field notes of the author.
12. Hough (141), p. 225.
13. Reichard (242), pp. 95, 127–128.
14. Loskeil (181), I, 15; Seaver (267), p. 23.
15. Curtis (62), p. 11.
16. Swanton (302), p. 78.

"My daughter, follow the advice that I give thee; I am old, I have the experience which life gives . . . . Engrave my advice on thy heart and thou wilt be happy . . . ." [17]

Certain Inca elders were assigned the task of remembering the important events of their history and recording, by knots and threads, all the laws, the succession of kings and the time in which each ruled, and other records of public interest. "It was a custom among them, and a law much kept and observed, for each king during his reign to select three or four old men, known for their intelligence and ability, who were instructed to retain in their memory all the events that happened in the provinces; whether they were prosperous, or whether they were the reverse, and to compose songs to be handed down, so that the history of the reign might be had in remembrance in after times." [18]

Among the Arawak certain information was known only to the very aged, some of whom were revered as great oracles of the tribe.[19] In the Witoto tribe the only thing that would save an aged and burdensome man from sore neglect by his people was that he "possess great wisdom and experience." [20] Old Lengua men had an explanation for every mystery. When, for example, Grubb showed a small compass to a group of natives, they turned to their elders. "One old man took it from me and examined it carefully. He noticed that whichever way he turned the little hand always pointed north . . . . The behavior of the little pointer puzzled him. Presently a fresh thought occurred to him, and he put the compass under his blanket. After turning it about and upside down, he peeped underneath it and watched the needle settle, but was surprised beyond means to find it still pointing north . . . . The old man declared it to be his firm opinion that, before I had left my own land, I had caught a little blue devil and had secured it in this case and that it was continually pointing out my road homeward with its finger." This explanation was received with great sobriety by the group.[21]

Old men and women among the Yukaghir were relied upon to know the legends, omens, and chronologies, even back to seven generations.[22] Old men among the Ainu were the chief dispensers

17. Bancroft (5), II, 152, 214; Saville (260), p. 221.
18. Locke (178), pp. 33, 42.
19. Im Thurn (151), p. 183; Brett (35), p. 400; *ibid.* (36), p. 7.
20. Whiffen (331), p. 170.
21. Grubb (119), pp. 99–101.
22. Jochelson (154), pp. 72–73, 136, 156–157.

of folklore and were prepared to give an explanation for every problem that arose.[23]

Ancient traditions of the Kazak were devoutly preserved by the old people either in the form of ancestral reminiscences and genealogical legends or in ballads.[24] It was the "old men who know" among the Sema Naga, and they had charge of the calendar records, a duty tabooed to young men.[25] Aged Toda were described as "the chief depositories of the mythological learning of the tribe";[26] and Rivers mentioned one who was renowned for his knowledge and genealogical lore. "I began my investigation with the aid of one of the most famous of these, Parkurs, an old man almost blind as the result of cataract and so feeble that he had to be carried when he came to me." [27] Jenks described one old Bontoc Igorot as representing the "knowledge and wisdom" of his people; another was greatly respected because he was "so old and wise and rich." The old men made a special effort to remember all the land transactions and were masters of native chronology and cosmology.[28] The customary ending of Iban legends was: "They say that all this is the tale of the old men, what they have dreamt in their dreams." Their system of omens was so complicated that "only the old men are able to tell what is to be done in all cases." During the discourse of the elders the young men "look gravely on, never indulging in a laugh, which would be regarded as a serious offense." [29]

When Trobrianders were asked whence they learned certain things, they usually answered "ancient talk." It was a common evening pastime for old men to relate the accounts and experiences of past generations.[30] An account of the Samoans states: "In the evening the old folks assembled under the bread-fruit trees, or sat cross-legged in the square, rehearsing the deeds of their ancestors, or listening to the legends of their gods—thus their ancient lore was handed down from generation to generation." If a young man were sufficiently talented, the council might deliberate and call him to "sit with the old men and learn

23. Batchelor (12), pp. 51, 54, 87, 154–155, 234, 407.
24. Spencer (290), No. 5, Div. I, Pt. 3A, p. 42.
25. Hutton (148), p. 360.
26. Breeks (34), p. 34.
27. Rivers (247), p. 462.
28. Jenks (153), pp. 39, 73, 74–79, 163, 216–219.
29. Roth (252), pp. 78, 195, 221, 293, 338.
30. Malinowski (190), p. 361; *ibid.* (191), p. 219

wisdom." Pritchard also talks of a time "when the old men of Samoa were the only depositories of lore, and the only teachers of the ethics of their country." He pictures a scene in which a legend was related by a "hoary headed, toothless, half-blind, wrinkle-faced old man in his native bush town, surrounded by his sons and grandsons, and great-grandsons, as they lay together on their mats in the dusk of the evening." Genealogies especially were preserved and taught by the oldest men.[31]

A young Samoan chief complained: "I had no old man to help me . . . . There was no old man in the house to sit with me in the evening and fill my ears with the things from the olden times. A young matia (house chief) should always have an old man beside him, who, even though he is deaf and cannot always hear his questions, can still tell him many things." [32]

The amount of knowledge retained by the aged Maori was very impressive. "Every plant and fern had its name in Maoriland; the knowledge in woodcraft displayed by the elderly men is most complete and such men are extremely interesting in the bush. They also have names for all the varieties of fungi, toadstools, etc." Best gave 100 bird names representing some 50 species known to the people, 280 plant names, 60 names of insects, earthworms, and the like, and 170 pages of botanical information gleaned from the natives. And he insisted that this represented "only the fragment of the knowledge of the old men." Of one it was said: "His mind was a storehouse of primitive lore." Another dictated 450 songs from memory and gave a genealogy of 1,400 names.[33]

Aged Dieri systematically kept certain portions of knowledge from the young in order to increase their power over them. Horne and Aiston in their investigations complained that most of the important information was stored with men eighty or ninety years of age and that their confidence was not easily won.[34] Miss Parker said of aged Euahlayi women: "How interesting those blacks made my bush walks for me. Every ridge, plain, and bend had its name and probable legend; each bird a past, every excrescence of nature a reason for its being. Those walks certainly . . . modified my conceit. I was always the dunce of the party . . . ." [35]

The Berber and Tuareg had their "old wise ones" who were

31. Pritchard (229), pp. 119, 125.
32. Mead (204), pp. 38, 56, 192–193.
33. Firth (100), pp. 42–43; Best (20), I, 12–17.
34. Horne and Aiston (138), pp. v–vi, 12–13.
35. Parker (218), p. 113.

respected as authorities.[36] Rattray said of the Ashanti that
". . . those that have accurate knowledge are the older men and
women." He further related: "I approached these old people and
this difficult subject [their religious beliefs] in the spirit of one
who came to them as a seeker after truths, the key to which . . .
they alone possessed . . . ." Their respect for the wisdom of the
aged was expressed in a proverb: "The words from the mouth of
an old man are better than an amulet." Venerable men were called
coiners and keepers of proverbs.[37]

Westermann wrote of the Shilluk that the best historical information was always to be found among the old men.[38] Bleek said
of the Bushmen: "Their history is bounded by the memory of
the oldest man." [39]

Akamba elders in the secret societies knew all the customs of
the people and a correct decision required their advice. These
aged men actually had a monopoly on knowledge and were in a
position to charge dearly for information. "When a man has need
of knowledge of a certain custom he will go to the elders . . . and
each time he does so he is required to pay a goat, or if he is rich,
a bull." Only by degrees could he learn all that was known by
these old people. "The whole learning of the elders of Ukuu is a
matter of great secrecy, and may only be imparted bit by bit to
those who have the necessary qualifications and who pay the fees.
When I was instructed in certain matters by the elders, I had to
pay a large fee for myself and a lesser fee for my interpreter,
whom I had to bind over faithfully to keep secrets that he had
learned; elders were also stationed around to keep off listeners,
and our conversation was carried on in low tones." [40]

Lindblom also wrote of the Akamba: "These old men and
women are the custodians of the tribe's traditions . . . . Anyone
who is in doubt as to how he ought to proceed in a certain case,
according to the custom of the tribe, goes to one of these old
persons for information, for which he pays . . . ." [41] Kidd
relates a typical incident: "Some controversy arose over an
ancient procedure. Immediately the old men recited the minutest
details of the case, which happened sixty or seventy years before.
They knew the exact color of the various cattle which had been the

36. Andrews (3), p. 145; Campbell (46), p. 208.
37. Rattray (237), pp. 7, 11; *ibid.* (236), pp. 9, 110.
38. Westermann (328), p. xxviii.
39. Bleek (24), p. 40.
40. Dundas (85), pp. 539–541.
41. Lindblom (174), p. 141.

subject of the dispute. One could see them mentally traveling back over the landscape of the past, and after ten minutes talk the old case was made to live again, so that all who heard the discussion would remember the various points for another sixty years." [42]

Holden gave an instructive account of the reception that aged Akamba natives accorded a young tribesman upon his return from abroad. "For some time the entire party sat in uninterrupted silence, the old men unwilling to admit curiosity . . . . 'Well, young man, it is said that you are older than we are; you have traveled farther and seen more; you have crossed the sea. Now tell us of your wanderings and what you have seen but do not pour lies upon us.' 'Yes, father,' replied the youth deferentially." After hearing the account of the wonders, an old man exclaimed: "Young man, if you speak the truth, you are old, you have seen much, we are but children." Finally the aged chief addressed him in the following words, "Young man, we thank you for your news. You have made us older than we were, but you are older still, for you have seen with your eyes what we only hear with our ears." [43]

From the foregoing it appears that accumulated wisdom may be regarded as a more important criterion of age than the passing of time itself, and that to have seen much with one's own eyes— to have acquired great experience—is, so to speak, a mark of having achieved an advanced "mental age." Although the ancient Hebrew would seem to have accepted this thesis they nevertheless insisted that ripe experience can only come with age. "I said days should speak and multitude of years should teach wisdom." [44] "With the ancient is wisdom; and in length of days understanding." [45]

Few generalizations concerning the aged in primitive societies can be made with greater confidence than that they have almost universally been regarded as the custodians of knowledge *par excellence* and the chief instructors of the people. Examples can be found everywhere, and it has been a common practice of ethnographers in their field investigations to search out these old people as the most reliable sources of information. The various ways by which the aged have utilized their advantage will bear further examination.

42. Kidd (161), pp. 280–281.
43. Holden (136), pp. 112–124.
44. Job 32:7.
45. *Ibid.* 12:12.

The old seem to have been peculiarly qualified for the practice of shamanism. They have been the ones with longest experience and most knowledge; sometimes, even, it has been believed that parts of their bodies have acquired fetish power. Not infrequently they themselves have claimed to be in communication with the dead and other spirits and even with gods. They have had strange and mysterious remedies for breaking taboos, treating disease, foretelling the future, and driving out spirits. Sometimes they boasted—more often have been accused—of possessing powers of sorcery and witchcraft. And, being so near the end of their lives, it has been quite generally believed that they would soon become spirits themselves, perhaps powerful ones, who would be able to punish those who had neglected or offended them.

Moreover, the problems most frequently treated by magic have not appeared solvable by purely physical means but have called for the more subtle methods at the command of the old and wise. It was not, for example, strength of brawn alone that could stave off bad luck, win the maiden's heart, heal the dreaded disease, remove the poisoned arrow, bring the rain or sunshine, divine omens, "fix" the enemy, cast out evil spirits, or propitiate the gods. It was a special power, strange, mysterious, and most potent—as well as safest—in the hands of the aged and when exercised in the light of wisdom and experience. Who were better qualified to use such power than the "old wise ones"? And, from the viewpoint of the aged themselves, these "supernatural" skills have been assets with which they might compensate for their own disabilities on the physical level. For the aged in certain social milieus, then, the "call to magic" has often seemed well-nigh irresistible; especially since their services in this field have been so commonly sought after. The old person who could "work miracles," or even appear to do so, could find plenty of younger and stronger persons both able and willing to do his bidding in order to secure his aid in situations where esoteric knowledge was at a premium and physical efforts of no avail. Here the aged possessed a further advantage, for with their superior knowledge, should a charm or a bit of counsel miscarry, they were in a position to explain away failure. Any wise old shaman could confidently affirm in the face of mishap that had it not been for this or that additional factor, for which he could not be responsible, the "medicine" would have worked; or, better still, except for his timely intervention something much worse might have happened.

The aleatory element, therefore, has been for age a most useful ally. Indeed, it may be that in the interpretation of good and bad luck the aged have exerted their greatest power in social relations. Especially where shamanism has been an established practice have the aged exploited the realm of the unknown where luck and chance hold sway. Not all magicians have been old nor have all aged persons been shamans; but superannuation and the supernatural have been very commonly linked. Therefore the aged have been afforded an excellent means for continued participation in the vital affairs of community life, to the mutual advantage of themselves and the younger generations.

It is not easy to distinguish sharply between shamanistic activities and priestly functions. The general rule here employed is to classify as shamanistic any practice which appears to deal with magic, and as priestly those functions which are more definitely related to ceremonial rites and organized religious institutions. Examples of the activities of the aged in shamanism will be examined first.

Certain old men among the Polar Eskimo were reputedly able to raise storms, produce calms, call up or drive off birds and seals, steal men's souls out of their bodies, and cripple anyone for life. They could fly up to heaven or dive down to the bottom of the sea, remove their skins like dirty garments and put them on again. Old women often made "soul flights" to the realm of the dead in order to save the lives of very sick persons. All these mighty works were said to be wrought by magic words. "I was told by one Eskimo . . . that the combination of words had been dreamt by old men, and afterwards acquired magic power in their mouths. New formulae are never invented now; old men die nowadays before their tongues acquire power. But the traditional formulae still pass from mouth to mouth. Old men are not eager to teach them, and the young ones know nothing of them; it is as they grow older that they ask to learn them, and then the teacher regards himself as the giver of a great gift . . . . After being with the oldest man in the tribe, Quilerneq, for a long time, I learnt some of his magic formulae . . . . It was when my departure was close at hand, that he gave me the following reason for this concession— 'Now I have grown fond of thee, and so I will give to thee the best that an old man can give to a young one. Soon thou wilt be going away, and one can never tell when thou mightest have need of them.' " [46]

The following example of the shamanistic performance of an

46. Rasmussen (233), pp. 49, 106, 149

old man was reported by Rasmussen: "Sagdloq was the greatest and oldest magician of the tribe, and he had just announced to his fellow-villagers that he was about to conjure up spirits. His wife was ill, and he wished . . . to cure her . . . . The people, therefore, collected down at the ice's edge; the sick woman was seated on a sledge among the rest, and her son stood by her side . . . . Sagdloq himself was alone in the house. All work in the settlement ceased; no one dared move. Every face bore the imprint of earnest reverence. 'Sagdloq was the only one still living,' said the countrymen, 'who had inherited the wisdom of his forefathers.' For instance, no other magician could crawl out of his skin, and then draw it on again. Any man who saw a magician in this state, 'flesh-bare,' would die, they declared. Such was the man Sagdloq. He had not conjured spirits for a long time for he had been ill. That very day he had been drawn about among the houses on a sledge, for his legs were stiff with rheumatism . . . ."

"When I had gone up to the house, I peeped in at him through the window. He was sitting alone on the raised stone sleeping-place, which in the day time serves as a seat in Eskimo houses, beating on his drum . . . . Kale (his assistant), sitting on the roof and waiting upon the words of the old wise man, looked down on us ignorant Christians, and said with dignity, 'Go aside, and be still. No one moves while spirit conjurations are proceeding . . . .' The people stood around listening silently. Soon a murmur mingled with the beating of the drum, and the old man's voice grew gradually louder and stronger. Then the drum stopped for a moment and there was a deep silence. The excitement of the auditors grew. But soon old Sagdloq seized his drum again, and, after a few introductory beats on the skin, called out, in a voice so loud that it might have been the effort of a young pair of lungs, 'The Evil Fate—Misfortune-Bringing Spirit— the white man.' Then again there was a long howl, and when the excitement was at its height, Sagdloq called out the whole pronouncement. It produced a shock. 'The white men brought the Evil Fate with them, they had a misfortune-bringing spirit with them. I saw it myself, there are no lies in my mouth.' " [47]

Rasmussen also related a visit he had from a very aged Eskimo woman: "Late in the evening, long after my house-mates were asleep, I heard creaking footsteps in the frozen snow. A little later the door opened, and when she had carefully convinced herself that everybody else was asleep, old Simigaq entered and sat

47. *Ibid.* (233), p. 16–22.

down by the head of my sleeping-place. It was her intention, she said, to make my sleep light. She wished to prepare my way toward the land of dreams with little sayings and legends; but first of all she wanted to give me for my journey the advice of an old woman, for she believed that age gives certain powers which one may hand on to the young . . . . If it be true that age gives to old people's words a strength which can be transmitted to the young, old Simigaq was certainly a tremendous source of power. Not only was she the oldest woman in the tribe—red-eyed, toothless, baldheaded, crooked with rheumatism, nearly blind, and thus in possession of every scar which a long and hard life leaves—but, in addition to all this she now had become so ugly and withered that they said she could not sink if she were thrown into the sea . . . . And now this weather-worn and hardened old woman . . . was sitting at my head, wanting me to share the benefit of her experiences, the results of her long life . . . . Therefore she came to me on this night with a few magic songs . . . and while possessed like a pagan priestess, she mumbled her songs through her toothless gums; and I lay close to her on my rug and listened." [48]

One native Eskimo explained the importance of the aged and their magic in the following words: "We do not all understand the hidden things, but we believe the people who say they do. We believe our Angakut (Medicine men), our magicians, and we believe them because we wish to live long, and because we do not want to expose ourselves to the danger of famine and starvation. We believe, in order to make our lives and our food secure. If we did not believe the magicians, the animals we hunt would make themselves invisible to us; if we did not follow their advice, we should fall ill and die." [49]

Aged Labrador men and women called up spirits from beneath the earth, discerned the causes of illness, and interpreted dreams.[50] Ray reported that among the Point Barrow Eskimo during the hunting season: "Daily the old men, especially those who are successful in curing the sick, meet on the sea-shore and talk for an east wind, so the ice will be driven off shore and a lead favorable for whales be opened up; and their faith remains unshaken through repeated failures; and when questioned as to the reason why their supplications remain unanswered they always attribute it to some offense they have given to the spirit." He also

48. *Ibid.* (235), pp. 38–41.
49. *Ibid.* (235), p. 123.
50. Hawkes (124), p. 137.

stated: "At their council gathering a fire is built in front of the house, and at the entrance is posted an old woman wise in ghost lore whose business is to keep out the evil spirits. She makes passes through the air with a long knife to keep them from entering. In each village there is a number of old women who are treated with the greatest consideration by all, they being credited with powers of divination and are consulted on all important affairs." [51]

Old Haida were said to know secret means for bringing success in fishing. The medicine men held their office for life and received special honors at burial. Even when dying they were considered quite powerful, and the bones of one old man were believed to be pregnant with magic ten years after his death.[52] Niblack stated: "They had great respect for the aged whose advice in most matters has great weight. Some of the older women, even bond women in former times, attain great influence in the tribe as soothsayers, due as much to their venerable appearance as to any pretense they may make of working medicine charms." [53]

The case was no different among the Kwakiutl. About 1900 an eclipse of the moon was visible at Fort Rupert, and Pawili, the oldest man of the village, was entreated to remedy matters. "Is it swallowed?" he inquired. They reported that it was not; and he declared, "Then I will make him vomit it." He ran outside where all the people were assembled, ordered them to kindle a fire and each person to throw into it some portion of his clothing or hair. Then he sang over and over, while the people, as they caught the air, joined in, "Vomit it, vomit it, or else you will be the younger brother of Pawili." The old man danced slowly around the fire and after awhile he called, "Is he vomiting it?" When the moon reappeared, he said proudly, "I made him vomit it . . . ." [54]

Curtis also quoted a native who claimed that the old men would dig up dead bodies and use them for magic. When fishermen were threatened by storms, the steersman, who was usually an old man of long experience, prayed to the sun: "Look down on us Chief. I beg that you be with us and take us across in safety." Then when they had landed he would say, "Thank you, Chief, that now we have reached the shore alive." The old man usually carried a small box of charms, including a piece of false hellebore and a bunch

51. Ray (241), pp. 39, 42–43.
52. Swanton (301), p. 57; Harrison (123), pp. 115–160; Dawson (68), p. 123.
53. Niblack (213), p. 240.
54. Curtis (63), pp. 62–63.

of shredded cedar-bark stained with menstrual blood, and in bad weather he would let one or the other float off astern to drive away danger.[55]

Aged medicine men were common among the Chippewa. They related how the Great Medicine Spirit once came to earth and lived a hundred years, going among the old men and teaching them many things, including magic.[56] It was common for the aged to have dreams in which they were told that the Great Spirit had chosen them for special missions, usually of a mystical nature.[57] In famines old women were accustomed to sing and pray all night for visions of places where game could be found. Once the parents of a sick boy sent tobacco to an old man, requesting that he give the child a new name. After talking and praying over the boy, he announced that he would name him the next day and that when he did so there would be a "clap of thunder." [58] Jones reported that whenever an aged witch or wizard was denied a request he might threaten someone with a disease, and that from fear of afflictions consent was often granted. "In this way . . . many of the old noted conjurers obtained more than one wife." [59]

Lowie wrote of the Crow: "Shamans are usually, but not always, old men." He mentioned competitions among them in which they performed tricks to prove who possessed the strongest medicine, and he cited persons renowned for their powers in prophecy and divination. "Thus there was an old man who knew when the enemy were approaching; he could tell in how many days and at what time they were going to come, and told the Crow when to watch for and kill them. Sometimes he prophesied that it would rain or snow on the following day. The sun was thought to be his medicine. He asked Indians to call him 'He-Sees-all-over-the-Earth.' " Some of these elders claimed to possess "Ghost Medicine" very potent for prophesying. The aged were in great demand for sending forth hunters on the chase, "because we had respect for the old and thought that behind them was some power that had brought them through the many dangers, and we wanted these powers to help us in the same way . . . ." Sometimes youths, desiring to get "medicine" from an old man, surrendered their marital rights to him. "Gray-bull secured some war-medicine from an old man, for which he first yielded possession of his

55. *Ibid.*, p. 63.
56. Densmore (73), p. 87.
57. Reid (243), pp. 108–109.
58. Tanner (304), pp. 51–53; Densmore (73), p. 57.
59. Jones (156), pp. 146–148.

mistress and later of his wife. The medicine was used for stealing horses from the enemy." [60]

Aged Crow women also engaged in shamanism. A certain old Crow was reported to have discovered a stone charged with property-acquiring powers. It became very famous, and in moving camp was carried along to guide the people to proper hunting grounds. War leaders would call upon the old lady with a special fee for "medicine" and for her dreams.[61] There was a Crow legend that once a heartbroken princess, wishing to learn the whereabouts of her lover, gave a party and invited several old women famed for wisdom and esoteric powers. Placing choice food before them, she entreated their counsel. One old granny gave her a root charged with charms sufficient to shield her from harm and directed her to the haunts of an old, old woman who was able to locate the lost lover.[62]

Medicine men were very influential in Navaho life. Anyone possessing the requisite ability could set up as an expert, but, owing to the elaborateness of the ceremonies, it took most of a long life to master them. At a feast the "old man of the songs" would take the lead, and he was paid for chant-cures.[63] The old women acquired knowledge of the minor chants, and often sang to cure lesser diseases in their families or to dispel the effects of bad dreams or of lightning.[64]

Among the Hopi aged people were often credited with great powers of healing, and were not infrequently accused of witchcraft, especially in the spread of misfortune and disease. One native reported: "Our medicine men are very wise and important people who spend years learning the healing arts and are able to save lives even when they are old and blind." The same informant spoke of witches (*Bowakas*), who were quite frequently old people, as the greatest threat to life and happiness: "They have tried to make me a member of their evil society; they have led others to suspect me of mischief; and they have caused the greatest sorrows of my life. A clan grandmother caused my death, and, later when I returned to life, she nearly ruined my back. An old-maid witch got a crush on me and shot poison lizard tails into my feet because I would not make love with her. My wife's uncle killed my children one by one. Then because of an angry and foolish

60. Lowie (185), Pt. I, p. 63; Curtis (62), pp. 73, 93.
61. Lowie (186), pp. 333, 390.
62. Curtis (62), p. 117.
63. *Ibid.* (61), p. 79; Stephen (294), pp. 352–353.
64. Reichard (242), pp. 53–90.

remark that I made, I could have no more children. When my old grandfather turned out to be a witch; shot poison arrows into my loins and ruined my private parts, it did not seem possible for me to stand it." [65]

One old Hopi related how he came to treat diseases: "While I was at First Mesa watching a Katcina dance, three old medicine men laid their hands on me and told me to follow them. They led me to a private place and informed me that they were getting very old and feeble and had chosen me to take their place and save life. They gave me much advice and finally said, 'Now our Hopi women are very pretty, and when they come to you and lie down for treatment their flesh will be tempting. You must be careful to put your hands only on the parts that are in pain. Think this over and tell us whether you will follow in our steps.' I hung my head and thought for a long time, finally replying that I was not sure that I could exercise such strict self control for the rest of my life. Then the old medicine men told me that when I had practiced eight years or more the people would trust me and permit me to take some liberties with patients. When I agreed to join the medicine society the old men took me into a room, emptied a large bag of herbs, roots, and other things on the floor, and said, 'Pick out the different plants, place them in separate piles, and explain their uses.' This was an examination that I feared I could not pass, but resolved to try and worked hard until late afternoon, while the old doctors watched and made comments. When I finished they seemed greatly pleased and told me that I would become a successful and highly respected medicine man. I have kept the rules, worked hard, and am happy to say that many people whom I have treated are still alive." This old man was still earning a living and supporting a sick relative and his family by treating the sick in 1941, although he was then becoming rather feeble.[66]

Pomo hunters, resigned to camp life because of their age, still contributed to the success of the chase by chanting magic songs.[67] The "Bear Doctors," always past middle age, were believed to be invulnerable to attack, could assume the form of bears, and boasted that they could die and return to life any number of times. There was a legend of an "Old She Bear Doctor" with very exceptional powers. "Both men and women of middle or old age

65. Don C. Talayesva; field notes of the author.
66. Field notes of author.
67. Loeb (180), pp. 171–172.

could become doctors. In fact it is said that women sometimes made very successful doctors. Even a woman so old and feeble that she could hardly walk would acquire great powers of endurance and swiftness through this magic." [68]

Kroeber described the trick of a Pomo magician with an eye for profits. "At times a woman of wealth would be told that her dead husband or brother would appear to her. She might be torn between fear and desire; if she yielded to the latter, she was directed to give beads for him to carry back with him. The old men then selected an initiate as like the deceased as possible in figure and concealed him in a hole covered with leaves. His body was painted black and white; his hair and face were completely whitened. As he raised himself from the excavation, the blanching completely disguised his features; the poor woman thought that she recognized her beloved, whitened by the ashes of his funeral pyre, and burst into tears and wailing." [69]

Aged Creek prophets sang magic songs to protect houses against evil spirits, witches, and wizards, and to control the weather. In 1840 a prophet was reported to have relieved the people of a severe drought by rain-making. "After performing his ceremony for a time, the old man published that he was about to be successful and that the country might be flooded, and he thought it best to desist, which he did. In the following winter it was very cold and he was asked to moderate the weather. A following winter was very mild and the old man explained it by saying that he blew off the cold of last winter so far that it had not come back." The Creek often kept their children away from certain old people, fearing witchcraft. "It was thought that an old man who had passed through as many fastings as most of them had undergone at that time of life might be a wizard. It was feared that he might shoot a pain into the child, or injure it in some manner. One of my informants said that he had often been slapped hard enough to be knocked down when standing near some of the old people." [70]

The Aztec had their aged medicine men and necromancers who constituted a regular fraternity and whose remedial agents and mystic formulas were transmitted by hereditary succession from father to son. When Montezuma, the ruler, was threatened by the Spaniards, "some old men immediately came forward with a

68. Barrett (10), pp. 444, 452–454.
69. Kroeber (166), p. 265.
70. Swanton (302), pp. 78, 508, 629–630, 632–634.

dream; certain old hags appeared with their interpretations; and it was decided that the city was doomed. They also have a legend of how God appeared to one of their rulers in the guise of an old man, revealed unto him the will of the Almighty, and offered him a beverage by means of which he might acquire immortality." [71]

In Jivaro society most old men were acquainted with the arts of medicine, sorcery, and witchcraft.[72] Up de Graff described, with obvious bias, the making of a medicine man: "Some old ambitious scamp, with his eyes on the coveted post (office of medicine man), takes a reed-flute and goes off down the river at dead of night, alone, for many miles, where he seats himself on a sand-bar and plays until the anacondas come out of the water and dance round him. Many times he tries until one morning he walks into the settlement and announces that his great powers have prevailed, and he has enticed the serpents to his very feet. In times of peace he is the official weather prophet, astrologer, and doctor." [73]

Shamanism was common among the Arawak, and was practiced by aged men and women. Curses could be pronounced by any very old person. Certain foods, tabooed under ordinary conditions, were rendered edible in times of scarcity by the simple procedure of getting a shaman, or even an old woman, to blow a number of times upon them.[74] "Red-Rattle," the oracle of his tribe, was the dispenser of information "which it was only in the power of an aged man of his class to communicate." [75]

Old women were the jugglers in Abipone society, and exaggerated reports say that they were as common as "the gnats of Egypt"![76] Whenever there was danger of attack from outside enemies, which was frequent, these old jugglers were asked to consult the spirits. "A light rumor, smoke seen from a distance, strange footmarks, or the unreasonable barking of dogs fills them with suspicions that their lives are in danger . . . especially when they dread the vengeance for slaughters which they themselves have lately committed. The task of tranquilizing and preparing their minds devolves upon the jugglers, who, whenever anything is to be feared, or anything to be done, consult the evil spirit. About the beginning of the night a company of old women

71. Featherman (98), p. 88; Bancroft (7), I, 109–110; Biart (22), p. 121.
72. Karsten (158), p. 9.
73. Up de Graff (319), pp. 235, 237.
74. Roth (253), p. 332; Im Thurn (151), p. 368.
75. Brett (35), p. 400.
76. Briffault (38), II, 523.

assemble in a huge tent. The mistress of the band, an old woman remarkable for wrinkles and gray hairs, strikes every now and then two large discordant drums . . . and whilst these instruments return a horrible bellowing, she, with a harsh voice, mutters kinds of songs, like a person mourning. The surrounding women, with their hair disheveled and their breasts bare, rattle gourds and loudly chant funeral verses which are accompanied by a continual motion of the feet and tossing about of the arms . . . . At daybreak all flock to the old woman's hut as to a Delphi oracle . . . . The replies of the old woman are generally of such doubtful report that whatever happens they may seem to have predicted the truth." Another rather famous old woman insisted that whenever an enemy approached she felt a strange pricking sensation in her left arm, and sometimes she aroused the whole town for the night. The chief juggler was reputed to be a hundred years old and was venerated for her wrinkles as well as her magic art.[77]

It was an Abipone custom to taboo the names of the dead and other words whose use was believed to be harmful, and a word once outlawed seemed never to be revived. New words sprang up to take the place of old ones, and the "mint of words" was in the hands of the old women; whatever terms they stamped with approval went into circulation and were accepted by high and low alike. The missionary Dobrizhoffer, reports that it was astonishing to see how meekly everyone "acquiesced in the decision of a withered old hag, and how completely the old familiar words fall instantly out of use and are never repeated . . . ."[78]

Shamanism was a customary activity of the aged among the Lengua. Old men with gourds and chants frightened ghosts from the village. "On a cloudy day when the sun has been obscured for some time an old man is sometimes seen to take a firebrand and hold it up to the sun; apparently with the intention of encouraging the luminary to show his face again." Some old men could eat poisonous roots that would "kill ordinary people." When an old woman dreamed that she saw ghosts, she caused a great commotion in the village. Old men claimed that they could suck bone splinters out of wounds which had been placed there by other unfriendly wizards, also old. Grubb vividly described a certain witch doctor: "Old grandfather looks as like a skeleton covered with parchment as it is possible to be. He is a greedy, crafty, hypo-

77. Dobrizhoffer (75), II, 71–73, 81, 145.
78. Frazer (107), pp. 254–255.

critical old creature . . . his wife was ill and he concluded that she was about to die. He had her removed outside the village and there with a knife . . . opened her side. He then thrust into the gaping wound some broken stones, dog's bones, etc., and covered up the wound with a piece of tin which he had picked up." [79]

Medicine men were very popular among the Witoto; and Whiffen doubted whether even a hostile tribe would wittingly put one of them to death, for fear of retaliation on the part of his ghost. The position of shaman was usually inherited by the eldest son, who was taught the art by his aged father but not permitted to practice until after the death of the old man.[80] Should an Indian wish to eat a forbidden food, he had to get an old woman to breathe upon it. If a child was sickly, a like procedure might restore its health. The task of cooking the human flesh of enemies slain in battle was delegated to old women, since they were believed to be better able to cope with offended spirits.[81]

Observers noted among the Yahgans "a tendency of almost all the old people to work cures, to prophesy, etc."; and Cooper reported that "nearly every old man was a wizard." [82]

The Iban of Borneo consulted omens at the commencement of almost all undertakings, and because of popular belief in occult powers an individual might feel "obstruction and restraint at every step of life." "The law and observance of omens occupy probably a greater share of his thoughts than any other part of his religion or superstition; and I cannot imagine that any tribe in any age ever lived in more absolute subservience to augury than do the Dyaks. The system, as carried out by them, is most elaborate and complicated, involving uncertainties innumerable to all who are not fully experienced in the science, and the younger men have constantly to ask the older ones how to act in unexpected coincidences of various and apparently contradictory omens." [83]

The Iban shamans might be old men or women and ranked next in importance to village chiefs. Gray-haired leaders examined the content of dreams, the flight of birds, and the hearts of pigs to predict future events. "Old men, industrious and sensible in ordinary matters of life, will sit for hours at a stretch discussing lawful or unlawful, lucky or unlucky combinations of these voices of

79. Grubb (119), pp. 16, 126, 132–133, 138, 153, 155, 165; *ibid.* (118), p. 128.
80. Whiffen (331), pp. 142, 145, 183.
81. *Ibid.* (332), pp. 53–54; *ibid.* (331), p. 181.
82. Lothrop (182), p. 173; Cooper (56), pp. 160, 178.
83. Perham (221), pp. 228, 234.

nature, and their effect upon the work and destiny of men. Only the older men are able to tell what is to be done in all cases . . . . And this involved system of life is thoroughly believed in as the foundation of all success." [84]

A curious divining custom was observed, for example, in planting rice. "Four water beetles, of the kind that skates on the surface of the still water, are caught in the river and placed on water in a large gong. Some old man especially wise in this matter watches the beetles, calling to them to direct their movements. The people crowd round deeply interested, while the old man interprets the movements of the beetles as forecasting good or ill luck with the crop of the following season, and invokes the good-will of Laki Ivong [a deity]." [85] Gomes wrote that the people had "a great dread of a curse which makes it quite easy for a feeble or decrepit person to exercise considerable influence over them." For instance, an old man or woman might place the following curse upon anyone accused of theft: "If the thief be a woman, may she be childless, or if she happen to be with child let her be disappointed and let her child be still-born, or better still, let her die in childbirth. May her husband be untrue to her, and despise her and ill-treat her, may her children all desert her if she live to grow old. May she suffer from such diseases as are peculiar to women, and may her eyesight grow dim as the years go on, and may there be no one to help her about when she is blind." The author reported that he could never forget the silence and awe of those who witnessed such a curse.[86]

At an Iban funeral feast the dead were invited to return, and a quantity of drink, which was reserved for them in a bamboo, was "drunk by an old man renowned for bravery or riches, or by other aged guests who are believed to possess a nature tough enough to encounter the risk of so near a contact with the shades of death." [87] Roth reported, quoting St. John: "Many of the priests are the blind and maimed for life, who by following this profession are enabled to earn a livelihood." [88]

In the Banks Islands magicians had great faith in their charms, and the art commonly passed from father to son. One of the magic gifts was the "power to make money out of nothing." A case has been cited of one old woman who was reputed to be a "money

84. *Ibid.* (221), p. 234; Roth (252), I, 231, 265; St. John (255), I, 63–64.
85. Hose and McDougall (140), I, 112–123.
86. Gomes (117), pp. 65–66.
87. Perham (222), p. 298.
88. Roth (252), I, 265.

spinner." She gave an exhibition of her power by dancing, singing, and rubbing her hands together, after which there came forth money, "apparently out of space." [89]

Aged men and women among the Kiwai Papuans of New Guinea also exercised great influence by means of magic rites. Without sorcery, it was believed, there could be little success in any undertaking. Those noted for such powers generally controlled the people and extracted from them gifts of food on the promise of withholding their curses. An aged person, it was held, could injure anyone at a long distance simply by chewing a little ginger and squirting the juice in his direction, repeating at the same time a special formula.[90]

Almost every vegetable was planted and cultivated under the magic rites of these old wonder-workers. The first yam in the garden had to be planted by an aged couple with the aid of a bull-roarer which had been smeared with "strength-fluid" from the old woman's vagina. When the first sprouts appeared, the old pair came again to the garden, and the woman smeared her hands with the same "fluid," after which she rubbed them over the plants. Then they went to tell the owner to put up the sticks. After a few days they returned and tied up the shoots of the first yam. This was done by the old lady who passed the string once around her own neck to "teach" the yam how to wind, and climb. When the leaves appeared, the old man came alone to the garden where he lighted a fire, boiled water and mixed it in a cocoanut bowl with ashes of a piece of dugong skin which he had placed in the fire. Then he dipped his hand into the bowl and, with dripping fingers, stretched out the leaf, saying at the same time, "Grow big." Another way to make the yam grow was for the owner's father and mother to remove the earth around the top of the tuber, and then for the old lady to take off her grass skirt and sit over the root, touching it with her genitalia, which had power to make it grow. The harvest of the first yam also had to be ceremonially performed by an aged couple.[91]

Eating the first yams of the harvest was also a serious matter and required the special service of the old people. When the crop was brought in an old man took water in his mouth and spurted it ɔver the roots, saying, "You no make him bell (stomach) swell up, no make him man sick, man and woman no sick, all he stop all

89. Coombe (55), pp. 64, 93.
90. Landtman (171), pp. 153, 324.
91. *Ibid.* (171), pp. 76–80, 85–86.

right." The roots were then roasted by an old woman, and, when they were thoroughly cooked, she opened them and inserted a little of the egg of a bush-fowl, after which she passed the roots once over her stomach and handed them to the men. All ate a little in order to make their stomachs "strong" so that they would not easily get hungry; otherwise the garden would be emptied too quickly.[92]

Aged Kiwai men had important duties to perform in hunting turtles. One would chew a special root and spit it upon a sharp stick cut from a certain vine. This was then pressed into the body of a turtle to "stupefy all the turtles in the sea," so that they would not sink when the fishermen approached. Old men and women were also in demand for ceremonial operations in felling trees for canoes, in house construction, and as mediums for communication with the dead. Warfare was never undertaken without their ministrations. "In order to foretell the results of a fighting expedition, an old man and woman may withdraw into the bush, where the latter takes off her petticoat and lies down . . . . If the man does not feel 'strong along woman,' he advises his friends to return home, for there will be a defeat . . . ." Another device was for an old man to smoke a pipe, inhaling, and if he choked, the people had to call off the expedition, for the omen predicted that they would have to run until they were breathless, with the enemy in hot pursuit. There was another rite which protected the warriors while at the same time causing destruction to the enemy. An old woman would lie down on the floor in the men's house with her head directly towards the east. An old man would stand over her straddle-legged, and place on her bare body an *ibaia*, a certain amphibian which moves with a curious limping action as if continually falling down and rising up again. The warriors then crawled on their hands and feet between the legs of the old man, and the first of them put his right hand upon the animal, seized it, jumped up, and walked a few steps toward the rising sun. This was powerful medicine sufficient to vanquish the foe.[93]

Aged shamans and necromancers were common among the Semang,[94] Trobrianders,[95] Samoans,[96] and Maori.[97] Old Arunta

92. *Ibid.* (171), p. 80.

93. Riley (245), pp. 110–111, 124; Landtman (169), pp. 13–14; *ibid.* (169), pp. 156, 288–290, 325.

94. Schebesta (262), pp. 66, 68, 72–73; Evans (96), p. 201.

95. Malinowski (191), p. 248; *ibid.* (192), I, 46.

96. Turner (315), p. 37.   97. Best (20), I, 332, 467.

men were also versed in ancient lore and skillful in magic, keeping possession of bull-roarers and sacred stones to increase their power. They communicated with the dead, and one aged shaman had a hole bored through his tongue to strengthen his powers of sorcery.[98] Dieri patriarchs communicated with spirits and read omens to discover when it would rain, where holes should be sunk for water, where to find game, and who was responsible for cases of sickness and death. It was said that by their songs they could compel fowls to lay their eggs, induce rains, and insure safety in battle. A special means of producing rain was to assemble a number of elders in a hut and draw blood from their arms, making it flow freely upon other members of the group. Old men dipped strings of rabbit fur in red ochre paste and wore them around their necks to induce spirits to sleep with them and instruct them in their dreams. If part of a corrobone ceremony was forgotten, a spirit would recall it to the mind of anyone who wore such a charm; and in times of drought such old dreamers might be thus guided to water-holes. When a tree was struck by lightning an old man would dig about its roots for lightning stones to bring good luck. One aged Dieri boasted that he could direct thunderbolts to strike down any of his foes. The old men were experts at "boning" enemies and discovering who had caused recent deaths.[99]

Old fetish men and women were common among the Euahlayi. Mrs. Parker tells of one who possessed two charmed reptiles, a snake and a lizard. "This man was the greatest of local wizards, and I think really the last of the very clever ones . . . . We always considered him a centenarian." The bag of an old shaman usually contained several fetish stones and bones, and a *dillee*— a large magic stone used for crystal gazing. Its "spirit" was said to seek out a person, wherever he might be, and clearly show his face and conduct in the crystal. There was also a death-dealing stone which knocked men insensible as quickly as a flash of lightning. To these were generally added a miscellaneous collection of medicinal herbs, and also a nose-bone to put through the cartilage of the nose whenever a new territory was entered, so that the wearer could smell out strangers more easily.[100]

The rain-making technique of one old charm-worker was described in detail: "Old Bootha has what she calls a *wi-mouyan*,

98. Spencer and Gillen (288), p. 12; *ibid.* (289), I, 26, 36, 92, 329.
99. Horne and Aiston (138), pp. 118–119, 125; Gason (113), p. 173; Woods (336), p. 278; Frazer (107), pp. 64–65.
100. Parker (218), pp. 30–31, 37.

clever stick. It is about six feet long, with great lumps of beef-wood gum making knobs on it at intervals; between each knob it is painted. Armed with this stick, a piece of crystal, some green twigs, sometimes a stick with a bunch of feathers on the tip, and a large flat stone, she goes out to make rain. The crystal and the stone she puts under the water in the creek, the feathered stick she erects on the edge of the water, then goes in and splashes about with green twigs, singing all the time. After awhile she gets out and parades the bank with the stick, singing a rain-song which charms some of the water out of the creek into the clouds, whence it falls where she directs." She also possessed a stick which she claimed was so powerful that anyone who touched it would break out with boils from head to toe.[101]

Magic-making by the aged was extremely common in Africa. Among the Berber of Morocco, according to Westermarck: "Old women are particularly dangerous. An old woman is worse than the Devil—nay the Devil himself is much afraid of her—she bottles him up . . . . When a man is a hundred years old he is surrounded by a hundred angels, and when a woman is a hundred years old she is surrounded by a hundred devils . . . . If a man meets an old woman on his way, he should say, 'In the name of God, be merciful and compassionate.' If he meets her in the morning when he sets out on a journey, he should not proceed on that day but should turn back." [102] The curses of these old people were greatly feared and even a stare from them was to be avoided. If a wife suspected her husband of love for another woman, she could secure the service of some old crone who would go at night to a cemetery with a dish of meal and water, unearth the hands of a recently buried corpse, and stir the dish with it. This dough was then made into bread and given to the errant husband to eat, often, it was said, with very good effects. Special potions were prepared and sold by old women to cause the death of an undesirable spouse. These old women also trafficked in remedies for restless wives, preparing for them a concoction from cemeteries and recommending that they feed it to their husbands in order to gain for themselves greater liberties, since when a man ate of this substance "his heart dies." A good contraceptive potion recommended for such pleasure-loving women was "a drink from the bath of a corpse." [103]

101. *Ibid.* (218), pp. 47, 49.
102. Westermarck (330), II, 7
103. *Ibid.* (330), I, 338–339, 420; II, 344, 544, 552–555.

Westermarck also reported: "In Hiaina an old woman sometimes goes to the cemetery, likewise at the full of the moon, carrying with her some *semolina* in a dish and water to pour over it;
she unearths a recently buried corpse, paints its right hand and
foot with henna, its right eye with antimony, and the teeth on the
right side of its mouth with walnut root. Then she stirs the dish
with the right hand of the dead body, all the time reciting an incantation in the 'devil's language,' and after the moon, which
must shine in the dish, has produced there a sort of foam, she covers the corpse with earth and leaves the grave. On the following
day she puts the contents of the dish in the sun, and when the
semolina has become dry she uses it to compel people to comply
with her wishes, since a person who eats of it will become silly." [104]

Baraka was a word used by the Berber to denote a wonder-
working force, a "Blessed Virtue" from God which age conferred
upon a man. This "power" could be transmitted by the exchange
of saliva. "Moreover, old age itself inspires a feeling of mysterious awe, which tends to make the man a saint and a woman a
witch." The young tended to submit to the old because of fear or
respect for gray hairs. Therefore, the curses of aged parents, as
well as their blessings, were potent forces to be reckoned with by
the rising generation. [105]

Aged Berber could travel about at will and in relative comfort.
Andrews, who in his journeys occasionally found it difficult to
purchase necessities, would take with him an old man who was of
great service in getting food out of the people. "We sometimes
send old Si Lhassen on alone to a village, for his patriarchal aspect and the reputed knowledge of secret things and occult necro-
mancies that always attaches to the very old, can often procure
food when the offer of money cannot." [106] It is obvious that wherever such magical powers have been attributed to the aged they
have possessed an instrument of social adjustment that has re-
inforced their security tremendously.

Old women among the Tuareg might lie on the tomb of a holy
man all night in order to receive messages from departed relatives. [107] Among the Dahomeans aged fetish women played important roles in the ceremony of "Head Worshiping" which was believed to bring good luck. [108] The Shilluk would let the oldest mem-

104. *Ibid.* (330), II, 553.
105. *Ibid.* (330), I, 46, 489.
106. Andrews (3), p. 171.
107. Campbell (46), p. 78.
108. Burton (42), II, 2, 149.

ber of a party eat first, so that if the "evil eye" had fallen upon
the food he might detect its presence and cleanse it. Their aged
medicine men were regarded as great assets to the community.[109]
Lango hunters were prepared for the chase and for warfare by
their elders who endeavored by magic to make them successful.
The healing of diseases was also in their hands.[110] Ashanti dreamers sought interpretations from the aged.[111] Old Bushmen blessed
the hunters as they went out, and in return received part of the
kill.[112] Sorcery and magic among the Bakongo were a monopoly
of "old wise ones," who arrogated to themselves all credit for
supernatural powers. Enfeebled parents would control their children by means of a curse, and one old man boasted that he successfully managed three vivacious wives by threats of curses and
the adept use of fetishes.[113]

Aged medicine men and witch doctors were common among the
Xosa, and with many of them it was said to be a matter of "No
pay, no cure." Alberti reported that: "Ordinarily it is the old
women who pretend to exercise magic, and they usually make this
pious fraud work to the end of profit to themselves." [114] Kidd described the mysterious divining ritual of one old woman: "In
front of this motley crowd a witch-doctor was dancing. She was
an ugly old withered hag, clad in a monkey-skin skirt, from which
a dozen long tails were flying in a tangent. Round her waist was
a belt of bead-work, and a couple of jangling bells were fastened
to her skirt. Round her ankles were some dozen circular cocoon-
like hollow balls filled with seeds which rattled as she moved. On
her head was perched a battered old hat of sailor type. In her
hand she held a native battle-axe which she brandished in the
faces of women and children. She stamped about the open space
with a vigor that was surprising. She suddenly stopped dancing,
placed her head to one side as if listening for some voice beneath
the ground, and then jumped about furiously and rushed at the
drummers or the women as they increased their noise. Suddenly
she pretended to be in a frenzy and in rapport with the ancestral
spirits . . . . Her body became seized with irregular jerking
spasms; her head kept quite steady as she stamped at a tremendous rate with her feet; then the lower part of her body vibrated

109. Oyler (217), II, 128, 136.
110. Driberg (82), pp. 57–58, 107–108, 112.
111. Bandelier (8), p. 192.
112. Bleek (24), p. 11.
113. Claridge (53), p. 158; Weeks (327), pp. 155–156; *ibid.* (326), p. 132.
114. Alberti (2), p. 96; Kidd (161), pp. 158–159.

rapidly as if the muscles were seized with tremendous motion. After this she stood still while the upper part of her body was racked with the most tempestuous jerks . . . ."[115]

Whenever an Akamba man was killed away from the village, his spirit was said to return and speak to the people through the medium of an old woman in a dance. Aged men and women were in great demand for special ceremonies before the planting of grain. The wood from a certain tree was believed to be so charged with power that it could be used only by a senior elder or a very old woman. If young people were to use this tree, they would become ill or die.[116] An aged mother could curse, and thereby control, her adult children. To do this she would place some vegetables, grains of maize, millet, and other seeds in a calabash over a fire; and then as the vessel cracked and was consumed, she muttered: "I gave birth to you; I have suckled you, washed you, carried you, and removed your motions when you were a child. But now, when you have eaten and grown strong, it is I who curse you; may you be destroyed thus (like the food in the fire), you and your children." Sometimes old people on their deathbeds cursed their relatives and others, and only certain old men of the class of elders could ever remove the ill effects of such a curse.[117]

Among the Chin the aged were often diviners, and whenever a new bride went to the house of her husband the old women and "wise people" watched her entrance into the house and noted "which foot enters first and what she first says and does," whereupon they prophesied good and evil accordingly.[118]

In each Palaung village one or more wise old men or women treated diseases, prepared love potions, helped women to conceive, named their children, and served as special godmothers or godfathers to those who did not thrive. They also predicted future events, produced countless "success charms," and sometimes bewitched recalcitrant members.[119]

Aged Lapp used the sacred drum with great magical effect. Old women were said to be able to drive serpents into the bodies of enemies by the repetition of magic formulas. They were also engaged to castrate reindeer by crushing the testes between their teeth.[120] Among the Albanians the worst curse that a mother could

115. *Ibid.* (161), pp. 171–173.
116. Hobley (131), pp. 31–33, 76.
117. Lindblom (174), p. 171; Hobley (131), p. 150.
118. Carey and Tuck (48), I, 189.
119. Milne (205), pp. 240–250.
120. Scheffer (263), pp. 149–150, 157; Taylor (306), p. 145.

impose upon her son was to say, "May my milk poison you." Though he might be a grown man, it was believed that she could thus harm him.[121]

Yakut shamans were often "dried-up old men." They performed rites, instructed young aspirants in magic, and pointed out favorite spots where they could communicate with the spirits.[122] They knew where certain "black" spirits dwelt, what diseases they caused, and how they could be propitiated. Aged women also engaged in magic rites. According to Czaplicka: "Nearly all writers on Siberia agree that the position of the female shaman in modern days is sometimes even more important than that occupied by the male." [123]

In a Chukchi family the oldest wife had care of the sacred things of the household and was called the "One with the fire tool." "The two oldest women of the tent must meet the cortege on its arrival from burying the dead. They present to the returning people a bunch of newly twisted sinew-thread which has been strengthened by incantations. Each member of the cortege carries a small twig of willow, around which he winds a piece of thread received from one of the old women. Then he removes the thread and winds it round his right wrist, but neither ties nor fastens it. The twig is put on the hearth as a purifying sacrifice . . . . The thread round the wrist is worn until it drops off . . . ." An old "knowing" woman was often engaged to relieve a homesick bride of her sorrow.[124]

Batchelor said of the Ainu: "It is really wonderful what an amount of power for evil the ghost of a deceased old woman is supposed to possess. Not only so, but strange though it may seem among such a people, even before death old women have a good deal of power over the opposite sex, and children are particularly afraid of them. Some of these ancient dames are veritable old witches if one offends them; and if they are against a person, the men will be found to be so too. The Ainu assert that in years long gone by the ancients used to burn down the hut in which the oldest woman of a family had died. This curious custom was followed because it was feared that the spirit of the woman would return to the hut after death, and, out of envy, malice, and hatred, bewitch her offspring and sons and daughters-in-law, together with

121. Durham (88), p. 279.
122. Sieroshevski (272), p. 102; Sauer (259), p. 119.
123. Sieroshevski (272), p. 243; Czaplicka (66), p. 185.
124. Bogoras (28), pp. 359, 454, 471, 528–529, 551, 595.

their whole families, and bring upon them various noxious diseases and many sad calamities. Not only would she render them unprosperous, but she would cause them to be unsuccessful in the hunt, kill all the fish, send the people into great distress, and render them childless. She would curse the labor of their hands both in the house, the gardens, and in the forest; she would blight all their crops, stop the fountains and springs of drinking water, make life a weary burden, and eventually slay all the children." [125]

Shamanistic tendencies were not entirely lacking among the ancient Hebrew. Their God made his revelations to aged patriarchs—a strong reinforcement of their authority in social and political affairs. By divine intervention Abraham's wife Sarah was said to have borne a son in extreme old age.[126] The establishment of the rite of circumcision is credited to this old man.[127] He constantly had visions in which the Almighty directed his course: "And when Abram was ninety years old and nine, Jehovah appeared to Abram, and said to him, 'I am God Almighty; walk before me, and be thou perfect.' " [128] Jacob, old and on his deathbed, had visions of things to come and prophesied.[129] King Saul went to a witch in his perplexities and requested that she call forth the shade of Samuel; and after appropriate rites she replied, "An old man cometh up; and he is covered with a mantle." [130]

A belief not infrequently associated with the aged has been that there is magical power in their personal exuviae. Thus has their prestige been increased and substantial benefits derived. The Polar Eskimo believed that a young child could be endowed with the vital force of an old man by smearing the latter's saliva around the child's mouth. The magical strength of age could also be imparted to youth by transferring some lice from an old man's head to that of a younger person. Rasmussen's old friend in his farewell discourse endeavored to bestow some of his own energy by rubbing his hands over the traveler's breast. He was quoted as saying, "I am an old man, but all within me, with forces that grow old, is strong yet; and now I stroke thee over the breast to make thee strong for a long life." [131]

125. Batchelor (11), pp. 222–224.
126. Gen. 18:10–11.
127. *Ibid.* 17:10.
128. *Ibid.* 17:1.
129. *Ibid.*, chap. 49.
130. I Sam., chap. 28.
131. Rasmussen (235), p. 131; *ibid.* (233), p. 50.

The bones of a certain medicine man among the Haida were regarded as very potent ten years after his death.[132] The Chippewa had legends of an old man who could bring a dead person back to life by breathing upon him.[133] Withered Witoto dames breathed over delicate children to make them grow. Whiffen stated that there was a universal belief among these Indians that the breath of human beings had great potency for expelling evil agencies.[134]

The spittle of aged Kiwai Papuans, as well as other excretions from their bodies, were considered indispensable to the growth of crops and were believed to work many other marvels.[135] In Samoa it was the custom for an old chief, at the point of death, to breathe on his son, saying, "Receive the succession of my office, with all the wisdom necessary for its fulfillment." [136] The blood of old Dieri men was thought very effective in instilling courage into younger men.[137] The saliva of certain aged Lango was held to be a powerful agent in the healing of diseases.[138] The Ashanti grandfather imparted some of his spirit to his infant grandchild by spitting into his mouth and at the same time giving him a name.[139] Among the Hottentot the urine of old men was used to purify relatives and mourners after a funeral. One of them would boil his dirty old night-cap, "which he had worn for half a century," to make a decoction that was declared to be an infallible cure for venomous snake bites.[140] Old Chukchi men imparted their power to the young by blowing on their eyes or into their mouths; or they stabbed themselves with knives and mixed their blood with that of younger persons.[141]

It is obvious from the cases cited that the widespread belief in and practice of magic has had important influences upon the role of the aged in primitive society. The vast majority of preliterate peoples, when faced with crises, have turned to their elders for help and guidance. And the old people have not hesitated to give counsel and aid. Those who have claimed to possess knowledge and special powers have done something, or made it appear that they could do something to temper bad luck and cushion hard

132. Dawson (68), p. 123.
133. Kohl (163), pp. 147–148.
134. Whiffen (332), pp. 59–60.
135. Landtman (169), pp. 125–126, 326–340.
136. Sumner and Keller (299), I, 489.
137. Woods (336), p. 270.
138. Driberg (82), pp. 157–158.
139. Rattray (238), p. 64.
140. Kolben (164), p. 40; Chapman (52), I, 389.
141. Bogoras (28), p. 425.

fate. At least they have made an attempt, and then have explained with confidence how matters might have been worse but for their intervention. It can be no great surprise that so many old people, with their vigor ebbing and their days numbered, should have grasped eagerly such opportunities to render service to their fellows and at the same time enhance their own security and prestige.

The aged have also found many opportunities to exercise their powers in more formalized religious and ceremonial roles. They have served as guardians of temples, shrines, and sacred paraphernalia, as officers of the priesthood, and as leaders in the performance of rites associated with prayers, sacrifices, feast days, annual cycles, historic celebrations, and the initiation of important and hazardous enterprises. They also have been prominent in ceremonies associated with critical periods in the life cycle—such as birth, puberty, marriage, and death. Although a sharp distinction cannot be drawn between lay shamanism and professional priestly functions, a limited number of cases will be cited to illustrate the range of activities in the latter spheres.

The medicine lodge of the Chippewa, with its bags, songs, and emblems, was guarded by one of their old men. Densmore speaks of an aged keeper as "one of the most eminent." [142] The sacred pipe ceremony of the Omaha was conducted by certain old men. According to Dorsey, there were many keepers of sacred pipes, tents, and the most sacred "pole." [143] A native vividly described the consternation of himself and a friend when, as boys, they disturbed one of these old men in the performance of his duty:

One bright summer afternoon the Omahas were traveling along the valley . . . on their annual Buffalo hunt. The mass of moving people and horses extended for nearly half a mile in width and some two miles in length. There was an old man walking in a space in the midst of this moving host. The day was sultry . . . but the solitary old man wore a heavy buffalo robe wrapped about his body. Around his shoulder was a leather strap about the width of my hand, to the ends of which was attached a dark object that looked like a long black pole. From one end hung a thing resembling a scalp with long hair. One of my playmates was with me and we talked in low tones about the old man and the curious burden on his back. He looked weary, and the perspiration dropped in profusion from his face, as

142. Densmore (71), p. 95; *ibid.* (74), p. 168.
143. Dorsey (78), p. 217.

with measured steps he kept apace with the cavalcade. The horses
that I was driving stopped to nibble the grass, when, partly from
impatience and partly out of mischief, I jerked the lariat . . . and
the end of it came with a resounding whack against the sleek side
of the gray. Startled at the sound, all of the five horses broke into a
swift gallop through the open space, and the gray and the black,
one after the other, ran against the old man, nearly knocking him
over. My friend turned pale; suddenly he became anxious to leave
me, but I finally persuaded him to remain with me until camp was
pitched. . . . We finished our dinner, but as we started to go out
our father stopped us and said, "Now you boys must go to the
sacred tent. Take both horses with you, the gray and the black, and
this piece of scarlet cloth. When you reach the entrance you must
say, 'Venerable Man, we have, without any intention of disrespect,
touched you and we have come to be asked to be cleansed from the
wrong that we have done.' " We did as we were instructed and appeared before the sacred tent in which was kept the "Venerable
Man," as the Sacred Pole was called, and repeated our prayer. The
old man who had been so rudely jostled by our horses came out in
response to our entreaty. He took from me the scarlet cloth, said a
few words of thanks, and re-entered the tent; soon he returned carrying in his hand a wooden bowl with warm water. He lifted his right
hand to the sky and wept, then sprinkled us and the horses with the
water, using a spray of artemisia. This act washed away the anger
of the "Venerable Man," which we had brought down upon ourselves.[144]

A keeper of the sacred pole was called "grandfather," and he
had to be extremely careful in all the rites "on account of his children, for it meant the loss of one of them by death should an error
occur." One old man said, "As I stand before the *Uzhieti* (Pole),
I seem to be listening for the words of the Venerable One who gave
us these rites." But a native later complained, "Our people no
longer flock to these sacred houses as in times past, bringing their
children laden with offerings that they might receive a blessing
from hallowed hands . . . ." The last keeper of the sacred pole,
when a very old man, is reported to have said:

The men whom I have associated in the keeping and teaching of the
two sacred houses have turned into spirits and departed, leaving me
to dwell in solitude the rest of my life. All that gave me comfort in

144. Fletcher and La Flesche (103), p. 245.

this lonely travel was the possession and care of the sacred Buffalo [Pole], one of the consecrated objects that once kept our people firmly united; but, as though to add to my sadness, rude hands have taken from me by stealth, this one solace, and I now sit empty handed, awaiting the call of those who have gone before me. For a while I wept for this loss, morning and evening, as though for the death of a relative dear to me, but as time passes my tears ceased to flow and I can now speak of it with some composure. . . . As I sit speaking with you, my eldest son, it seems as though the spirits of the old men have returned and are hovering about me. I feel their courage and strength in me, and the memory of the songs revives. Make ready, I shall once more sing the songs of my fathers. . . ." Fletcher adds, "As I listened to the old priest his voice seemed as full and resonant as when I heard him years ago. . . . Now the old man sang with his eyes closed, and watching him there was like watching the last embers of the religious rites of a vanishing people.[145]

Among the Creek it was the "Beloved Old Men" who conducted the ceremonies and had charge of the chants and sacrifices around the sacred fire.[146] At the head of the Hopi societies and religious fraternities were chiefs or priests whose offices were held for life. During their very elaborate ceremonies, the needs of the people were made known to the gods through the prayers of these aged priests. Hough has drawn an excellent pen picture of an old ceremonial leader: "Great must be Supela's ability, since he is capable of counseling the numerous societies on any doubtful points in their rites and ceremonies. In fact it seems that no observance in Walpi can get along without his aid, and even the farther towns call upon him to assist them in delicate points involved in the conduct of their religious celebrations. Short of stature, he has thick, gray hair, hanging to his shoulders around a not unpleasant, mobile face. Nervous of movement, cordial, but occupied with pressing business . . . he seems to have the burden of Atlas on his shoulders. He resembles a promoter or a ward politician . . . . If Supela seems head and front of everything religious in the summer, in winter he plays a more prominent part in the Soyaluma [Solstice ceremony] . . . . At this time Supela is in his element and proud of himself to the last degree, for does

145. *Ibid.* (103), pp. 241, 249, 251.
146. Adair (1), p. 107.

he not regulate the rites that are to bring back the sun from his winter wanderings?" [147]

Old men held the highest offices in the religious organization of the Aztec and were referred to as "the ancients of the temple." A high priest was described as a man of venerable aspect with a bushy white beard. In certain orders of the priesthood "only men above sixty" were admitted, and their pronouncements were regarded as divine revelation.[148] Bancroft wrote: ". . . it was the province of the priests to attend to all matters relating to religion and the instruction of youths. Some took charge of the sacrifices, others were skilled in the arts of divination, certain of them were entrusted with the arrangement of festivals and the care of the temple and sacred vessels; others applied themselves to the composition of hymns and attended to the singing and music. The priests who were learned in science superintended the schools and colleges, made the calculations for the annual calendar, and fixed the feast-days." [149]

The high priest of the Inca was described as "an old man aged a hundred years . . . clothed in a dress reaching down to the ground, very woolly and covered with sea-shells. He was the priest of the oracle . . . who had made the reply." [150]

In Morocco: "Holy men, both living and dead, are of the greatest importance . . . . Their simple hearts turn toward the hundred tombs of old saints . . . . These saints were withered old men living in desolate graveyards or under some hollow tree, subsisting by alms of the charitable, wrapping their hearts ever in holy dreams, as they spent their last years counting over old black rosaries the ninety-nine Excellent Names of God. And when they died the villagers built them humble tombs on the hill side, bare and crude like their own dwellings. And here the devout will come and sit beside the coffin, knock three times to wake the sleeping saint and whisper their hopes and needs." [151]

Old Lango men had leading roles in practically all the ceremonies.[152] The grave shrines of Shilluk kings were tended by aged men and women.[153] The aged had charge of the sacred golden

147. Hough (141), pp. 223–225.
148. Frazer (107), p. 458; Bancroft (5), II, 203, 209, 214.
149. *Ibid.* (5), II, 203, 209.
150. Sarmiento d Gamboa (258), p. 176.
151. Andrews (3), pp. 203–204.
152. Driberg (82), pp. 243–263.
153. Frazer (107), p. 268.

stool of the Ashanti, and one of them was keeper of the sacred shrine of the dead. Old women had very important parts in priestly orders. "On the morning of the (Adae) ceremony an old woman brought a pot of water, and standing outside the 'palace' waved it over her head, quickly inverted it, put it on the ground bottom side upwards, and placed a stone upon it. This, I was informed, was to prevent any quarrelling or disagreement arising among those who attend the ceremony." The wave offering was quite generally observed throughout Ashanti. Water was poured upon the ground outside the stool house by the head carrier, with the words, "Ghost grandfathers, today is the Sunday Adae, receive this water and wash your hands." Rattray added, "Quite apart from these ceremonial occasions, I do not suppose that a single day passes among any of the old folk upon which some little offering is not cast upon the roof of the hut or placed on the altar beside the door to "the Great God of the Sky." [154]

No Xosa was supposed to eat the *amasi* made from the new season's milk until the grandfather or some other old man duly appointed had performed a certain ceremony over it. [155]

Hobley has described the graduated scale of stages through which a native Akamba passed during his life. When he had circumcised children he entered upon the various grades of the council—first the *kisuka* and later the *nzama*. "The final degree which he reaches in old age is the leader of the shrine and his duty then is to offer the sacrifices at the sacred grove. Among the Akamba the members of this grade take but little part in the affairs of the tribe . . . . If an elder becomes so old as to fall into his dotage, and has a son who is qualified to take his place, the son is often elected in his stead. The elders are very few in number; there are rarely more than two for each grove." [156] Dundas stated that the most important functions of the senior elders were the "offering of sacrifice at the *ithembo*, and these are more important to the community as a whole than the medicine craft of any medicine man." [157] Many other lesser ceremonial duties devolved upon the elders. If a woman lost a young child by death, it was necessary for her to have her breasts ceremonially purified by a qualified elder, or, it was believed, any future children she might bear would die. If a hyena defecated in a village during

154. Rattray (237), pp. 9, 107, 144; *ibid.* (238), p. 116.
155. Kidd (162), p. 40.
156. Hobley (130), pp. 414–415.
157. Dundas (86), p. 241.

the night, it placed a curse upon the people, and the elders had to kill a goat and administer purification rites. Irregular sex relations had to be ritually absolved lest the cattle all die.[158] Prayers by the graveside were offered by very old men or women, and huts in which death occurred were sprinkled and purified by an elder.[159]

Lindblom gave an example of Akamba village purifications after a death. "The old man who is performing the rite slaughters a goat, which is consecrated by being given some purifying medium to drink . . . . The contents of the small stomach, which is called *kipatea*, are taken out and mixed in a calabash with a certain sort of plant. Those present all sit on their hams in a circle, and the old man first sprinkles them with the mixture, and then the walls and bed in the hut where the death took place." [160] If a stranger came to a village and died in a hut, it might be abandoned or even destroyed, and the men who tore it down would be considered unclean just as if they had handled the corpse. Thus they had to be purified by the elders and have their heads ceremonially shaved by a very old woman.[161]

Among the Iban elderly men officiated at sacrifices and religious ceremonies, but these were not bound up with priestly orders. Anyone might conduct them, but old men were generally selected, because of respect for their age and powers.[162] When the land had been fully cleared it was left to dry, and if it rained heavily for several weeks without any indication of ceasing, the people would imagine that some impurity had defiled the tribe and thus angered the great spirit. Then the elders would get together and "adjudicate on all cases of incest and bigamy, and purify the earth with the blood of pigs." Prayers would be offered from one end of the country to the other. Aged men also officiated at festivals. One traveler reported: "At Sennah a great feast was given in my honor. On my arrival a pig had been killed, and when I joined the festival gathering at night an old man approached me with some of its blood in a cup. He then made a speech, the purport of which, I was informed, meant good luck, happiness, and prosperity to me and my followers." [163] Gomes reported that "at marriages or at burials the *manang* (medicine

158. Hobley (130), pp. 412–413.
159. *Ibid.* (129), p. 66; Dundas (85), p. 525.
160. Lindblom (174), pp. 100–101.
161. Hobley (130), p. 409.
162. Roth (252), I, 190, 401.
163. *Ibid.* (252), I, 243.

man) is not the officiant, but some old man of standing who has a reputation for being fortunate in his undertakings." An old and "successful" man officiated in the baptismal ceremony for infants. A fowl was slaughtered, its blood made to drip into the stream, and the old man waded out in the water with the child in his arms and performed the rite.[164]

The leading ceremony in the construction of a Kiwai men's house was performed by a very old man and woman whose tasks involved a mournful fate, for it was believed that both would die soon after.[165] In Samoa the father of the family was the high priest. "In every house there was a fireplace in the center. Before beginning to eat, the fire was made to blaze up well and the patriarch began, addressing first the family-gods and then the whole host of gods . . . ." [166] Among the Maori of New Zealand there were many aged priests.[167]

Aged patriarchs were family priests among the Ainu of Japan. As soon as a child was born, the father or the grandfather would go to the bank of a river, where he would seat himself upon the ground and pray to the gods. Then he would cut a green stick of willow about a foot long, reverently bring it home, and whittle out a fetish. He would worship devoutly, offer prayers to the goddess of the fire, and then set up the willow stick at the sleeping place of the baby as its tutelary god, for "this birth fetish is looked upon as the angel of the child's growth." [168]

According to Batchelor, at the east end of every hut, near the sacred east window, the Ainu had what might be called his temple; for to him it was a special place of worship. It consisted of a few poles, upon which were placed the skulls of deer, bears, foxes, and other animals killed in the hunt, and also a large number of offerings to the gods. Twice a year, at least, the owner of the hut, together with his immediate friends and relatives, reverently approached these skulls and shavings and offered worship. This took place in the early spring and autumn, and also whenever there was a birth, a sickness, or death in the family. "It is a touching sight to see the old men with grave and reverent faces sitting before those sun-dried skulls, and praying to their gods." [169]

Old men performed priestly functions among the Sema Naga.

164. Gomes (117), pp. 101, 181.
165. Pritchard (229), p. 124.
166. Turner (315), p. 18.
167. Cowan (58), pp. 118–119.
168. Batchelor (12), pp. 183–184.
169. *Ibid.* (11), pp. 60–61.

They conducted rituals during the sowing and reaping of crops. People of an old village would not eat in a new one until the elders had purified it with rites. During the erection of the center post in a new house two old men selected the finest red cock obtainable and killed it by striking its head against the post, repeating the words, "May you [the owner] have a long life; let dogs increase; let pigs be multiplied; let riches increase; let illness and decline be forbidden." Whenever a fire went out in a house a village elder was called to rebuild it.[170]

At a Sema Naga betrothal the prospective bridegroom, when he went to the house of the girl's parents to eat and drink, was accompanied by a person called *anisu*—an old man or woman— who drank and ate before others and blessed the union. An attempt is made "to assure, if possible, that any evil influences attending the proposed match shall fall on the *anisu,* who is old and therefore unimportant or less susceptible, rather than on the bridegroom, just as the reaping and sowing of crops are initiated by old persons who have in any case little to expect of life, are of little value to the community as fighters, workers or breeding units, or perhaps are so tough as to be able better to withstand evil influences . . . ." In the ceremonial slaying of a bull an old man gave the mortal stroke. In 1906 someone discovered a black stone which was believed to possess great powers. Within six years a well-established cult had grown up about the stone and it was guarded by three old men who made regular sacrifices to it.[171]

Elderly men officiated at Toda ceremonies in which buffalo calves were sacrificed; and the priest of the dairy was always an old man.[172]

Aged men among the Palaung were regarded as priests with very special powers. When a paddy crop was harvested a small portion was left standing for the oldest man to cut and make into a fetish representing a man. This was set up on the threshing floor where the harvesters would kneel before it in thanksgiving. Anyone who reached great age was believed to have led a very good life in previous existences, and it was firmly held that the presence of such a person brought good fortune to a household. "Children are therefore taught to kneel before old people while they ask for their blessing and help. A child often goes, without any prompting into the house of an old man or woman, taking

170. Hutton (148), pp. 43–45, 155, 239, 242.
171. *Ibid.* (148), pp. 229, 238–239, 255.
172. Rivers (247), pp. 40, 276.

some little offering, a bamboo joint full of water, a few sticks for the fire, or the tender leaves of some wild plant to be cooked as vegetables. The child makes its little offering then kneels down quite simply for the expected blessing." When the young left the house of an aged person, they always expected good advice and never resented it. Indeed, they would be much surprised if no advice were offered, and the older the person the more respectfully was his counsel heeded. When starting on a journey, a young man or woman generally called on all the old men of the village. He or she would go from house to house and make an offering of a little rice or tobacco, explain the journey to the old people, and ask them for a special blessing. Milne explained: "Merit—acquired through countless lives—forms, as it were, a coat of mail around the body, which the darts of evil and mischievous spirits cannot pierce. An old man is generally revered, because the number of his years shows that he has been a really good man in many previous existences. The fact of his age is proof of previous merit, and for this reason his blessing is asked by the young. If his present life is not good, he will suffer for it in his next existence. Old people have happy lives among the Palaung; they are asked to all the festivals and to all the weddings, because their very presence brings a good and helpful influence to all the younger people, and, as we have already said, the blessing of the elders is the last stage in the marriage ceremony. Elders are heartily welcomed to all the feasts, and are offered the best seats and the best food." [173]

Old men performed priestly functions among the ancient Hebrew. "And Noah was six hundred years old [!] when the flood of waters was upon the earth." [174] "And Noah built an altar unto Jehovah, and took of every clean beast, and of every clean bird, and offered burnt-offerings on the altar. And Jehovah smelled the sweet savor . . . ." [175] Abraham, an old man of ninety-nine, entertained angels of the Lord and pled for mercy upon Sodom and Gomorrah.[176] The Hebrew believed that aged parents, and especially fathers, could by their blessing or curse determine the fate of their children: "And it came to pass, that when Isaac was old, and his eyes were dim, so that he could not see, he called Esau his eldest son, and said unto him: 'Behold now, I am old, I know

173. Milne (205), pp. 49, 198, 224, 314.
174. Gen. 7:6.
175. *Ibid.* 8:20–21.
176. *Ibid.*, chap. 18.

not the day of my death . . . make me savory food, such as I love, and bring it to me, that I may eat; that my soul may bless thee before I die.' " [177] The blessing, which through clever deception fell upon the younger son Jacob, was regarded as a tragic misfortune for Esau. King David's dying charge to his son Solomon may be regarded as a priestly blessing: "Now the days of David drew nigh that he should die; and he charged Solomon his son, saying, 'I am going the way of all the earth; be thou strong therefore, and show thyself a man; and keep the charge of Jehovah thy God, to walk in his ways, to keep his statutes, and his commandments, and his ordinances, according to that which is written in the Law of Moses, that thou mayest prosper in all that thou doest, and whithersoever thou turnest thyself . . . .' " [178]

It has been stressed repeatedly that opportunities for the aged to continue their participation in group activities have been dependent upon both personal qualifications and impersonal external factors. Concrete cases give a vivid impression of the role of the aged in the exercise of knowledge, magic, and religious or ceremonial functions; and the statistical data afford a base for further generalizations.

Belief in and fear of ghosts and unfriendly spirits have apparently been universal in primitive societies. Few other cultural traits have shown a wider and more regular distribution (Table VI, trait 92). In fact, fear of ghosts and spirits has been so common that neither its presence nor its intensity has been greatly affected by such factors as severity of climate, permanency of residence, stage of economic development, form of family organization, or existence of an organized priesthood—factors which have regularly influenced many other social phenomena. The universality of ghost-fear appears clearly in the many low and irregular coefficients of association (Cor. 368–379). Thus not only has the fear of ghosts and other occult powers provided opportunities for the aged to participate actively and profitably in human affairs, but this form of adjustment has been available to them in all preliterate groups.

Shamanism as an adjustment to occult and mysterious powers that threaten mankind has been equally universal, irrespective of such physical or cultural determinants as climatic conditions, permanency of residence, stage of maintenance, form of family organization, or presence of an organized priesthood (Table VI,

177. *Ibid.* 27:1–4.
178. I Kings 2:1–3.

trait 82, Cor. 280–291). As an available means of adjustment for the aged, therefore, recognized and accredited shamanistic practices have been as common as beliefs in ghosts and spirits.

The development of an organized priesthood, however, seems to have been quite strongly influenced, and even determined, by certain cultural factors. The priesthood has tended to be undeveloped in the severest climates; under nomadic conditions; among collectors, hunters, and fishers; and generally where the family system has been based upon matrilocal residence and matrilineal descent. Contrariwise, positive coefficients of association exist between organized priesthood and favorable climate, permanency of residence, herding, agriculture, grain, and a constant food supply. Similarly high positive coefficients are linked strongly with developed priesthood, with powerful chieftainship, government by restricted councils, secret societies, codified laws, the patriarchal family system, hereditary castes and classes, and plutocratic economy. The same association is found with ancestor worship and great elaboration of ceremonial rites (Cor. 392–413). In short, organized priesthood appears as a product of more complex and highly developed social systems, and it is in these that the aged have found the best opportunities for the exercise of priestly functions. The development of elaborate ceremonies and rituals has followed the same trends, although not so consistently (Cor. 414–434).

Following the establishment of these trends in the spheres of ghost-fear, magic, religion, and ceremonialism, a more specific examination was made of the role of the aged in them. However, statistical analysis of the activities of the aged as seers, magicians, shamans, and priests indicates that it would be pointless to calculate coefficients of association because there were no instances in which the statement was definitely made that the aged did not participate, and almost never was there an assertion that their participation was slight. The following generalizations were made, therefore, without any calculation of the usual coefficients.

Aged men were reported to be authoritative dispensers of information in 55 tribes while aged women were mentioned as similarly occupied in 27. It appears, then, that aged men have been generally in greater demand than women as recognized sources of information. At any rate this has been the impression gained by ethnographers and other informants; although the evidence is not conclusive, since special investigations have not been made. Still, in almost every count of cases, and irrespective of other cultural determinants, aged men have made a better showing than old women (Cor. 435–452). Probably the truth is that the aged of either sex, with some preference for males, have regularly been in demand as sources of information and possessors of experience especially where no better means for the preservation and transmission of knowledge has been available. Such variables as climate, residence, stage of maintenance, and family system have exercised no marked influence on these special prerogatives of age.

The aged have also been active in shamanism. Old men are reported as shamans in 60 tribes with aged women in 47 (Table VII, traits 153, 154). Here again various countings indicate that aged men have been more occupied in magic and shamanism than women, and their opportunities for participation would appear to have been influenced by other cultural factors (Cor. 453–476). In virtually all preliterate societies aged persons with appropriate qualifications, especially men, have been able to derive considerable advantage from the practice of magic.

Aged men are also reported to be active in priestly and ceremonial functions in 35 tribes, while aged women are found to be fairly active in 10, especially so in 1, very slightly in 1, and excluded from ceremonial participation in 2 (Table VII, traits 149, 150). The advantage has been very definitely in favor of aged men; and their opportunities have been greatest in a favorable climate, under permanent conditions of residence, in a herding or agricultural economy, and under a patriarchal family system. They have attained even further advantages with the development of organized priesthood and elaborate rituals, and wherever ancestor worship has prevailed (Cor. 477–502).

In final summary, it can be stated explicitly that in primitive societies aged men and women have been generally regarded as repositories of knowledge and imparters of valuable information, as specialists in dealing with the uncertain aleatory element, and as mediators between their fellows and the fearful supernatural powers. These qualifications have operated to give them key positions in a wide range of social activities. They have been esteemed as experts in solving the problems of life. They have supervised and instructed in the arts and crafts; and have initiated hazardous and important undertakings, such as housebuilding, boat construction, the planting and harvesting of crops, and warfare. They have been in constant demand for treating diseases, exorcising spirits, working charms, controlling the weather, conjuring enemies, and predicting the future. They have been accredited officiators in the great events of life, such as childbirth, child-naming, initiations, weddings, funerals, and the "laying of ghosts." They have also functioned frequently as leaders at social gatherings, and as directors of games, songs, dances, and festivals. In fact, hardly any of the great and critical occasions of life have not been presided over and supervised by some aged men or women. Truly have they been the guardians of life's emergencies, the custodians of knowledge, and the directors of ceremonies and pastimes. In possession of such great influence, they have been the chief conservators of the status quo. And finally, after death, they have become supernatural agents themselves, still expert in the tried and tested wisdom of the ages, and very jealous of any young upstarts who might presume to challenge or change the ancient folkways.

VII

THE FUNCTIONS OF THE FAMILY

SOCIAL relationships have provided the strongest securities to the individual, especially in old age. With vitality declining, the aged person has had to rely more and more upon personal relations with others, and upon the reciprocal rights and obligations involved. The strongest reinforcement of these has been through continued performance of useful tasks; retention of property interests and civic functions; exercise of knowledge, skill, and experience in supervision and instruction; and general participation in politics, religion, magic, and other common interests. To withstand the strain of obligations, social ties have had to be continuously revitalized, and for the aged the surest move to this end has been continued execution of socially useful work.

In the late stages of life, however, with the body feeble and the mind hazy, even the lightest chores might become burdensome, the most firmly entrenched property rights difficult to enforce, and the simplest prerogatives hard to retain. Thus, even in societies where the aged have possessed firmly entrenched rights, the very decrepit have faced the threat of indifference, neglect, and actual abuse. It is of interest, therefore, to discover which prerogatives have tended to sustain a person farthest along in life.

Throughout human history the family has been the safest haven for the aged. Its ties have been the most intimate and longlasting, and on them the aged have relied for greatest security. When other supports have crumbled and disappeared, the aged have clung to kith and kin as their last saviors; and the astute old man or woman has not infrequently manipulated such bonds to great personal advantage. Indeed, many individuals have been able to find in family relationships opportunities for effective social participation well into senility, and even to exploit some rights which have outlasted life itself, for the last wishes of aged parents have seldom been ignored by their offspring.

One way in which the aged have been able to gain advantage through family relationships has been by marriage to younger mates. This has been a rather widespread practice, especially of

men. And where old women have been unable to marry younger
men they have sometimes encouraged their aged husbands to take
younger wives in order to lighten their own labors and perhaps to
enhance their position in the family hierarchy. Examples of the
marriage of youth and age are plentiful.

The Labrador Eskimo were said to prefer young wives, and
Hutton relates how one young woman sought help in behalf of her
husband, saying: "The old man has such feeble knees, they totter
and shake when he gets up out of bed in the morning I
want some good knee medicine to cure that." Another old gentleman had two wives of whom "one was very old—his life-long
companion, in fact, and past work—almost as feeble as the old
man himself; so he married a young wife as well, so as to have
somebody at home to do the work." [1]

A Haida widower was expected to marry the eldest daughter of
his deceased wife's sister, provided she was of marriageable age.[2]
Mary Jemison, a white woman captured when young by the
Iroquois, related how she was given in marriage to an old man who
was reported to have reached the age one hundred and three.[3]
Beauchamp said of the Onondagas, a tribe of the Iroquois
Federation, that young men often attached themselves to elderly
women with the idea that the experience of an old wife was
valuable—"and the rule worked both ways." [4]

A Navaho woman, when enfeebled, might give her own daughter
to her husband, a provision which Reichard believes was made in
order to keep the affair in the family, since the old lady would
have greater authority over the young girl than over a stranger.[5]
Lipps explained that the young girls commanded higher prices
and that the old men, having most of the property, were in a
position to acquire them. "Old men marry the young girls and the
young men frequently marry the old women." [6]

Fletcher's interpretation of the Omaha custom was quite
matter-of-fact: "Looking at the duties and customs of the tribe,
it seems that the question of domestic labor had a great deal to
do with the practice of polygamy. 'I must take another wife. My
old wife is not strong enough now to do all the work alone,' was a
remark made not as offering an excuse for taking another wife,

1. Hutton (149), pp. 41, 292–293.
2. Curtis (64), p. 128.
3. Seaver (267), pp. 150–151.
4. Beauchamp (14), p. 91.
5. Reichard (242), p. 59.
6. Lipps (177), p. 43.

but as stating a condition that must be met, and remedied in the only way that custom permitted." [7]

Among the Creek it was customary for an elderly man to marry a young girl, or sometimes a child.[8] It was said of the Abipone that "should a man cast his eyes upon a handsome woman, the old wife must remove merely on account of her fading form or advancing years." [9] Smith mentioned an Araucanian who was very old and the possessor of eight wives.[10] Witoto men chose, as a rule, girls considerably younger than themselves, and Whiffen stated that the general disparity of age was from five to fifteen years: "For a man will choose an undeveloped girl, perhaps only nine or ten years of age, and hand her over to the women of his own tribe." [11] Bridges wrote of the Yahgans: "Because of the common custom of marrying young girls to elderly men, it often happens that the young men can only marry widows. It brings it about that in most cases aged persons are bound to the young by marriage ties." [12]

The custom of old men marrying young mates was common in Africa. The aged Berber often secured young wives;[13] old Lango women encouraged their husbands to take younger mates to help with the work;[14] and the custom was also very popular among both the Shilluk[15] and the Fan. Among the latter it was reported that a headman died leaving seven widows, three of middle age, and four young ones.[16] Ashanti infants were not infrequently married to the older men;[17] and some Dahomean rulers had "many young wives." [18]

Dundas reported that the aged Akamba often married young women; and Lindblom explained: "If a man has only one wife and, later when she is old, buys a young girl, the latter usually stays in the elder wife's hut, and is treated as a daughter by her, but must do most of the work under her direction." [19] Xosa girls were said to be "literally dragged off" to be married to elderly

7. Fletcher and La Flesche (103), p. 326.
8. Swanton (303), p. 368.
9. Dobrizhoffer (75), II, 211.
10. Smith (282), p. 252.
11. Whiffen (332), p. 48; *ibid.* (331), p. 162.
12. Bridges (37), p. 174.
13. Westermarck (330), I, 534.
14. Driberg (82), p. 155.
15. Westermann (328), p. xxxvii.
16. Bennett (19), p. 78.
17. Becham (17), p. 125.
18. Duncan (84), II, 48.
19. Dundas (85), p. 519; Lindblom (174), p. 77.

men, "usually an old polygamist," and households were listed in which the oldest wife was seventy and the youngest seventeen.[20] Holden described the proud position of an aged Xosa: "The man is then supported in Kafir pomp and plenty; he can eat, drink, and be merry, bask in the sun, sing, and dance at pleasure, spear bucks, plot mischief, or make bargains for his daughters; to care and toil he can say farewell, and so go on to the end of life. As age advances he takes another young wife or concubine, and then another, to keep up eternal youth, for he is never supposed to grow old as long as he can obtain a youthful bride; she by proxy imparts her freshness to his withered frame and throws her bloom over his withered brow." [21]

Weeks reported of the Bakongo: "It must be remembered that in a country where polygamy is recognized a large number of virile young women are often tied to an old man." [22] Claridge explained that a man's wealth was measured by the number of wives he owned, so that his marital appetite was seldom satisfied: "Children and women are the most valuable stock that a heathen possesses." [23] He wrote further: "Plurality of wives make a negro big and important among his fellows. His subsistence is more secure, too, because there are more to farm for him, and more to feed him." The Negro would say: "To own one wife is as big a risk as to own only one belt for palm climbing. If it breaks you are done for." Claridge told of a girl betrothed to an old man who was afflicted with a loathsome disease and suffering from a number of functional disorders. She ran away from him, but was caught and sent back, and tied in a basket after the manner in which pigs and goats were delivered. One old man dickered for the wife of the missionary himself and was puzzled to learn that she was not for sale at any price. Wives were said to be the safest property investment that a man could make: "When a wife dies, the negro expects those who provided her to also supply him with another without extra charge. If there be no one suitable, he gets his money back." [24]

In a Chukchi family in Siberia the first wife was generally much older and had several children when a second wife was obtained. Then the old woman became the mistress of the house-

20. Kidd (161), pp. 204, 221; Shooter (270), pp. 58–59.
21. Holden (136), pp. 203–204.
22. Weeks (327), p. 108.
23. Claridge (53), pp. 81–82.
24. *Ibid.*, pp. 81–84.

hold while the younger one was treated almost like a maid. "The first wife sits with the husband in the warm sleeping room, while the second works outside in the cold . . . prepares the food, and serves it. Sometimes the aged husband takes a second young wife for the express purpose of giving a helper and maid to his wife, who is getting old and cannot get through with the housework by herself. Cases have occurred where the first wife insisted that the husband marry a younger and more able-bodied woman." [25]

Milne wrote concerning a Palaung couple: "In a village near Namshan I met a civil and most obliging head-man and his wife. I asked the wife if she had many sweethearts when she was a girl. She smiled and said, 'Yes,' adding, 'when they came to sit with me in the evenings, I never listened for any other footsteps but HIS.' Here she nodded her head to her old husband, saying, 'I cared only for him.' The husband smiled and said, 'When I went to sit with the other girls the time seemed long, but it went as quickly as a chew of betel-nut when I was with her.' " Mrs. Milne added, as a sort of anticlimax to the romance: "Their children being all dead, the old lady persuaded her husband to take another wife, and he agreed, stipulating that she choose the young lady. This was done, and they appeared to be a happy family. The young woman did all the housework." [26]

The custom for old men to marry youthful wives was common among the Iban.[27] Best reported of the Maori that "in former times middle aged and elderly men in a good many cases married women much younger than themselves." [28] Samoan girls of tender age were often affianced to men old enough to be their grand-fathers. Mead reported that an old man, a widower or divorcee, would frequently be a girl's first lover; and the first marital relations of a young man were often with an older woman. A form of punishment which a parent might inflict on an unruly daughter was to marry her off to an old man.[29]

The domination of old men in Australia has been widely reported. Briffault was of the opinion that because of the success of the older men in monopolizing the younger women it became difficult for young men to obtain wives at all. "Far from endeavoring to remedy the situation, the older men, on the contrary, ex-

25. Borgoras (28), p. 600.
26. Milne (205), p. 103.
27. Roth (252), I, 288.
28. Best (20), I, 468.
29. Mead (204), pp. 88–89; Stair (292), p. 171.

pressly prevent the younger ones, sometimes, it appears, on the pain of death from marrying at all." [30] Mrs. Parker reported of the Euahlayi that it was customary for graybeards to add younger mates to their households, and that these women were usually placed under the control of the older wife. "Should the young wife in the absence of her husband speak to a young man, she will probably get a scolding from the old wife and a 'real hiding' from the old man . . . . Quite young men often marry quite old women; a reason sometimes given is that these young men were on the earth before and loved these same women, but died before their initiation, so could not marry until now in their reincarnation. Certainly amongst the blacks, age is no disqualification for a woman; she never seems to be too old to marry, and certainly with age gains power." [31]

Rivers, summing up the situation among the Banks Islanders, concluded "We seem therefore driven to assume a state of society in which these elders had in some way acquired so predominant a position in the community that they were able to monopolize all the young women. It is in such a condition that I believe marriage with a granddaughter, as an organized practice, to have had its origin . . . . The most natural way of explaining the granddaughter marriage is by the supposition that at one time such a dominance not only existed in Melanesia, but reached a pitch far surpassing anything which has been recorded in Australia; a dominance so great that the elders were able to monopolize all the young women of the community, the young women of each moiety becoming as a matter of course the wives of the elders of the other moiety. My first supposition, then, is that the marriage with the daughter's daughter is the immediate and natural result of the monopoly by the old men of all the young women of the community. As I have already mentioned, the obvious consequence of such a condition is that as the young men grow up, they will find the young women who would naturally have been their wives already appropriated by the old men. Their only chance of obtaining wives will be that women may be given them who have already been the wives of their elders." [32]

Whether marriage to younger mates has proved an asset or a liability has depended very largely upon the prerogatives vouchsafed in the marriage bond and upon other rights and privileges

30. Briffault (38), I, 744–745
31. Parker (218), p. 56.
32. Rivers (248), II, 59.

within the family circle. The authority of parents over their children, for example, has prevailed in the most rudimentary as well as the most complex societies. Other vested interests have often affected a wide circle of relatives—in-laws, siblings, nephews, nieces, grandchildren, and others who came within the orbit of the kinship system. Family prerogatives for the aged have varied greatly and no classification of particular rights and privileges is provided here; but an ample sampling is presented as a forerunner to statistical analysis of trends. Cases are presented first from tribes characterized by matrilineal descent, and these are followed by cases from patrilineal societies.

In matrilineal tribes of North America, both aged men and women exercised considerable authority and often received remarkable care from members of their family within a wide range of kinship. Aged Haida of both sexes enjoyed great authority and respect and were well cared for by their relatives. It was the duty of young women to look after the comfort of their ageing parents and their husbands were required by custom to assume responsibility for their support.[33] The Iroquois cherished and cared for their aged and incapacitated, and killed or abandoned them only under pressure of dire necessity. According to Morgan, the control of domestic affairs was practically the business of aged matrons, "certain elderly and prudent women being set apart more or less formally as rulers of the house." Young men often knew nothing of matrimonial plans in which they were involved until the ceremony was at hand and their mothers instructed them to prepare for marriage. Their aged leaders taught, "It is the will of the Great Spirit that you reverence the aged even though they be helpless as infants." Old people were entitled to a home among any of their kindred wherever and whenever they chose to take it. The crime regarded as most horrible by the Iroquois, indeed almost too horrible to occur was rebelliousness of a son against his mother. When she grew old he provided for her; and the customary assurance of a son to his ageing father was, "I will cherish your old age with plenty of venison, and you shall live easy." [34]

Aged Omaha did not have to work and were supported by their relatives who never abandoned them on the prairie if they could possibly avoid it, fearing that the deity would punish them for it.

33. Murdock (208), p. 252; Curtis (64), p. 120; Harrison (123), p. 79.
34. Murdock (208), p. 312; Morgan (207), I, 165, 220, 311–312, 319; Briffault (38), I, 148; Seaver (267), p. 128.

When it was absolutely necessary to leave them behind, they were provided with shelter and food, water, and fuel.[35]

Among the Crow, old people depended upon their property and their children to keep them from want, and they had a saying: "How can a man be poor when he has . . . many children to look after him when he is old?" Their children and other relatives were expected to provide them with the best food—stripped tenderloin, dried, pounded, and mixed with bone marrow.[36]

Creek women owned the houses in which they lived and occupied them until death, enjoying the homage and support of younger members of the family. Old men whose wives were dead and whose children had grown up and scattered could return to the homes of their childhood or, as frequently happened, they might move from house to house among their female relatives. A typical Creek household would consist, therefore, of a man and woman, their children, one or more sons-in-law, some grandchildren, perhaps an orphan or two, and some aged or dependent person of the kinship group. "In case a stranger visited the town and made known to what clan he belonged, it was the duty of the man married into that clan to invite him to his house." Although neither he nor his wife had set eyes on the man before, he would say to him, "Come to your home." Sometimes an old man whose children had grown up, or who for any reason was alone in the world, would travel about from one to another of the houses of his female kin. He would say, "Well, I am going to my home," and make for the house of someone who had never seen him before. "In later times this struck the young people as very presumptuous, but it was the old law. It not only served to provide for the old, infirm, and indigent, but enabled the adventurous to travel and see more of the world than would otherwise be possible." Swanton asserted that there were no instances on record of an aged person being killed to save his family the trouble of supporting him; and although Bartram claims that such cases did occur occasionally, they were only in dire emergencies and at the earnest request of the old man or woman.[37]

Aged women exercised much authority in a Seri family. A young man lived in the household of his wife and was expected to become provider and protector of her family, including dependent children, and the crippled, aged, and invalid.[38]

35. Dorsey (78), pp. 274–275, 325, 369.
36. Curtis (62), p. 57; Linderman (175), pp. 138–139.
37. Swanton (302), pp. 79, 171, 345.   38. McGee (188), pp. 272, 280.

The aged Navaho woman played an important role in the economic and social life of her family. She owned much of the property in herds, and her influence was said to be so great that a feeling prevailed that "wherever the mother is, is home." Her daughters remained near her after marriage and their husbands were generally subservient to her wishes until her death.[39] It was also the duty of even distant relatives to provide for their aged kin. Reichard wrote: "As provision is always made for the care of young children, so old people are usually made comfortable. The duty devolves upon members of the family according to convenience. The daughter or granddaughter customarily assumes the responsibility, but if the old man or woman has no daughter or granddaughter the sister's daughter would be looked to next. I have seen old blind and crippled men who were kindly, often tenderly, led about by the young men or women of the family. They usually have a large pile of sheepskins and blankets upon which to recline—the other members of the family have one or two—they occupy the warmest place in the *hogan* and they are patiently waited on. One very old man near Keam's Canyon was very troublesome. He was blind, very deaf, and feeble. He often wandered about trying to get from one *hogan* to another. Upon these occasions he would get lost and then the young people were obliged to hunt for him. They did this without complaint or outward indication of annoyance. Near the same place another helpless old man lived with his deceased daughter's husband and his second wife who was no blood or clan relative of his . . . . There are in the Navajo tribe those who are poor, there are others who are helpless such as small children and aged persons, cripples and the like, and there are a few who are subnormal in mentality. The care of the unfit is a family matter which is taken over by individuals who feel themselves responsible usually because of relationship to the person concerned." [40]

Hough said of the Hopi: "Another law of the greater family was that of mutual help, providing for the weak, infirm, and unprotected members." [41] Although in more recent times relatives might neglect and even abuse helpless and useless old people, family and kinship ties remained strong supports in senescence. Children were expected to provide for their aged parents and to bury them appropriately after death. The aged generally agreed

39. Reichard (242), pp. 51–52, 69–70.
40. *Ibid.* (242), pp. 51, 57; Lipps (177), p. 44.
41. Hough (141), p. 37.

that it was better to live with a daughter because a son might get into trouble with his wife's people and be driven out of the house, in which case one would be left with "strangers." It was also better to live with a younger sister than a brother, for then one would always be among his own relatives. Aged women remained with their daughters, and retained some authority. Aged Hopi would remark: "Long ago relatives were good to their old people, for they realized that they were dependent upon us." In recent times cases of dire neglect, and even exploitation of the aged, have been reported; but nearly every old man or woman would still rely, above all else, upon kinfolk for support, especially upon sisters and daughters, but not infrequently upon brothers and sons.[42]

Among the Arawak of South America, Roth reported that natives tended to regard their parents, when too old to work, as more of a nuisance than anything else. "There is one great failing . . . neglect of old persons and the sick. They are stowed away in corners of the house, neglected and left to themselves, where weakness keeps them to their hammocks, perhaps often without the necessaries of life." Im Thurn also wrote that "powerless old age meets with no respect. When old and past work, they are indeed allowed to remain in their hammocks in the houses which, once perhaps, belonged to them, and are fed by their younger relations in a rough and grudging manner, but no further care or kindness is shown to them." It is important to note, however, that they were fed and sheltered by relatives, and it has been stated elsewhere that a father would not willingly lose his son-in-law, whose duty it was to maintain and support him in old age.[43] The Araucanians also found support in family and kinship which lightened the burdens of age. One old man boasted, "Even I, who am poor, have two wives." [44]

In Africa, Rattray reported that "no Ashanti woman stands alone . . . for behind the woman stands the united family, bound by the tie of blood, which has a power and meaning that we can hardly grasp . . . ." Aged men and women were cared for by their families. Property interests, vested in the authority of the uncle, safeguarded individuals from danger of being reduced to extreme poverty. "This is one reason why, up to the present [1929], we have not had any paupers or workhouses in West

42. Field notes of author.
43. Roth (254), pp. 684, 698, 703; Im Thurn (151), p. 224; Spencer (290), Div. I, Pt. 4A, p. lvi.
44. Smith (282), pp. 188, 205–206.

Africa." Even if a widow was very old, she had every right to remain in her former husband's house. Rattray further explained: "The whole conception of 'mother right' affords the woman a protection and status that is more than an adequate safeguard against ill-treatment by any male or group of males. Her children belong to her and her clan, not to that of her husband. All her individually acquired and inherited property is hers and her clan's, and her husband cannot touch it . . . . 'I am the mother of a man,' she says, and her meaning we cannot understand until a fuller knowledge of Ashanti social and religious organization shows us what is meant. 'I alone can transmit the blood to a king. If my sex die in the clan then that very clan becomes extinct, for be there one or one thousand male members left, not one can transmit the blood, and the life of the clan becomes measured on this earth by the span of a man's life.' " The power of the legitimate wife was so great that Ashanti husbands and fathers were known to say, "I prefer my slave wife and my children by her to my free wife and free children because I have undisputed right over them." An uncle usually found it to his advantage to arrange marriage between his nephews and nieces and his daughters and sons, for he thereby maintained his influence over his own children and insured their assistance. While fathers had almost no rights over their children, uncles on the maternal side could even pawn their nephews and nieces. After the death of a husband, the widow had the right to remain in the house, and even though very old, she could compel the heir to marry her, though perhaps merely *pro forma*.[45]

Matrilineal avunculate rights also afforded security to the aged among the Bakongo by providing the maternal uncle with a substantial income from the sale of marriageable nieces. He might also pawn a nephew to secure a loan. Daughters remained under the control of their mothers, whom they served until they married; and even afterwards a mother-in-law could make life quite unbearable for her daughter's husband should he fail to show her proper consideration. Children were greatly desired and a girl was called a "redeemer," signifying that she would some day bring gain to the family in the marriage market. Proverbs rated a boy as "a piece of string, always useful." The aged could always find food and shelter with younger relatives. "The return of the women from the fields to the town seems to arouse it to life. The old, young and sick, that have been drowsing in the shade through

45. Rattray (237), pp. 78–80; *ibid.* (239), pp. 18–19, 29, 33.

the hot hours of the afternoon, come out of their cool hiding places to greet the women and scan with hungry inquisitive eyes the contents of the baskets that are now on the ground." [46]

Seligmann rote of the Vedda of Ceylon: "Certainly at first sight it seems as if all game were equally divided among members of the group, but after a little time one perceived that while an unmarried man looked especially to his mother, a married man's father-in-law had at least an equal claim on his son-in-law and in practice often received more attention, since a man generally spent most of his time with his wife's family. The relationship between father-in-law and son-in-law is very close . . . thus when discussing children and their bringing up a man was asked whether a Vedda preferred to have a son or a daughter, the answer was prompt and decided, 'A daughter, for thus a man obtained a son-in-law.' But in theory sons should take at least as large a part in looking after their aged and infirm fathers as do the latter's sons-in-law." [47]

Aged people in the Banks Islands could usually count upon the support of relatives. If a man with children died while his own parents were still alive, they had first claim on his possessions and the children did not succeed to his land until they had bought off the rights of the grandparents.[48]

It was customary among the Trobrianders for brothers to cultivate gardens for their married sisters and to help support them and their husbands as long as they lived. Thus, for an old man to marry a woman with several young and healthy brothers was about the safest insurance possible. Men hesitated to marry into families without able-bodied men, saying, "Where are the brothers to make a garden for my wife?" Widows and especially widowers married as soon as possible, for "marriage brings with it a considerable yearly tribute in staple food, given to the husband by the wife's family." Great consideration was shown to a senior wife, even when she became old and ugly, evidently because of the income gained from her family. One old man explained the advantage of cross-cousin marriage in terms of old-age security: "I wanted when I got old to have someone of my family to look after me, to cook my food, to bring me my lime-pot and lime-stick, to pull out my grey hairs. It is bad to have a stranger do that; when it is someone of my own people, I am not afraid."

46. Weeks (327), pp. 98, 105, 118–119, 147, 155–156; *ibid.* (324), p. 414.
47. Seligmann (269), pp. 66–67
48. Rivers (248), I, 36–37.

Malinowski explained: "The man may have to rely in his old age on the attentions of his son and son's wife, but neither of them are his real kindred (according to their system) unless the daughter-in-law is also his sister's child. In spite of his personal affection for his son, he prefers to have someone of his own maternal kindred about him, and this can only be achieved if the son married the right cross-cousin, that is the father's sister's daughter, or her daughter." Here is an obvious case of manipulating family ties to gain security.[49]

Foregoing instances drawn from societies with matrilineal descent indicate that in such tribes aged men and women both have been able to realize considerable security through family and kinship ties; and that the women appear to have enjoyed fully as much authority and security as the men, perhaps even somewhat more. A more precise statistical analysis will be presented later on.

Moving on to patrilineal societies we find that here aged men have been able to realize a great deal of power and security, more indeed than in matrilineal groups; but there is some question as to whether aged women have enjoyed equal consideration. We turn now to a sampling of concrete cases.

Aged Kwakiutl men were prominent in family affairs and were well cared for my their children.[50] Chippewa relatives dealt kindly with their aged, and crippled old women were supported by their children, who in their wanderings carried them on their backs.[51]

The Aztec never married without parental consent; and the father, however aged, had the power to pawn or sell his children into slavery for his material support. Young persons might even be hanged for squandering the family income.[52] And Inca law forbade the marriage of any young person without parental consent.[53] Each Jivaro father was, theoretically, "absolute ruler of his own house," and a son-in-law had to slave for his father-in-law for many months.[54]

Grown-up Akamba sons in Africa built their huts near the residence of their fathers, and were under his authority. Dundas stated that marriage was strictly by bride-price, which provided a special source of profit to the father. The father held the

49. Malinowski (192), I, 81, 103; Seligmann (268), p. 705.
50. Boas (26), p. 581; Curtis (63), p. 139.
51. Jones (156), p. 69; Densmore (73), p. 60.
52. Bancroft (5), II, 220; Biart (22), pp. 127–128, 201, 232–234.
53. Westermarck (329), I, 607.
54. Up de Graff (319), p. 215.

property for the purchase of his sons' wives and had much to say about their choices. As head of the family he had authority over all his children, could control his sons' earnings, and when they were disobedient he might resort to the most dreaded recourse—a curse—to bring them to terms. The Akamba father was described as a despot of the family, "knowing no authority but his own." As a mark of his position he might carry a forked stick and a three-legged stool. Family prerogatives were not so favorable for aged women. When a man died his widow became the spouse of his eldest brother; or he might dispose of her to another. "If she is old, so that he does not care to keep her for himself and has no prospect of selling her, he may lend her to someone." [55]

In a Vai family the father was the sole authority, and he could pawn a child for his support.[56] The same was reported of the Shilluk, who in times of famine were known to have sold their children for food.[57]

Xosa who had the misfortune to lose their cattle could count with confidence on the assistance of their sons and relatives. Kidd stated that when age overtook a man he was "quite safe" in handing over his possessions and affairs to his sons.[58] But old women had fewer rights, and their lot was described as "sad indeed." Natives sometimes called them "cast-off things," and regarded them as of "no more use." They were "frequently left to starve or die of exposure or neglect," and were often killed as witches.[59]

A venerable Xosa patriarch explained that no man would kill his own son, but that if he were very undutiful the father might drive him off and retain his cattle. Girls could be married off against their will "to fill the harems" of aged patriarchs.[60] An elderly father could select wives for his sons and force compliance.[61] Alberti stated that when a Xosa became old, he would usually turn over his herd to the son who had married last and who had not yet left the paternal hut. In making this gift he reserved for himself only some cows to milk, leaving everything else to the son. If a son acted badly towards his father or refused to obey his orders, he was sure to suffer the contempt of the

55. Lindblom (174), pp. 36–37, 81, 133, 170–171; Dundas (85), pp. 493–494, 520.
56. Ellis (92), pp. 59, 192, 217.
57. Westermann (328), pp. xxxiii–xxxvi.
58. Kidd (161), pp. 22–23, 29.
59. *Ibid.* (161), pp. 22–23, 29.
60. Shooter (270), pp. 58–59, 82, 92.
61. MacDonald (187), p. 271.

group.[62] Kidd adds: "If the son neglected the father in his old age, he would be hounded out of the tribe as an utterly worthless fellow." [63]

Aged men enjoyed special consideration among the Arunta of Australia. They possessed most of the young women, whose business it was to gather food for them; and they exercised strong control over the children. It was also customary for a young man to prove his gratitude by frequently presenting to his father-in-law a part of his hunting booty, "helping thus to provide for him in his old age." [64]

The Dieri said: "The more wives the more food with less work for the husbands." Horne and Aiston gave the example of an old man who was "hopelessly imbecile" and had to be led about like a child; but, "His woman looks after him and manages to collect enough food for the two." Such old men might lend their wives to younger men for a consideration.[65]

Kiwai Papuan sons and daughters helped their parents with the work and looked after them when they were ill or aged. If a father became too old to work his gardens, they were taken over by the sons, who then supported him until his death. "Children appear to be very devoted to parents, show them respect and obedience, and take care of them in their old age." It was also customary for friends to pledge themselves to provide for each other's dependents in case of misfortune. "Two boys that have grown up together since they began to crawl and have become great chums are called *kége*, which is the word to denote close friendship. They constantly give each other food and other presents, and whatever the one asks for the other must give him. On parting for any length of time they exchange arm guards or bracers. If the one is killed, the other is bound to take revenge . . . . At the death of a *kége* the surviving friend moves with his wife and children into the dead man's house. He becomes the guardian of the friend's children and also looks after his parents; his new 'father and mother' apparently being his first care, before his own parents, although he does not neglect these either . . . . The new parents call him by the name of their dead son, whose place he in fact assumes.[66]

Aged Maori men were often comfortably situated with two or

62. Alberti (2), pp. 116–117.
63. Kidd (161), p. 29.
64. Spencer and Gillen (289), I, 39; Schulze (265), p. 236.
65. Gason (113), pp. 169–170; Horne and Aiston (138), p. 16.
66. Landtman (171), pp. 178, 197, 201, 228, 233, 236.

more wives; and they usually arranged the marriages of their sons. It was customary for an old man to live in a house with his children and grandchildren.[67]

Aged Samoans were well endowed with family prerogatives, and old women were said to possess more rights than men. The oldest female progenitor had special rights over the distribution of a dowry coming into the family, and also exercised a veto on the sale of land. Whenever a household matriarch's desires were thwarted, she could coerce other members of the family by threats of a curse—a most dreaded calamity for she had the power to "cut the line" and "make the name extinct." [68]

Family ties provided insurance in old age among the Semang. Schebesta mentioned a man of seventy, a widower, blind and a cripple, who lived under a shelter behind the house of his son and was assisted by him. "He and his son had married into the Jahai family group and were parasites on that family." Another "grey-haired, half-blind old man" lived alone and was looked after by his unmarried daughter, who had a hut next to his. Aged women stayed with their children and grandchildren.[69]

It was a "universal custom" among the Bontoc Igorot "for relatives to feed and otherwise care for the aged." A widow usually lived in a small hut of her own but took her meals with married children. Bontoc youths and maidens received little permanent property during the lives of their parents until the old people were too feeble to work; then their lands were turned over to married sons and daughters, who assured them that their wants would be faithfully met.[70]

The father possessed great authority in the old Ainu families of Japan. He could divorce his wives or disinherit his children. Even when old and blind, he was entirely supported by his children "and received until his dying day filial reverence and obedience." [71] Aged women did not exert so much influence nor did they fare so well generally. Left to the mercy of their sons and daughters, they were often regarded as worthless creatures. A vivid example of this was provided in an account of a feeble old woman who was found crouched in the dark corner of a hut. Landor relates: "As I got closer I discovered a mass of white hair and two

67. Cowan (58), p. 2; Best (20), I, 463; Firth (100), p. 96.
68. Mead (204), pp. 82, 194; Turner (315), p. 161.
69. Schebesta (262), pp. 35, 63, 72–73.
70. Jenks (153), pp. 47, 70–71, 74, 164.
71. Bird (23), p. 103; Batchelor (12), p. 36.

claws, almost like thin human feet with long hooked nails. A few fish bones were scattered on the ground and a lot of filth was massed together in that corner, the disgusting odors of which were beyond measure horrible. I could hear someone breathing heavily under that mass of white hair, but I could not make out the shape of a human body. I touched the hair, I pulled it, and with a groan, two thin bony arms suddenly stretched out and clasped my hand . . . her limbs were merely skin and bones, and her long hair and long nails gave her a ghastly appearance. I dragged her out and she made little resistance . . . . Nature could not have inflicted more evils on that wretched creature. She was nearly blind, deaf, and dumb; she was apparently suffering from rheumatism, which had doubled her body and stiffened her bony arms and legs; and moreover, she showed many symptoms of leprosy. Altogether, she was painful, horrible, disgusting, and humiliating to contemplate . . . . She was neither ill treated, nor taken care of by the village or by her son, who lived in the same hut; but she was regarded as a worthless object and treated accordingly. A fish was occasionally flung to her . . . ." [72] Even at that, however, it was a son who kept her alive.

Kazak daughters were desired more than sons because of the bride-price received for them.[73] Mongol brides also brought handsome sums to their families. Sons, even after marriage, generally lived near their parents and were obedient to them.[74] A Rwala's children were his own property, and it was said that a father might even kill his son or daughter with impunity. If a son slew his father, however, he had to leave the clan or tribe forever. The older a Rwala became, the more extended grew the circle of relatives upon whom he could rely for support. "There are no beggars among the Rwala. An impoverished man is helped by his kin, his clan, and his chief. Aged widows may return to the house of their own kin." [75]

In Sema Naga families the aged lived out their last days among relatives; and in eating from a common dish the oldest started first.[76] Chin parents had the right to sell their daughters, and seldom paid much attention to considerations of love and romance in the marriage of their children. "The facts are that a girl culti-

72. Landor (168), pp. 53–55.
73. Spencer (290), No. 5, Div. I, Pt. 3A, p. 34.
74. Howorth (145), Pt. IV, pp. 194–195, 201.
75. Musil (212), pp. 49, 456, 494–495, 663–664.
76. Hutton (148), p. 97.

vates her parents' fields and performs the household duties, and if any man wants her to do the same for him, he must compensate the parents for the loss of an able-bodied servant." [77]

A certain corner in a Palaung house was reserved for the oldest man, who was head of the family, and no other person would dare use.it.[78] Among the Toda, it was the duty of the youngest son to dwell with his parents and support them as long as they lived. A widow could live with her sons or a married daughter.[79]

Members of a Munda family shared all they had in common until the death of the father. Complete control of all property remained in his hands as long as he lived, and he could expel an unruly son. The sons with their wives and children lived under the paternal roof, cooperated in cultivating the family fields, had their meals cooked in the same family pot, and contributed their separate earnings to the common fund. Very old men unfit for work did nothing except sit at home, but they exercised absolute control over the family. When a sonless Munda got old, he might choose one of his cousins, nephews, or grandnephews to take the place of a son, care for him in his dotage, and inherit his property.[80]

Aged men wielded authority in Kazak families, and the principle of seniority in clan and family relations was rigidly upheld. Homage was paid to the aged: "The son is never entirely emancipated from his father, although when he reaches the age of twenty he usually has a tent set aside for himself, and cattle and sheep are given to him for his subsistence. He does not reach full age until he is thirty . . . but as long as his father may live, he is supposed to be acting only as his deputy." [81]

Among the Chukchi, according to Bogoras: "There is a fair number of old men. Sometimes four generations live together in the same family, the great-grandfather being from seventy to seventy-five years of age." The old men demanded and received great consideration, for they retained possession of the herd and the general direction of the family until they were very old, usually until death. The position of old women was "much inferior to that of old men." "All families of the Reindeer Chukchee," wrote Bogoras, were "connected among themselves by ties of relationship. Thus a poor family without relatives is almost impossi-

77. Carey and Tuck (48), I, 189.
78. Milne (205), pp. 186–187.
79. Rivers (247), pp. 559–560; Thurston (308), p. 158.
80. Belcher (18), pp. 73, 79; Sarat (257), pp. 364, 427–429, 435.
81. Huntington (147), p. 117; Jochelson (155), p. 84; Schuyler (266), I, 139.

ble. Nearly always some relative, however distant, will take them to his camp and give them means of subsistence." [82]

In Yukaghir families an older man's orders were promptly obeyed. "Generally each younger member of the family or group looks on his or her elder as his or her protector or ruler." A young man would go to live in the house of his father-in-law, where, although he was received as a son, his position remained subordinate. "He must neither look at or speak to the parents and older relatives. The products of his hunting and fishing are under the control of his mother-in-law, and the furs of the animals killed by him he must bring to his father-in-law. Only when he becomes a father himself can he use some of the furs without asking." A father in accepting a son-in-law would often use the following terms: "I will say, the bride-groom shall be admitted to my house if he is willing to stay with me till the end of my life, till my death." Jochelson further explained: "The position of the young man in the house of his father-in-law is a very subordinate one. In fact he appears to be 'serving' for his wife as long as any member of the family older than he is alive. He has to do the bidding of his father-in-law, his wife's elder brothers, and elder members of the family; but after the death of his father-in-law, his wife's elder brothers, or after the latter marry and go away to live with their fathers-in-law, he himself becomes the head of the family." When old, weak, and no longer able to hunt or fish, "he sits in the house doing nothing but commanding, advising, and directing the work." Should he have children, he might live in their house as the head of the family and enjoy a guarded and respected old age. "This is one of the reasons the Yukaghir love their children so much. Those who are left without children and have to live their old age with relatives occupy no enviable position and have no authority in household matters." Elders with no children often adopted them. Old women with children received honor, respect, and support. Their advice and guidance in all household matters were sought by the young women, and they were faithfully cared for. "In the spring wanderings or hunting expeditions the old people are carried on sledges drawn by young women in conjunction with dogs." One native remarked: "The parents love the oldest child the most; but it is the youngest one that is the most faithful, and cares for them when they are old." The advantages of possessing children were said to extend even beyond the grave, "for people are believed to live in the other world in the same fam-

82. Bogoras (28), pp. 37–38, 544–548, 551, 555, 600–601, 624–625.

ily groups in which they lived on earth. The old parents will therefore enjoy in the other world, after their children's death, the same respectful position as heads of their families; while during their children's lives they will receive offerings from them." [83]

Conditions were also favorable for old men among the Yakut. "If the head of the household has grown-up children, the amount of work which he does is very insignificant . . . . Inside the house he is treated with almost slavish respect . . . . The Yakuts say that a father may deprive a son of his inheritance." If an old man's power should be threatened by an especially aggressive son, he might give him a small allotment to be rid of him, and then take in his place a grandson, nephew, or even a hired man who would occupy a more subordinate position than a real son. Instances were common in which a father, an older brother, or an uncle forced the younger members of the family into marriages or put them out to work for others under very hard conditions, collecting the payments for himself. "In the *Kergen* (family) the younger is subject to the older and all are subject to the head, whether it be a father, older brother, grown-up son, or in rare cases, a mother if she is a clever and energetic widow . . . . The head can give away and squander anything he chooses. He can even give away his children as laborers to outside persons." [84]

The male economic unit in a Yakut family usually consisted of about four persons: two adult laborers, one youth, and a boy or old man incapable of doing full work. Where there were large herds the rule of the father was strengthened and maintained for a long time, until he became completely decrepit and lost the capacity to comprehend even the simplest things. His position was upheld largely by property rights within the family system. The Yakut were averse to writing wills, feeling that such an act would "bury them alive" and deprive them of the right to manage their property. Sauer commented: "I have never seen an old man contradicted or opposed, but always implicitly obeyed as a father of a family. A young man even gives his opinion with the greatest respect and caution; and even when asked, he submits his ideas to the judgment of the old." [85]

On the other hand, there was no deep-rooted feeling of respect for the old. It has been reported that when the young had the

83. Jochelson (154), pp. 70, 87–92, 107, 119.
84. Sieroshevski (272), pp. 75–76, 78.
85. Sauer (259), p. 124.

chance they dealt very badly with decrepit and "feeble-minded" parents, wresting from them any bits of property that they might still possess. The lot of defenseless old women was also very hard. One native, reproached for neglect of his aged mother, replied: "Let her cry, let her go hungry. She made me cry more than once, and she begrudged me my food. She used to beat me for trifles." [86]

Open conflict between the old and the young sometimes arose in Yakut society, especially in more recent times. "If the parents, on account of their own deficiencies, or the exceptional hard-heartedness of a son, have not been able to discipline him, then sooner or later strife arises in the family. The women are in such cases more yielding. They are physically weaker and have scarcely any rights. As members of the sib, they have no rights to land, property, or independent existence. They surrender very soon. Most frequently, they make no attempt to resist; there is no place for them outside the family." [87]

Sieroshevski further states: "I know cases . . . where sons beat their old relatives . . . . I know cases where old people did not dare sell a pound of butter, a wagonload of hay, did not dare to buy anything for themselves without begging permission from a grown son." "The Yakuts treat their old relatives, who have grown stupid, very badly. Usually they try to take from them the remains of their property, if they have any; then constantly, in measure, as they become unprotected they treat them worse and worse. Even in houses relatively self-sufficient, I found such living skeletons, wrinkled, half-naked, or even entirely naked, hiding in corners, from where they crept out only when no strangers are present, to get warm by the fire, to pick up together with children bits of food thrown away, or to quarrel with them over the licking of the dish emptied of food." [88]

In spite of all familial conflict, however, the greatest security for an aged Yakut, man or woman, was to marry and have as many sons and daughters as possible. They feared childlessness, dreading dependence in old age upon strangers or distant relatives. Of such relatives they said: "They begrudge you food, they drive you away from the fire, they begin to curse you for every trifle, they do not care for your illnesses . . . and so, hiding in the corner, you die slowly from cold, from hunger, not like a man,

86. Sieroshevski (272), pp. 65, 75–78, 94–95; *ibid.* (271), p. 522.
87. *Ibid.* (271), p. 78.
88. *Ibid.* (271), pp. 510–513.

but like cattle . . . in silence . . . . The only hope for us Yakut is children, the love of our children: You bring up a little one and he gets used to you." [89]

Family ties were strong among the Norsemen, and they had a saying: "Bare is the back of the brotherless." Williams reported that "paternal superiority was supreme in many ways." According to Norse law: "A man was bound to support his parents, children, and brothers and sisters, if they were in want and unable to work, even if such an obligation resulted in his going into debt-thraldom; and if his income exceeded a certain minimum he was required to maintain still more distant kindred." [90]

An Albanian mother of many sons was said to be sure of the lasting affection of her husband, to enjoy respect and consideration from all the family, and to exercise much authority in the household. Since her sons never permanently left the parental roof, she could look forward to their support and care in her old age, spending her last days in the midst of her grandchildren. Aged men who were heads of families held very advantageous positions, but those who had no sons might face neglect in their senescence. A married widow who had borne only daughters had no right to stay in the family house, although she might be permitted to do so, and as her daughters went to the homes of their husbands, she was left alone without relatives. In the event that she was forced out, her nearest male relative had the right to sell her again—cheaply. Therefore, her greatest guarantee of security was to bear many sons.[91]

The ancient Hebrew also found security in their old age through kinship ties and the possession and control of children. Their wise men preached: "Children's children are the crown of old men." When Naomi's daughter-in-law refused to forsake her she was exalted as a model of filial devotion; and later when she bore a man child friends gathered about the grandmother and exclaimed: "He shall be unto thee a restorer of life and a nourisher of thine old age." Aged patriarchs possessed well entrenched family prerogatives. The blessing or the curse of a dying father was of the utmost seriousness. Property rights were often not disposed of until the dying hour; and a chief Hebrew axiom was: "Honor thy father and mother both in word and deed that a blessing may come upon thee from them." Hebrew laws safeguarded

89. Sieroshevski (271), p. 516.
90. Williams (333), pp. 23, 26–27, 98–99.
91. Garnett (111), p. 28; Durham (88), p. 193.

parental rights in the following unequivocal terms: "If a man have a stubborn and rebellious son, which will not obey the voice of his mother, and that, when they have chastened him, will not hearken unto them, then shall his father and his mother lay hold on him and bring him out unto the elders of his city, and unto the gate of his place. And they shall say unto the elders of his city, 'This our son is stubborn and rebellious; he will not obey our voice, he is a glutton and a drunkard.' And all the men of his city shall stone him with stones, that he die." [92]

Another family relationship of great significance for the aged has been the commonly observed intimate association between the very young and the very old. Frequently they have been left together at home while the able-bodied have gone forth to earn the family living. These oldsters, in their wisdom and experience, have protected and instructed the little ones; while the children, in turn, have acted as the "eyes, ears, hands, and feet" of their feeble old friends. Care of the young has thus very generally provided the aged with a useful occupation and a vivid interest in life during the long dull days of senescence.

In a social sense, one might say, the aged have often returned to childhood, when, with the little ones, they have kept house for the breadwinners. In broad cultural perspective, this relationship has been almost universal; and the youth-age partnership has been of advantage to both childhood and old age. Here again we find that for the aged social participation, rather than withdrawal, has been the course of greatest reward. Old men and women, casting their lot with the children, have thus had something to live for, and by contributing service to the group, have achieved security for themselves.

The childhood-old-age relationship has been so common that illustrations could be cited in great abundance. Among the Polar Eskimo, for example, old men and women were the constant companions and teachers of the children.[93] Aged Labrador women cared for and sang over the babies to make them strong and successful hunters and industrious housewives; illegitimate children especially came under their care.[94] Grandparents were welcomed in Chippewa homes as companions and guides for the very young. Children were especially admonished to "listen to the advice of

92. Gen., chaps. 24, 27, 49; Deut. 21:18–21; Prov. 17:6; Ruth 4:13–16; Westermarck (329), I, 622.

93. Rasmussen (233), p. 158.

94. Hawkes (124), p. 91; Turner (316), p. 189.

the old." Kohl added, "Nor is there any want of warnings and lessons of every description, and it is frequently quite edifying to listen to the speeches which an old Indian will make to his children and children's children." The aged grandfather was usually the sole counselor of a boy during his puberty fast. One native reported: "Father gathered us children around him in the evening and instructed us as we sat on the soft hides. He instructed us to be kind to the poor and aged and to help those who were helpless. This made a deep impression on me, and I have always helped the old people . . . . During the winter my grandmother made lots of fish nets of nettle-stalks fiber. As winter came on grandmother had a supply of thorn apple's thorns, and she got these out and pinned up the children's coats so they would be warm, and we started off in the snowstorm and went to the sugar bush. Grandmother had charge of storing the fish and made the young girls do the work." [95]

Crow children were frequently cared for by their aged grandparents. "It was a standing custom for the first child of any young couple to be given as a present to the paternal grandparents when he became about a year old and could be weaned . . . . Other children, if enough came to be a burden, could be disposed of in the same manner." Marquis states that "the young mothers ordinarily did not carry babies, this burden being assumed by the old women . . . ." It was said that an old woman was in past times "one of the essential elements of a full-fledged Crow Indian household." [96]

The aged Omaha were found in constant association with children, admonishing them on conduct and entertaining them with games, stories, and dances. Fletcher described a typical evening scene with a grandfather singing and slapping his thighs to keep time while the children danced about. "The baby crows and jumps, and the old man sings the songs over and over again, and finally, the dancers flag and sleep comes easily to the tired children." [97]

The relationship between the aged and children in Hopi society was most intimate. Old people, even when blind and crippled, were in frequent demand as baby-watchers while the mothers worked. They sang to them in the evening, told them stories, and diligently instructed them in the Hopi way of life. Children, in

95. Densmore (73), pp. 60–61; Kohl (163), pp. 235, 276; Densmore (73), p. 122.
96. Marquis (197), pp. 37, 165–167.
97. Fletcher (102), pp. 120–121.

turn, assisted the aged in many tasks, led them about when they were blind, and often teased them with their simple pranks. When an old man treated a child for disease or accident, or performed a ritual over him to keep off evil spirits, he usually "adopted" the child and thus established a life-long relationship of reciprocal assistance and companionship.[98]

Pomo boys were instructed by old men in skillful ways of hunting, and were provided with special charms. When a boy became old enough to hunt alone, the old teacher would take him to the secret spot where he kept his hunting costumes, false deer heads, and other charms. There the elder built a fire in a little hole and burned four sacred ingredients—turtle eggs, yana, pine burr seeds, and angelica—sweated the boy over the fire, prayed over him, and imparted to him the secret skills.[99]

Among the Creek it was reported: "In every clan in each town there was one man who looked to keep his eyes on the young people in his clan, lecture them at the annual busk and at other times, and if necessary chastize them. This man would theoretically be the oldest male clansman, but in fact, probably the oldest influential member." One old native complained: "Young people are not so orderly and obedient to the old people now as they used to be in the old nation. When we tell them to do anything they seem to stop and think about it. Formerly they always went at once and did as they were told." [100]

Much attention was given to the care and instruction of children by the Aztec, and they were especially enjoined to trust and respect the old people. Young girls were usually accompanied by an aged matron who directed their behavior.[101] Old Arawak women taught girls their domestic duties and frequently relieved mothers of the care of their children, sometimes even providing milk from their own breasts.[102]

Aged Jivaro house-fathers repeated the following discourse to their sons morning after morning when they arose from sleep, in order, it was said, to instill hatred in their hearts and make them brave vendetta warriors: "The Shuara So-and-so killed my father, my grandfather, my brothers while I was a child, carried off my mother, my sisters, and burnt our house. This blood guilt is not yet washed off. It is the duty of you, my sons, to avenge

98. Field notes of author.
99. Loeb (180), p. 181.
100. Swanton (303), pp. 365–367.
101. Featherman (98), p. 93.
102. Im Thurn (151), pp. 219–223.

this crime and to kill the enemy or his sons, who are still threatening our family. If you do this, blessings and good luck will follow you in all your undertakings; you will have a long life, and be able to kill many other enemies; your plantations will be richly fruitful, your domestic animals, the swine, and the chickens will prosper and grow numerous; there will never be lack of food in your house." [103]

It was a common sight among the Lengua to see an old man sitting cross-legged and patiently making ingenious string puzzles for the entertainment of the little ones, or instructing them in the names of various objects.[104]

Among the Dahomeans it was considered proper that a girl's genitalia, from her earliest years, should be "manipulated" by some old woman. It is reported that whenever this was not done, friends would deride the mother, declaring that she had neglected her child's education.[105] Bakongo children were left with the aged while the men went forth to hunt and the women to work in the gardens.[106] Aged Bushmen attended their grandchildren and often adopted them when weaned.[107] Little Xosa children sat around the fire at night to hear tales by grandparents; and Kidd observed that it rarely ever occurred to a Xosa child to question the words of an aged person, the first axiom of the people being, "the old men know best." [108] Aged women taught girls to dance and certain old ladies were appointed to train them in the duties of wifehood.[109]

Dundas stated that in Akamba society there was "a feast at which the youths and girls performed dances and were instructed by an old man and woman in the art of criminal cunning. The extent to which it is carried on is almost inconceivable. Thus I am told that a man who has not been through the *Ndzaiko va nene* will not steal, seemingly because he is too unversed in such matters." [110]

Aged Andamanese remained in camp with the children while the able-bodied went off to hunt and collect firewood.[111] Milne re-

103. Karsten (158), p. 141.
104. Grubb (120), p. 187.
105. Burton (43), p. 319.
106. Weeks (327), p. 270; *ibid.* (324), p. 425.
107. Bleek (24), p. 34.
108. Bourhill and Drake (31), p. v; Kidd (162), p. 156.
109. Müller (211), p. 23; Kidd (161), p. 210.
110. Dundas (85), p. 523.
111. Brown (40), p. 28.

ported the tenderest relationship between Palaung grandparents and the children. "The aged and children engage in gossip, riddles, and story-telling after supper in the evenings. The boys and girls and all unmarried folks of a Palaung village are looked after, as to their conduct, by certain elderly men and women . . . . They are chosen to the office by the chief and usually hold it for life. When chosen they receive from the chief a staff of office . . . . They also preside at all the gatherings and festivals peculiar to young people, for whose behavior they are responsible." [112]

Old Bontoc Igorot women cared for their grandchildren and often took the babies to the river banks to bathe them. Little work was required of the old folk, but they frequently tended the little ones about the pueblo.[113] During the heavy work of the Iban harvest the very old stayed at home to take care of the children.[114] Kiwai Papuans took great pains to instruct their young in sexual matters. A long house was partitioned off with mats into two divisions, and the boys and girls were placed there under the care of certain old women. At night they were dressed appropriately and brought to the central part of the house, where they sat about a group of older people. Some old man who "savvied much" would tell them what they should know, his narrative being frequently interrupted by the other elders who confirmed the truth of his counsel.[115]

In Samoa it was the special responsibility of the old people to stay about the house supervising the children and giving advice, and as a disciplinary measure they sometimes threatened the children with, "May Sepo (the God) eat you." Mead reported that "feebleness hinders the old man from teaching the youth the technique of fishing, etc. . . . while he can teach the lore . . . . The old woman, on the other hand, is mistress of household crafts and to her must go the girl who is ambitious to become a skilled weaver." Girls were carefully attended and guarded by old women appointed to the task in order to guarantee their virginity until marriage. At the time of the wedding the chastity of the bride was put to the test, and if she passed the requirements successfully the old lady who had long guarded her proclaimed with song the triumph of her charge.[116]

112. Milne (205), pp. 60, 196–197.
113. Jenks (153), pp. 61, 136.
114. St. John (255), p. 49.
115. Landtman (171), pp. 353–356.
116. Mead (204), pp. 192–193; Pritchard (229), pp. 113, 138.

Very soon after an Arunta male child's birth, the paternal grandfather would go out into the bush with two or three old men and make a wooden churinga [fetish object] for him. When he began to walk his grandfather presented him with a wooden stick over which he had sung. Certain old men bore the title of "grand instructors" to the young.[117] Aged Euahlayi women were very attentive to small children. When a baby clutched at anything and then tried to give it to someone, the grandmother, or some elderly woman, would take what the baby offered, make a muffled clicking sort of noise with the tongue rolled over against the roof of the mouth, and utter a charm which was believed to inculcate generosity in the heart of the child.[118]

In New Zealand the Maori grandmother, or some other old crone, started soon after the baby's birth to make it beautiful. The infant was placed face downward on the old woman's lap and carefully massaged, a procedure which might last intermittently for weeks.[119] The grandfather would take a keen interest in a small boy's training. "Many kind lessons were employed with the children to impress upon them desirable habits and qualities. Generosity and hospitality were admired virtues; thus, when a child was given some delectable article of food, an elder might ask him for a portion thereof in order to accustom the child to be unselfish." One old sage explained that the story of Hine-poupou swimming across Cook Straits was simply a tale related to children in order to render them fearless of the water. Another native stated that when he was taught certain formulas in his youth it was customary for the old teacher to conclude: "Be careful to retain these treasured recitations of your ancestors. They and your elders prize them highly." Or a worthy old sage might remark to one whom he had taught: "O son, carefully retain the tapu lore I have imparted to you. Should any person condemn these teachings, then may the sun wither him, may the moon consign him to the pit of darkness. He is not condemning me, but Taine and Parent, from whom this sacred lore was derived." According to Best, an old man would often sit under a tree teaching a boy, and, as he talked, he might dip his fingers in a human skull filled with liquid and pass them over the lad's forehead as a symbolic, perhaps magical, demonstration of what age could give to youth.[120]

117. Spencer and Gillen (289), I, 486, 646.
118. Parker (218), p. 52.   119. Tregear (313), p. 48.
120. Best (20), I, 71, 84, 125, 376, 411.

In the light of these extensive and varied examples of the status and treatment of the old within the family it appears that kinship relationships have profoundly affected the role and status—indeed, the whole social destiny—of the aged in primitive societies. In every human group people have found themselves "placed" within the framework of some form of kinship system and have lived out their lives in a more or less patterned network of interpersonal rights and privileges, duties and obligations. A brief survey of the salient features of kinship systems as they have impinged upon the aged would seem essential, therefore, to a complete understanding of the position and behavior of the old in their more intimate personal adjustments.

Even a cursory analysis of types of family organization and kinship systems must begin with consideration of the basic question of descent and sex-status. Indeed, descent itself seems to have been the pivotal factor determining both the form of any kinship system and the status of women in society. The so-called mother-family and father-family have both rested upon the conception of blood relationship reckoned through one or the other parent. The purest types of the mother-family have existed in societies where inheritance, succession, and descent have all been matrilineal and residence matrilocal. Under such conditions the wife and mother have usually exercised considerable authority in the family circle and have not infrequently owned the dwelling and other property, while in questions of major concern deference has been paid to an uncle or brother rather than a father or husband. In the father-family, on the other hand, inheritance and succession, following descent, have generally been reckoned in the paternal line, residence has usually been patrilocal, and leading authority has been vested in the father or husband. Bilineal or bilateral descent, the third possible plan, has shown considerable variability with respect to combinations of inheritance, succession, and authority; but in the matrilineal and patrilineal systems all features have tended to follow the pattern set by the line of descent.[121]

Statistically, in these two forms of family organization, the interdependence or cohesion of all the traits of either system is quite apparent. When, for example, the above-mentioned traits of the mother family are inter-correlated, remarkably high positive coefficients of association appear (Cor. 503–522). Similar results follow the inter-correlation of the standard features of the father-

121. Sumner and Keller (299), III, 1996.

family (Cor. 523–532). Conversely, when traits of one system are correlated with corresponding traits in the other, such as matrilocal and patrilocal residence, equally high *negative* coefficients are consistently obtained (Cor. 533–567). Undoubtedly, then, the characteristic features of each system tend to occur in close association.

Now since descent, and the other factors linked with it, make such a distinct cleavage in social organization, it is important to inquire just what effect it may have had upon sex-status and the treatment of aged men and women in family situations. While it has been generally held that sex-status cannot be defined precisely or properly evaluated apart from a particular cultural context, and also that it is difficult to subject such a matter to exact cross-cultural comparison, nevertheless anthropologists have come to regard certain types of culturally patterned behavior as favorable to the status of women and others as unfavorable. Considered as conducive to high status of women have been ownership of the dwelling or other property by the wife, matripotestal family authority, and dominant influence of women in government; and, under statistical analysis, it is found that these particular traits are indeed positively inter-correlated (Cor. 568–569). Moreover, when these traits are correlated with matrilineal descent and its associated features, consistent and relatively high positive coefficients of association appear (Cor. 570–588). But when the same traits are correlated with patrilineal descent and its related characteristics, the coefficients all shift to very high negative values (Cor. 589–603).

Proceeding to an analysis of cultural traits which have generally been regarded as unfavorable to the status of women, we find a significant reversal in coefficients. For example, subjection and social inferiority of women, property rights in women, wife capture, and marriage by wife-purchase or bride-price, when inter-correlated, show consistent and positive coefficients of association (Cor. 604–607). When correlated separately with matrilineal descent and its associated traits, the same traits show almost as consistent and as relatively high negative coefficients (Cor. 608–624). Contrariwise, in correlating them with patrilineal descent and its related features, we find coefficients which are nearly all positive and usually high (Cor. 625–639).

When patripotestal family authority, wife-lending or exchange, and difficulty of divorce for women are correlated with matrilineal kinship systems, all but two of the coefficients appear as negative, most of them significantly so (Cor. 640–662). As might now be expected, however, when the same traits are correlated with patrilineal kinship systems, the results are even more marked positive coefficients (Cor. 663–679).

Such a cumulative array of consistent coefficients (177 correlations) demonstrates impressively the pivotal role of descent in both kinship systems and sex-status. Indeed, it provides very strong evidence that when descent has been reckoned exclusively in the female line, woman has regularly gained status with respect to property, civil rights, and social position. "To the sex that carries descent and what goes with it a distinct importance is accorded." Sumner and Keller further remark: "If . . . anyone wants to understand the process of societal evolution in its long perspective, he should ponder upon the reversal in adjustment represented by the transition from mother-right to father-right in family organization, for it is undoubtedly one of the most striking cases of right-about-face ever executed by mankind." [122]

But what lies back of descent? Since social forces do not run their courses independently—being always interrelated and interwoven—and since the life of society roots down in the fundamentals of maintenance, it would seem logical to seek more basic determinants in the economic sphere. Even as descent has been largely determinative in sex-status, so types of maintenance may have conditioned descent and the forms of family organization. Descent itself, as well as sex-status, appears to have represented modes of adjustment, over ages of variation and selection in the mores, to the major life conditions of both bisexuality and the necessities of maintenance. But what of the evidence?

The statistical evidence indicates that matrilineal descent and the mother-type of family organizations have tended to occur in association with the simpler forms of maintenance, such as collection, hunting, and possibly fishing; and that, on the other hand, among farmers and especially herders, the trend has been toward patrilineal descent and the associated characteristics of the father-family. When, for instance, matrilocal residence is correlated successively with collection, hunting, fishing, herding, and agriculture, the swing from positive to negative coefficients is pronounced (Cor. 680–684). The same shift in coefficients, even more strongly marked, occurs with respect to matrilineal descent, up to the point where it is correlated with agriculture, when the trend recedes toward a neutral association (Cor. 685–689). Simi-

122. *Ibid.* (299), III, 1951, 1997.

lar trends with slight exceptions appear clearly when correlations are drawn between types of maintenance and matrilineal inheritance and succession, matripotestal authority, the avunculate, and ownership of the dwelling by the wife (Cor. 690–714). Most of the coefficients thus support the conclusion that matrilineal descent and related traits of the mother-family have tended to predominate among collectors, hunters, and possibly fishers; while a shift to patrilineal descent and the father-family has tended to occur among farmers and herders, especially the latter.

Further evidence demonstrating the influence of types of maintenance on the kinship system is provided by correlations of modes of economy with patrilineal descent and related traits of the father-family. Here strong negative coefficients of association are usually found with collection, hunting, and fishing; a shift to positive coefficients appears with herding, while again the association with agriculture tends to be nearly neutral (Cor. 715–739). Little doubt can remain, then, that the manner of maintenance has been closely related to mode of descent and type of family organization and that it has had at least an indirect bearing upon sex-status. It would seem likely, therefore, that economic organization has also exercised influence upon the position and treatment of aged men and women; and the available evidence concerning this will be presented later.

At this point it must be stated that, while there is good reason for assuming that the maintenance mores have exerted an effect upon the types of family systems prevailing in primitive societies, this influence should not be over-stressed. Especially would it be misleading and unjustified to assume that maintenance factors were the sole determinants of kinship systems in general or of their particular configurations in given areas. "In their adjustments the mores move forward in rank, not in file, though that rank may not be without its irregularities." "Property, law, rights, government, classes, marriage, religion—are all born together and linked together." Forms of the family, of property, and of political organization "all march together for the sake of expediency and under the strain of consistency . . . ." [123] Considering the importance of the "total configuration" of culture, as brought out in these quotations, it would seem to be necessary to carry our correlations further, in order to discover whether other factors than types of economy may have exercised influence upon

123. *Ibid.* (299), I, 260, 502; III, 1997.

family form and kinship organization. It is possible that the dichotomy between the matrilineal and patrilineal systems, as reflected in the correlations already established, is more broadly associated with what might be termed "general cultural level." It may be, for instance, that more complex and "advanced" cultures have tended to favor or to be associated with the ascendancy of the father-family system and with accompanying limitations on the status of woman.

Statistical coefficients indeed support such a generalization. When correlations are drawn between form of family organization and sex-status, on the one hand, and certain traits generally presumed to be characteristic of "advanced" culture, on the other, the resulting coefficients are impressively consistent. If such a trait as codified laws (trait 38)—which has commonly been regarded as an "advanced" cultural adaptation—is correlated with typical features of the matrilineal family system, the resulting coefficients are all negative, the majority of them substantially so (Cor. 740–746). If, then, the existence of codified laws is correlated with patrilineal systems, all but one coefficient are appreciably positive (Cor. 747–751). Likewise, such social handicaps of women as "subjection and inferiority," "wife-purchase and bride-price," and "difficulty of divorce for women" are all positively correlated with codified laws (Cor. 752–755). It seems, therefore, that as cultures have become more advanced, judging this by the development of codified laws, there has been a tendency —not invariable to be sure—to shift from matrilineal to patrilineal family organization, with a corresponding loss in status for women.

Further support for this generalization is found when attention is turned to such traits as concentration of political power in a chief or other centralized authority, the rise of hereditary castes and classes, and the development of an organized priesthood, all of which have been generally regarded as characteristic of more advanced cultures. Here we find the same general tendency to shift from matrilineal to patrilineal types of family organization, and an accompanying loss in the status and rights of women (Cor. 756–798). Various other statistical correlations reported elsewhere substantiate the conclusion that a transition from matrilineal to patrilineal types of social organization has occurred with the development of herding, possibly agriculture, and what are generally regarded as more advanced forms of societal adaptations; and that this change has been reflected in the status and rights of women.[124]

In summary, then, the statistical data, as treated here, indicate that descent has been the basic determinant of the form of family organization—whether mother-centered or father-centered—and that the family system has, in turn, strongly affected the relative status of the sexes. Underlying these forces we find the conditioning factors of maintenance and the more generalized and complex determinants involved in total cultural development. In broad perspective, the mother-family system which has safeguarded higher rank and more rights for women, has generally tended to be associated with simpler types of maintenance such as collection, hunting, and possibly fishing. The father-family system, which has usually enhanced rank and rights of men—not infrequently at the expense of women—has shown a strong tendency to prevail among herders and probably farmers. This economically determined process, however, has been only a part—even though probably a dominant part—of the total complex of interrelated social forces involved in cultural evolution. In broader view, it is generally apparent that with advance in cultural complexity the father-family system and male sex dominance have tended to gain, usually at the expense of the female descent and status. All but a very few of the above 296 statistical correlations (Cor. 503–798) support this general conclusion. This is not to imply that there are no exceptions, or even no significant exceptions, to the rule. But the general trend is so pronounced as to leave little doubt that it must have been accompanied by important changes in the role and treatment of the aged, particularly of women.

As stated before, the aged have found their safest haven in home and the family. In cross-cultural perspective the range of potentially successful adaptation to family life and mores has been wide indeed for them—so wide that a detailed and exhaustive analysis of the manifold possibilities cannot be made here. It seems preferable, therefore, to limit the investigation to these inquiries: What opportunities have the aged had (1) to marry young mates, (2) to exercise a managerial role in the family, (3) to rely upon family care and support, and (4) to rely on the support of their sons-in-law. These questions are discussed in the order listed.

Old men have had much better opportunities to marry young mates than have aged women (Table VII, traits 135, 136); but

124. Simmons (274), pp. 495–517; Murdock (209), pp. 445–471.

the success or failure of either has been conditioned by cultural circumstances. What little chance aged women have had to marry younger spouses has occurred mainly in the mother-type of family organization; here all but one of the coefficients of association are positive (Cor. 799–805). Under the patrilineal system every coefficient is strongly negative (Cor. 806–810). Furthermore, when correlations are drawn between the marital potentialities of old women seeking young mates, on the one hand, and different types of maintenance on the other, we find strong coefficients in collecting, hunting, and fishing tribes; a negative coefficient in herding groups; and a more nearly neutral association in agricultural societies (Cor. 811–815). Aged women also appear to have possessed some advantage in acquiring young mates where they have shared important property rights, where polygyny has prevailed, where the betrothal of infants and children has been a common practice, and where aged women have been free to pursue shamanistic activities (Cor. 816–819). We find a moderately high coefficient of association in societies where centralized authority has been vested in a chief (Cor. 820); but the coefficients are lower when correlations are drawn between the marriage of aged women to young mates and the existence of codified laws and of hereditary castes and classes (Cor. 820–822). Finally, the coefficients are all negative when we correlate such marriages with plutocratic economy, marriage by wife-purchase or bride-price, difficulty of divorce for women, subjection and inferiority of women, and development of an organized priesthood (Cor. 823–827).

The conclusion may safely be ventured, therefore, that aged women have generally been at a distinct disadvantage in seeking young and vigorous husbands as co-laborers, providers, and protectors in their old age; and that this disadvantage has been greatest among herders and farmers, in patriarchal societies, and within cultures generally regarded as more advanced. Their opportunities in this regard thus appear to have followed about the same course as the general trend in the status of women. In many societies the mores have simply been set against an aged matron who would seek security by such an alliance.

Old men, however, have had far more success in marrying younger women. Still, their opportunities have tended to be much greater in patriarchal societies, and among herders (Cor. 828–837). The same has been true of societies characterized by the existence of codified laws, hereditary castes and classes, plutocracy, polygyny, betrothal of infants and children, marriage by wife-purchase or bride-price, and the recognition of women's rights (Cor. 838–844). Aged men have had fair opportunities for securing young women as wives even in some matrilineal groups as well as among hunters and fishers (Cor. 845–850, cf. 833–835). They have been at greatest disadvantage in this regard wherever the mother-family system has been combined with the wife's ownership of the dwelling (Cor. 851). Thus marriage with young mates as a form of old-age security has been generally more possible for men than for women, but especially so among herders, in patriarchal societies, and in cultures which would be generally regarded as more advanced. The same chances for aged women in this respect have been offered mainly among collectors, hunters, and fishers—less frequently among agriculturists—where the matriarchal family system has prevailed, and in less advanced societies. As in all matters of sex-status, the trends are more significant in the case of women than of men.

More important for security in old age than marriage with youthful spouses has been the possession of authority within the family circle, particularly the aged person's own family of procreation. Here old men have been at a disadvantage in matrilineal societies, where in every correlation the coefficients are extremely low or strongly negative (Cor. 852–858). The same situation is found among collecting and hunting groups, and to a lesser degree among fishers (Cor. 859–861). On the other hand, among herders and farmers, where residence has been permanent, where grain has been cultivated, and where the food supply has been more or less stable, aged men have gained in domestic authority (Cor. 862–866). Especially is this so—here we have our more significant finding—where patrilineal descent and the father-family have prevailed (Cor. 867–870). Furthermore, consistently positive coefficients are found in the case of societies where the aged father has exercised authority in the family, where political power has been concentrated in the chief or ruler, and where government by restricted council, codified laws, hereditary castes and classes, and plutocratic economy have existed (Cor. 871–878). The coefficients are no less significantly positive when correlations are drawn with marriage by wife-purchase or bride-price, the levirate, difficulty of divorce for women, subjection and inferiority of women, and property rights in women (Cor. 879–883). Finally, the same trend appears in societies with organized priesthoods, and ancestor worship, and also wherever aged men have controlled property rights (Cor. 884–886).

This impressive and virtually consistent array of coefficients provides unquestionable evidence that the simpler forms of maintenance and the matriarchal type of family organization have been unfavorable to the exercise of domestic power by aged men; but the development of more complex types of maintenance, a shifting from matrilineal to patrilineal descent with accompanying changes in related traits, and elaboration of government, laws, property rights, and religion have all been accompanied by a trend toward ever-increasing domination by old men over family affairs, and a corresponding enhancement of their security.

The evidence is quite different in the case of aged women. Like as with status of women in general, feminine domestic authority has been greatest in societies with matrilineal descent and related traits (Cor. 887–893), and among hunters and fishers; but somewhat less marked among collectors and farmers (Cor. 894–898). It is least in patriarchal societies (Cor. 899–903), where polygyny has occurred, where the levirate has existed, where property rights in women have been recognized, and where general subjection and inferiority of women have prevailed (Cor. 904–907). Correlations with other traits, such as permanency of residence, constancy of food supply, government by restricted council, castes and classes, monogamy, and organized priesthood yield coefficients which are irregular and by no means consistent (Cor. 908–920). But where women have shared in government and where aged women have customarily owned considerable property, they have also exercised important authority in the family (Cor. 921–922).

On the whole, then, it would appear that the domestic authority of aged women has followed more irregular trends than that of old men. In simpler societies and where the mother-family has prevailed, old women have wielded considerable power over family affairs; but among herders and under the patriarchal system they have lost dominance. In the case of most other cultural traits (e.g., agricultural economy), the trends are irregular. In cross-cultural perspective old women appear much less prominently as family leaders than old men. Nevertheless, they have had greater advantage in this regard than in opportunities to marry younger mates.

Family responsibility for the care and support of the old is not necessarily related to domestic dominance of the aged, and therefore must be treated separately. Here the relative status of the sexes seems to have made little difference. Even mode of descent would appear to have had no appreciable influence upon the extent of family support enjoyed by men as compared with women; although the coefficients are more consistent and slightly higher for both in patriarchal societies (Cor. 923–946). A general assessment of the coefficients indicates that in the matter of family care and support aged men and women have fared almost alike in both matrilineal and patrilineal societies; but that both have been a little better off in the latter. Varying types of economy have caused little difference also; but both sexes have tended to receive better care in agricultural societies, and where residence has been permanent, grain available, and the food supply constant (Cor. 947–962). Family care and support seem also to have improved for aged men and women alike wherever there have existed strongly centralized political authority, codified laws, hereditary castes and classes, and plutocratic economy (Cor. 963–972). No significant changes in trends appear when correlations are drawn between family care and support of aged men and women and polygyny, monogyny, marriage by wife-purchase or bride-price, difficulty of divorce for women, property rights in women, and even general subjection and inferiority of women (Cor. 973–982). Finally, positive coefficients are yielded when family support of old men or women is correlated with the existence of an organized priesthood and ancestor worship, and ownership of property by the aged (Cor. 983–988). The truth of the matter seems to be that in primitive societies aged men and women have everywhere relied on the family for care and support and that such assistance is very nearly a universal social phenomenon, irrespective of the form of the family or any other cultural variations.

One other kind of family assistance deserves special examination, namely support by sons-in-law. Here it appears that both aged parents have possessed greater claims on the service of sons-in-law in matrilineal than in patrilineal societies, and particularly where residence has been matrilocal (Cor. 989–1002). When correlations are drawn with the characteristic traits of patrilineal societies, the coefficients are nearly all negative or neutral, with the rather interesting exception of patrilineal succession, for which no ready explanation can be found (Cor. 1003–1012).

The general impression that support of the aged by their sons-in-law has been more prevalent in relatively simple societies and in matrilineal groups is supported by correlations with types of maintenance. In the case of collectors, hunters, and fishers the coefficients are consistently and substantially positive; but the correlations with herding yield strongly negative coefficients, while those with farming show negative or neutral trends (Cor. 1013–1022). In the thirty-three correlations just reviewed no significant difference appears between aged men and women. One possible reason for the fact that women have been treated as well in this regard as men is that son-in-law support has occurred more commonly in matriarchal societies. The decreasing importance of son-in-law support with advancing culture is demonstrated by the fact that when this practice is correlated with permanency of residence, possession of grain, and constant food supply, the coefficients are approximately neutral or negative (Cor. 1023–1028). Finally, additional statistical evidence emphasizes this trend when son-in-law support is correlated with the series of traits which are usually regarded as characteristic of more advanced cultures, such as centralization of authority in the chief, government by restricted council, existence of hereditary castes and classes, plutocracy, marriage by wife-purchase or bride-price, difficulty of divorce for women, subjection and inferiority of women, and the presence of an organized priesthood. (Cor. 1029–1043). Throughout these correlations again, the relative status of the sexes in general caused no difference in treatment. In broad background, therefore, support of the aged by their sons-in-law seems to have been a rather precarious form of security and safely reliable only under certain cultural conditions, such as primitive types of economy, simple general culture, and the matriarchal family system. It has declined in importance with cultural advances, and possibly also with the decline of the mother-family.

In conclusion, the caution is reiterated that the above correlations should be regarded only as evidence of very general trends. Glaring exceptions could be found in particular societies. Moreover, many of the coefficients of association are not especially strong, nor are they always consistent, a fact which may lend support to the claim that the reliance of the old upon younger members of the family group has been so nearly universal a human adjustment that it has cut across the manifold social and cultural determinants and has been little influenced by any combination of them. Furthermore, the need of the aged for family support has always been most compelling and has therefore forced sharp decisions and exceptions to general rules. The aged have suffered a steady loss in both physical and mental powers, without hope of ever regaining them. In this respect they have differed from the young, the sick, and the temporarily enfeebled. With the advance of age they have been forced to withdraw from active enterprise and to retreat within the bosom of the family. There they have taken their last stand, relying more and more upon their kinsmen to keep soul and body together.

Nevertheless, even though the aged have had to withdraw from the rigors of life and betake themselves to domestic shelter, they have not been entirely doomed to passivity. The aged have not been mere social parasites. By the exercise of their knowledge, wisdom, experience, property rights, and religious or magical powers they have often played useful roles. Enterprising oldsters have found essential household chores to perform; they have held on to their property rights, they have married off their children to their own advantage; and might even take to themselves fresh young mates. They have often been able to dominate the younger members of the family and by force of custom to call upon these relatives for care far into the extremity of life. Indeed, in broad cultural perspective, it would seem that few social expedients have been left untried by the aged in their search for security within the confines of the family; and it is just here, in the home and the circle of kinship, that the old have always found their greatest security during the closing years of life.

VIII

REACTIONS TO DEATH

THE closing scene in the drama of old age is death. By dying honorably, courageously, even heroically, men have had a final opportunity to inspire respect and admiration, and, not infrequently, especially in primitive society, actual worship among their survivors. Vanity has thus played a part even in death, for not only security, but also post-mortem prestige, has been sought by those departing the mundane sphere for the ghostly realm. The young, of course, have often had the chance to die heroically—as in warfare—but the price has been high, for the best of their life has still been before them. The aged have been able to do so too, but usually in different ways and at the end of a long life, which is not without advantage to them. It is pertinent to our study, therefore, to examine the various means which society has offered old people to achieve through death itself a last great measure of prestige.

To understand the full implications of such a situation, it is necessary to examine the attitude held toward death by primitive peoples. In many of the simpler societies death has come abruptly to a large proportion of the population. The necessities of group survival have often demanded quick and drastic elimination of seriously handicapped persons. The hardships of climate, lack of food, accidents, migrations, and the hazards of warfare and disease have forced the weaker members to drop out of the ranks and die alone. Moreover, under primitive conditions death has commonly struck children, youths, and persons in the prime of life more frequently than the very old; for few ever got to be old. Thus in many societies death has been more usually associated with youth than with age, and life has been more often snuffed out suddenly than left to flicker and fade out by degrees.

Owing in part to its early, sudden, and unexpected impact, primitive people have not frequently accepted the phenomenon of death as a natural and normal event. Even though it has been recognized as the ultimate fate of every man, it has quite generally been thought to originate from some blunder or oversight on the part of someone, and to be caused primarily by magic and sorcery.

Countless legends have grown up to explain the origin of death. The Abipone, for example, denied that death ever resulted from age alone; and, even in cases of extreme senility, they insisted that it must be caused by accident or witchcraft.[1] Among the Araucanians it was claimed that although a person should die peacefully at the age of a hundred, even then it would be proof of sorcery.[2] The Arunta denied the possibility of a natural death. "However old or decrepit a man or woman may be when this takes place, it is at once supposed that it has been brought about by the magic influence of some enemy." The dying man would often whisper into the ear of a shaman the name of the witch whose magic was killing him.[3] Dornan reported that the Bushmen of Africa denied that there could be such a thing as natural death even for the oldest.[4] And Bennett described how among the Fan a highly trusted medicine man performed a post-mortem examination on an old woman by opening her abdomen with a rusty knife and cutting away the uterus which he held up to the anxious crowd with the declaration, "Six witches!"[5] Malinowski wrote of the Trobrianders, "Natural death caused by old age is admittedly possible, but when I asked in several concrete cases, in which age was obviously the cause, why such a man died I was always told that a *bwaga'u* (sorcerer) was at the back of it." He also stated, "When I asked about M'tabaly, a very old and decrepit man, whether he was going to die soon, I was told that, if no evil spell were thrown on him, there was no reason why he should not go on living."[6]

In the legends we find many accounts of how death first occurred as an accident, or as an evil foisted upon man; and there are also very detailed explanations of how old age originated. Natives of the Banks Islands explained that once people never died; for they renewed their youth by casting off their skins like snakes and crabs. But an unhappy change occurred at last through the folly of an old woman who went to a stream to renew herself. There she stripped off her wizened old hide, threw it upon the water, and watched it float down stream and catch on a stick.

1. Dobrizhoffer (75), II, 84.
2. Frazer (106), I, 35.
3. Spencer and Gillen (289), I, 454.
4. Dornan (77), p. 144.
5. Bennett (19), p. 95.
6. Malinowski (191), p. 78; *ibid.* (190), p. 360.

Later a child, whom she had left at home, failed to recognize her and set up such a prodigious squalling that, to quiet it, she went straight back to the river, fished out the cast-off thing and put it on again. From that day on people have ceased to cast off their skins and renew their youth in eternal life.[7] The Ainu told of ancient heroes who, when they reached a hundred, would shed their hair, whiskers, teeth, and skin and make a fresh start.[8] The Yukaghir of Siberia did not believe in natural death and spoke often of an old woman who once possessed the "water of youth" which could change the most decrepit matron back into a spry young maiden; but, alas, this water was eventually lost.[9] The Trobrianders also claimed that long ago they could rejuvenate themselves by shedding their skins; but the art was finally lost through the carelessness of a certain ancestor. Then Topileta, their ruler of the underworld, mixed a medicine which could restore youth to himself and his wife and children, but he kept it from others.[10] The Semang said that there was a land beyond the setting sun where men grew old and young again, and never had to die.[11]

In Navaho myths an old woman could renew herself by passing back and forth through a door which faced to the north; and two clever old men discovered how they could, by smoking a magic pipe, periodically remove the marks of age and win for themselves new and very attractive wives.[12] The Haida also had legends of a great magician who could make the aged spry again by spitting powerful medicine over their parched skins.[13] And the ancient Hebrew in their sacred lore made references to a "Tree of Life" planted in the Garden of Eden, a story which is believed to be a modification of the earlier Gilgamesh epic of Semitic origin. The latter account related how the hero came into possession of a life-giving plant which had the miraculous power of renewing youth; but, unfortunately, he lost it through the wiles of a serpent.[14]

It would seem, then, that the fact of the naturalness of death, even for the aged, has not been generally accepted by men. Of 47 tribes on which information could be obtained, in 17 death was

7. Frazer (106), I, 70; Codrington (54), p. 265.
8. Batchelor (11), pp. 201–202.
9. Bogoras (29), pp. 55–58.
10. Malinowski (192), II, 434; *ibid.* (190), p. 361.
11. Skeat and Blagden (277), II, 292; Schebesta (262), p. 105.
12. Matthews (201), p. 845; Buxton (45), p. 302; Curtis (61), pp. 106–111.
13. Swanton (301), p. 204.
14. Gen. 2:9; Frazer (108), p. 18.

not regarded as natural; in 26 others the possibility was only partially admitted; while in only 4 did it appear that death was frankly recognized as a natural occurrence (Table VI, trait 99).

Furthermore, the conviction has been perhaps even more widespread and persistent that remedies were known, or could be devised, for checking the unwelcome onset of age, and for prolonging life if not actually rejuvenating it. Although the more glowing accounts of rejuvenation have usually been set in a golden age long past, or in a very distant future, remedies which have promised to extend life even a little have rarely been left untried; and such prescriptions have been extremely varied.

Some people have confidently sought longer life through prayer and the careful observance of rituals and divine precepts. The Chippewa believed that a guardian spirit appeared at the danger points of life and only those who carefully heeded his warnings ever attained longevity.[15] The dying Maori priest promised long life to those who clung to his teachings.[16] One aged Euahlayi insisted that she might live forever by faithfully observing the orders of a certain ancestral spirit.[17] The ancient Hebrew proclaimed "length of days" to be the reward of those who obeyed the Almighty.[18] A Palaung was taught to pray before the ancestral altar: "Thou are gone, my father, but I still respect these things that belong to thee. Give me long life and health, O my father." [19] The Ainu prayed to their dead: "O ye ancestors, now dwelling in the underworld, we offer you beer and lees, receive them and rejoice. Your grandchildren have met together especially to offer these things. Rejoice! Watch over us and keep us from sickness. Give us a long life so that we may continue to offer such gifts." [20] Part of the Iroquois prayer to the Great Spirit was: "Preserve us from all pestilential diseases. Give strength to us all that we may not fall. Preserve our old men among us . . . ." [21]

The keynote of practically every Hopi prayer and ceremony was a petition for long life; and their fondest hope was to "fall asleep" peacefully in extreme old age. Even in infancy a godmother put sacred cornmeal on a new baby's face and, waving an

15. Densmore (73), p. 90.
16. Best (20), I, 245, 389.
17. Parker (218), p. 47.
18. I Kings 3:14; Prov. 3:1.
19. Milne (205), p. 189.
20. Hitchcock (128), p. 154.
21. Morgan (207), I, 188.

ear of corn, prayed over mother and child: "May you live to old age . . . ."[22] Throughout life the sun was frequently petitioned for longevity.[23] Symbols of old age, three small sticks curved at the upper ends like canes, were placed on ceremonial sand paintings and in the shrines on mesa tops, where the people touched them, beginning with the longest and ending with the shortest, praying, "I want to be old"; or, as they reached the shortest crook, they might say, "I want to be like you, very old," referring to the crook which represented the head bowing to the ground in extreme old age and looking for the world below from which it came.[24] Sacred prayer meal was rubbed on the face and head to insure longevity; and once annually the Crier Chief called out for everybody to get up, go toward the sunrise, sacrifice prayer feathers and corn meal, and "pray to have a long life, to get to be an old man or woman."[25]

Longevity has also been very widely regarded as a just reward to those who led good moral lives and obeyed all the rules. According to the beliefs of the Berber, a man lived longer who always told the truth; indeed, anyone who lied too much might even beget bald-headed children.[26] The Dieri said that a man could escape gray hair by properly avoiding his mother-in-law.[27] The Labrador Eskimo recommended courageous conduct: "He who encounters head winds will live a long life."[28] An important admonition and promise of the ancient Hebrew was, "Honor thy father and thy mother, that thy days may be long in the land . . . ."[29]

The Hopi earnestly asserted that "whoever is not mean will live long." Good thoughts and peace of mind were stressed above all else. A dictum denied by no Hopi was that "a worried life is a short one." No one should become preoccupied with his own age or ask the age of another. An old man would vividly relate events of long ago: "But when you ask him when was all this, he says indifferently, 'A long time ago, maybe a hundred years, who knows, it is not well to count the years, it makes one old.' "[30] Peace and cooperation with one's neighbors were particularly important. A child was admonished to obey his parents, work hard, and

22. Hough (141), p. 117.
23. Parsons (220), I, 180.
24. Voth (322), pp. 101–103; Stephen (295), I, 47.
25. Parsons (219), p. 115.
26. Westermarck (330), II, 13.
27. Howitt (143), p. 296.
28. Hawkes (124), p. 135.
29. Ex. 20:12.
30. Stephen (295), pp. 11, 598, 1019.

treat everybody right. "If you do these things you will live to be
an old man yourself and pass away in sleep without pain. This is
the trail that every good Hopi follows." [31] It was constantly repeated in public ceremonies: "We must take good care of each
other and be kind to each other, and so we will have a long life." [32]
Kennard concluded: "All these ideas of unanimity of will directed
to attaining health, long life and happiness, and holding fast
to the Hopi road are made explicit in so far as they concern the
people as a whole. But they are equally true of individual lives
which are the whole writ small. Every individual has his own road
to follow, his own will which he concentrates on keeping happy,
healthy, and arriving at old age. He too must live without mental
conflict, worry or trouble, since these destroy his will and consequently lead to unhappiness, sickness, and death. A man who
thinks of the dead or of the future life instead of being concerned
with worldly activities is thereby bringing about his own
death." [33]

Another popular aid to long life has been the possession of a
fetish—a powerful object or word. Crow women would keep a
"rattle" or an "otter" which was regarded as "big medicine" and
able to preserve one until such an old age that "her body would
crack when she moved about." [34] An old Arunta might have a
churinga (fetish) brought from its storehouse and scraped, the
small particles being mixed with dust and water and taken as an
elixir.[35] An aged Yukaghir would keep a few vermin on his body
to prolong his life.[36] The Labrador Eskimo believed that those
who were "wished" a long life would reach very old age.[37] And it
was said that Hottentot who sneezed should repeat the magical
phrase, "Live to old age." [38]

More mundane remedies have also been prescribed. The Samoans drank a concoction of *'ava* root, which had been chewed up,
mixed with saliva, and left to ferment, believing that it promoted
longevity.[39] A Kwakiutl would bathe his face in urine and dip
himself in salt water.[40] The Hopi exercised by running and took

31. Simmons (275), p. 51.
32. Parsons (219), p. 38.
33. Kennard (160), p. 492.
34. Lowie (185), pp. 119, 182.
35. Spencer and Gillen (289), I, 134.
36. Jochelson (154), p. 26.
37. Hawkes (124), p. 135.
38. Spencer (290), IV, Div. I, Pt. 2A, p. xix.
39. Turner (315), p. 114.
40. Boas (27), p. 456.

early morning baths in a spring or, better still, in ice-cold water. Old men could be seen breaking the ice in basins to take their baths, or rubbing their naked bodies with snow; for they strongly affirmed that a soft life produced flabby flesh and warm water made wrinkles.[41]

To forestall or at least to delay old age, the Xosa recommended the removal of all gray hairs and frequent marriages with fresh young wives. A Xosa patriarch with the advance of age: "takes another wife or concubine and then another to keep up eternal youth, for he is never supposed to grow old so long as he can obtain a youthful bride. She by proxy imparts her freshness to his withered frame and throws her bloom over his withered brow." [42] Even the Hebrew are reported to have sought out a fair maiden to warm the blood of their favorite king when he was "old and stricken in years." [43]

From these cases it is evident that, in the first place, people have frequently denied the necessity of death as a natural event; and, in the second place, they have fervently maintained that something could be done to forestall old age or at least to prolong life. Furthermore, the conviction has been equally strong and widespread, and even more persistent throughout all stages of culture, that although death might destroy the body, no serious damage could be done to the spirit or ghost. Indeed, death might even render a service, since the spirit—the real essence of a person—would thereby be freed from the bondage of the flesh. Moreover, this ghost might return to mortal life by reincarnation; it might undergo a transmigration and become another living creature; or, much more generally, it might continue on in spirit form. These beliefs, firmly held, have been so nearly world wide that they need no special illustration.[44]

On a statistical basis, it appears that belief in the survival of ghosts has been far more common than theories of either reincarnation or transmigration. Belief in reincarnation was found to be strong in 6 tribes, moderate in 5, slight in 4, absent in 2, and unreported in 54. Belief in transmigration was even rarer (Table VI, traits 91, 105). But belief in and fear of ghosts were reported as marked in 49 tribes, moderate in 13, slight in 2, and absent in none (Table VI, traits 91, 92). Very probably all that would be

41. Field notes of author.
42. Holden (136), pp. 203–204.
43. I Kings, chap. 9.
44. See Frazer (106); Tyler (317); Spencer (291); Sumner and Keller (299).

needed for an almost unanimous affirmative report on these traits would be more complete information. It seems, therefore, that belief in ghosts, or in the future life of the spirit, has been about as universal in primitive societies as any trait could be; and it has obviously played no small part in the reactions of people to death, including death in old age.

Finally, it has been quite commonly held that the life of a spirit could be, under favorable conditions, more noble and desirable than an earthly existence which had already become burdensome at best; that both self-interest and personal dignity might well favor the exchange of an enfeebled dotage for an afterlife that promised richer rewards. Then there has been the additional expectation that as a spirit one's power over mortals would be greatly enhanced. It has been very generally believed that in its disembodied state a ghost could expect and demand greater deference and more substantial services—even sacrifices—from its mortal survivors. By the promise of rewards or the threat of revenge, ghosts could enforce their commands to the living. Such beliefs, obviously, have at least smoothed, if not removed, the sting of death; and whether regarded as a natural or supernatural event, death has thus not always been viewed as an unmitigated tragedy, especially for the aged and ailing.

Belief not only in a future life, but also its general attractiveness, has been widespread. Of 61 tribes on which information could be tabulated, the future status of the ghost was regarded as attractive, or even enviable, in 15; it was believed to be moderately desirable in 28 more; and slightly so in 17 others; while a wholly pessimistic view was reported in none. The statements of certain Christian missionaries tended to discount the attractiveness of the "heathen's heaven"; but other evidence in their own reports or the accounts of more impartial investigators usually corrected this bias (Table VI, trait 98). In fact, belief in a future life among primitive peoples has been generally so firm and matter-of-fact that it is difficult for modern man to appreciate it fully; and with the consequence that death has often been regarded as a welcome release from the fetters of age and a direct means of enhancing one's personal interests.

Opportunities for gaining prestige through death have been further augmented in some societies by the development of customs and procedures which have prescribed appropriate, respectable, and even honorific ways of dying. Not infrequently the occasion and the manner of a man's death have been regarded by both himself and his contemporaries as much more significant than the fact of death itself. Certain cultures have prescribed for the aged the precise manner of death which would guarantee them future respect and deference. Such mortuary prescriptions might even be compulsory for old men and women. In some instances the social pressure for a particular type of death has been so strong that persons who postponed it or cringed from it were regarded as queer, abnormal, or even despicable.

Nevertheless, while dignified and glorious death for the aged has been possible, and even obligatory, such instances have been exceptional and have required a favorable combination of both personal qualities and cultural circumstances. In the great majority of instances, and over a wide range of culture, death has usually been even in old age a sad and trying experience, particularly when too long delayed.

Actual neglect, or even abandonment, has been a rather common, and not necessarily disrespectful, mode of treatment of the aged. Of the 39 tribes on which definite information could be obtained, neglect or abandonment was customary in 18. (Table VII, traits 217, 218). Such treatment was well known among North American Indians, particularly nomadic groups; but it could be found also in some sedentary, agricultural tribes. Even the Hopi, who placed such a high premium on old age, made a distinction between the useful period and the "helpless stage;" and when this point was reached by any person, he or she was apt to be sorely neglected, sometimes even maltreated.

The Omaha hesitated to leave their aged alone on the prairie, fearing punishment from their god (Wakanda); but the very feeble were customarily left at a camp site provided with shelter, food, water, and a fire. It was considered even better treatment to leave them a growing cornfield or a cache of dried meat, promising to return within a month or so.[45] The Kutenai abandoned their aged who could not follow when they moved from place to place in search of game and good fishing.[46] The choice between abandonment and a voluntary death was reported to be a common procedure among the Creek.[47] And a Crow Indian stated that abandonment was an approved custom of his people: "I have heard my grandmother tell of the days when old women, too worn out and weak to travel afoot . . . had to be left to die.

45. Dorsey (78), pp. 274–275, 369.
46. Bancroft (6), I, 279.
47. Swanton (303), p. 345.

She told me that when an old woman was used up, no good any more, the people set up a lodge for her, gave her meat and wood for a fire, and then left her there to finally die. They could do nothing else." [48]

In South America the very aged among the Arawak were "stowed away in small corners of the house, neglected, and left to themselves." [49] Wiffen said of the Witoto: "Old people are not killed but they are left to die. . . . If they are unable to tend themselves, not an Indian will go out of his way to render any help or service. Cassava may be thrown to them occasionally, or it may be forgotten . . . ." [50] Because of their great fear of the ghost, the Abipone abandoned the house in which any person was believed to be dying.[51]

In northern Europe the Lapp, when moving camp, felt obliged to abandon their sick and very old. "To carry the sick or disabled persons such a long journey is impossible, and so there is no choice but that he or she, whoever it may be, perhaps one's own father or mother, must be left behind, provided with food, in some miserable hut on the mountain, with the alternative of following later or else dying entirely alone . . . . But a father or mother does not think this being left alone on the mountain is a sign of cruelty or ingratitude on the part of their children. It is a sad necessity and a fate which perhaps has befallen their parents before them." [52]

In Africa the Bushmen forsook their aged and decrepit when moving from place to place; but it was their custom to build little shelters for them, and provide them with firewood, a piece of meat, and a shell or an ostrich egg filled with water. [53] The Xosa carried their helpless aged to the bush to die, and extremely frail old women were almost entirely ignored.[54] Very old Hottentot who could be of no more service were carried to solitary huts and left with scanty provisions. When white missionaries tried to rescue them, some of them declined aid, saying: "My children have left me here to die. I am old you see, and am no longer able to serve them . . . . It is our custom. I am nearly dead; I do not want to die again." Moffat reported: "I have often reasoned with the

48. Linderman (175), pp. 82–83.
49. Roth (254), p. 702.
50. Whiffen (331), p. 170.
51. Dobrizhoffer (75), II, 265.
52. Friis (109), p. 64.
53. Ratzel (240), II, 275; Bleek (24), p. 35.
54. Kidd (161), pp. 22–23, 247, 391

natives on this cruel custom to which they would only laugh." [55]
Kolben explained that it was the fate of the rich as well as the
poor, and added: "They consider it an act of mercy and are
filled with astonishment when they hear it reprobated by Euro-
peans." [56]

The Yakut in Siberia who were without near relatives complained of the treatment they received from others. "They
begrudge you food, they drive you away from the fire, they begin
to curse you for every trifle, they do not care for your illness, and
so bedded in the corner, you die slowly from cold . . . ." [57]

In Japan it was an Ainu custom to place very old people in
little isolated huts and feed them there until they died. The huts
were burned down and "sent to heaven" for their convenience—
more especially in order that the ghosts of old women might not
return and prowl around the village.[58]

When among the Euahlayi of Australia an infirm old person
had become too feeble to accompany the group, he or she was left
behind in the charge of a younger companion who would finally
bury the corpse when death occurred.[59] The Tasmanians abandoned very old or diseased persons, depositing them in hollow
trees, or under rock ledges "to pine and die." [60]

The available data, although sketchy, would thus seem to leave
little doubt that neglect and abandonment have played a large
part in the elimination of aged and enfeebled persons. To move
on and leave behind any permanently helpless and useless person
has been the simplest and perhaps most humane method of dealing
with inescapable necessity. The method has probably been
resorted to at some time in the past history of most groups; and it
might recur at any time that conditions seemed to become sufficiently critical. On the whole, the procedure has tended to be
discarded under more favorable circumstances; but when associated with fear of the dead, and when established through wont
and custom, it has often survived long after conditions which once
required it have changed.

Neglect and abandonment of the aged has probably been
related to the custom of exposure of the dying and abandonment
of the house of death. Both of these adjustments arose in part, no

55. Moffat (206), pp. 97–98.
56. Kolben (164), I, 318–324.
57. Sieroshevski (271), p. 516.
58. Batchelor (12), pp. 48–49, 152, 222–224.
59. Howitt (143), pp. 466–467.
60. Roth (251), p. 74.

doubt, from fear of the ghost. In fact, when statistical correlations are drawn between exposure of the dying and abandonment of the aged, the coefficients of association are exceptionally
high (Cor. 1045–1046). Abandonment of the house of death
seems, however, to have been much more common than either of
these two practices (Table VII, traits 93, 94); but even here the
coefficients are positive when correlations are made with abandonment of the aged (Cor. 1047–1048). The question might be
raised, then, as to what general cultural conditions have been
associated with exposure of the dying and abandonment of houses
blighted by death. Statistical coefficients reveal that exposure of
the dying has been much more likely to occur under conditions of
shifting residence, and among collectors, hunters, and usually
herders. Where residence has been permanent, apparently among
fishers, certainly among farmers, and usually where a society has
a well-established priesthood, exposure of the dying has tended to
disappear (Cor. 1049–1055). The general trends in abandonment of the house of death are almost the same (Cor. 1056–1062).
Both practices seem to have been associated with impermanency
of residence, collecting, hunting, and possibly fishing and herding,
and also with the absence of an organized priesthood. Most likely
the coefficients would be negative if these customs were correlated
with cultural traits commonly found in advanced societies.

On the basis of recorded data we are probably justified in
asserting that actual abandonment of the aged has not been very
common, especially since the practice is sufficiently dramatic not
to have escaped the notice of investigators where it has occurred.
It is mentioned in only 38 of 71 tribes; of these it is reported as a
regular practice in 7 or 8, fairly common in 5 or 6, rare in 4 or 5,
and nonexistent in 21. Aged women have been slightly more likely
to be abandoned than old men, but the differential is very small
(Table VII, traits 217, 218). In general, we find that such treatment of the aged follows virtually the same trends as exposure of
the dying and abandonment of the house of death. Abandonment
of the aged and decrepit, men and women alike, has been more
prevalent among nomads and among collectors and hunters;
somewhat less so among fishers and herders. Wherever groups
have settled down, relied upon cultivation of the soil, and had an
established priesthood—which probably gave them other means
of coping with the feared ghosts—abandonment of the aged has
tended to disappear (Cor. 1063–1076). The custom seems also

to have declined under patriarchal social organization, but here the statistical results are not entirely clear (Cor. 1077–1090).

Suicide by the aged might result from neglect, abandonment, or any other trying circumstance; and it has sometimes been encouraged by custom and by popular belief in an attractive hereafter. Various means of suicide have found favor among different peoples. Curtis, in his account of the Crow, related how "a tottering old woman gazed long at the swirling river and, declaring that she was not afraid to die, but feared the water, stabbed herself and fell lifeless." [61] "Old men who could take care of themselves sometimes dressed in their finest clothes and went to war among their enemies, often alone, until they found an opportunity to die in combat. Sometimes these old men went out with war-parties of young men just to find a chance to get killed while fighting." [62] Even among the Hopi, where suicide was strongly discouraged, instances were known in which the aged jumped from high mesas to end their lives.[63] The Hudson Bay Eskimo when aged, might pitch themselves from cliffs or resort to strangulation.[64] The Polar Eskimo believed that it was right to take one's life "when it became heavier than death." [65] To the Norsemen, suicide appears to have been more honorable than a prolonged and pathetic old age. In Njal's Saga the hero, an old man, preferred to perish in a burning house rather than live enfeebled, dishonored, and unable to avenge the death of his son.[66] Among the Yakut: "The greatest number of suicides are old people who fear a lonely old age." [67] Chukchi custom permitted young people to take their own lives, "but for the older people, assistance [in dying] is considered more becoming than death by their own hands." [68]

On the whole, information concerning the suicide of aged people in primitive societies is rather meager; but of the 17 tribes on which data could be tabulated, the practice was reported to be frequent in 11, rare in 4, and nearly nonexistent in 2. There is no noticeable difference on the basis of sex (Table VII, traits 179,

61. Curtis (64), p. 8.
62. Linderman (175), p. 83.
63. Field notes of author.
64. Turner (316), p. 127.
65. Rasmussen (233), p. 127.
66. Elton and Powell (93), p. xxxvi.
67. Sieroshevski (272), p. 78.
68. Bogoras (28), p. 562.

180). Since suicide has almost always been possible as a last resort for harassed mortals, one would expect its occurrence to be reported more frequently, especially for the aged.

Neglect and abandonment of the aged, as well as their suicide, have probably offered to relatives and other responsible persons the comforting rationalization that they had not caused the death and might therefore escape revenge by the ghost or other spirits. Such a fear, however, has not always restrained individuals from actual assaults on the aged, sometimes for purely exploitative purposes; but this has seldom occurred among members of the in-group. The following is an example among the Yahgans, if the report can be regarded as reliable. Jimmie Button, a native in the custody of Captain Fitzroy of the Beagle, was said to have stated: "During a severe winter, when a hard frost and deep snow prevents their obtaining food as usual, and a famine is staring them in the face, extreme hunger impels them to lay violent hands on the oldest woman of the party, hold her head over a thick smoke, made by burning green wood, and pinching her throat, choke her. Then they devour every particle of her flesh . . . ." [69] Although such incidents might occur occasionally, they do not appear to have been common or to have met with much social approval. Cases of aged men or women being killed by members of their own group for cannibalistic purposes or for the sake of trophies, such as heads, are quite rare (Table VII, traits 231–234).

A much more common provocation for violent attacks on the aged has been the accusation of witchcraft, and persecution of this kind has often received strong social approval. But even this was not found to be anything like as common in primitive societies as one might expect. Violent attacks on aged men for sorcery or witchcraft were reported as customary in 8 tribes, rare in 4, and never occurring in 8; the subject was not mentioned in 51. The same treatment of aged women was stated to be frequent in 13 tribes, rare in 3, and absent in 8; nothing was said of it in 47. It should be observed that this is not a mode of conduct likely to have gone unnoticed by ethnographers if it had 'been practiced at all (Table VII, traits 215, 216).

In a sense it may be claimed that persecution for witchcraft has been a risk accompanying the practice of shamanism by the aged, for individuals might bring it upon themselves whenever they failed to produce socially approved results as reputed

69. Fitzroy (101), II, 183.

magicians and wonder workers. Witchcraft, so viewed, is shamanism gone awry. This may explain in part why old women have
been more frequently persecuted as witches than aged men; perhaps they have not been so successful in shamanism and in defend-
ing themselves against accusations of witchcraft.

A few examples of persecution of witches will illustrate the
range of treatment. Belief in sorcery was very pronounced
among the Hopi and persons accused of such a practice might be
subjected to social ostracism, pointed contempt, and cruel neglect,
even in a last illness and by nearest relatives. Anyone might
publicly challenge a suspicious old person; revile him to his face;
and even persuade others to spit upon him. It was not unusual for
a son to accuse a sick and dying father of witchcraft and refuse to
feed him or have anything more to do with him.[70]

Swanton related that among the Creek a father, at the sudden
death of his child, "went to a poor helpless old woman who was
sitting innocent, and unsuspectingly, and sunk his tomahawk
into her head without the least fear of being called to account." [71]
Among the Yahgans nearly every old man was a wizard, and
occasionally an old woman practiced the art, enjoying a certain
amount of fear and respect but at times being subjected to rude
and severe treatment.[72] The Munda were reported to have tried
witches and beat them to death.[73] In Africa, according to all
reports, the aged have suffered severely from charges of witchcraft. The Vai believed that old witches would enter their houses
at night and ride them in their sleep, and that they would even
steal babies and sacrifice them. In all cases of death: "Somebody
is usually convicted and suffers the death and disgrace of a
witch." [74] Many old Akamba women and some men were killed for
witchcraft by a form of lynching. "When such an execution was
foreseen other aged women would gather and hold the witch dance
partly for self-protection and partly to invoke the vengeance of
the spirits of the ancestors on the guilty parties . . . ." [75] An
Ashanti priest confided to Rattray that the majority of witches
were women who sucked the blood from other people, and for this
they were often killed.[76] Kolben told how the Hottentot attributed

70. Simmons (275), pp. 327, 334, 345.
71. Swanton (302), 633–634.
72. Cooper (56), p. 160.
73. Sarat (257), p. 487.
74. Ellis (92), pp. 63, 215–216.
75. Lindblom (174), p. 167; Vanden-Bergh (321), p. 216.
76. Rattray (238), p. 30.

all pain, sickness, and accidents to witchcraft, "an art which they believe is taught by their Devil, and under the imputation of which their old women suffer more than any others." [77] Kidd related that among the Xosa, when the cattle in a kraal were ill, the diviner was called. He came and concluded that an old woman was guilty. She was placed between hot stones, compelled by torture to confess, and killed by a blow on the head. Kidd concluded, "Nothing is easier than to get a witch doctor to 'smell-out' any old hag who makes herself objectionable." [78] Holden adds that if a young chief was powerful enough he might get rid of disturbing old counselors by seeing that they fell victims to the accusation of witchcraft. [79] In general it would appear that persecution for witchcraft has virtually always imposed upon the suspects severe social stigma, and often an ignominious death. Though notorious, it has certainly never been a dignified way to die; indeed it has been regarded as perhaps the least desirable death anyone could experience.

While the aged have sometimes suffered the ignominy of death for witchcraft, some societies, as stated above, have provided honorable, even though equally abrupt and violent, forms of death for the old. Not infrequently relatives and friends have regarded these acts as deeds of mercy, and it has been indicated already that the aged have sometimes welcomed and even demanded them. Although such killing of the aged has been by no means common, examples are easy to find.

The aged among the Labrador Eskimo were sometimes "quietly put to death." When an old woman became a burden on the community she was apt to be neglected until so weak that she could not keep up with the group. Then three or four male relatives would retrace their steps to recover a lost whip or a forgotten ammunition bag. "They rarely go further than where they find the helpless person, and if their tracks be followed, it will be found that the corpse has stones piled around it and is bound with thongs." Turner also related how one old woman had such a badly diseased eye that her associates "proposed to strangle her to relieve her of her misery." [80] Hawkes insisted that the aged Eskimo were treated with great respect; but did admit: "This does not prevent them, however, from putting the old folks out of

77. Spencer (290), No. 4, Div. I, Pt. 11A, p. 29.
78. Kidd (161), p. 22–23, 176–177.
79. Holden (136), p. 326.
80. Turner (316), p. 186.

the way, when life becomes a burden to them, but the act is usually done in accordance with the wish of the persons concerned and is thought to be proof of devotion." He also indicated that these people believed that there were special compensations for anyone who died a violent death; he would be transported to the highest heaven, in the vicinity of the Aurora Borealis, and there spend his time with other courageous spirits who had died in like manner, "playing football with a walrus head." [81]

The Haida believed that those who suffered a slow death of old age or disease were obliged to "go west" over a much more difficult course and overcome special barriers; and even then they would find the afterlife less satisfactory than would those who had died in full vigor.[82]

The aged among the Chippewa might be killed by their sons, "and when an old man was reluctant to die, his children would sometimes offer him the alternative of being put ashore on some island with a canoe and paddles, bow and arrows, and a bowl from which to drink, and to run the risk of starving." Old people generally elected to die according to custom, with the usual dog feast and smoking of the peace pipe. At the conclusion of songs, dances, and the chanting of prayers, a son would dispatch his aged father with a tomahawk in order that he might enter the land of spirits and find himself youthful again.[83] When the Iroquois moved camp they are said to have killed any aged or helpless person who could not follow them.[84] The Seri, whenever the exigencies of travel made it necessary, "systematically exterminated weaklings and oldsters." [85] Concerning the Pomo, Kroeber wrote: "The decrepitly aged are said to have been sometimes strangled with a stick pressed down at each end." He added, however, that where there was wealth the practice probably was rare.[86]

The Hopi probably never deliberately killed their aged through either resentment or sympathy, but the death of old people was sometimes hastened by the conduct of their relatives. Daughters-in-law could be "very mean"; sons might refuse to support their father; and when he was very feeble he might be forced to lie in vermin and filth, or be left alone in a small house apart from others. Not infrequently a blind old person was per-

81. Hawkes (124), pp. 109, 117
82. Goddard (115), p. 134.
83. Skinner (278), p. 152.
84. Morgan (207), II, 286.
85. McGee (188), p. 157.
86. Kroeber (166), p. 253.

mitted to wander off alone and was later found dead. A missionary who had lived many years in Hopiland recited instances of "abuse" of the aged. An old woman was found weeping, and when asked why she cried said, "Nobody cares for me, and my son has just thrown me out of the house." She was helped in her misery; but a few days later she sulked and said to the missionary: "The Katcinas (masked individuals personifying spirits) who whip the children also whip us old people who are friendly with Whites. It is your fault that I am still alive." One old man described how his grandmother died when he was a boy: "She lay upon a mat and at each mealtime I was sent to her with a little food which I placed in her hand. One morning she was asleep and when I poked her she did not move. Then I ran to tell my parents and they said, 'Thanks, thanks, now she sleeps.'" The old people often complained and would say: "We always looked forward to old age, but see how we suffer. It is foolish to look forward to such a time." It has also been reported that sometimes very old people, even though only half-dead, would be buried before sunset because of the fear of ghosts after dark.[87]

There are a few accounts among the Hopi of aged persons who were "helped" to die. One native described the death of an old uncle who had been of "no use to anybody" for two or three years. "He lay in the corner of my mother's house, very dirty and full of lice. My mother placed food beside him, sometimes fed him, and kept dirty rags tucked between his thighs which she changed like diapers. One afternoon in November . . . my sister Mabel came to tell me that our uncle was dying. Naquima was with him and said, 'It is good that you came. Uncle has been dying since morning, but his heart still beats and there is a little breath left in him. I have covered his face with a blanket.' I removed the cover, placed my ear close to his mouth and listened. Then I said to Naquima, 'His breath is about the length of my finger, and he is getting cold. He must be on the road to our dear ones. I hate to bury him in the dark. I will prop him up against the wall so that the breath will escape quickly. Let's not worry for he is too old and too weak to feel any pain; and it is better for him to be on his way.' As I raised him up, the last breath came out." [88]

The Araucanians considered it no crime for a son to kill his father, since it was allowable for one to "shed his own blood." [89]

87. Field notes of author.
88. Simmons (275), pp. 312–322.
89. Latcham (172), p. 356.

The aged among the Lengua were said to be well cared for; but Grubb cited cases of incurable sickness and senility in which they were suffocated or strangled. He wrote of one infirm old man: "His children have no means whatever of relieving his pain . . . so they take steps to hasten his end . . . . Taking the old man unawares, the son-in-law suddenly wrapped a blanket round his head, while the brother at the same time sat upon his chest so that he was suffocated." On another occasion the missionary rescued an old woman, much against her wishes, who was about to be killed. "She stoutly refused, maintaining that any attempt to save her life was useless, and that she wanted to die." Grubb added, however, that she did recover and lived twelve years. He further explained that when anyone was incapacitated or decrepit, and there were doubts as to whether he would live through the night, he might be buried alive before sunset in order to avoid danger from his ghost in the dark. Indeed, once the natives attempted to bury the missionary himself. "The people were convinced that I was about to die, and, according to their custom decided to bury me before sunset, and remove their village to a safe distance. About three o'clock in the afternoon the old men gathered round me, assured me solemnly that I was about to leave this world and that it was necessary forthwith to bury me . . . ." [90]

The Arawak sometimes buried their aged before they were entirely dead.[91] If a Witoto man or woman suffered from an "uncurable" disease or was rendered helpless by age he was apt to be buried alive.[92] A slow and tiresome death was not viewed with favor by the Aztec, who believed that the hereafter for such persons would be rather gloomy—a vast pathless plain where darkness and desolation reigned, "the abiding place of the ghost of those mortals who die a natural death either from disease or old age." [93]

To prevent certain calamities it used to be the regular custom of the Shilluk to put their king to death whenever he showed signs of ill health or failing strength. "One of the fatal symptoms of decay was taken to be an incapacity to satisfy the sexual passions of his wives, of whom he had very many . . . . When the ominous weakness manifested itself, the wives reported it to the chiefs, who are popularly said to have intimated to the king

90. Grubb (120), pp. 76–77; *ibid.* (119), p. 101; *ibid.* (118), pp. 45, 162.
91. Roth (254), p. 698.
92. Farabee (97), p. 143.
93. Featherman (98), p. 134.

his doom by spreading a white cloth over his face and knees as he lay slumbering in the heat of the sultry afternoon. Execution soon followed the sentence of death. A hut was specially built for the occasion; the king was led into it and lay down with his head resting on the lap of a nubile virgin; the door of the hut was then walled up; and the couple were left without food, water, or fire and to die of hunger and suffocation." [94]

Codrington wrote of the Banks Islanders: "Nothing seems more inhuman than the practice of burying sick and aged people alive, yet it is certain that when this was done there was generally a kindness intended. It is true that sometimes the relatives of the sick became tired of waiting upon them, and buried them when they thought they ought to be ready for it; but even in such cases the sick and aged acquiesced. It was common for them to beg their friends to put them out of their misery. Some years ago a man at Mota buried his brother, who was in extreme weakness from influenza; but he heaped the earth loosely over his head, and wept, and went from time to time to ask him whether he were still alive. Of late years, though old people ask for it, their friends will not consent." [95]

Among the Samoans the aged were buried alive at their own request. It was even considered a disgrace to the family of an aged chief if he were not so honored. "When an old man felt sick and infirm, and thought he was dying, he deliberately told his children and friends to get all ready and bury him. They yielded to his wishes, dug a round deep pit, wound a number of fine mats around his body, and lowered down the poor old man into his grave in a sitting posture. Live pigs were then brought, and tied, each with a separate cord, the one end of the cord to the pig, and the other end to the arm of the old man. The cords were cut in the middle, leaving the one half hanging at the arm of the old man, and the pigs were taken to be killed and baked for the burial feast; the old man, however, was supposed still to take the pigs with him to the world of spirits. The greater the chief the more numerous the pigs, and the more numerous the pigs, the better reception in their hades of heathenism . . . . His grave was filled up, and his dying groans drowned amid the weeping and wailing of the living." [96]

94. Frazer (107), pp. 266–268.
95. Codrington (54), p. 347.
96. Turner (315), pp. 335–337.

Among the Kiwai Papuans the construction and dedication of their special men's house involved the sacrifice of an old man and woman selected because of their age and position in the community. They were given leading parts in the ceremonies and, at the completion of the house, they were not slain, but they would sicken and die very soon, for "the endowment of the house with its various magical properties [had] consumed their vitality." [97]

It was a tradition among the Yakut that in ancient times, if a person became extremely decrepit, or if anyone became ill beyond hope of recovery, he generally begged his beloved children or relatives to bury him. Then the neighbors were called together, the best and fattest cattle were slaughtered, and a three-day feast was celebrated, during which time the one who was to die, dressed in his traveling clothes, sat in the foremost place and received from all who were present marks of respect and the best pieces of food. At the conclusion of the ceremonies the relatives chosen by him led him into the wood and suddenly thrust him into a hole previously prepared. Sometimes an old man and his wife were interred together; sometimes an ox or horse was buried alive with them; or a saddle horse might be tied to a tree near by and left to die of hunger.[98]

Voluntary death was deemed praiseworthy by the Chukchi on the ground that in the next world those who died thus would be given "the best dwelling places." Strangulation was a popular method of dying. "The wife of the man who is to die holds his head on her knees wrapped in a shawl, while two men pull from both sides at a rope put around his neck." After the desire to die had been proclaimed, the execution had to be performed promptly, lest the spirits, hovering about as a result of the promise, might lose their patience and take some other person. It was stoutly maintained that the Chukchi system of ethics required this, and that the old considered such a death a right to be claimed of their kinsmen. Sometimes a victim would take a lively interest in the preparations for his own death. One investigator wrote: "An old man, whose strangulation I witnessed, was as interested as anybody in the preparations for his own death. I was speaking to him on the shore about it a few days before the ceremony. He did not seem dejected, but merely remarked in English, 'Me die Monday.' He even set out the whisky barrels and prepared the

97. Landtman (171), pp. 8–10, 210
98. Sieroshevski (272), p. 100; Czaplicka (66), p. 161.

walrus thong for his execution. He was rendered insensible with drink before being dispatched." [99]

Another method employed in slaying the aged has been stabbing. This was also found among the Chukchi. "When death is inflicted by stabing the mortal stroke must be given by a man." When a man was slain·with his own knife in the hands of his son, the ordeal was believed to be much less painful. When death at the point of the spear was chosen, the face of the victim was usually covered with a piece of skin or shawl. He would take his place in the inner room close to the entrance and the executioner would stand in the outer room, holding his spear forward. The man seeking death would take the spearhead with both hands, and pointing it against his heart, give the signal for the death-stroke. In stabbing with either knife or spear, the blow was made from the front, never from behind. "When a man shows a desire to die a voluntary death, his house-mates usually show much fear, and often try to dissuade him. This is done in good earnest, because the duty of killing, and by a near relative at that, is considered something terrible. When a person has no sons and wants to die by stabbing, there is often some difficulty in having his desire executed. Nobody wants to deal the mortal blow. In two cases mentioned before, the hand of the son who had to kill his father was unsteady and the wound inflicted was not immediately mortal." One native related: "Among our people, when a father is very angry with his lazy and bad son, he says, 'I do not want to see him any more. Let me go away.' Then he asks to be killed, and charges the very son who offended him with the execution of his request. 'Let him give me the mortal blow, let him suffer from the memory of it.' " The people defended their custom as right and proper. When Hooper, hearing of an old Chukchi woman who was stabbed by her son, made some remark on the frightful nature of the act, his native companions answered: "Why should not the old woman die? Aged and feeble, weary of life, and a burden to herself and others, she no longer desired to encumber the earth, and claimed of him who owned nearest relationship the friendly stroke which should let out her scanty remnant of existence." [100]

The Lapp in their arduous wanderings often, in preference to abandonment, disposed of any decrepit person by a "blow on the head." [101] And the Norsemen in their legends of the hero Stara-

99. Sumner and Keller (299), IV, 1162–1163.
100. Borgoras (28), pp. 561–565; Sumner and Keller (299), IV, 1162.
101. Leem (173), p. 227.

kad, glorified voluntary death at the point of the sword. The hero, "worn out with extreme age . . . but loathe to lose his ancient glory through the fault of his eld, thought it would be a noble thing if he could make a voluntary end, and hasten his death by his own free-will . . . . Having so often fought nobly, he thought it would be mean to die a bloodless death, and, wishing to enhance the glory of his past life by the lustre of his end, he preferred to be slain by some man of gallant birth rather than wait the tardy shaft of nature." In order to buy an executioner, he hung all his gold about his neck and finally met a noble youth whose father he had slain in a former bout. With jibes, taunts, and rewards he belabored the young man to strike the mortal blow: "Moreover, Hather, I robbed thee of thy father . . . requite me this, I pray, and strike down the old man who longs to die; aim at my throat with the avenging steel. For my soul chooses the service of a noble smiter, and shirks to ask its doom at a coward's hand. Righteously may a man choose to forestall the ordinance of doom. What cannot be escaped it will be lawful also to anticipate . . . . Death is best when it is sought; and when the end is loved, life is wearisome. Let not the troubles of age prolong the miserable lot." So saying, he took money from his pouch and gave it to the other, eagerly handed over his sword, and, stooping his neck beneath it, counseled the young man not to do the smiter's work timidly, telling him that if he could spring between the head and the trunk before the corpse fell, he would be rendered proof against arms. Thus could an aged hero die a noble death.[102]

The cases show that violent killing of the aged, either enforced or voluntary, has been prevalent among a considerable number of peoples. But the custom has been by no means uniform throughout any extensive area of the world—unless it be in the extreme north—and it is improbable that a majority of the aged in any society have been able to attain prestige by this manner of death. Such a dramatic custom is not likely to have been overlooked or left unreported by observers, and yet killing of the aged was attested in less than one third of the tribes covered in the present survey. The practice was said to be frequent or fairly common in 11 tribes, occasional in 10 others, and nonexistent in 22; while it was not mentioned in 28 (Table VII, traits 219, 33).

We may well consider the question: Under what environmental and cultural conditions has killing of the aged been most likely

102. Elton and Powell (93), pp. 323–329.

to occur, and under what circumstances has such a death contributed prestige to the victims? Statistically, analysis reveals that the practice has been most prevalent where the climate has been severe, where residence has been impermanent, and the food supply irregular; it has also been observed not infrequently among collectors, hunters, herders, and fishers (Cor. 1091–1104). On the other hand, the custom has tended to occur less frequently among people possessing permanent residences, a constant food supply, agriculture, and grain cultivation. In all such instances the coefficients are substantially negative (Cor. 1093–1096; 1105–1108). Infrequency or absence of killing of the aged is found in association with such advanced cultural adaptations as property rights in land, establishment of a strongly centralized authority, and development of codified laws (Cor. 1109–1114). The trends were not at all clear, however, with respect to variations in the kinship system and such associated traits as descent, inheritance, succession, and authority within the family (Cor. 1115–1136). One might have expected the practice to decline quickly with the establishment of an organized priesthood and ancestor worship, and with more elaborate and ritualistic means of adjustment to death, but such a trend is not clearly portrayed (Cor. 1137–1140). It also appears that tribes who have held attractive views of a future life have tended not to kill the aged except under urgent necessity (Cor. 1141–1142). The statistical trends would suggest, therefore, that killing of the aged has resulted more often from environmental and social necessities than from either the vision of a bright hereafter or the callous indifference or vindictiveness of relatives. In other words, it might be stated with confidence that abandonment, exposure, or killing of the aged has been practiced more because of dire necessity than because of personal whims; the hardness of primitive life, not the hardness of savage hearts, has been the main reason for it.

Furthermore, the gaining of sympathy and prestige by the aged through violent death has depended largely upon a combination of necessity and willingness on the part of the old to die courageously when circumstances have required it. This is demonstrated by the fact that when sympathy for and prestige of the dying are correlated with permanency of residence and constancy of food supply, the coefficients are strongly negative (Cor. 1143–1144). But where there has existed a willingness to die, coupled with necessity, the coefficients are positive (Cor. 1145–1146). Still, the necessity of dying seems to have been in itself no sure

guarantee of popular sympathy and prestige; for only in about
half of the tribes in which the aged have been killed has any
special respect or honor been associated with the event (Table
VII, traits 219, 220, cf. 223, 224).

Thus, the opportunities for the aged to gain glory by violent
death have been relatively rare and have generally required a
certain combination of circumstances. Environmental conditions
should make it a necessity; cultural beliefs about life, death, gods,
and the hereafter should inspire the deed and cushion the blow;
established precedent should prescribe the manner of dying and
delegate the proper agents to perform the execution. An audience
and possibly a celebration should attend the ceremony. Finally,
the aged person should demonstrate sufficient force of character
to meet the hard challenge courageously; and the act should not be
put off too long. The very senile who have lost their courage or
returned to childish ways have not been able to play the proper
part.

The prestige of the aged in death has been frequently enhanced
by the significance attributed to their "last words." These final
statements have often dealt with disposition of property, choice
of successors, impartation of special knowledge or counsel, pledge
of special favors from the spirit realm, and pronouncement of
blessings—sometimes curses—upon close relatives.

Ashanti patriarchs frequently withheld decisions on property
rights until just before death.[103] The Akamba believed that while
dying anyone could place a malediction upon his own property
or upon the person of a relative. "If the head of a family feels that
he is nearing his end, he will assemble his sons and to the eldest he
will probably say, 'The goats belonging to such a hut shall be
yours.' He would then call another son and say, 'The goats of such
and such a hut shall be yours, and if any of you break these wishes
he shall surely die.' " He might curse any son or daughter who
incurred his displeasure by invoking upon them poverty, barren-
ness, and early death. A dying curse upon property was believed
to retain its harmful effects to the third and fourth generations.[104]

Honey was placed in the mouths of the dying Berber, a chapter
of the Koran was read, and messages were whispered into their
ears which they were requested to take to departed relatives.[105] A
Shilluk legend described an old man who, when dying, promised

103. Rattray (239), p. 15; Ellis (90), p. 237.
104. Hobley (130), pp. 427–429.
105. Westermarck (330), II, 434–435.

that if he were buried in the cattle kraal he would insure regular and fruitful calving of the cows.[106]

Close relatives of a dying Vedda gathered eagerly and respectfully to hear the statement of inheritance rights. The dying man might distribute locks of his hair as tokens of title, saying solemnly, "If there is any dispute after my death, show this to whoever troubles you." [107]

A Samoan chief, when about to die, would breathe on his son, saying, "Receive the succession of my office with all the wisdom necessary for its fulfillment." [108] A dying Euahlayi might promise to send rain in three days.[109] The Iban showed great dread of a dying curse and tried to dissuade a dying person from pronouncing one. An old man, "with one foot in the grave," would seek favors from his associates by pledging that he would "mention their names with respect" to certain powerful spirits in the hereafter. A person might place a brass ring on the finger of an old man who was dying and say, "Here, grandfather, take this ring, and in Hades remember that I am very poor, and send me some paddy medicine that I may get better harvests." [110]

The last statements of a dying Maori were regarded as an unbreakable testament. The aged Maori priest held back bits of wisdom and special counsel to impart to hushed and awed listeners at the very end of his life. Then he would even urge favored persons to bite some part of his body as life left him, "believing that the act had the effect of transmitting the powers of knowledge." Anything a dying Maori might fancy would be procured for him. If he chose a drink from a far distant stream, swift runners were dispatched to fetch it. The request for any favored food was promptly granted—a piece of dog, a mess of rat, a stew of earthworms, or a slice of human flesh. "Many a man (slave) has been slain to provide a last meal for persons of influence." [111]

The Yakut often waited to pronounce with their last breath decrees concerning property and personal goods.[112] A dying Chukchi was treated to dainty morsels of fat meat, and all his wishes were promptly observed. The people tried not to annoy him, and, even though he chided them, they kept silent.[113]

106. Westermann (328), p. 232.
107. Seligmann (269), p. 114.
108. Sumner and Keller (299), I, 489.
109. Parker (218), pp. 80–90.
110. Gomes (117), pp. 65–66; Roth (252), I, 139; Perham (222), p. 300.
111. Best (20), I, 245, 349; II, 52–53.
112. Sieroshevski (272), p. 79.   113. Bogoras (28), pp. 564–565.

The ancient Hebrew patriarchs appear to have waited until near death for the making of bequests, the announcement of successors, the deliverance of special charges, and the bestowal of blessings. They maintained that a father could by curses or blessings determine the fate of his children: "The blessings of the father establisheth the houses of children; but the curse of the mother rooteth out the foundations." Jacob, as a young man, worked deception to cheat his brother out of the dying blessing of an aged father, and this was regarded as a great calamity by the unfortunate Esau who begged the blind old man for even a second-rate blessing. Years later, when Jacob had finished commanding his sons, "he gathered up his feet in bed, and yielded up the ghost . . . ." Still later, King David delivered final charges to Solomon, his son, "when the days drew nigh that he should die." [114]

Among the Hopi at Walpi, on July 4, 1928, Supela, the aged Sun Priest, died. "The people were suffering from a prolonged drought, and since old Supela was soon to go through the *sipapu* to the underworld where lived the spirits who control rain and germination, he promised that he would without delay explain the situation to the gods and intercede for his people and that they might expect results immediately after his arrival there. Since his life had been duly religious and acceptable to the gods, it was the belief of both Supela and his friends that he would make the journey in four days, which is the record time for the trip, when one has no obstacles in the way of atonement or punishment to work off enroute. Supela promised this, and the people looked for its fulfillment. Four days after Supela's death the long drought was broken by a terrific rain storm accompanied by heavy thunder and lightning. Did the Hopi show astonishment? On the contrary, they were aglow with satisfaction and exchanged felicitations on the dramatic assurance of Supela's having 'gotten through' in four days, the most wonderful eulogy possible." [115]

In summary, therefore, among primitive societies death in old age has presented neither simple nor uniform problems; nor has the role of either the aged or their relatives been entirely passive. Both the circumstances of and the attitudes toward death have been extremely variable. In fact, the social significance of dying, for the aged, has ranged all the way from the height of homage to the depth of degradation. Under varying circumstances, and

114. Gen., chap. 27; 48:22; 49:33; Ecc. 3:9.
115. Lockett (179), pp. 41–42.

often entirely beyond personal control, an aged person faced with death might be neglected, abandoned, cast out, or killed by his closest of kin; or, instead, he might be protected by them and nursed along to the very moment of expiration. In the hour of death the aged might be feared or loved, despised or honored, reviled or even worshiped. And he in turn might deny death as a natural necessity, resist it as a curse, submit to it as the hand of fate, embrace it as a golden opportunity, or even demand it as a right. His dying treatment and his reaction to death have been conditioned in part by his personal characteristics, but even more so by the impersonal environmental and cultural factors of his particular social milieu.

As the records have shown, certain cultural developments have made it possible for the aged, by confronting the Great Reaper heroically, to make of death a victory. But much has depended upon the social setting and the opportunities of the occasion. For an old man or woman to die in some societies has been like making a great adventure in state; but in other groups the march toward death has been a pathetic and ignominious struggle every inch of the way. In death, as in life, man's fate has been decided by the mores of his time and place.

APPENDIX A

Cor. No.	Traits		Ratio +=/+=	Ratio −0/+=	Coef.
1	30–193	Communal sharing of food and community support of aged men	32/19	13/1	+.92
2	30–194	Communal sharing of food and community support of aged women	32/18	13/1	+.92
3	0–30	Severity of climate and communal sharing of food	24/14	47/17	+.30
4	0–193	Severity of climate and community support of aged men	24/13	47/12	+.53
5	0–194	Severity of climate and community support of aged women	24/11	47/11	+.50
6	6–30	Collection and communal sharing of food	22/11	32/15	+.49
7	8–30	Fishing and communal sharing of food	35/19	28/10	+.45
8	7–30	Hunting and communal sharing of food	47/24	23/8	+.14
9	9–30	Herding and communal sharing of food	26/8	43/23	−.54
10	10–30	Agriculture and communal sharing of food	42/15	28/17	−.44
11	6–193	Collection and community support of aged men	22/10	32/11	+.64
12	6–194	Collection and community support of aged women	22/8	32/10	+.60
13	8–193	Fishing and community support of aged men	35/14	28/7	+.54
14	8–194	Fishing and community support of aged women	35/13	28/6	+.57
15	7–193	Hunting and community support of aged men	47/18	23/7	−.07
16	7–194	Hunting and community support of aged women	47/16	23/6	−.06
17	9–193	Herding and community support of aged men	26/8	43/15	−.06
18	9–194	Herding and community support of aged women	26/8	43/14	−.02
19	10–193	Agriculture and community support of aged men	42/11	28/13	−.78
20	10–194	Agriculture and community support of aged women	42/10	28/12	−.79
21	1–193	Permanency of residence and community support of aged men	47/12	24/12	−.33
22	1–194	Permanency of residence and community support of aged women	47/11	24/11	−.33
23	12–193	Constancy of the food supply and the community support of aged men	53/18	15/7	−.08
24	12–194	Constancy of the food supply and the community support of aged women	52/15	15/7	−.17
25	11–193	Use of grain as food and the community support of aged men	37/9	29/14	−.71

Cor. No.	Traits		Ratio +=/+=	Ratio −0/+=	Coef.
26	11–194	Use of grain as food and the community support of aged women	37/8	29/13	−.66
27	29–193	Private property in land and community support of aged men	22/3	32/10	−.25
28	29–194	Private property in land and community support of aged women	22/3	32/10	−.25
29	28–193	Private property in objects other than land and community support of aged men	55/15	8/6	−.52
30	28–194	Private property in objects other than land and community support of aged women	55/14	8/6	−.55
31	25–193	Trade and community support of aged men	56/15	11/8	−.62
32	25–194	Trade and community support of aged women	56/13	11/8	−.66
33	26–193	Use of money as a means of exchange and community support of aged men	32/6	25/13	−.62
34	26–194	Use of money as a means of exchange and community support of aged women	32/5	25/9	−.50
35	24–193	Debt-relations and community support of aged men	28/8	11/6	−.20
36	24–194	Debt-relations and community support of aged women	28/7	11/6	−.26
37	23–193	Slavery and community support of aged men	23/5	35/16	−.31
38	23–194	Slavery and community support of aged women	23/4	35/15	−.38
39	0–203	Severity of climate and food taboos favorable to aged men	24/8	47/14	+.06
40	0–204	Severity of climate and food taboos favorable to aged women	24/4	47/6	−.50
41	6–203	Collection and food taboos favorable to aged men	22/8	32/12	+.45
42	6–204	Collection and food taboos favorable to aged women	22/3	32/6	−.33
43	7–203	Herding and food taboos favorable to aged men	47/15	23/8	−.14
44	7–204	Herding and food taboos favorable to aged women	47/8	23/2	+.33
45	8–203	Fishing and food taboos favorable to aged men	35/9	28/12	−.53
46	8–204	Fishing and food taboos favorable to aged women	35/3	28/5	−.53
47	9–203	Herding and food taboos favorable to aged men	26/7	43/12	−.33
48	9–204	Herding and food taboos favorable to aged women	26/3	43/5	−.25
49	10–203	Agriculture and food taboos favorable to aged men	42/12	28/10	−.25
50	10–204	Agriculture and food taboos favorable to aged women	42/4	28/5	+.23
51	12–203	Constancy of food supply and food taboos favorable to aged men	53/19	15/4	+.65

Cor. No.	Traits		Ratio += / +=	Ratio −0/+=	Coef.
52	12–204	Constancy of food supply and food taboos favorable to aged women	53/8	15/1	+.88
53	0–127	Severity of climate and property rights of aged men	24/15	47/32	−.68
54	0–128	Severity of climate and property rights of aged women	24/3	47/12	−.68
55	12–127	Constancy of the food supply and property rights of aged men	53/39	15/7	+.47
56	12–128	Constancy of the food supply and property rights of aged women	53/14	15/1	+.83
57	6–127	Collection and property rights of aged men	22/8	32/26	−.43
58	6–128	Collection and property rights of aged women	22/5	32/6	+.51
59	7–127	Hunting and property rights of aged men	47/25	23/21	−1.00*
60	7–128	Hunting and property rights of aged women	47/11	23/4	+.20
61	8–127	Fishers and property rights of aged men	35/20	28/22	−.21
62	8–128	Fishers and property rights of aged women	35/9	28/5	+.44
63	9–127	Herding and property rights of aged men	26/23	43/22	+.71
64	9–128	Herding and property rights of aged women	26/1	33/13	−.90
65	10–127	Agriculture and property rights of aged men	42/31	28/15	+.68
66	10–128	Agriculture and property rights of aged women	42/9	28/6	+.02
67	30–127	Communal sharing of food and property rights of aged men	32/18	13/11	−.42
68	30–128	Communal sharing of food and property rights of aged women	32/8	13/2	+.24
69	27–127	Communal ownership of land and property rights of aged men	46/27	9/8	−1.00*
70	27–128	Communal ownership of land and property rights of aged women	46/11	9/2	+.24
71	28–127	Property rights in objects other than land and property rights of aged men	46/43	8/3	+.91
72	28–128	Property rights in objects other than land and property rights of aged women	46/13	8/2	+.20
73	29–127	Property in land and property rights of aged men	22/20	26/20	+1.00*
74	29–128	Property in land and property rights of aged women	22/5	32/7	−.17
75	14–127	Mining and smelting of metals and property rights of aged men	21/19	39/18	+1.00*
76	14–128	Mining and smelting of metals and property rights of aged women	21/2	39/9	−.64
77	23–127	Slavery and property rights of aged men	23/19	35/22	+.64
78	23–128	Slavery and property rights of aged women	23/4	35/8	−.20
79	26–127	Money and property rights of aged men	32/29	25/10	+.84
80	26–128	Money and property rights of aged women	32/9	25/3	+.33
81	24–127	Debt-relations and property rights of aged men	28/27	11/4	+1.00*

* Coefficients with an asterisk indicate that where a zero has appeared in one corner of the correlational box, 1 has been added all round. See p. 14.

Cor. No.	Traits	Ratio +=/+=	Ratio −0/+=	Coef.
82	24–128 Debt-relations and property rights of aged women	28/6	11/3	.00
83	25–127 Trade and property rights of aged men	56/44	11/3	+.76
84	25–128 Trade and property rights of aged women	56/12	11/3	+.09
85	42–127 Matrilocal residence and property rights of aged men	20/9	32/26	−.49
86	42–128 Matrilocal residence and property rights of aged women	20/9	32/4	+.87
87	44–127 Matrilineal descent and property rights of aged men	28/18	18/16	−.45
88	44–128 Matrilineal descent and property rights of aged women	28/12	18/1	+.97
89	46–127 Matrilineal inheritance and property rights of aged men	20/15	23/19	−.12
90	46–128 Matrilineal inheritance and property rights of aged women	20/12	23/1	+.98
91	48–127 Matrilineal succession and property rights of aged men	14/12	18/15	−.11
92	48–128 Matrilineal succession and property rights of aged women	14/7	18/1	+.94
93	53–127 Ownership of dwelling by wife and property rights of aged men	12/8	31/23	−.18
94	53–128 Ownership of dwelling by wife and property rights of aged women	12/8	31/6	+.88
95	50–127 Matripotestal authority and property rights of aged men	14/9	16/14	−.65
96	50–128 Matripotestal authority and property rights of aged women	14/7	16/2	+.71
97	52–127 Avunculate and property rights of aged men	20/16	16/10	+.03
98	52–128 Avunculate and property rights of aged women	20/10	16/2	+.90
99	43–127 Patrilocal residence and property rights of aged men	57/39	10/5	+.71
100	43–128 Patrilocal residence and property rights of aged women	57/6	10/7	−.90
101	45–127 Patrilineal descent and property rights of aged men	36/24	17/10	+.85
102	45–128 Patrilineal descent and property rights of aged women	36/3	17/9	−.95
103	47–127 Patrilineal inheritance and property rights of aged men	46/31	15/6	+1.00*
104	47–128 Patrilineal inheritance and property rights of aged women	46/6	15/6	.00
105	49–127 Patrilineal succession and property rights of aged men	45/34	10/6	+.79
106	49–128 Patrilineal succession and property rights of aged women	45/5	10/6	−.76
107	51–127 Patripotestal authority and property rights of aged men	50/36	8/5	+.65
108	51–128 Patripotestal authority and property rights of aged women	50/5	8/6	−.89

Cor. No.	Traits	Ratio += / +=	Ratio −0/+=	Coef.
109	66–127 Bride price and property rights of aged men	50/39	15/8	+.66
110	66–128 Bride price and property rights of aged women	50/9	15/6	−.67
111	80–127 Property rights in women and property rights of aged men	18/15	17/10	+.71
112	80–128 Property rights in women and property rights of aged women	18/1	17/3	−.80
113	81–127 Organized priesthood and property rights of aged men	21/16	34/24	+.54
114	81–128 Organized priesthood and property rights of aged women	21/2	34/10	−.47
115	83–127 Ancestor worship and property rights of aged men	15/14	21/16	+1.00*
116	83–128 Ancestor worship and property rights of aged women	15/1	21/7	−.75
117	0–191 Severity of climate and prestige for aged men	24/20	47/41	−.32
118	0–192 Severity of climate and prestige for aged women	24/12	47/30	−.33
119	1–191 Permanency of residence and prestige for aged men	47/41	24/20	+.34
120	1–192 Permanency of residence and prestige for aged women	47/30	24/10	+.51
121	6–191 Collection and prestige for aged men	22/18	32/29	−.23
122	6–192 Collection and prestige for aged women	22/13	32/21	+.30
123	7–191 Hunting and prestige for aged men	47/38	23/22	−.07
124	7–192 Hunting and prestige for aged women	47/30	23/12	+.11
125	8–191 Fishing and prestige for aged men	35/29	28/25	+.04
126	8–192 Fishing and prestige for aged women	35/24	28/10	+.79
127	9–191 Herding and prestige for aged men	26/22	42/37	+.29*
128	9–192 Herding and prestige for aged women	26/11	43/31	−.70
129	10–191 Agriculture and prestige for aged men	42/36	28/24	+.20
130	10–192 Agriculture and prestige for aged women	42/26	28/16	+.34
131	12–191 Constancy of the food supply and prestige for aged men	53/47	15/11	+.84*
132	12–192 Constancy of the food supply and prestige for aged women	53/34	15/5	−.86
133	24–191 Debt-relations and prestige for aged men	28/26	11/9	+1.00
134	24–192 Debt-relations and prestige for aged women	28/16	11/8	+.14
135	25–191 Trade and prestige for aged men	56/49	11/8	+.47*
136	25–192 Trade and prestige for aged women	56/31	11/8	−.48*
137	26–191 Use of money and prestige for aged men	32/29	25/19	+.64*
138	26–192 Use of money and prestige for aged women	32/15	25/14	+.36
139	28–191 Private property in objects other than land and prestige for aged men	55/47	8/7	+.33*
140	28–192 Private property in objects other than land and prestige for aged women	55/29	8/5	−.16
141	29–191 Private property in land and prestige for aged men	22/20	32/27	+.38*
142	29–192 Private property in land and prestige for aged women	22/14	32/30	+.64

Cor. No.	Traits		Ratio +=/+=	Ratio −0/+=	Coef.
143	127–191	Property rights held by aged men and respect for aged men	46/41	7/5	+.90*
144	128–192	Property rights held by aged women and respect for aged women	49/44	6/4	+.93*
145	38–191	Codified laws and respect for aged men	34/30	20/14	+.72*
146	38–192	Codified laws and respect for aged women	34/22	20/10	+.57
147	33–191	Government by restricted council and respect for aged men	52/47	6/5	+.81
148	33–192	Government by restricted council and respect for aged women	52/33	6/4	+.08
149	34–191	Women in government and respect for aged men	22/20	26/24	+.25
150	34–192	Women in government and respect for aged women	22/14	26/17	+.66
151	40–191	Authority of judges and respect for aged men	44/39	10/7	+.70
152	40–192	Authority of judges and respect for aged women	44/28	10/4	+.62
153	123–191	Aged men in councils and respect for aged men	54/50	3/2	+.70*
154	123–192	Aged men in councils and respect for aged women	54/34	3/1	+.66
155	131–191	Aged men in control of secret societies and respect for aged men	12/12	7/6	+.57*
156	131–192	Aged men in control of secret societies and respect for aged women	12/7	7/5	+.47
157	42–192	Matrilocal residence and respect for aged women	20/19	32/18	+.79*
158	44–192	Matrilineal descent and respect for aged women	28/20	18/10	+.60
159	46–192	Matrilineal inheritance and respect for aged women	20/17	23/12	+.78*
160	48–192	Matrilineal succession and respect for aged women	14/13	18/8	+.72*
161	50–192	Matrilineal authority and respect for aged women	14/11	16/10	+.05
162	52–192	Avunculate and respect for aged women	20/16	16/8	+.50
163	53–192	Ownership of house and respect for aged women	12/12	31/19	+.59*
164	43–192	Patrilocal residence and respect for aged women	57/30	10/9	−.53*
165	45–192	Patrilineal descent and respect for aged women	36/19	17/14	−.57
166	47–192	Patrilineal inheritance and respect for aged women	46/25	15/12	+.02
167	49–192	Patrilineal succession and respect for aged women	45/22	10/9	−.53
168	51–192	Patrilineal authority and respect for aged women	50/28	8/7	−.42*
169	42–191	Matrilocal residence and respect for aged men	20/18	32/27	+.34*
170	44–191	Matrilineal descent and respect for aged men	28/27	18/16	+.53*

Cor. No.	Traits	Ratio +=/+=	Ratio −0/+=	Coef.
171	46–191 Matrilineal inheritance and respect for aged men	20/20	23/19	+.35*
172	48–191 Matrilineal succession and respect for aged men	14/14	18/15	+.30*
173	50–191 Matrilineal authority and respect for aged men	14/13	16/15	.00
174	52–191 Avunculate and respect for aged men	20/16	16/8	+.50
175	43–191 Patrilocal residence and respect for aged men	57/49	10/9	+.25*
176	45–191 Patrilineal descent and respect for aged men	36/31	17/17	−.05*
177	47–191 Patrilineal inheritance and respect for aged men	46/41	15/13	+.80*
178	49–191 Patrilineal succession and respect for aged men	45/40	10/9	+.63
179	51–191 Patrilineal authority and respect for aged men	50/43	8/8	+.42*
180	61–191 Polygyny and respect for aged men	52/44	17/15	+.49
181	61–192 Polygyny and respect for aged women	52/26	17/14	−.63
182	80–191 Property rights in women and respect for aged men	18/17	17/14	+.56*
183	80–192 Property rights in women and respect for aged women	18/10	17/11	+.06
184	127–191 Aged men with property rights and respect for aged men	46/41	7/5	+.90*
185	133–191 Rights of aged men in the family and respect for aged men	49/44	6/4	+.93*
186	135–191 Marriage of aged men to young mates and respect for aged men	40/34	3/2	+.89
187	6–169 Collection and collecting activities of aged men	22/3	32/0	.00
188	7–165 Hunting and hunting activities of aged men	47/15	23/2	+.45*
189	8–165 Fishing and fishing activities of aged men	35/12	28/5	+.62*
190	9–167 Herding and herding activities of aged men	26/5	43/1	+.95
191	10–163 Agriculture and farming activities of aged men	42/9	28/0	+.94*
192	6–170 Collection and collecting activities of aged women	22/3	32/1	.00
193	7–166 Hunting and hunting activities of aged women	47/4	23/1	.00
194	9–163 Herding and herding activities of aged women	26/4	43/0	+.93*
195	10–164 Agriculture and farming activities of aged women	42/13	28/0	+.97*
196	6–173 Collection and manufacturing of implements by aged men	22/5	32/6	−.40*
197	7–173 Hunting and manufacturing of implements by aged men	47/11	23/3	+.20*
198	9–173 Herding and manufacturing of implements by aged men	26/4	33/8	.00
199	10–173 Agriculture and manufacturing of implements by aged men	42/7	28/6	.00
200	6–174 Collection and manufacturing of implements by aged women	22/2	32/2	.00

Cor. No.	Traits	Ratio +=/+=	Ratio −0/+=	Coef.
201	7–174 Hunting and manufacturing of implements by aged women	43/3	23/2	.00
202	9–174 Herding and manufacturing of implements by aged women	26/2	33/3	.00
203	10–174 Agriculture and manufacture of implements by aged women	42/3	28/2	.00
204	6–171 Collection and household services of aged men	22/4	32/4	.00
205	7–171 Hunting and household services of aged men	47/8	23/3	.00
206	9–171 Herding and household services of aged men	26/4	43/7	.00
207	10–171 Agriculture and household services of aged men	42/8	28/3	.00
208	6–172 Collection and household services of aged women	22/7	32/17	.00
209	7–172 Hunting and household services of aged women	47/19	23/13	.00
210	9–172 Herding and household services of aged women	26/13	43/18	.00
211	10–172 Agriculture and household services of aged women	42/19	28/13	.00
212	0–140 Severity of climate and midwifery by aged women	24/15	47/28	+.30
213	1–140 Permanency of residence and midwifery by aged women	47/30	24/12	+.43
214	6–140 Collection and midwifery by aged women	22/14	32/18	+.22
215	7–140 Hunting and midwifery by aged women	47/30	23/12	+.43
216	9–140 Herding and midwifery by aged women	24/15	43/27	+.05
217	10–140 Agriculture and midwifery by aged women	42/27	28/15	+.28
218	0–139 Severity of climate and childbirth services by aged men	24/4	47/13	−.40
219	1–139 Permanency of residence and childbirth services by aged men	47/15	24/2	+.76
220	6–139 Collection and childbirth services by aged men	23/4	32/6	+.18
221	7–139 Hunting and childbirth services by aged men	47/14	23/3	+.75
222	9–139 Herding and childbirth services by aged men	26/4	43/12	−.76
223	10–139 Agriculture and childbirth services by aged men	42/13	28/3	+.70
224	42–139 Matrilocal residence and childbirth services by aged men	20/6	32/6	+.71
225	44–139 Matrilineal descent and childbirth services by aged men	28/7	18/5	+.78*
226	46–139 Matrilineal inheritance and childbirth services by aged men	20/6	23/6	+.75
227	48–139 Matrilineal succession and childbirth services by aged men	14/4	18/5	+.52
228	50–139 Matripotestal authority and childbirth services by aged men	14/2	16/4	+.20
229	52–139 Avunculate and childbirth services by aged men	20/6	16/3	+.71

Cor. No.	Traits		Ratio +=/+=	Ratio −0/+=	Coef.
230	43–139	Patrilocal residence and childbirth services by aged men	57/12	10/4	−.33
231	45–139	Patrilineal descent and childbirth services by aged men	36/11	17/3	−.40*
232	47–139	Patrilineal inheritance and childbirth services by aged men	46/13	15/2	+.04
233	49–139	Patrilineal succession and childbirth services by aged men	45/11	10/1	+.29
234	51–139	Patripotestal family authority and childbirth services by aged men	50/12	8/2	−.26*
235	42–140	Matrilocal residence and midwifery by aged women	20/20	32/21	+.48
236	44–140	Matrilineal descent and midwifery by aged women	28/19	18/12	+.52
237	46–140	Matrilineal inheritance and midwifery by aged women	20/12	23/15	+.23
238	48–140	Matrilineal succession and midwifery by aged women	14/19	18/10	−.05
239	50–140	Matripotestal authority and midwifery by aged women	14/10	16/8	+.42*
240	52–140	Avunculate and midwifery by aged women	20/14	16/10	−.18*
241	43–140	Patrilocal residence and midwifery by aged women	57/33	10/8	+.11
242	45–140	Patrilineal descent and midwifery by aged women	36/21	17/11	−.02
243	47–140	Patrilineal inheritance and midwifery by aged women	46/28	15/11	+.12
244	49–140	Patrilineal succession and midwifery by aged women	45/29	10/6	+.41
245	51–140	Patripotestal family authority and midwifery by aged women	50/27	8/6	−.11
246	1–31	Permanency of residence and authority of chief	47/37	24/11	+.68
247	6–31	Collection and authority of chief	22/11	32/24	−.55
248	7–31	Hunters and authority of chief	47/30	23/20	−.54
249	8–31	Fishers and authority of chief	35/24	28/13	+.10
250	9–31	Herders and authority of chief	26/21	43/28	+.32
251	10–31	Agriculture and authority of chief	42/37	28/13	+.82
252	36–31	Extent of warfare and authority of chief	55/43	13/6	+.57
253	33–31	Restricted councils and authority of chief	52/43	6/1	+.94
254	1–36	Permanency of residence and extent of warfare	47/39	24/15	+.50
255	6–36	Collection and extent of warfare	22/16	32/23	−.01
256	7–36	Hunting and extent of warfare	47/36	23/18	+.06
257	8–36	Fishing and extent of warfare	35/26	28/22	−.19
258	9–36	Herding and extent of warfare	26/22	43/32	+.35
259	10–36	Agriculture and extent of warfare	42/38	28/17	+.74
260	1–33	Permanency of residence and restricted council	47/41	24/11	+.76
261	6–33	Collection and restricted councils	22/11	32/27	−.10
262	7–33	Hunting and restricted councils	47/31	23/20	−.52

Cor. No.	Traits		Ratio += / +=	Ratio -0/ +=	Coef.
263	8–33	Fishing and restricted councils	35/22	28/22	.00
264	9–33	Herding and restricted councils	26/20	33/23	+.27
265	10–33	Agriculture and restricted councils	42/38	28/13	+.87
266	1–38	Permanency of residence and codified laws	47/26	24/7	+.58
267	6–38	Collection and extent of codified laws	22/4	32/20	−.82
268	7–38	Hunting and extent of codified laws	47/18	23/16	−.78
269	8–38	Fishing and extent of codified laws	35/13	28/18	−.47
270	9–38	Herding and extent of codified laws	26/17	33/17	+.50
271	10–38	Agriculture and extent of codified laws	42/27	28/7	+.80
272	1–40	Permanency of residence and authority of judges	47/33	24/11	+.64
273	6–40	Collection and authority of judges	22/8	32/24	+.78
274	7–40	Hunting and authority of judges	47/23	23/20	−.77
275	8–40	Fishing and authority of judges	35/19	28/19	−.11
276	9–40	Herding and authority of judges	26/19	33/24	−.09
277	10–40	Agriculture and authority of judges	42/32	28/11	+.74
278	31–40	Authority of chief and authority of judges	51/39	18/5	+.90
279	33–40	Restricted council and authority of judges	52/39	6/1	+.87
280	38–40	Extent of codified laws and authority of judges	34/30	20/6	+.96
281	31–38	Authority of chief and codified laws	51/29	18/5	+.78
282	33–38	Restricted council and codified laws	52–29	6/2	+.63
283	31–39	Authority of chief and group responsible for crimes	51/23	18/5	+.33
284	6–31	Collection and authority of chief	22/11	32/24	−.55
285	6–121	Collection and aged men as chiefs	22/17	32/22	+.65
286	7–121	Hunting and aged men as chiefs	47/26	23/17	+.12
287	8–121	Fishing and aged men as chiefs	35/29	28/18	+.60
288	9–121	Herding and aged men as chiefs	26/15	43/28	−.06
289	10–121	Agriculture and aged men as chiefs	42/35	28/18	+.53
290	1–121	Permanency of residence and aged men as chiefs	47/38	24/16	+.41
291	36–31	Prevalence of warfare and authority of chief	55/43	13/6	+.57
292	36–121	Prevalence of warfare and aged men as chiefs	55/43	13/10	+.26
293	33–121	Restricted council and aged men as chiefs	52/43	6/2	+.88
294	31–121	Authority of chief and aged men as chiefs	51/44	18/9	+.94
295	34–121	Influence of women in government and aged men as chiefs	22/17	26/20	−.08
296	35–121	Secret societies and aged men as chiefs	19/18	20/13	+.78
297	39–121	Group responsibility for crimes and aged men as chiefs	28/24	10/6	+.60
298	38–121	Codified laws and aged men as chiefs	34/25	20/15	+.38
299	40–121	Authority of judges and aged men as chiefs	44/36	10/6	+.85
300	54–121	Age-grades and aged men as chiefs	17/15	6/5	.00
301	55–121	Hereditary caste and classes and aged men as chiefs	29/23	16/13	−.06
302	42–121	Matrilocal residence and aged men as chiefs	20/15	31/25	−.54
303	43–121	Patrilocal residence and aged men as chiefs	57/43	10/9	−.02
304	44–121	Matrilineal descent and aged men as chiefs	28/25	18/13	+.32
305	45–121	Patrilineal descent and aged men as chiefs	36/27	17/15	−.39*

Cor. No.	Traits	Ratio +=/+=	Ratio −0/+=	Coef.
306	46–121 Matrilineal inheritance and aged men as chiefs	20/17	23/17	.00
307	47–121 Patrilineal inheritance and aged men as chiefs	46/35	15/13	+.15
308	48–121 Matrilineal succession and aged men as chiefs	14/12	18/12	.00
309	49–121 Patrilineal succession and aged men as chiefs	45/36	10/8	+.36
310	50–121 Matripotestal authority and aged men as chiefs	14/13	16/10	+.44
311	51–121 Patripotestal authority and aged men as chiefs	50/35	8/7	−.09
312	52–121 Avunculate and aged men as chiefs	20/19	16/17	+.69
313	53–121 Ownership of dwelling by wife and aged men as chiefs	12/9	31/26	−.07
314	28–121 Property rights and aged men as chiefs	55/43	8/5	+.48
315	127=121 Property rights of aged men and aged men as chiefs	56/35	8/4	+.74
316	1–123 Permanency of residence and aged men as councilmen	47/41	24/14	+.85
317	6–123 Collectors and aged men as councilmen	22/15	32/26	+.07
318	7–123 Hunting and aged men as councilmen	48/33	23/20	−.44*
319	8–123 Fishing and aged men as councilmen	35/26	28/22	+.65
320	9–123 Herding and aged men as councilmen	26/19	43/32	+.09
321	10–123 Agriculture and aged men as councilmen	42/35	28/18	+.77
322	12–123 Constancy of the food supply and aged men as councilmen	53/43	15/10	+.88*
323	28–123 Property rights and aged men as councilmen	55/45	8/5	+.89
324	127–123 Property rights of aged men and aged men as councilmen	46/45	7/4	+.91*
325	36–123 Extent of warfare and aged men as councilmen	55/43	13/10	+.26
326	33–123 Government by restricted council and aged men as councilmen	52/45	6/3	+.96*
327	31–123 Authority of chiefs and aged men as councilmen	51/42	18/11	+.87*
328	34–123 Influence of women in government and aged men as councilmen	22/19	26/20	+.58*
329	35–123 Secret societies and aged men as councilmen	19/17	20/15	+.54
330	39–123 Group responsibility for crimes and aged men as councilmen	28/23	10/8	+.48
331	38–123 Extent of codified laws and aged men as councilmen	34/29	20/12	+.66
332	40–123 Authority of judges and aged men as councilmen	44/39	10/5	+.90*
333	54–123 Age-grades and aged men as councilmen	17/17	6/4	+.76*
334	55–123 Hereditary caste and classes and aged men as councilmen	29/23	16/13	+.55*
335	42–123 Matrilocal residence and aged men as councilmen	20/15	32/25	+.25
336	43–123 Patrilocal residence and aged men as councilmen	57/41	10/9	+.17*
337	44–123 Matrilineal descent and aged men as councilmen	28/23	18/15	+.50*

Cor. No.	Traits		Ratio += /+=	Ratio −0/+=	Coef.
338	45–123	Patrilineal descent and aged men as councilmen	36/29	17/14	.00*
339	46–123	Matrilineal inheritance and aged men as councilmen	20/17	23/18	+.31*
340	47–123	Patrilineal inheritance and aged men as councilmen	46/36	15/13	+.13*
341	1–125	Permanency of residence and aged men as judges	47/28	24/13	+.62
342	6–125	Collection and aged men as judges	22/11	32/21	+.02
343	7–125	Hunting and aged men as judges	47/26	23/15	−.07
344	8–125	Fishing and aged men as judges	35/20	28/17	+.65*
345	9–125	Herding and aged men as judges	26/16	33/24	+.14
346	10–125	Agriculture and aged men as judges	42/25	28/15	+.54
347	12–125	Constancy of the food supply and aged men as judges	53/31	15/8	+.77
348	28–125	Property rights and aged men as judges	55/33	8/5	+.53
349	127–125	Property rights of aged men and aged men as judges	46/30	7/3	+.90
350	34–125	Influence of women in government and aged men as judges	22/12	26/17	−.17
351	36–125	Extent of warfare and aged men as judges	55/29	13/10	+.49
352	33–125	Government by restricted councils and aged men as judge	52/31	6/4	+.77
353	31–125	Authority of chiefs and aged men as judges	51/30	18/10	+.71
354	35–125	Secret societies and aged men as judges	19/12	20/15	+.42*
355	39–125	Group responsibility for crimes and aged men as judges	28/17	10/6	+.77*
356	38–125	Extent of codified laws and aged men as judges	34/24	20/9	+.45
357	55–125	Hereditary caste and classes and aged men as judges	29/16	16/9	+.56
358	54–125	Age-grades and aged men as judges	17/10	6/4	+.63*
359	40–125	Authority of judges and aged men as judges	44/31	10/4	+.88
360	42–125	Matrilocal residence and aged men as judges	20/12	32/18	−.20
361	43–125	Patrilocal residence and aged men as judges	57/31	10/7	+.16*
362	44–125	Matrilineal descent and aged men as judges	28/16	18/11	−.22*
363	45–125	Patrilineal descent and aged men as judges	36/22	17/10	.00*
364	46–125	Matrilineal inheritance and aged men as judges	20/10	23/14	+.37*
365	47–125	Patrilineal inheritance and aged men as judges	46/30	15/8	−.58
366	131–125	Aged men as officials of secret societies and as judges	12/8	7/5	+.63*
367	149–125	Aged men as priests and ceremonial leaders and as judges	35/24	0/0	+.72*
368	0–92	Severity of climate and prevalence of ghost fear	24/21	47/40	−.23*
369	1–92	Permanency of residence and prevalence of ghost fear	47/40	24/22	−.23*
370	6–92	Collection and prevalence of ghost fear	22/21	32/28	−.14
371	7–92	Hunting and prevalence of ghost fear	47/44	23/18	+.42

Cor. No.	Traits		Ratio +=/+=	Ratio −0/+=	Coef.
372	8–92	Fishing and prevalence of ghost fear	45/33	28/23	+.18
373	9–92	Herding and prevalence of ghost fear	26/21	43/39	−.30
374	10–92	Agriculture and prevalence of ghost fear	42/35	28/26	−.33*
375	42–92	Matrilocal residence and prevalence of ghost fear	20/19	32/28	−.18*
376	44–92	Matrilineal descent and prevalence of ghost fear	28/24	18/15	+.22*
377	43–92	Patrilocal residence and prevalence of ghost fear	57/49	23/20	−.12*
378	45–92	Patrilineal descent and prevalence of ghost fear	36/30	17/15	−.01*
379	81–92	Organized priesthood and prevalence of ghost fear	21/18	34/31	+.08*
380	0–82	Severity of climate and the practice of shamanism	24/24	47/46	−.03*
381	1–82	Permanency of residence and the practice of shamanism	47/46	24/24	−.01*
382	6–82	Collection and the practice of shamanism	22/22	32/32	.00
383	7–82	Hunting and the practice of shamanism	47/46	23/23	−.01*
384	8–82	Fishing and the practice of shamanism	35/35	28/27	.00
385	9–82	Herding and the practice of shamanism	26/26	43/42	.00
386	10–82	Agriculture and the practice of shamanism	42/41	28/28	.00
387	42–82	Matrilocal residence and the practice of shamanism	20/19	32/3:	.00
388	44–82	Matrilineal descent and the practice of shamanism	28/27	18/18	.00
389	43–82	Patrilocal residence and the practice of shamanism	57/56	10/10	.00
390	45–82	Patrilineal descent and the practice of shamanism	36/35	17/17	.00
391	81–82	Organized priesthood and the practice of shamanism	21/20	34/34	.00
392	0–81	Severity of climate and organized priesthood	24/4	47/17	−.45
393	1–81	Permanency of residence and organized priesthood	47/16	24/4	+.39
394	6–81	Collection and organized priesthood	22/1	32/11	−.87
395	7–81	Hunting and organized priesthood	47/11	23/19	−.26
396	8–81	Fishing and organized priesthood	35/5	28/11	−.50
397	9–81	Herding and organized priesthood	26/11	33/9	+.48
398	10–81	Agriculture and organized priesthood	42/17	28/3	+.63
399	11–81	Use of grain and organized priesthood	37/15	29/3	+.71
400	12–81	Constancy of the food supply and organized priesthood	53/19	15/1	+.75
401	31–81	Authority of chief and organized priesthood	51/20	18/1	+.82
402	33–81	Government by restricted council and organized priesthood	52/20	6/0	+.67*
403	35–81	Secret societies and organized priesthood	19/5	20/3	+.37
404	36–81	Extent of warfare and organized priesthood	55/16	12/4	+.18
405	38–81	Codified laws and organized priesthood	34/16	20/1	+.86
406	42–81	Matrilocal residence and organized priesthood	20/1	32/12	−.77
407	44–81	Matrilineal descent and organized priesthood	28/5	18/9	−.61

Cor. No.	Traits		Ratio +=/+=	Ratio −0/+=	Coef.
408	43–81	Patrilocal residence and organized priesthood	21/19	32/24	+.69
409	45–81	Patrilineal descent and organized priesthood	36/15	17/4	+.46
410	55–81	Hereditary caste and classes and organized priesthood	29/12	16/1	+.86
411	56–81	Plutocracy and organized priesthood	43/16	11/1	+.73
412	83–81	Ancestor worship and organized priesthood	15/9	21/4	+.74
413	84–81	Elaboration of ceremonial rites and organized priesthood	44/17	14/1	+.81
414	0–84	Severity of climate and elaboration of ceremony and ritual	24/15	47/29	+.13
415	1–84	Permanency of residence and elaboration of ceremony and ritual	47/32	24/13	+.30
416	6–84	Collection and elaboration of ceremony and ritual	22/10	32/24	−.54
417	7–84	Hunting and elaboration of ceremony and ritual	47/29	23/14	−.09
418	8–84	Fishing and elaboration of ceremony and ritual	35/22	28/17	+.16
419	9–84	Herding and elaboration of ceremony and ritual	26/16	33/26	+.39
420	10–84	Agriculture and elaboration of ceremony and ritual	42/28	28/15	+.14
421	11–84	Use of grain and elaboration of ceremony and ritual	37/25	29/14	+.71
422	12–84	Constancy of food supply and elaboration of ceremony and ritual	53/35	15/7	+.62
423	31–84	Authority of chief and elaboration of ceremony and ritual	51/33	18/9	+.47
424	33–84	Government by restricted council and elaboration of ceremony and ritual	52/36	6/2	+.80
425	35–84	Secret societies and elaboration of ceremony and ritual	19/13	20/13	+.56
426	38–84	Codified laws and elaboration of ceremony and ritual	34/24	20/7	+.84
427	42–84	Matrilocal residence and elaboration of ceremony and ritual	20/13	32/20	+.32
428	44–84	Matrilineal descent and elaboration of ceremony and ritual	28/17	18/12	−.17
429	43–64	Patrilocal residence and elaboration of ceremony and ritual	57/30	10/7	−.12
430	45–84	Patrilineal descent and elaboration of ceremony and ritual	36/24	17/12	−.50
431	55–84	Hereditary caste and classes and elaboration of ceremony and ritual	29/17	16/9	+.48
432	56–84	Plutocracy and elaboration of ceremony and ritual	43/32	11/5	+.78
433	81–84	Organized priesthood and elaboration of ceremony and ritual	21/17	34/20	+.80
434	83–84	Ancestor worship and elaboration of ceremony and ritual	15/13	21/14	+.70

Cor. No.	Traits		Ratio +=/+=	Ratio −0/+=	Coef.
435	0–177	Severity of climate and aged men as dispensers of information	24/17	47/37	
436	0–178	Severity of climate and aged women as dispensers of information	24/8	47/19	
437	1–177	Permanency of residence and aged men as dispensers of information	52/37	24/16	
438	1–178	Permanency of residence and aged women as dispensers of information	47/19	24/6	
439	6–177	Collection and aged men as dispensers of information	22/16	32/26	
440	6–178	Collection and aged women as dispensers of information	22/6	32/15	
441	7–177	Hunting and aged men as dispensers of information	47/36	23/19	
442	7–178	Hunting and aged women as dispensers of information	47/20	21/8	
443	8–177	Fishing and aged men as dispensers of information	26/18	28/20	
444	8–178	Fishing and aged women as dispensers of information	35/28	28/7	
445	9–177	Herding and aged men as dispensers of information	26/18	43/34	
446	9–178	Herding and aged women as dispensers of information	26/8	43/19	
447	10–177	Agriculture and aged men as dispensers of information	42/35	28/19	
448	10–178	Agriculture and aged women as dispensers of information	42/17	28/10	
449	44–177	Matrilineal descent and aged men as dispensers of information	28/22	18/15	
450	44–178	Matrilineal descent and aged women as dispensers of information	28/10	18/7	
451	45–177	Patrilineal descent and aged men as dispensers of information	36/27	17/15	
452	45–178	Patrilineal descent and aged women as dispensers of information	36/12	17/7	
453	0–153	Severity of climate and aged men as shamans	24/19	47/40	
454	0–154	Severity of climate and aged women as shamans	24/15	47/30	
455	1–153	Permanency of residence and aged men as shamans	47/37	24/19	
456	1–154	Permanency of residence and aged women as shamans	47/27	24/17	
457	6–153	Collection and aged men as shamans	22/20	32/28	
458	6–154	Collection and aged women as shamans	22/12	32/20	
459	7–153	Hunting and aged men as shamans	47/41	23/18	
460	7–154	Hunting and aged women as shamans	47/29	23/15	
461	8–153	Fishing and aged men as shamans	35/29	28/22	
462	8–154	Fishing and aged women as shamans	35/23	28/13	
463	9–153	Herding and aged men as shamans	26/17	43/37	
464	9–154	Herding and aged women as shamans	26/16	43/27	

Cor. No.	Traits	Ratio +=/+=	Ratio −0/+=	Coef.
465	10–153 Agriculture and aged men as shamans	42/25	28/25	
466	10–154 Agriculture and aged women as shamans	42/27	28/17	
467	44–153 Matrilineal descent and aged men as shamans	28/22	18/15	
468	44–154 Matrilineal descent and aged women as shamans	28/19	18/10	
469	45–153 Patrilineal descent and aged men as shamans	36/29	17/12	
470	45–154 Patrilineal descent and aged women as shamans	36/18	17/13	
471	82–153 Shamanism and aged men as shamans	70/59	1/0	
472	82–154 Shamanism and aged women as shamans	70/45	1/0	
473	81–153 Organized priesthood and aged men as shamans	21/16	34/30	
474	81–154 Organized priesthood and aged women as shamans	21/14	34/21	
475	84–153 Elaboration of ceremony and aged men as shamans	44/37	14/12	
476	84–154 Elaboration of ceremony and aged women as shamans	44/28	14/11	
477	0–149 Severity of climate and aged men as priests	24/10	47/25	
478	0–150 Severity of climate and aged women as priests	24/3	47/8	
479	1–149 Permanency of residence and aged men as priests	47/29	24/10	
480	1–150 Permanency of residence and aged women as priests	47/9	24/2	
481	6–149 Collection and aged men as priests	22/6	32/18	
482	6–150 Collection and aged women as priests	22/0	32/7	
483	7–149 Hunting and aged men as priests	47/20	23/14	
484	7–150 Hunting and aged women as priests	47/5	23/6	
485	8–149 Fishing and aged men as priests	35/12	28/11	
486	8–150 Fishing and aged women as priests	35/6	28/4	
487	9–149 Herding and aged men as priests	26/14	33/20	
488	9–150 Herding and aged women as priests	26/3	33/8	
489	10–149 Agriculture and aged men as priests	42/26	28/8	
490	10–150 Agriculture and aged women as priests	42/10	28/1	
491	44–149 Matrilineal descent and aged men as priests	28/11	18/9	
492	44–150 Matrilineal descent and aged women as priests	28/3	18/5	
493	45–149 Patrilineal descent and aged men as priests	36/20	17/7	
494	45–150 Patrilineal descent and aged women as priests	36/7	17/3	
495	82–149 Shamanism and aged men as priests	70/32	1/1	
496	82–150 Shamanism and aged women as priests	70/11	1/0	
497	81–149 Organized priesthood and aged men as priests	21/17	34/14	
498	81–150 Organized priesthood and aged women as priests	21/6	34/4	
499	84–149 Elaboration of ceremony and aged men as priests	44/24	14/6	

Cor. No.	Traits		Ratio +=/+=	Ratio −0/+=	Coef.
500	84–150	Elaboration of ceremony and aged women as priests	44/9	14/1	
501	83–149	Ancestor worship and aged men as priests	15/10	21/10	
502	83–150	Ancestor worship and aged women as priests	15/4	21/4	
503	42–44	Matrilocal residence and matrilineal descent	20/10	32/6	+.88
504	42–46	Matrilocal residence and matrilineal inheritance	20/8	32/11	+.75
505	42–48	Matrilocal residence and matrilineal succession	20/6	32/8	+.83
506	42–50	Matrilocal residence and matripotestal family authority	20/5	32/7	+.73
507	42–53	Matrilocal residence and ownership of dwelling by wife	20/9	32/2	+.90
508	44–46	Matrilineal descent and matrilineal inheritance	28/15	18/3	+.88
509	44–48	Matrilineal descent and matrilineal succession	28/13	18/1	+.99
510	44–50	Matrilineal descent and matripotestal family authority	28/10	18/2	+.93
511	44–52	Matrilineal descent and avunculate	28/16	18/2	+.93
512	44–53	Matrilineal descent and ownership of dwelling by wife	28/11	18/0	+.81*
513	46–48	Matrilineal inheritance and matrilineal succession	20/11	23/1	+.95
514	46–50	Matrilineal inheritance and matripotestal family authority	20/10	23/2	+.89
515	46–52	Matrilineal inheritance and avunculate	20/12	23/4	+.82
516	46–53	Matrilineal inheritance and ownership of dwelling by wife	20/8	23/2	+.87
517	48–50	Matrilineal succession and matripotestal family authority	14/9	18/0	+.97*
518	48–52	Matrilineal succession and avunculate	14/11	18/0	+.97*
519	48–53	Matrilineal succession and ownership of dwelling by wife	14/7	18/0	+.87*
520	50–52	Matripotestal family authority and avunculate	14/13	16/1	+.97*
521	50–53	Matripotestal family authority and ownership of dwelling by wife	14/5	16/1	+.79
522	52–53	Avunculate and ownership of dwelling by wife	20/8	16/0	+.80*
523	43–45	Patrilocal residence and patrilineal descent	57/33	10/7	+.89*
524	43–47	Patrilocal residence and patrilineal inheritance	57/40	10/3	+.74
25	43–49	Patrilocal residence and patrilineal succession	57/38	10/4	+.60
526	43–51	Patrilocal residence and patripotestal family authority	57/45	10/3	+.87
527	45–47	Patrilineal descent and patrilineal inheritance	36/32	17/5	+.90
528	45–49	Patrilineal descent and patrilineal succession	36/34	17/4	+.97

Cor. No.	Traits		Ratio +=/+=	Ratio −0/+=	Coef.
529	45–51	Patrilineal descent and patripotestal family authority	36/32	17/6	+.96
530	47–49	Patrilineal inheritance and patrilineal succession	46/38	15/4	+.97
531	47–51	Patrilineal inheritance and patripotestal family authority	46/39	15/5	+.96
532	49–51	Patrilineal succession and patripotestal family authority	45/37	10/3	+.97
533	42–43	Matrilocal residence and patrilocal residence	20/8	32/19	−.86*
534	42–45	Matrilocal residence and patrilineal descent	20/4	32/22	−.65
535	42–47	Matrilocal residence and patrilineal inheritance	20/9	32/23	−.26
536	42–49	Matrilocal residence and patrilineal succession	20/8	32/24	−.33
537	42–51	Matrilocal residence and patripotestal family authority	20/10	32/26	−.44
538	44–43	Matrilineal descent and patrilocal residence	28/21	18/17	−.70
539	44–45	Matrilineal descent patrilineal descent	28/7	18/18	−.95
540	44–47	Matrilineal descent and patrilineal inheritance	28/13	18/16	−.74
541	44–49	Matrilineal descent and patrilineal succession	28/12	18/18	−.84
542	44–51	Matrilineal descent and patripotestal family authority	28/13	18/18	−.83
543	46–43	Matrilineal inheritance and patrilocal residence	20/12	23/22	−.85
544	46–45	Matrilineal inheritance and patrilineal descent	20/4	23/20	−.97
545	46–47	Matrilineal inheritance and patrilineal inheritance	20/8	22/21	−.85
546	46–49	Matrilineal inheritance and patrilineal succession	20/8	23/21	−.89
547	46–51	Matrilineal inheritance and patripotestal family authority	20/8	23/22	−.91
548	48–43	Matrilineal succession and patrilocal residence	14/10	18/17	−.74
549	48–45	Matrilineal succession and patrilineal descent	14/2	18/17	−.98
550	48–47	Matrilineal succession and patrilineal inheritance	14/6	18/16	−.83
551	48–49	Matrilineal succession and patrilineal succession	14/4	18/18	−.94*
552	48–51	Matrilineal succession and patripotestal family authority	14/6	18/18	−.91*
553	50–43	Matripotestal family authority and patrilocal residence	14/8	16/15	−.83
554	50–45	Matripotestal family authority and patrilineal descent	14/2	16/14	−.97

Cor. No.	Traits		Ratio $+=/+=$	Ratio $-0/+=$	Coef.
555	50–47	Matripotestal family authority and patrilineal inheritance	14/6	16/13	−.89
556	50–49	Matripotestal family authority and patrilineal succession	14/6	16/14	−.84
557	50–51	Matripotestal family authority and patripotestal family authority	14/5	16/16	−.92*
558	52–43	Avunculate and patrilocal residence	20/12	16/14	−.59
559	52–45	Avunculate and patrilineal descent	20/6	16/13	−.72*
560	52–47	Avunculate and patrilineal inheritance	20/10	16/11	−.53
561	52–49	Avunculate and patrilineal succession	20/10	16/12	−.79
562	52–51	Avunculate and patripotestal family authority	20/10	16/12	−.86
563	53–43	Ownership of dwelling by wife and patrilocal residence	12/5	31/28	−.83
564	53–45	Ownership of dwelling by wife and patrilineal descent	12/2	31/19	−.83
565	53–47	Ownership of dwelling by wife and patrilineal inheritance	12/6	31/21	−.37
566	53–49	Ownership of dwelling by wife and patrilineal succession	12/4	31/22	−.63
567	53–51	Ownership of dwelling by wife and patripotestal family authority	12/5	31/24	−.65
568	50–34	Matripotestal family authority and influence of women in government	14/6	16/6	+.14
569	53–34	Ownership of dwelling by wife and influence of women in government	12/5	31/8	+.33
570	42–50	Matrilocal residence and matripotestal family authority	20/5	32/7	+.73
571	44–50	Matrilineal descent and matripotestal family authority	28/10	18/2	+.93
572	46–50	Matrilineal inheritance and matripotestal family authority	20/10	23/2	+.89
573	48–50	Matrilineal succession and matripotestal family authority	14/9	18/0	+.97*
574	50–52	Matripotestal family authority and avunculate	14/13	16/1	+.97*
575	50–53	Matripotestal family authority and ownership of dwelling by wife	14/5	16/1	+.79
576	42–53	Matrilocal residence and ownership of dwelling by wife	20/9	32/2	+.90
577	44–53	Matrilineal descent and ownership of dwelling by wife	28/11	18/0	+.81*
578	46–53	Matrilineal inheritance and ownership of dwelling by wife	20/8	23/3	+.87
579	48–53	Matrilineal succession and ownership of dwelling by wife	14/7	18/0	+.87*
580	50–53	Matripotestal family authority and ownership of dwelling by wife	14/5	16/1	+.79
581	52–53	Avunculate and ownership of dwelling by wife	20/8	16/0	+.80*

Cor. No.	Traits		Ratio +=/+=	Ratio −0/+=	Coef.
582	42–34	Matrilocal residence and influence of women in government	20/8	32/10	+.30
583	44–34	Matrilineal descent and influence of women in government	28/12	18/3	+.53
584	46–34	Matrilineal inheritance and influence of women in government	20/12	23/4	+.69
585	48–34	Matrilineal succession and influence of women in government	14/8	18/5	+.47
586	50–34	Matripotestal family authority and influence of women in government	14/6	16/6	+.14
587	52–34	Avunculate and influence of women in government	20/9	16/3	+.30
588	53–34	Ownership of dwelling by wife and influence of women in government	12/5	31/8	+.33
589	43–50	Patrilocal residence and matripotestal family authority	57/7	10/6	−.81
590	45–50	Patrilineal descent and matripotestal family authority	36/2	17/7	−.97
591	47–50	Patrilineal inheritance and matripotestal family authority	46/6	15/6	−.89
592	49–50	Patrilineal succession and matripotestal family authority	45/6	10/5	−.84
593	51–50	Patripotestal family authority and matripotestal family authority	50/5	8/8	−.92*
594	43–53	Patrilocal residence and ownership of dwelling by wife	57/5	10/6	−.83
595	45–53	Patrilineal descent and ownership of dwelling by wife	36/2	17/8	−.83
596	47–53	Patrilineal inheritance and ownership of dwelling by wife	46/6	15/5	−.37
597	49–53	Patrilineal succession and ownership of dwelling by wife	45/4	10/4	−.63
598	51–53	Patripotestal family authority and ownership of dwelling by wife	50/5	8/4	−.65
599	43–34	Patrilocal residence and influence of women in government	57/17	10/4	−.44
600	45–34	Patrilineal descent and influence of women in government	36/9	17/9	−.47
601	47–34	Patrilineal inheritance and influence of women in government	46/11	15/9	−.59
602	49–34	Patrilineal succession and influence of women in government	45/11	10/7	−.84
603	51–34	Patripotestal family authority and influence of women in government	50/12	8/5	−.60
604	65–74	Marriage by capture and subjection or inferiority of women	6/2	48/9	+.10
605	80–74	Property rights in women and subjection or inferiority of women	18/12	17/5	+.60
606	74–66	Subjection or inferiority of women and marriage by wife purchase or bride price	35/27	32/22	+.24

Cor. No.	Traits	Ratio +=/+=	Ratio −0/+=	Coef.
607	80–66	Property rights in women and marriage by wife purchase or bride price	18/16	17/10	+.81
608	42–74	Matrilocal residence and subjection or inferiority of women	20/7	33/13	−.13
609	44–74	Matrilineal descent and subjection or inferiority of women	28/6	18/10	−.65
610	46–74	Matrilineal inheritance and subjection or inferiority of women	20/4	23/13	−.73
611	48–74	Matrilineal succession and subjection or inferiority of women	14/1	18/11	−.92
612	50–74	Matripotestal family authority and subjection or inferiority of women	14/1	16/11	−.93
613	53–74	Ownership of dwelling by wife and subjection or inferiority of women	12/3	31/14	−.50
614	42–80	Matrilocal residence and property rights in women	20/2	32/11	−.53
615	44–80	Matrilineal descent and property rights in women	28/3	18/8	−.45
616	46–80	Matrilineal inheritance and property rights in women	20/3	23/8	−.19
617	48–80	Matrilineal succession and property rights in women	14/3	18/6	+.20
618	50–80	Matripotestal family authority and property rights in women	14/4	16/6	−.09
619	53–80	Ownership of dwelling by wife and property rights in women	12/0	31/9	−.66*
620	42–65	Matrilocal residence and marriage by capture	20/1	32/2	−.05
621	44–65	Matrilineal descent and marriage by capture	28/0	18/1	−.43*
622	42–66	Matrilocal residence and marriage by wife-purchase or bride-price	20/11	32/16	−.26
623	44–66	Matrilineal descent and marriage by wife-purchase or bride-price	28/17	18/14	−.30
624	46–66	Matrilineal inheritance and marriage by wife-purchase or bride-price	20/13	23/20	−.56
625	43–74	Patrilocal residence and subjection or inferiority of women	57/26	10/2	+.58
626	45–74	Patrilineal descent and subjection or inferiority of women	36/18	17/2	+.73
627	47–74	Patrilineal inheritance and subjection or inferiority of women	46/24	15/1	+.90
628	49–74	Patrilineal succession and subjection or inferiority of women	45/23	10/0	+.89*
629	51–74	Patripotestal family authority and subjection or inferiority of women	50/24	8/1	+.74
630	43–80	Patrilocal residence and property rights in women	57/16	10/0	+.73*
631	45–80	Patrilineal descent and property rights in women	36/11	17/2	+.25
632	47–80	Patrilineal inheritance and property rights in women	46/14	15/2	+.58

Cor. No.	Traits	Ratio +=/+=	Ratio −0/+=	Coef.
633	49–80	Patrilineal succession and property rights in women	45/13	10/2	+.16
634	51–80	Patripotestal family authority and property rights in women	50/16	8/2	−.20
635	43–65	Patrilocal residence and marriage by capture	57/4	10/0	+.12*
636	45–65	Patrilineal descent and marriage by capture	36/2	17/0	+.13*
637	43–66	Patrilocal residence and marriage by wife-purchase or bride-price	57/42	10/6	+.44
638	45–66	Patrilineal descent and marriage by wife-purchase or bride-price	36/26	17/11	+.41
639	47–66	Patrilineal inheritance and marriage by wife-purchase or bride-price	46/36	15/10	+.29
640	42–51	Matrilocal residence and patripotestal family authority	20/10	32/26	−.44
641	44–51	Matrilineal descent and patripotestal family authority	28/13	18/18	−.83
642	46–51	Matrilineal inheritance and patripotestal family authority	20/8	23/22	−.91
643	48–51	Matrilineal succession and patripotestal family authority	14/6	18/18	−.91*
644	50–51	Matripotestal family authority and patripotestal family authority	14/5	16/16	−.92*
645	53–51	Ownership of dwelling by wife and patripotestal family authority	12/5	31/24	−.65
646	42–61	Matrilocal residence and polygyny	21/10	32/25	−.61
647	44–61	Matrilineal descent and polygyny	28/20	18/15	−.50
648	46–61	Matrilineal inheritance and polygyny	20/12	23/19	−.62
649	48–61	Matrilineal succession and polygyny	14/9	18/13	−.29
650	50–61	Matripotestal family authority and polygyny	14/11	16/11	+.14
651	52–61	Avunculate and polygyny	20/15	16/9	+.35
652	53–61	Ownership of dwelling by wife and polygyny	12/5	31/25	−.63
653	42–68	Matrilocal residence and wife-lending or wife-exchange	20/3	32/8	−.26
654	44–68	Matrilineal descent and wife-lending or wife-exchange	28/4	18/4	−.05
655	46–68	Matrilineal inheritance and wife-lending or wife-exchange	20/2	23/7	−.61
656	42–72	Matrilocal residence and difficulty of divorce for women	20/8	32/18	−.24
657	44–72	Matrilineal descent and difficulty of divorce for women	28/10	18/14	−.70
658	46–72	Matrilineal inheritance and difficulty of divorce for women	20/10	23/14	−.30
659	48–72	Matrilineal succession and difficulty of divorce for women	14/7	18/12	−.35
660	50–72	Matripotestal family authority and difficulty of divorce for women	14/7	16/10	−.28
661	52–72	Avunculate and difficulty of divorce for women	20/9	16/10	−.38

Cor. No.	Traits		Ratio +=/+=	Ratio −0/+=	Coef.
662	53–72	Ownership of dwelling by wife and difficulty of divorce for women	12/4	31/16	−.33
663	43–51	Patrilocal residence and patripotestal family authority	57/45	10/3	+.87
664	45–51	Patrilineal descent and patripotestal family authority	36/32	17/6	+.96
665	47–51	Patrilineal inheritance and patripotestal family authority	46/39	15/5	+.96
666	49–51	Patrilineal succession and patripotestal family authority	45/37	10/3	+.97
667	43–61	Patrilocal residence and polygyny	57/46	10/4	+.74
668	45–61	Patrilineal descent and polygyny	36/27	17/12	+.23
669	47–61	Patrilineal inheritance and polygyny	46/34	15/10	+.26
670	49–61	Patrilineal succession and polygyny	45/33	10/6	+.38
671	51–61	Patripotestal family authority and polygyny	50/39	8/7	−.21
672	43–68	Patrilocal residence and wife-lending or wife-exchange	57/18	10/0	+.63*
673	45–68	Patrilineal descent and wife-lending or wife-exchange	36/8	17/4	−.08
674	47–68	Patrilineal inheritance and wife-lending or wife-exchange	46/11	15/2	+.45
675	43–72	Patrilocal residence and difficulty of divorce for women	57/32	10/2	+.82
676	45–72	Patrilineal descent and difficulty of divorce for women	36/21	17/5	+.51
677	47–72	Patrilineal inheritance and difficulty of divorce for women	46/29	15/5	+.57
678	49–72	Patrilineal succession and difficulty of divorce for women	43/28	10/3	+.68
679	51–72	Patripotestal family authority and difficulty of divorce for women	50/31	8/2	+.73
680	6–42	Collection and matrilocal residence	22/9	32/8	+.56
681	7–42	Hunting and matrilocal residence	47/15	23/2	+.67
682	8–42	Fishing and matrilocal residence	35/13	28/6	+.45
683	9–42	Herding and matrilocal residence	26/3	43/16	−.61
684	10–42	Agriculture and matrilocal residence	42/8	28/11	−.45
685	6–44	Collection and matrilineal descent	22/12	32/7	+.92
686	7–44	Hunting and matrilineal descent	47/17	23/7	+.24
687	8–44	Fishing and matrilineal descent	35/17	28/8	+.45
688	9–44	Herding and matrilineal descent	26/4	43/23	−.76
689	10–44	Agriculture and matrilineal descent	42/16	28/12	−.08
690	6–46	Collection and matrilineal inheritance	22/5	32/9	+.22
691	7–46	Hunting and matrilineal inheritance	47/12	23/8	+.03
692	8–46	Fishing and matrilineal inheritance	35/11	28/7	+.31
693	9–46	Herding and matrilineal inheritance	26/3	43/16	−.75
694	10–46	Agriculture and matrilineal inheritance	42/14	28/6	+.11
695	6–48	Collection and matrilineal succession	22/6	32/3	+.93
696	7–48	Hunting and matrilineal succession	47/8	23/5	+.29
697	8–48	Fishing and matrilineal succession	35/11	28/2	+.77
698	9–48	Herding and matrilineal succession	26/2	43/12	−.81
699	10–48	Agriculture and matrilineal succession	42/8	28/6	−.03

Cor. No.	Traits		Ratio +=/+=	Ratio −0/+=	Coef.
700	6–50	Collection and matripotestal family authority	22/4	32/6	+.45
701	7–50	Hunting and matripotestal family authority	47/10	23/4	+.32
702	8–50	Fishing and matripotestal family authority	35/11	28/4	+.66
703	9–50	Herding and matripotestal family authority	26/3	43/11	−.65
704	10–50	Agriculture and matripotestal family authority	42/9	28/5	+.50
705	6–52	Collection and avunculate	22/5	32/9	+.10
706	7–52	Hunting and avunculate	47/14	23/6	+.17
707	8–52	Fishing and avunculate	35/12	28/8	+.32
708	9–52	Herding and avunculate	26/3	33/17	−.63
709	10–52	Agriculture and avunculate	42/14	28/6	+.43
710	6–53	Collection and ownership of dwelling by wife	22/5	32/3	+.61
711	7–53	Hunting and ownership of dwelling by wife	47/10	23/2	+.61
712	8–53	Fishing and ownership of dwelling by wife	35/6	28/5	−.11
713	9–53	Herding and ownership of dwelling by wife	26/2	43/10	−.57
714	10–53	Agriculture and ownership of dwelling by wife	42/7	28/5	−.06
715	6–43	Collection and patrilocal residence	22/18	32/20	−.04
716	7–43	Hunting and patrilocal residence	47/36	23/20	−.67
717	8–43	Fish:ng and patrilocal residence	35/28	28/22	−.47
718	9–43	Herding and patrilocal residence	26/23	43/32	+.31
719	10–43	Agriculture and patrilocal residence	42/33	28/23	−.02
720	6–45	Collection and patrilineal descent	22/8	32/22	−.61
721	7–45	Hunting and patrilineal descent	47/20	23/16	−.37
722	8–45	Fishing and patrilineal descent	35/15	28/16	−.36
723	9–45	Herding and patrilineal descent	26/18	43/17	+.78
724	10–45	Agriculture and patrilineal descent	42/23	28/12	+.02
725	6–47	Collection and patrilineal inheritance	22/11	32/25	−.46
726	7–47	Hunting and patrilineal inheritance	47/26	23/19	−.34
727	8–47	Fishing and patrilineal inheritance	35/19	28/21	−.47
728	9–47	Herding and patrilineal inheritance	26/23	43/22	+.61
729	10–47	Agriculture and patrilineal inheritance	42/28	28/16	+.08
730	6–49	Collection and patrilineal succession	22/10	32/24	−.71
731	7–49	Hunting and patrilineal succession	47/25	23/20	−.30
732	8–49	Fishing and patrilineal succession	35/21	28/19	−.52
733	9–49	Herding and patrilineal succession	26/19	43/25	+.51
734	10–49	Agriculture and patrilineal succession	42/31	28/13	+.41
735	6–51	Collection and patripotestal family authority	22/14	32/27	+.22
736	7–51	Hunting and patripotestal family authority	47/30	23/19	−.31
737	8–51	Fishing and patripotestal family authority	35/23	28/22	−.23
738	9–51	Herding and patripotestal family authority	26/22	43/28	+.69
739	10–51	Agriculture and patripotestal family authority	42/29	28/21	−.67
740	38–42	Codified laws and matrilocal residence	34/7	20/7	−.33
741	38–44	Codified laws and matrilineal descent	34/10	20/10	−.43
742	38–46	Codified laws and matrilineal inheritance	34/10	20/5	−.27
743	38–48	Codified laws and matrilineal succession	34/5	20/5	−.57
744	38–50	Codified laws and matripotestal family authority	34/8	20/4	−.06
745	38–52	Codified laws and avunculate	34/12	20/5	+.38

Cor. No.	Traits		Ratio += /+=	Ratio −0/+=	Coef.
746	38–53	Codified laws and ownership of dwelling by wife	34/5	20/4	−.37
747	38–43	Codified laws and patrilocal residence	34/27	20/15	+.28
748	38–45	Codified laws and patrilineal descent	34/20	20/9	+.23
749	38–47	Codified laws and patrilineal inheritance	34/24	20/25	+.26
750	38–49	Codified laws and patrilineal succession	34/24	20/11	+.46
751	38–51	Codified laws and patripotestal family authority	34/23	20/13	−.50
752	38–74	Codified laws and subjection or inferiority of women	34/17	20/7	+.32
753	38–80	Codified laws and property rights in women	34/15	20/3	+.90
754	38–66	Codified laws and marriage by wife-purchase or bride-price	34/26	20/13	+.18
755	38–72	Codified laws and difficulty of divorce for women	34/21	20/8	+.51
756	31–42	Power vested in the chief and matrilocal residence	51/10	18/10	−.68
757	31–44	Power vested in the chief and matrilineal descent	51/20	18/6	−.20
758	31–46	Power vested in the chief and matrilineal inheritance	51/16	18/3	+.19
759	31–48	Power vested in the chief and matrilineal succession	51/10	18/8	−.58
760	31–50	Power vested in the chief and matripotestal family authority	51/10	18/4	−.09
761	31–43	Power vested in the chief and patrilocal residence	51/42	18/13	+.17
762	31–45	Power vested in the chief and patrilineal descent	51/29	18/7	+.02
763	31–47	Power vested in the chief and patrilineal inheritance	51/35	18/10	+.12
764	31–49	Power vested in the chief and patrilineal succession	51/37	18/8	+.51
765	31–74	Power vested in the chief and subjection or inferiority of women	51/23	18/5	+.41
766	31–80	Power vested in the chief and property rights in women	51/15	18/3	+.70
767	31–66	Power vested in the chief and marriage by wife-purchase or bride-price	51/37	18/10	+.19
768	31–72	Power vested in the chief and difficulty of divorce for women	51/27	18/9	+.23
769	55–42	Hereditary caste & classes and matrilocal residence	29/3	16/7	−.69
770	55–44	Hereditary castes and classes and matrilineal descent	29/11	16/7	+.08
771	55–46	Hereditary castes and classes and matrilineal inheritance	29/12	16/3	+.51
772	55–48	Hereditary castes and classes and matrilineal succession	29/7	16/4	−.22
773	55–50	Hereditary castes and classes and matripotestal family authority	29/6	16/5	−.14

Cor. No.	Traits		Ratio +=/+=	Ratio −0/+=	Coef.
774	55–53	Hereditary castes and classes and ownership of dwelling by wife	29/1	16/5	−.83
775	55–43	Hereditary castes and classes and patrilocal residence	29/26	16/11	+.84
776	55–45	Hereditary castes and classes and patrilineal descent	29/17	16/10	−.22
777	55–47	Hereditary castes and classes and patrilineal inheritance	29/23	16/9	+.44
778	55–49	Hereditary castes and classes and patrilineal succession	29/21	16/11	+.06
779	55–51	Hereditary castes and classes and patripotestal family authority	29/23	16/12	−.02
780	55–74	Hereditary castes and classes and subjection or inferiority of women	29/12	16/3	+.57
781	55–80	Hereditary castes and classes and property rights in women	29/12	16/23	+.81
782	55–66	Hereditary castes and classes and marriage by wife-purchase or bride-price	29/25	16/8	+.72
783	55–72	Hereditary castes and classes and difficulty of divorce for women	29/19	16/9	+.23
784	81–42	Organized priesthood and matrilocal residence	21/1	34/11	−.77
785	81–44	Organized priesthood and matrilineal descent	21/5	34/17	−.63
786	81–46	Organized priesthood and matrilineal inheritance	21/5	34/12	−.23
787	81–48	Organized priesthood and matrilineal succession	21/2	34/9	−.71
788	81–50	Organized priesthood and matripotestal family authority	21/4	34/8	−.20
789	81–53	Organized priesthood and ownership of dwelling by wife	21/2	34/7	−.19
790	81–43	Organized priesthood and patrilocal residence	21/19	34/24	+.69
791	81–45	Organized priesthood and patrilineal descent	21/15	34/14	+.46
792	81–47	Organized priesthood and patrilineal inheritance	21/17	34/19	+.28
793	81–49	Organized priesthood and patrilineal succession	21/17	34/21	+.42
794	81–51	Organized priesthood and patripotestal family authority	21/16	34/23	−.03
795	81–74	Organized priesthood and subjection or inferiority of women	21/12	34/9	+.70
796	81–80	Organized priesthood and property rights in women	21/10	34/6	+.82
797	80–66	Organized priesthood and marriage by wife-purchase or bride-price	21/16	34/24	+.28
798	81–72	Organized priesthood and difficulty of divorce for women	21/14	34/16	+.50
799	42–136	Matrilocal residence and marriage of aged women to young mates	20/5	32/6	+.16

Cor. No.	Traits		Ratio +=/+=	Ratio −0/+=	Coef.
800	44–136	Matrilineal descent and marriage of aged women to young mates	28/11	18/0	+.80*
801	46–136	Matrilineal inheritance and marriage of aged women to young mates	20/7	23/1	+.79
802	48–136	Matrilineal succession and marriage of aged women to young mates	14/7	18/0	+.85*
803	50–136	Matripotestal family authority and marriage of aged women to young mates	14/7	16/2	+.27
804	52–136	Avunculate and marriage of aged women to young mates	20/8	16/2	+.60
805	53–136	Ownership of dwelling by wife and marriage of aged women to young mates	11/2	31/8	−.33
806	43–136	Patrilocal residence and marriage of aged women to young mates	57/10	10/3	−.41
807	45–136	Patrilineal descent and marriage of aged women to young mates	36/1	17/8	−.96
808	47–136	Patrilineal inheritance and marriage of aged women to young mates	46/2	15/7	−.94
809	49–136	Patrilineal succession and marriage of aged women to young mates	45/3	10/5	−.87*
810	51–136	Patripotestal family authority and marriage of aged women to young mates	50/5	8/6	−.83*
811	6–136	Collection and marriage of aged women to young mates	22/6	32/2	+.80
812	7–136	Hunting and marriage of aged women to young mates	47/10	23/3	+.38
813	8–136	Fishing and marriage of aged women to young mates	35/9	28/2	+.86
814	9–136	Herding and marriage of aged women to young mates	26/1	33/12	−.93
815	10–136	Agriculture and marriage of aged women to young mates	42/7	28/6	+.10
816	128–136	Property rights of aged women, including slaves, and marriage of aged women to young mates	15/5	17/2	+.76
817	61–136	Polygyny and marriage of aged women to young mates	52/11	17/2	+.40
818	63–136	Betrothal of infants and children and marriage of aged women to young mates	27/10	14/0	+.83*
819	154–136	Shamanistic practices of aged women and marriage of aged women to young mates	45/10	3/0	+.29*
820	31–136	Power vested in the chief and marriage of aged women to young mates	51/8	18/2	+.52
821	38–136	Codified laws and marriage of aged women to young mates	34/5	20/3	+.14
822	55–136	Hereditary castes and classes and marriage of aged women to young mates	29/5	16/3	.00
823	56–136	Plutocracy and marriage of aged women to young mates	43/7	11/2	−.44
824	66–136	Marriage by wife-purchase or bride-price and marriage of aged women to young mates	50/9	15/3	−.45

Cor. No.	Traits	Ratio +=/+=	Ratio −0/+=	Coef.
825	72–136 Difficulty of divorce for women and marriage of aged women to young mates	37/2	22/6	−.75
826	74–136 Subjection or inferiority of women and marriage of aged women to young mates	30/3	32/7	−.35
827	81–136 Organized priesthood and marriage of aged women to young mates	21/2	34/9	−.38
828	43–135 Patrilocal residence and marriage of aged men to young mates	57/33	10/5	+.31
829	45–135 Patrilineal descent and marriage of aged men to young mates	36/19	17/11	−.05
830	47–135 Patrilineal inheritance and marriage of aged men to young mates	46/23	15/10	+.07
831	49–135 Patrilineal succession and marriage of aged men to young mates	45/25	10/5	+.43
832	51–135 Patripotestal family authority and marriage of aged men to young mates	50/30	8/7	+.12
833	6–135 Collection and marriage of aged men to young mates	22/12	32/10	−.34*
834	7–135 Hunting and marriage of aged men to young mates	47/26	23/13	+.60*
835	8–135 Fishing and marriage of aged men to young mates	35/15	28/18	+.54*
836	9–135 Herding and marriage of aged men to young mates	26/16	43/23	+.48*
837	10–135 Agriculture and marriage of aged men to young mates	42/25	28/14	+.05
838	38–135 Codified laws and marriage of aged men to young mates	34/24	20/9	+.45
839	55–135 Hereditary castes and classes and marriage of aged men to young mates	29/20	16/7	+.66*
840	56–135 Plutocracy and marriage of aged men to young mates	43/26	11/4	+.53
841	61–135 Polygyny and marriage of aged men to young mates	52/27	17/5	+.46
842	63–135 Betrothal of infants and children and marriage of aged men to young mates	27/20	14/6	+.74*
843	66–135 Marriage by wife-purchase or bride-price and marriage of aged men to young mates	50/31	15/6	+.58
844	80–135 Property rights in women and marriage of aged men to young mates	18/13	17/7	+.77*
845	42–135 Matrilocal residence and marriage of aged men to young mates	20/9	32/19	−.03
846	44–135 Matrilineal descent and marriage of aged men to young mates	28/15	18/10	+.49
847	46–135 Matrilineal inheritance and marriage of aged men to young mates	20/13	23/10	+.44
848	48–135 Matrilineal succession and marriage of aged men to young mates	14/7	18/12	−.24*
849	50–135 Matripotestal family authority and marriage of aged men to young mates	13/11	16/10	.00*

Cor. No.	Traits	Ratio +=/+=	Ratio −0/+=	Coef.
850	52–135 Avunculate and marriage of aged men to young mates	20/13	16/8	+.24*
851	53–135 Ownership of dwelling by wife and marriage of aged men to young mates	12/4	31/19	−.60
852	42–133 Matrilocal residence and family rights of aged men, including seniority rights	20/10	32/26	−.68
853	44–133 Matrilineal descent and family rights of aged men, including seniority rights	28/18	18/15	−.25
854	46–133 Matrilineal inheritance and family rights of aged men, including seniority rights	20/13	23/19	−.49
855	48–133 Matrilineal succession and family rights of aged men, including seniority rights	14/8	18/15	−.58
856	50–133 Matripotestal family authority and family rights of aged men, including seniority rights	14/11	16/14	−.46
857	52–133 Avunculate and family rights of aged men, including seniority rights	20/15	16/13	+.07
858	53–133 Ownership of dwelling by wife and family rights of aged men, including seniority rights	12/5	31/24	−.52
859	6–133 Collection and family rights of aged men, including seniority rights	22/13	32/26	−.14
860	7–133 Hunting and family rights of aged men, including seniority rights	47/29	23/20	−.66*
861	8–133 Fishing and family rights of aged men, including seniority rights	35/24	28/17	+.17
862	9–133 Herding and family rights of aged men, including seniority rights	26/22	43/28	+.52
863	10–133 Agriculture and family rights of aged men, including seniority rights	42/30	28/19	+.52
864	1–133 Permanency of residence and family rights of aged men, including seniority rights	47/33	24/15	+.83
865	11–133 Use of grain for food and family rights of aged men, including seniority rights	37/27	29/21	+.73
866	12–133 Constancy of food supply and family rights of aged men, including seniority rights	53/40	15/9	+.80
867	43–133 Patrilocal residence and family rights of aged men, including seniority rights	57/41	10/5	+.78
868	45–133 Patrilineal descent and family rights of aged men, including seniority rights	36/29	17/9	+.73
869	47–133 Patrilineal inheritance and family rights of aged men, including seniority rights	46/36	15/8	+.92*
870	49–133 Patrilineal succession and family rights of aged men, including seniority rights	45/37	10/4	+.93
871	51–133 Patripotestal family authority and family rights of aged men, including seniority rights	50/40	8/5	+.68
872	31–133 Power vested in the chief and family rights of aged men, including seniority rights	51/36	18/12	+.71

Cor. No.	Traits	Ratio +=/+=	Ratio −0/+=	Coef.
873	33–133 Government by restricted council and family rights of aged men, including seniority rights	52/33	6/3	+.76
874	38–133 Codified laws and family rights of aged men, including seniority rights	34/27	20/12	+.74
875	55–133 Hereditary castes and classes and family rights of aged men, including seniority rights	29/25	16/9	+.88*
876	56–133 Plutocracy and family rights of aged men, including seniority rights	43/32	11/7	+.86
877	61–133 Polygyny and family rights of aged men, including seniority rights	52/41	17/12	+.24*
878	62–133 Monogamy and family rights of aged men, including seniority rights	52/35	10/8	−.27*
879	66–133 Marriage by wife-purchase or bride-price and family rights of aged men, including seniority rights	50/41	15/5	+.78
880	70–133 Levirate and family rights of aged men, including seniority rights	37/33	13/5	+.94
881	72–133 Difficulty of divorce for women and family rights of aged men, including seniority rights	37/29	22/12	+.57
882	74–133 Subjection or inferiority of women and family rights of aged men, including seniority rights	30/23	32/21	+.64
883	80–133 Property rights in women and family rights of aged men, including seniority rights	18/17	17/12	+.70
884	81–133 Organized priesthood and family rights of aged men, including seniority rights	21/17	34/14	+.91*
885	83–133 Ancestor worship and family rights of aged men, including seniority rights	15/13	21/16	+.24*
886	127–133 Property rights of aged men, including slaves, and family rights of aged men including seniority rights	46/38	7/2	+.98
887	42–134 Matrilocal residence and family rights of aged women, including seniority rights	20/9	31/15	+.41
888	44–134 Matrilineal descent and family rights of aged women, including seniority rights	28/13	18/10	+.53
889	46–134 Matrilineal inheritance and family rights of aged women, including seniority rights	20/16	23/6	+.90*
890	48–134 Matrilineal succession and family rights of aged women, including seniority rights	14/11	18/8	+.81*
891	50–134 Matripotestal family authority and family rights of aged women including seniority rights	14/11	16/7	+.81
892	52–134 Avunculate and family rights of aged women including seniority rights	20/13	18/8	+.53
893	53–134 Ownership of dwelling by wife and family rights of aged women including seniority rights	12/7	31/12	+.72*

Cor. No.	Traits	Ratio +=/+=	Ratio −0/+=	Coef.
894	6–134 Collection and family rights of aged women including seniority rights	22/5	32/13	+.01
895	7–134 Hunting and family rights of aged women including seniority rights	47/16	23/9	+.28
896	8–134 Fishing and family rights of aged women including seniority rights	35/15	28/10	+.45
897	9–134 Herding and family rights of aged women including seniority rights	26/6	43/19	−.75
898	10–134 Agriculture and family rights of aged women including seniority rights	42/16	28/9	+.21
899	43–134 Patrilocal residence and family rights of aged women including seniority rights	57/17	10/7	−.66
900	45–134 Patrilineal descent and family rights of aged women including seniority rights	36/13	17/10	−.68
901	47–134 Patrilineal inheritance and family rights of aged women including seniority rights	46/15	15/9	−.29
902	49–134 Patrilineal succession and family rights of aged women including seniority rights	45/17	10/6	−.59
903	51–134 Patripotestal family authority and family rights of aged women including seniority rights	50/15	8/7	−.71*
904	61–134 Polygyny and family rights of aged women including seniority rights	52/15	17/10	−.33*
905	70–134 Levirate and family rights of aged women including seniority rights	37/16	13/7	−.51
906	80–134 Property rights in women and family rights of aged women including seniority rights	18/7	17/8	−.23
907	74–134 Subjection or inferiority of women and family rights of aged women including seniority rights	30/5	22/18	−.89
908	1–134 Permanency of residence and family rights of aged women including seniority rights	47/19	24/5	+.53
909	11–134 Use of grain for food and family rights of aged women including seniority rights	37/10	29/13	−.29
910	12–134 Constancy of food supply and family rights of aged women including seniority rights	53/21	15/4	+.64
911	31–134 Power vested in the chief and family rights of aged women including seniority rights	51/18	18/7	−.13
912	33–134 Government by restricted council and family rights of aged women including seniority rights	52/21	6/2	+.40
913	38–134 Codified laws and family rights of aged women including seniority rights	34/14	20/7	−.20
914	55–134 Hereditary castes and classes and family rights of aged women including seniority rights	29/12	16/9	−.14
915	56–134 Plutocracy and family rights of aged women including seniority rights	43/19	11/3	+.59
916	62–134 Monogamy and family rights of aged women including seniority rights	52/21	10/4	+.4C

Cor. No.	Traits	Ratio +=/+=	Ratio −0/+=	Coef.
917	63–134 Betrothal of infants and children and family rights of aged women including seniority rights	27/12	14/5	+.41
918	66–134 Marriage by wife-purchase or bride-price and family rights of aged women including seniority rights	50/17	15/7	−.16
919	72–134 Difficulty of divorce for women and family rights of aged women including seniority rights	37/15	22/7	+.28
920	81–134 Organized priesthood and family rights of aged women, including seniority rights	21/8	34/13	−.15
921	34–134 Influence of women in government and family rights of aged women including seniority rights	22/11	26/9	+.62
922	128–134 Property rights of aged women, including slaves and family rights of aged women including seniority rights	15/12	17/7	+.85*
923	42–195 Matrilocal residence and general family support of aged men	20/17	32/26	−.21
924	42–196 Matrilocal residence and general family support of aged women	20/18	32/26	−.18
925	43–195 Patrilocal residence and general family support of aged men	57/49	10/7	+.75
926	43–196 Patrilocal residence and general family support of aged women	57/45	10/9	+.66*
927	44–195 Matrilineal descent and general family support of aged men	28/22	18/15	+.48*
928	44–196 Matrilineal descent and general family support of aged women	28/23	18/15	+.50*
929	45–195 Patrilineal descent and general family support of aged men	36/30	17/12	+.09*
930	45–196 Patrilineal descent and general family support of aged women	36/28	17/13	+.61*
931	46–195 Matrilineal inheritance and general family support of aged men	20/14	23/22	−.22*
932	46–196 Matrilineal inheritance and general family support of aged women	20/16	23/21	−.13*
933	47–195 Patrilineal inheritance and general family support of aged men	46/40	15/10	+.84*
934	47–196 Patrilineal inheritance and general family support of aged women	46/36	15/12	+.83*
935	48–195 Matrilineal succession and general family support of aged men	14/10	18/14	+.19*
936	48–196 Matrilineal succession and general family support of aged women	14/12	18/14	+.27*
937	49–195 Patrilineal succession and general family support of aged men	45/39	10/6	+.73
938	49–196 Patrilineal succession and general family support of aged women	45/32	10/9	+.56*
939	50–195 Matripotestal family authority and general family support of aged men	14/13	16/13	.00

Cor. No.	Traits	Ratio +=/+=	Ratio −0/+=	Coef.
940	50–196 Matripotestal family authority and general family support of aged women	14/12	16/14	−.08*
941	51–195 Patripotestal family authority and general family support of aged men	50/37	8/7	+.40*
942	51–196 Patripotestan family authority and general family support of aged women	50/41	8/7	+.68*
943	52–195 Avunculate and general family support of aged men	20/17	16/14	+.09
944	52–196 Avunculate and general family support of aged women	20/17	16/14	+.10*
945	53–195 Ownership of dwelling by wife and general family support of aged men	12/9	31/2	+.93*
946	53–196 Ownership of dwelling by wife and general family support of aged women	12/11	31/25	+.16*
947	6–195 Collection and general family support of aged men	22/19	32/29	+.14*
948	6–196 Collection and general family support of aged women	22/15	32/30	−.33
949	7–195 Hunting and general family support of aged men	47/39	23/19	+.20*
950	7–196 Hunting and general family support of aged women	47/36	23/19	−.24*
951	8–195 Fishing and general family support of aged men	35/26	28/25	−.48*
952	8–196 Fishing and general family support of aged women	35/26	28/17	−.33*
953	9–195 Herding and general family support of aged men	26/21	43/35	−.25
954	9–196 Herding and general family support of aged women	26/21	43/23	−.04
955	10–195 Agriculture and general family support of aged men	42/35	28/22	+.23
956	10–196 Agriculture and general family support of aged women	42/33	28/22	+.16
957	1–195 Permanency of residence and general family support of aged men	47/39	24/10	+.37
958	1–196 Permanency of residence and general family support of aged women	47/37	24/16	+.40
959	11–195 Use of grain for food and general family support of aged men	37/33	29/21	+.64
960	11–196 Use of grain for food and general family support of aged women	37/32	29/20	+.65*
961	12–195 Constancy of food supply and general family support of aged men	53/46	15/11	+.84
962	12–196 Constancy of food supply and general family support of aged women	53/43	15/10	+.85*
963	31–195 Power vested in the chief and general family support of aged men	51/40	18/15	+.45
964	31–196 Power vested in the chief and general family support of aged women	51/39	18/15	+.22

Cor. No.	Traits		Ratio += /+=	Ratio -0/+=	Coef.
965	33–195	Government by restricted council and (general) family support of aged men	52/40	6/4	+.82
966	33–196	Government by restricted council and general family support of aged women	52/40	6/4	+.82
967	38–195	Codified laws and general family support of aged men	34/29	20/13	+.62*
968	38–196	Codified laws and general family support of aged women	34/27	20/14	+.70*
969	55–195	Hereditary castes and classes and general family support of aged men	29/23	16/13	+.69*
970	55–196	Hereditary castes and classes and general family support of aged women	29/23	16/13	+.67*
971	56–195	Plutocracy and general family support of aged men	43/35	11/8	+.85*
972	56–196	Plutocracy and general family support of aged women	43/46	11/8	+.85*
973	61–195	Polygyny and general family support of aged men	52/46	17/11	+.84*
974	61–196	Polygyny and general family support of aged women	52/42	17/12	+.79*
975	66–195	Marriage by wife-purchase or bride-price and general family support of aged men	50/41	15/11	+.58
976	66–196	Marriage by wife-purchase or bride-price and general family support of aged women	50/40	15/12	+.54*
977	72–195	Difficulty of divorce for women and general family support of aged men	37/32	22/17	+.69*
978	72–196	Difficulty of divorce for women and general family support of aged women	37/30	22/17	+.67*
979	80–195	Property rights in women and general family support of aged men	18/17	17/14	+.56*
980	80–196	Property rights in women and general family support of aged women	18/16	17/14	+.58*
981	74–195	Subjection or inferiority of women and general family support of aged men	30/28	32/22	+.58*
982	74–196	Subjection or inferiority of women and general family support of aged women	30/24	32/26	+.47*
983	81–195	Organized priesthood and general family support of aged men	31/19	34/26	+.19*
984	81–196	Organized priesthood and general family support of aged women	31/17	34/16	+.66*
985	83–195	Ancestor worship and general family support of aged men	15/14	21/16	+.67*
986	83–196	Ancestor worship and general family support of aged women	15/12	21/16	+.21*
987	127–195	Property rights of aged men, including slaves, and general family support of aged men	46/40	7/4	+.92*
988	128–196	Property rights of aged women, including slaves, and general family support of aged women	15/13	17/14	+.47*

Cor. No.	Traits	Ratio +=/+=	Ratio −0/+=	Coef.
989	42–197 Matrilocal residence and son-in-law support of aged men	20/10	32/2	+.89*
990	42–198 Matrilocal residence and son-in-law support of aged women	20/10	32/1	+.91*
991	44–197 Matrilineal descent and son-in-law support of aged men	28/5	18/3	+.05
992	44–198 Matrilineal descent and son-in-law support of aged women	28/4	18/2	.00
993	46–197 Matrilineal inheritance and son-in-law support of aged men	20/5	23/3	+.43
994	46–198 Matrilineal inheritance and son-in-law support of aged women	20/5	23/2	+.76
995	48–197 Matrilineal succession and son-in-law support of aged men	14/3	18/2	−.17
996	48–198 Matrilineal succession and son-in-law support of aged women	14/4	18/1	+.60
997	50–197 Matripotestal family authority and son-in-law support of aged men	14/5	16/3	+.54
998	50–198 Matripotestal family authority and son-in-law support of aged women	14/5	16/2	+.60*
999	52–197 Avunculate and son-in-law support of aged men	20/5	16/4	−.41
1000	52–198 Avunculate and son-in-law support of aged women	20/6	16/2	+.20
1001	53–197 Ownership of dwelling by wife and son-in-law support of aged men	12/5	31/6	+.62*
1002	53–198 Ownership of dwelling by wife and son-in-law support of aged women	12/5	31/5	+.68*
1003	43–197 Patrilocal residence and son-in-law support of aged men	57/8	10/6	−.69*
1004	43–198 Patrilocal residence and son-in-law support of aged women	57/18	10/5	−.22*
1005	45–197 Patrilineal descent and son-in-law support of aged men	36/5	17/3	−.09
1006	45–198 Patrilineal descent and son-in-law support of aged women	36/3	17/4	−.60
1007	47–197 Patrilineal inheritance and son-in-law support of aged men	46/7	15/2	+.27
1008	47–198 Patrilineal inheritance and son-in-law support of aged women	46/6	15/2	.00
1009	49–197 Patrilineal succession and son-in-law support of aged men	45/10	10/1	+.66
1010	49–198 Patrilineal succession and son-in-law support of aged women	45/6	10/2	.00
1011	51–197 Patripotestal family authority and son-in-law support of aged men	50/11	8/2	−.24
1012	51–198 Patripotestal family authority and son-in-law support of aged women	50/7	8/2	−.30*
1013	6–197 Collection and son-in-law support of aged men	22/4	32/	+.43

Cor. No.	Traits	Ratio +=/+=	Ratio −0/+=	Coef.
1014	6–198 Collection and son-in-law support of aged women	22/4	32/7	+.26
1015	7–197 Hunting and son-in-law support of aged men	47/11	23/6	+.91*
1016	7–198 Hunting and son-in-law support of aged women	47/9	22/4	+.85
1017	8–197 Fishing and son-in-law support of aged men	35/10	28/5	+.60
1018	8–198 Fishing and son-in-law support of aged women	35/9	28/3	+.50
1019	9–197 Herding and son-in-law support of aged men	26/1	43/15	−.87
1020	9–198 Herding and son-in-law support of aged women	26/0	43/12	−.86*
1021	10–197 Agriculture and son-in-law support of aged men	42/8	28/8	−.33
1022	10–198 Agriculture and son-in-law support of aged women	42/6	28/6	.00
1023	1–197 Permanency of residence and son-in-law support of aged men	47/9	24/4	−.28
1024	1–198 Permanency of residence and son-in-law support of aged women	47/9	24/3	.00
1025	11–197 Use of grain for food and son-in-law support of aged men	37/7	29/9	−.12
1026	11–198 Use of grain for food and son-in-law support of aged women	37/6	29/5	+.09
1027	12–197 Constancy of food supply and son-in-law support of aged men	53/10	15/6	−.50
1028	12–198 Constancy of food supply and son-in-law support of aged women	53/8	15/4	.00
1029	31–197 Power vested in the chief and son-in-law support of aged men	51/7	18/8	−.77*
1030	31–198 Power vested in the chief and son-in-law support of aged women	51/5	18/6	−.71*
1031	33–197 Government by restricted council and son-in-law support of aged men	52/7	6/4	−.63*
1032	33–198 Government by restricted council and son-in-law support of aged women	52/7	6/3	−.43*
1033	55–197 Hereditary castes and classes and son-in-law support of aged men	29/4	16/5	−.87*
1034	55–198 Hereditary castes and classes and son-in-law support of aged women	29/1	16/5	−.82*
1035	56–197 Plutocracy and son-in-law support of aged men	43/6	11/3	−.50
1036	56–198 Plutocracy and son-in-law support of aged women	43/6	11/4	−.33
1037	66–197 Marriage by wife-purchase or bride-price and son-in-law support of aged men	50/9	15/6	−.14
1038	66–198 Marriage by wife-purchase or bride-price and son-in-law support of aged women	50/5	15/6	−.56
1039	72–197 Difficulty of divorce for women and son-in-law support of aged men	37/5	22/5	−.36
1040	72–198 Difficulty of divorce for women and son-in-law support of aged women	37/5	22/5	−.33

Cor. No.	Traits		Ratio +=/+=	Ratio −0/+=	Coef.
1041	74–197	Subjection or inferiority of women and son-in-law support of aged men	30/7	32/9	−.12
1042	74–198	Subjection or inferiority of women and son-in-law support of aged women	30/4	32/6	−.64
1043	81–197	Organized priesthood and son-in-law support of aged men	21/1	34/7	−.06
1044	81–198	Organized priesthood and son-in-law support of aged women	21/1	34/7	.00
1045	93–217	Exposure of the dying and abandonment and exposure of aged men to the natural elements	6/3	39/4	+.88*
1046	93–218	Exposure of the dying and abandonment and exposure of aged women to the natural elements	6/4	39/5	+.88*
1047	94–217	Abandonment of the house of the dead and abandonment and exposure of aged men to the natural elements	19/4	33/5	+.23
1048	94–218	Abandonment of the house of the dead and abandonment and exposure of aged women to the natural elements	19/4	33/6	+.18
1049	1–93	Permanency of residence and exposure of the dying	47/2	24/4	−.33
1050	6–93	Collection and exposure of the dying	22/3	32/1	+.79
1051	7–93	Hunting and exposure of the dying	47/6	21/0	+.66*
1052	8–93	Fishing and exposure of the dying	35/3	28/3	−.05
1053	9–93	Herding and exposure of the dying	26/3	43/3	+.23
1054	10–93	Agriculture and exposure of the dying	42/2	28/4	−.70
1055	81–93	Organized priesthood and exposure of the dying	21/1	34/14	−.51
1056	1–94	Permanency of residence and abandonment of house of the dead	47/6	34/13	−.88
1057	6–94	Collection and abandonment of house of the dead	22/12	32/3	+.96
1058	7–94	Hunting and abandonment of house of the dead	47/19	23/0	+.88
1059	8–94	Fishing and abandonment of house of the dead	35/10	28/5	+.27
1060	9–94	Herding and abandonment of house of the dead	28/6	43/11	+.04
1061	10–94	Agriculture and abandonment of house of the dead	42/5	28/13	−.87
1062	81–94	Organized priesthood and abandonment of house of the dead	21/3	34/13	−.60
1063	1–217	Permanency of residence and abandonment and exposure of aged men to the natural elements	47/4	24/8	−.64
1064	1–218	Permanency of residence and abandonment and exposure of aged women to the natural elements	47/6	24/8	−.53
1065	6–217	Collection and abandonment and exposure of aged men to the natural elements	22/4	32/6	+.01

Cor. No.	Traits	Ratio +=/+=	Ratio −0/+=	Coef.
1066	6–218 Collection and abandonment and exposure of aged women to the natural elements	22/4	32/7	−.03
1067	7–217 Hunting and abandonment and exposure of aged men to the natural elements	47/10	23/2	+.38
1068	7–218 Hunting and abandonment and exposure of aged women to the natural elements	47/12	23/2	+.50
1069	8–217 Fishing and abandonment and exposure of aged men to the natural elements	35/8	28/4	+.18
1070	8–218 Fishing and abandonment and exposure of aged women to the natural elements	35/9	28/4	+.27
1071	9–217 Herding and abandonment and exposure of aged men to the natural elements	26/4	43/8	+.33
1072	9–218 Herding and abandonment and exposure of aged women to the natural elements	26/5	43/9	+.35
1073	10–217 Agriculture and abandonment and exposure of aged men to the natural elements	42/4	27/8	−.63
1074	10–218 Agriculture and abandonment and exposure of aged women to the natural elements	42/6	27/8	−.45
1075	81–217 Organized priesthood and abandonment and exposure of aged men to the natural elements	21/2	34/7	−.24
1076	81–218 Organized priesthood and abandonment and exposure of aged women to the natural elements	21/3	34/8	−.06
1077	42–217 Matrilocal residence and abandonment and exposure of aged men to the natural elements	20/4	32/6	−.02
1078	42–218 Matrilocal residence and abandonment and exposure of aged women to the natural elements	20/4	32/8	−.20
1079	43–217 Patrilocal residence and abandonment and exposure of aged men to the natural elements	57/9	10/2	−.05
1080	43–218 Patrilocal residence and abandonment and exposure of aged women to the natural elements	57/11	10/2	+.10
1081	44–217 Matrilineal descent and abandonment and exposure of aged men to the natural elements	28/2	18/3	−.37
1082	44–218 Matrilineal descent and abandonment and exposure of aged women to the natural elements	28/3	18/3	−.18
1083	45–217 Patrilineal descent and abandonment and exposure of aged men to the natural elements	36/3	17/2	−.16
1084	45–218 Patrilineal descent and abandonment and exposure of aged women to the natural elements	36/5	17/2	+.11
1085	46–217 Matrilineal inheritance and abandonment and exposure of aged men to the natural elements	20/2	23/2	+.20

Cor. No.	Traits	Ratio +=/+=	Ratio −0/+=	Coef.
1086	46–218 Matrilineal inheritance and abandonment and exposure of aged women to the natural elements	20/3	23/4	+.12
1087	47–217 Patrilineal inheritance and abandonment and exposure of aged men to the natural elements	46/4	15/5	−.66
1088	47–218 Patrilineal inheritance and abandonment and exposure of aged women to the natural elements	46/6	15/5	−.57
1089	50–218 Matripotestal family authority and abandonment and exposure of aged women to the natural elements	14/3	16/1	+.50
1090	53–218 Ownership of dwelling by wife and abandonment and exposure of aged women to the natural elements	12/1	31/8	−.67
1091	0–219 Severity of climate and killing of aged men	35/4	36/3	+.26
1092	0–220 Severity of climate and killing of aged women	35/6	36/5	+.22
1093	1–219 Permanency of residence and killing of aged men	42/2	24/5	−.75
1094	1–220 Permanency of residence and killing of aged women	47/4	24/7	−.70
1095	12–219 Constancy of food supply and killing of aged men	53/3	15/4	−.66
1096	12–220 Constancy of food supply and killing of aged women	53/5	15/6	−.64
1097	6–219 Collection and killing of aged men	22/3	22/2	+.41
1098	6–220 Collection and killing of aged women	22/3	22/4	+.04
1099	7–219 Hunting and killing of aged men	47/5	23/2	+.09
1100	7–220 Hunting and killing of aged women	47/7	23/4	−.22
1101	8–219 Fishing and killing of aged men	35/6	28/1	+.60
1102	8–220 Fishing and killing of aged women	35/6	28/1	−.20
1103	9–219 Herders and killing of aged men	26/3	43/4	+.47
1104	9–220 Herding and killing of aged women	26/7	43/4	+.84
1105	10–219 Agriculture and killing of aged men	42/3	28/5	−.47
1106	10–220 Agriculture and killing of aged women	42/4	28/7	−.50
1107	11–219 Use of grain and killing of aged men	37/0	29/7	−.82*
1108	11–220 Use of grain and killing of aged women	37/2	29/9	−.69
1109	29–219 Property rights in land and killing of aged men	22/1	32/3	−.55
1110	29–220 Property rights in land and killing of aged women	22/1	32/6	−.76
1111	31–219 Power vested in chief and killing of aged men	51/3	18/4	−.45
1112	31–220 Power vested in chief and killing of aged women	53/3	18/4	−.56
1113	38–219 Codified laws and killing of aged men	34/2	20/3	−.50
1114	38–220 Codified laws and killing of aged women	34/4	20/4	−.28
1115	42–219 Matrilocal residence and killing of aged men	20/2	32/3	−.05
1116	42–220 Matrilocal residence and killing of aged women	20/2	32/6	−.42
1117	44–219 Matrilineal descent and killing of aged men	28/1	18/2	−.53

Cor. No.	Traits	Ratio +=/+=	Ratio −0/+=	Coef.
1118	44–220 Matrilineal descent and killing of aged women	28/3	18/4	−.27
1119	46–219 Matrilineal inheritance and killing of aged men	20/2	23/1	+.58
1120	46–220 Matrilineal inheritance and killing of aged women	20/2	23/3	+.04
1121	48–219 Matrilineal succession and killing of aged men	14/1	18/2	−.27
1122	48–220 Matrilineal succession and killing of aged women	14/1	18/3	−.55
1123	50–219 Matripotestal family authority and killing of aged men	14/1	16/1	.00
1124	50–220 Matripotestal family authority and killing of aged women	14/2	16/2	+.06
1125	53–219 Ownership of dwelling by wife and killing of aged men	12/0	31/5	−.60*
1126	53–220 Ownership of dwelling by wife and killing of aged women	12/0	31/7	−.64*
1127	43–219 Patrilocal residence and killing of aged men	57/6	10/1	+.07
1128	43–220 Patrilocal residence and killing of aged women	57/10	10/1	+.39
1129	45–219 Patrilineal descent and killing of aged men	36/3	17/1	+.17
1130	45–220 Patrilineal descent and killing of aged women	36/5	17/1	+.47
1131	47–219 Patrilineal inheritance and killing of aged men	46/4	15/2	−.28
1132	47–220 Patrilineal inheritance and killing of aged women	46/8	15/2	+.17
1133	49–219 Patrilineal succession and killing of aged men	45/3	10/1	−.25
1134	49–220 Patrilineal succession and killing of aged women	45/7	10/4	−.19
1135	51–219 Patripotestal family authority and killing of aged men	50/4	8/1	−.33
1136	51–220 Patripotestal family authority and killing of aged women	50/8	8/1	+.04
1137	81–219 Organized priesthood and killing of aged men	21/1	34/3	−.02
1138	81–220 Organized priesthood and killing of aged women	21/3	34/5	+.31
1139	83–219 Ancestor worship and killing of aged men	15/3	21/3	+.29
1140	83–220 Ancestor worship and killing of aged women	15/3	21/3	+.29
1141	98–219 Attractiveness of future life and killing of aged men	43/2	17/4	−.68
1142	98–220 Attractiveness of future life and killing of aged women	43/5	17/6	−.55
1143	1–223 Permanency of residence and sympathy or prestige associated with a violent death	47/5	24/8	−.83*
1144	12–223 Constancy of food supply and sympathy or prestige associated with violent death	53/6	15/7	−.40
1145	179–223 Willingness to die and sympathy or prestige associated with a violent death	10/3	7/1	+.60*
1146	180–224 Willingness to die and sympathy or prestige associated with a violent death	10/3	7/0	+.20*

APPENDIX B

INDEX OF CORRELATIONS

Trait Numbers	Correlation Numbers	Trait Numbers	Correlation Numbers	Trait Numbers	Correlation Numbers
0– 30	3	1–149	479	6– 93	1050
0– 81	392	1–150	480	6– 94	1057
0– 82	380	1–153	455	6–121	285
0– 84	414	1–154	456	6–123	317
0– 92	368	1–177	437	6–125	342
0–127	53	1–178	438	6–127	57
0–128	54	1–191	119	6–128	58
0–139	218	1–192	120	6–133	859
0–140	212	1–193	21	6–134	894
0–149	477	1–194	22	6–135	833
0–150	478	1–195	957	6–136	811
0–153	453	1–196	958	6–139	220
0–154	454	1–197	1023	6–140	214
0–177	435	1–198	1024	6–149	481
0–178	436	1–217	1063	6–150	482
0–191	117	1–218	1064	6–153	457
0–192	118	1–219	1093	6–154	458
0–193	4	1–220	1094	6–169	187
0–194	5	1–223	1143	6–170	192
0–203	39			6–171	204
0–204	40	6– 30	6	6–172	208
0–219	1091	6– 31	247 (284)	6–173	196
0–220	1092	6– 33	261	6–174	200
		6– 36	255	6–177	439
1– 31	246	6– 38	267	6–178	440
1– 33	260	6– 40	273	6–191	121
1– 36	254	6– 42	680	6–192	122
1– 38	266	6– 43	715	6–193	11
1– 40	272	6– 44	685	6–194	12
1– 81	393	6– 45	720	6–195	947
1– 82	381	6– 46	690	6–196	948
1– 84	415	6– 47	725	6–197	1013
1– 92	369	6– 48	695	6–198	1014
1– 93	1049	6– 49	730	6–203	41
1– 94	1056	6– 50	700	6–204	42
1–121	290	6– 51	735	6–217	1065
1–123	316	6– 52	705	6–218	1066
1–125	341	6– 53	710	6–219	1097
1–133	864	6– 81	394	6–220	1098
1–134	908	6– 82	382		
1–139	219	6– 84	416	7– 30	8
1–140	213	6– 92	370	7– 31	248

Trait Numbers	Correlation Numbers	Trait Numbers	Correlation Numbers	Trait Numbers	Correlation Numbers
7– 33	262	7–197	1015	8–195	951
7– 36	256	7–198	1016	8–177	443
7– 38	268	7–203	43	8–178	444
7– 40	274	7–204	44	8–196	952
7– 42	681	7–217	1067	8–197	1017
7– 43	716	7–218	1068	8–198	1018
7– 44	686	7–219	1099	8–203	45
7– 45	721	7–220	1100	8–204	46
7– 46	691			8–217	1069
7– 47	726	8– 30	7	8–218	1070
7– 48	696	8– 31	249	8–219	1101
7– 49	731	8– 33	263	8–220	1102
7– 50	701	8– 36	257		
7– 51	736	8– 38	269	9– 30	9
7– 52	706	8– 40	275	9– 31	250
7– 53	711	8– 42	682	9– 33	264
7– 81	395	8– 43	717	9– 36	258
7– 82	383	8– 44	687	9– 38	270
7– 84	417	8– 45	722	9– 40	276
7– 92	371	8– 46	692	9– 42	683
7– 93	1051	8– 47	727	9– 43	718
7– 94	1058	8– 48	697	9– 44	688
7–121	286	8– 49	732	9– 45	723
7–123	318	8– 50	702	9– 46	693
7–125	343	8– 51	737	9– 47	728
7–127	59	8– 52	707	9– 48	698
7–128	60	8– 53	712	9– 49	733
7–133	860	8– 81	396	9– 50	703
7–134	895	8– 82	384	9– 51	738
7–135	834	8– 92	372	9– 52	708
7–136	812	8– 84	418	9– 53	713
7–139	221	8– 93	1059	9– 81	397
7–140	215	8– 94	1052	9– 82	385
7–149	483	8–121	287	9– 84	419
7–150	484	8–123	319	9– 92	373
7–153	459	8–125	344	9– 93	1053
7–154	460	8–127	61	9– 94	1060
7–165	188	8–128	62	9–121	288
7–166	193	8–133	861	9–123	320
7–171	205	8–134	896	9–125	345
7–172	209	8–135	835	9–127	63
7–173	197	8–136	813	9–128	64
7–174	201	8–149	485	9–133	862
7–177	441	8–150	486	9–134	897
7–178	442	8–153	461	9–135	836
7–191	123	8–154	462	9–136	814
7–192	124	8–165	189	9–139	222
7–193	15	8–191	125	9–140	216
7–194	16	8–192	126	9–149	487
7–195	949	8–193	13	9–150	488
7–196	950	8–194	14	9–153	463

Trait Numbers	Correlation Numbers	Trait Numbers	Correlation Numbers	Trait Numbers	Correlation Numbers
9–154	464	10–127	65	12–125	347
9–167	190	10–128	66	12–127	55
9–168	194	10–133	863	12–128	56
9–171	206	10–134	898	12–133	866
9–172	210	10–135	837	12–134	910
9–173	198	10–136	815	12–191	133
9–174	202	10–139	223	12–192	132
9–177	445	10–140	217	12–193	23
9–178	446	10–149	489	12–194	24
9–191	127	10–150	490	12–195	961
9–192	128	10–153	465	12–196	962
9–193	17	10–154	466	12–197	1027
9–194	18	10–163	191	12–198	1028
9–195	953	10–164	195	12–203	51
9–196	954	10–171	207	12–204	52
9–197	1019	10–172	211	12–219	1095
9–198	1020	10–173	199	12–220	1096
9–203	47	10–174	203	12–223	1144
9–204	48	10–177	447		
9–217	1071	10–178	448	14–127	75
9–218	1072	10–191	129	14–128	76
9–219	1103	10–192	130		
9–220	1104	10–193	19	23–127	77
		10–194	20	23–128	78
10– 30	10	10–195	955	23–193	37
10– 31	251	10–196	956	23–194	38
10– 33	265	10–197	1021		
10– 36	259	10–198	1022	24–127	81
10– 38	271	10–203	49	24–128	82
10– 40	277	10–204	50	24–191	133
10– 42	684	10–217	1073	24–192	134
10– 43	719	10–218	1074	24–193	35
10– 44	689	10–219	1105	24–194	36
10– 45	724	10–220	1106		
10– 46	694			25–127	83
10– 47	729	11 –81	399	25–128	84
10– 48	699	11– 84	421	25–191	135
10– 49	734	11–133	865	25–192	136
10– 50	704	11–134	909	26–193	31
10– 51	739	11–193	25	25–194	32
10– 52	709	11–194	26		
10– 53	714	11–195	959	26–127	79
10– 81	398	11–196	960	26–128	80
10– 82	386	11–197	1027	26–191	137
10– 84	420	11–198	1026	26–192	138
10– 92	374	11–219	1107	26–193	33
10– 93	1054	11–220	1108	26–194	34
10– 94	1061				
10–121	289	12– 81	400	27–127	69
10–123	321	12– 84	422	27–128	70
10–125	346	12–123	322		

Trait Numbers	Correlation Numbers	Trait Numbers	Correlation Numbers	Trait Numbers	Correlation Numbers
28–121	314	31–198	1030	38– 52	745
28–123	323	31–219	1111	38– 53	746
28–125	348	31–220	1112	38– 66	754
28–127	71			38– 72	755
28–128	72	33– 31	253	38– 74	752
28–191	139	33– 38	282	38– 80	753
28–192	140	33– 40	279	38– 81	405
28–193	29	33– 81	402	38– 84	426
28–194	30	33– 84	424	38–121	298
		33–121	293	38–123	331
29–127	73	33–123	326	38–125	356
29–128	74	33–125	352	38–133	874
29–191	141	33–133	873	38–134	913
29–192	142	33–134	912	38–135	838
29–193	27	33–191	147	38–136	821
29–194	28	33–192	148	38–191	145
29–219	1109	33–195	965	38–192	146
29–220	1110	33–196	966	38–195	967
		33–197	1031	38–196	968
30–127	67	33–198	1032	38–219	1113
30–128	68			38–220	1114
30–193	1	34–121	295		
30–194	2	34–123	328	39–121	297
		34–125	350	39–123	330
31– 38	281·	34–134	921	39–125	355
31– 39	283	34–191	149		
31– 40	278	34–192	150	40–121	299
31– 42	756			40–123	332
31– 43	761	35– 81	403	40–125	359
31– 44	757	35– 84	425	40–191	151
31– 45	762	35–121	296	40–192	152
31– 46	758	35–123	329		
31– 47	763	35–125	354	42– 34	582
31– 48	759			42– 43	533
31– 49	764	36– 31	252 (291)	42– 44	503
31– 50	760	36– 81	404	42– 45	534
31– 66	767	36–121	292	42– 46	504
31– 72	768	36–123	325	42– 47	535
31– 74	765	36–125	351	42– 48	505
31– 80	766			42– 49	536
31– 81	401	38– 40	280	42– 50	506 (570)
31– 84	423	38– 42	740	42– 51	537 (640)
31–121	294	38– 43	747	42– 53	507 (576)
31–123	327	38– 44	741	42– 61	646
31–125	353	38– 45	748	42– 65	620
31–133	872	38– 46	742	42– 66	622
31–134	911	38– 47	749	42– 68	653
31–136	820	38– 48	743	42– 72	656
31–195	963	38– 49	750	42– 74	608
31–196	964	38– 50	744	42– 80	614
31–197	1029	38– 51	751	42– 81	406

Trait Numbers	Correlation Numbers	Trait Numbers	Correlation Numbers	Trait Numbers	Correlation Numbers
42- 82	387	43-136	806	44-177	449
42- 84	427	43-139	230	44-178	450
42- 92	375	43-140	241	44-191	170
42-121	302	43-191	175	44-192	158
42-123	335	43-192	164	44-195	927
42-125	360	43-195	925	44-196	928
42-127	85	43-196	926	44-197	991
42-128	86	43-197	1003	44-198	992
42-133	852	43-198	1004	44-217	1081
42-134	887	43-217	1079	44-218	1082
42-135	845	43-218	1080	44-219	1117
42-136	799	43-219	1127	44-220	1118
42-139	224	43-220	1128		
42-140	235			45- 34	600
42-191	169	44- 34	583	45- 47	527
42-192	157	44- 43	538	45- 49	528
42-195	923	44- 45	539	45- 50	590
42-196	924	44- 46	508	45- 51	529 (664)
42-197	989	44- 47	540	45- 61	668
42-198	990	44- 48	509	45- 53	595
42-217	1077	44- 49	541	45- 65	636
42-218	1078	44- 50	510 (571)	45- 66	638
42-219	1115	44- 51	542 (641)	45- 68	673
42-220	1116	44- 52	511	45- 72	676
		44- 53	512 (577)	45- 74	626
43- 34	599	44- 61	647	45- 80	631
43- 45	523	44- 65	621	45- 81	409
43- 47	524	44- 66	623	45- 82	390
43- 49	525	44- 68	654	45- 84	430
43- 50	589	44- 72	657	45- 92	378
43- 51	526 (663)	44- 74	609	45-121	305
43- 53	594	44- 80	615	45-123	338
43- 61	667	44- 81	407	45-125	363
43- 64	429	44- 82	388	45-127	101
43- 65	635	44- 84	428	45-128	102
43- 66	637	44- 92	376	45-133	868
43- 68	672	44-121	304	45-134	900
43- 72	675	44-123	337	45-135	829
43- 74	625	44-125	362	45-136	807
43- 80	630	44-127	87	45-139	231
43- 81	408	44-128	88	45-140	242
43- 82	389	44-133	853	45-149	493
43- 92	377	44-134	888	45-150	494
43-121	303	44-135	846	45-153	469
43-123	336	44-136	800	45-154	470
43-125	361	44-139	225	45-177	451
43-127	99	44-140	236	45-178	452
43-128	100	44-149	491	45-191	176
43-133	867	44-150	492	45-192	165
43-134	899	44-153	467	45-195	929
43-135	828	44-154	468	45-196	930

Trait Numbers	Correlation Numbers	Trait Numbers	Correlation Numbers	Trait Numbers	Correlation Numbers
45–197	1005	47– 66	639	48–195	935
45–198	1006	47– 68	674	48–196	936
45–217	1083	47– 72	677	48–197	995
45–218	1084	47– 74	627	48–198	996
45–219	1129	47– 80	632	48–219	1121
45–220	1130	47–121	307	48–220	1122
		47–123	340		
46– 34	584	47–125	365	49– 34	602
46– 43	543	47–127	103	49– 50	592
46– 45	544	47–128	104	49– 51	532 (666)
46– 47	545	47–133	869	49– 53	597
46– 48	513	47–134	901	49– 61	670
46– 49	546	47–135	830	49– 72	678
46– 50	514 (572)	47–136	808	49– 74	628
46– 51	547 (642)	47–139	232	49– 80	633
46– 52	515	47–140	243	49–121	309
46– 53	516 (578)	47–191	177	49–127	105
46– 61	648	47–192	166	49–128	106
46– 66	624	47–195	933	49–133	870
46– 68	655	47–196	934	49–134	902
46– 72	658	47–197	1007	49–135	831
46– 74	610	47–198	1008	49–136	809
46– 80	616	47–217	1087	49–139	233
46–121	306	47–218	1088	49–140	244
46–123	339	47–219	1131	49–191	178
46–125	364	47–220	1132	49–192	167
46–127	89			49–195	937
46–128	90	48– 34	585	49–196	938
46–133	854	48– 43	548	49–197	1009
46–134	889	48– 45	549	49–198	1010
46–135	847	48– 47	550	49–219	1133
46–136	801	48– 49	551	49–220	1134
46–139	226	48– 50	517 (573)		
46–140	237	48– 51	552 (643)	50– 34	568 (586)
46–191	171	48– 52	518	50– 43	553
46–192	159	48– 53	519 (579)	50– 45	554
46–195	931	48– 61	649	50– 47	555
46–196	932	48– 72	659	50– 49	556
46–197	993	48– 74	611	50– 51	557 (644)
46–198	994	48– 80	617	50– 52	520 (574)
46–217	1085	48–121	308	50– 53	521 (575 580)
46–218	1086	48–127	91		
46–219	1119	48–128	92	50– 61	650
46–220	1130	48–133	855	50– 72	660
		48–134	890	50– 74	612
47– 34	601	48–135	848	50– 80	618
47– 49	530	48–136	802	50–121	310
47– 50	591	48–139	227	50–127	95
47– 51	531 (665)	48–140	238	50–128	96
47– 53	596	48–191	172	50–133	856
47– 61	669	48–192	160	50–134	891

Trait Numbers	Correlation Numbers	Trait Numbers	Correlation Numbers	Trait Numbers	Correlation Numbers
50–135	849	52–133	857	55– 50	773
50–136	803	52–134	892	55– 51	779
50–139	228	52–135	850	55– 53	774
50–140	239	52–136	804	55– 66	782
50–191	173	52–139	229	55– 72	783
50–192	161	52–140	240	55– 74	780
50–195	939	52–191	174	55– 80	781
50–196	940	52–192	162	55– 81	410
50–197	997	52–195	943	55– 84	431
50–198	998	52–196	944	55–121	301
50–218	1089	52–197	999	55–123	334
50–219	1123	52–198	1000	55–125	357
50–220	1124			55–133	875
		53– 34	569 (588)	55–134	914
51– 34	603	53– 43	563	55–135	839
51– 50	593	53– 45	564	55–136	822
51– 53	598	53– 47	565	55–195	969
51– 61	671	53– 49	566	55–196	970
51– 72	679	53– 51	567 (645)	55–197	1033
51– 74	629	53– 61	652	55–198	1034
51– 80	634	53– 72	662		
51–121	311	53– 74	613	56– 81	411
51–127	107	53– 80	619	56– 84	432
51–128	108	53–121	313	56–133	876
51–133	871	53–127	93	56–134	915
51–134	903	53–128	94	56–135	840
51–135	832	53–133	858	56–136	823
51–136	810	53–134	893	56–195	971
51–139	234	53–135	851	56–196	972
51–140	245	53–136	805	56–197	1035
51–191	179	53–192	163	56–198	1036
51–192	168	53–195	945		
51–195	941	53–196	946	61–133	877
51–196	942	53–197	1001	61–134	904
51–197	1011	53–198	1002	61–135	841
51–198	1012	53–218	1090	61–136	817
51–219	1135	53–219	1125	61–191	180
51–220	1136	53–220	1126	61–192	181
				61–195	973
52– 34	587	54–121	300	61–196	974
52– 43	558	54–123	333		
52– 45	559	54–125	358	62–133	878
52– 47	560			62–134	916
52– 49	561	55– 42	769		
52– 51	562	55– 43	775	63–134	917
52– 53	522 (581)	55– 44	770	63–135	842
52– 61	651	55– 45	776	63–136	818
52– 72	661	55– 46	771		
52–121	312	55– 47	777	65– 74	604
52–127	97	55– 48	772		
52–128	98	55– 49	778	66–127	109

Trait Numbers	Correlation Numbers	Trait Numbers	Correlation Numbers	Trait Numbers	Correlation Numbers
66–128	110	81– 47	792	83–220	1140
66–133	879	81– 48	787		
66–134	918	81– 49	793	84– 81	413
66–135	843	81– 50	788	84–149	499
66–136	824	81– 51	794	84–150	500
66–195	975	81– 53	789	84–153	475
66–196	976	81– 72	798	84–154	476
66–197	1037	81– 74	795		
66–198	1038	81– 80	796	93–217	1045
		81– 82	391	93–218	1046
70–133	880	81– 84	433		
70–134	905	81– 92	379	94–217	1047
		81– 93	1055	94–218	1048
72–133	881	81– 94	1062		
72–134	919	81–127	113	98–219	1141
72–136	825	81–128	114	98–220	1142
72–195	977	81–133	884		
72–196	978	81–134	920	123–191	153
72–197	1039	81–136	827	123–192	154
72–198	1040	81–149	497		
		81–150	498	127–121	315
74– 66	606	81–153	473	127–123	324
74–133	882	81–154	474	127–125	349
74–134	907	81–195	983	127–133	886
74–136	826	81–196	984	127–191	143 (184)
74–195	981	81–197	1043	127–195	987
74–196	982	81–198	1044		
74–197	1041	81–217	1075	128–134	922
74–198	1042	81–218	1076	128–136	816
		81–219	1137	128–196	988
80– 66	607 (797)	81–220	1138		
80– 74	605			131–125	366
80–127	111	82–149	495	131–191	155
80–128	112	82–150	496	131–192	156
80–133	883	82–153	471		
80–134	906	82–154	472	133–191	185
80–135	844			133–192	144
80–191	182	83– 81	412		
80–192	183	83– 84	434	135–191	186
80–195	979	83–127	115		
80–196	980	83–128	116	149–125	367
		83–133	885		
81– 42	784	83–149	501	154–136	819
81– 43	790	83–150	502		
81– 44	785	83–195	985	179–223	1145
81– 45	791	83–196	986		
81– 46	786	83–219	1139	180–224	1146

BIBLIOGRAPHY

Key to Abbreviations

AA: *American Anthropologist.* Washington, New York, Lancaster, Menasha.

AAAG: *Annals of the Association of American Geographers.* Madison.

AN: *American Naturalist.* Salem.

APAM: *Anthropological Papers of the American Museum of Natural History.* New York.

ARBAE: *Annual Reports of the Bureau of American Ethnology.* Washington.

ARSI: *Annual Reports of the Board of Regents of the Smithsonian Institution.* Washington.

BAMNH: *Bulletin of the American Museum of Natural History.* New York.

BBAE: *Bulletin of the Bureau of American Ethnology.* Washington.

BSAP: *Bulletin de la Société d'Anthropologie.* Paris.

CMAI: *Contributions from the Museum of the American Indian, Heye Foundation.* New York.

CNAE: *Contributions to North American Ethnology, Department of the Interior, United States Geographical and Geological Survey of the Rocky Mountain Region.* Washington.

CUCA: *Columbia University Contributions to Anthropology.* New York.

FL: *Folk-lore.* London.

FMAS: *Field (Columbian) Museum (of Natural History) Anthropological Series.* Chicago.

G: *Globus.* Braunschweig.

HAS: *Harvard African Studies.* Cambridge.

INM: *Indian Notes and Monographs, Museum of the American Indian, Heye Foundation.* New York.

JAI: *Journal of the (Royal) Anthropological Institute of Great Britain and Ireland.* London.

JAFL: *Journal of American Folklore.* Boston, New York.

MAAA: *Memoirs of the American Anthropological Association.* Lancaster, Menasha.

MAMNH: *Memoirs of the American Museum of Natural History.*
New York.

MASL: *Memoirs of the Anthropological Society of London.*
London.

MCDM: *Memoirs of the Canada Department of Mines, Geological Survey.* Ottawa.

PMP: *Peabody Museum Papers* (Archaeological and Ethnological Papers of the Peabody Museum, Harvard University). Cambridge.

RBAAS: *Report of the British Association for the Advancement
of Science.* London.

RCDM: *Canadian Department of Mines, Geological Survey Reports.* Montreal.

RGSC: *Report of the Geological Survey of Canada.* Montreal.

RPM: *Reports of the Peabody Museum of American Archaeol-
ogy and Ethnology, Harvard University.* Cambridge.

RUSNM: *Reports of the United States National Museum.* Washington.

TESL: *Transactions of the Ethnological Society. London.*

TPRSSA: *Transactions and Proceedings of the Royal Society of
South Australia.* Adelaide.

UCP: *University of California Publications in American Ar-
chaeology and Ethnology.* Berkeley.

UPMAP: *University of Pennsylvania Museum Anthropological
Publications.* Philadelphia.

1. Adair, J. *The History of the American Indians.* London, 1775.
2. Alberti, L. *Description physique et historique des Cafres sur la
   côte meridionale de l'Afrique.* Amsterdam, 1811.
3. Andrews, C. E. *Old Morocco and the Forbidden Atlas.* London,
   1922.
4. Atkinson, T. W. *Oriental and Western Siberia.* Philadelphia,
   1860.
5. Bancroft, H. H. *The Native Races of the Pacific States of
   North America.* New York, 1875. 3 vols.
6. ———— *The Native Races,* Vol. I. San Francisco, 1883.
7. ———— "The History of Mexico," Vol. I, In *Works of H. H.
   Bancroft,* Vol. IX. San Francisco, 1883.
8. Bandelier, A. F. "The Art of War and Mode of Warfare of the
   Ancient Mexicans." *RPM,* Vol. II. 1880.
9. Barbeau, C. M. "On Iroquoian Field-Work." *RCDM,* Report
   for 1912.

10. Barrett, S. A. "Ceremonies of the Pomo Indians." *UCP*, Vol. XII. 1917.
11. Batchelor, J. *The Ainu of Japan*. London, 1895.
12. —— *Ainu Life and Lore*. Tokyo, 1927.
13. Beaglehole, E., and P. "Ethnology of the Pukapuka." *Bernice P. Bishop Museum Bulletin*, No. 20. 1938.
14. Beauchamp, W. M. "Onondago Tale of the Pleiades." *JAFL*, Vol. XIII. 1900.
15. —— "The Good Hunter and the Iroquois Medicine." *JAFL*, Vol. XIV. 1901.
16. Beaver, W. N. *Unexplored New Guinea*. London, 1920.
17. Becham, J. *Ashantee and the Gold Coast*. London, 1841.
18. Belcher, E. "Notes on the Andaman Islands." *TESL*, n.s., Vol. V. 1867.
19. Bennett, A. L. "Ethnological Notes on the Fang." *JAI*, Vol. XXIX. 1899.
20. Best, E. *The Maori*. Wellington, 1924. 2 vols.
21. —— *The Maori As He Was*. Wellington, 1924.
22. Biart, L. *The Aztecs*. Chicago, 1892.
23. Bird, I. L. *Unbeaten Tracks in Japan*. New York, 1881.
24. Bleek, D. G. *The Naron: A Bushman Tribe of the Central Kalahari*. Cambridge, 1928.
25. Boas, F. "First General Report of the Indians of British Columbia." *RBAAS*, Vol. LIX. 1890.
26. —— "Social Organization and the Secret Societies of the Kwakiutl Indians." *RUSNM*, Vol. L. 1895.
27. —— "The Kwakiutl of Vancouver Island." *MAMNH*, Vol. VIII. 1909.
28. Bogoras, W. "The Chukchee." *MAMNH*, Vol. XI. 1904.
29. —— "Tales of the Yukaghir, Lamut and Russianized Natives of Eastern Siberia." *MAMNH*, Vol. XX. 1918.
30. Bonwick, J. *Daily Life and Origin of the Tasmanians*. London, 1870.
31. Bourhill, E. J., and Drake, J. B. *Fairy Tales from South Africa*. London, 1908.
32. Bourke, J. G. *The Snake-Dance of the Moquis of Arizona*. London, 1884.
33. Bowdich, T. E. *Mission from Cape Coast Castle to Ashanti*. London, 1819.
34. Breeks, J. W. *An Account of Primitive Tribes and Monuments of the Nilagiris*. London, 1873.

35. Brett, W. H. *The Indian Tribes of Guiana: Their Conditions and Habits.* London, 1868.

36. ——— *Legends and Myths of the Aboriginal Indians of British Guiana.* London, 1880.

37. Bridges, T. "Moeurs et coutumes des Fuegiens." *BSAP*, Vol. VII, Sec. 3. 1884.

38. Briffault, R. *The Mothers: A Study of the Origins of Sentiments and Institutions.* New York, 1927. 3 vols.

39. Broughton, J. C. M. *Travels in Albania,* Vol. I. London, 1855.

40. Brown, A. R. *The Andaman Islanders.* Cambridge, 1922.

41. Bunzel, R. "The Role of Alcoholism in Two Central American Cultures." *Psychiatry,* Vol. III. 1941.

42. Burton, R. F. *A Mission to Gelele, King of Dahome.* London, 1864. 2 vols.

43. ——— "Notes on Certain Matters Connected with the Dahomans." *MASL*, Vol. I. 1865.

44. Bushnell, D. I., Jr., "Native Cemeteries and Forms of Burial East of the Mississippi." *BBAE*, Vol. LXXI, 1920.

45. Buxton, D. "Some Navajo Folk-Tales and Customs." *FL*, Vols. XXXIII–XXXIV. 1923.

46. Campbell, D. *On the Trail of the Veiled Tuareg.* London, 1918.

47. Cardinall, A. W. *In Ashanti and Beyond.* London, 1927.

48. Carey, B. S., and Tuck, H. N. *The Chin Hills,* Vol. I. Rangoon, 1896.

49. Carruthers, D. *Unknown Mongolia.* London, 1913. 2 vols.

50. Chalmers, J. "Notes on the Natives of Kiwai Island, Fly River, British New Guinea." *JAI*, Vol. XXXI. 1903.

51. Chamberlain, A. F. "Report of the Kootenay Indians of Southeastern British Columbia." *RBAAS*, Vol. LXII. 1892.

52. Chapman, J. *Travels in the Interior of South Africa.* London, 1868. 2 vols.

53. Claridge, G. C. *Wild Bush Tribes of Tropical Africa.* London, 1922.

54. Codrington, R. H. *The Melanesians.* Oxford, 1891.

55. Coombe, F. *Islands of Enchantment.* London, 1911.

56. Cooper, J. M. "Analytical and Critical Bibliography of the Tribes of Tierra Del Fuego and Adjacent Territory." *BBAE*, Vol. LXIII. 1917.

57. Copway, G. *The Traditional History and Characteristic Sketches of the Ojibway Nation.* London, 1850.

58. Cowan, J. *The Maoris of New Zealand.* London, 1910.

59. Crane, L. *Indians of the Enchanted Desert.* Boston, 1925.

60. Curtin, J. *Seneca Indian Myths*. New York, 1923.
61. Curtis, E. S. *The North American Indians*, Vol. I Cambridge, 1907.
62. ———— *The North American Indians*, Vol. IV. Cambridge, 1909.
63. ———— *The North American Indians*, Vol. X. Norwood, 1915.
64. ———— *The North American Indians*, Vol. XI. Norwood, 1916.
65. ———— *The North American Indians*, Vol. XII. Norwood, 1922.
66. Czaplicka, M. A. *Aboriginal Siberia*. London, 1914.
67. ———— *My Siberian Year*. London, 1914.
68. Dawson, G. M. "Report of the Queen Charlotte Islands." *RGSC*, Report for the year 1878–79. Montreal, 1880.
69. Delafosse, M. "Les Vaï: leur langue et leur système d'écriture." *L'Anthropologie*, Vol. X. 1899.
70. Dennis, W. *The Hopi Child*. New York, 1941.
71. Densmore, F. "Chippewa Music." *BBAE*, Vol. XLV, 1910.
72. ———— "Chippewa Music." *BBAE*, Vol. LIII. 1913.
73. ———— "Chippewa Customs." *BBAE*, Vol. LXXXVI. 1920.
74. ———— "Uses of Plants by the Chippewa Indians." *ARBAE*, Vol. XLIV. 1926–27.
75. Dobrizhoffer, M. *An Account of the Abipones. An Esquestrian People of Paraguay*. London, 1822. 2 vols.
76. Donne, T. E. *The Maori, Past and Present*. London, 1927.
77. Dornan, S. S. *Pygmies and Bushmen of Kalahari*. London, 1925.
78. Dorsey, J. O. "Omaha Sociology." *ARBAE*, Vol. III. 1881–82.
79. ———— "A Study of Siouan Cults." *ARBAE*, Vol. XI. 1894.
80. ———— "Omaha Dwellings, Furniture and Implements." *ARBAE*, Vol. XIII. 1898.
81. Dowd, J. *The Negro Races*. New York, 1907. 2 vols.
82. Driberg, J. H. *The Lango*. London, 1923.
83. Du Chaillu, P. B. *The Land of the Midnight Sun*. London, 1882. 2 vols.
84. Duncan, J. *Travels in Western Africa in 1845–46*. London, 1847. 2 vols.
85. Dundas, C. "History of Kitui." *JAI*, Vol. XLIII. 1913.
86. ———— "The Organization and Laws of Some Bantu Tribes of East Africa." *JAI*, Vol. XLV. 1915.
87. ———— "Native Laws of Some Bantu Tribes of East Africa." *JAI*, Vol. LI. 1921.
88. Durham, M. E. *The Burden of the Balkans*. New York, 1905.

89. Ekblaw, W. E. "The Material Response of the Polar Eskimo to Their Far Arctic Environment." *AAAG*, Vols. XVII, XVIII. 1927–28.

90. Ellis, A. B. *The Tshi-Speaking Peoples of the Gold Coast of West Africa.* London, 1887.

91. —— *The Ewe-speaking People of the Slave Coast of West Africa.* London, 1890.

92. Ellis, G. W. *Negro Culture in West Africa.* New York, 1914.

93. Elton, O., and Powell, F. Y. *The First Nine Books of the Danish History of Saxo Grammaticus.* London, 1893.

94. Emaneau, M. B. "Toda Culture Thirty-five Years After." *Annals of the Bhandarkar. Oriental Research Institute*, Vol. XIX, Pt. II. 1938.

95. Enock, C. R. *Peru.* London, 1928.

96. Evans, I. H. N. *Studies in Religion, Folk-Lore and Customs in British North Borneo and the Malay Peninsula.* Cambridge, 1923.

97. Farabee, W. C. "Indian Tribes of Eastern Peru." *PMP*, Vol. X. 1922.

98. Featherman, A. *Social History of the Races of Mankind,* Vol. III. London, 1890.

99. Fewkes, J. W. "Fire Worship of the Hopi Indians." *Report of the Smithsonian Institute*, Vol. LXXV, Pt. I. 1920.

100. Firth, R. *Primitive Economics of the New Zealand Maori.* New York, 1929.

101. Fitzroy, R., ed. *Narrative of the surveying voyages of His Majesty's ships Adventure and Beagle, between the years 1826 and 1836, describing their examination of the southern shores of South America, and the Beagle's circumnavigation of the globe.* London, 1839. 3 vols.

102. Fletcher, A. C. "Glimpses of Child-Life among the Omaha Tribe of Indians." *JAFL*, Vol. I. 1888.

103. Fletcher, A. C., and La Flesche, F. "The Omaha." *ARBAE*, Vol. XXVII. 1905–6.

104. Ford, C. S. *Smoke from Their Fires.* New Haven, 1941.

105. Frazer, J. G. *The Golden Bough. A Study in Magic and Religion.* London, 1890. 2 vols.

106. —— *Belief in Immortality and the Worship of the Dead.* London, 1913–24. 3 vols.

107. —— *The Golden Bough; A Study in Magic and Religion.* New York, 1927. 1 vol.

108. —— *Folk-Lore in the Old Testament* (Abridged ed.) New York, 1927.

109. Friis, J. A. *Lajla; A Tale of Finmark.* London, 1888.

110. Furness, W. H. "The Ethnography of the Nagas of Eastern Assam." *JAI*, Vol. XXXII. 1902.

111. Garnett, L. M. J. *Balkan Home-Life.* London, 1917.

112. Garson, J. G. "On the Inhabitants of Tierra Del Fuego." *JAI*, Vol. XV. 1886.

113. Gason, S. "Of the Tribes, Dieyerie, Auminie, Yandrawontha, Yarawuarka, Pilladapa." *Jai*, Vol. XXIV .1894.

114. Gillin, J. "The Barama River Caribs of British Guiana." *PMP*, Vol. XIV, No. 2. 1936.

115. Goddard, P. E. *Indians of the Northwest Coast.* New York, 1924.

116. —— *Indians of the Southwest.* New York, 1931.

117. Gomes, E. H. *Seventeen Years among the Sea Dyaks of Borneo.* London, 1910.

118. Grubb, W. B. *Among the Indians of the Paraguayan Chaco.* London, 1904.

119. —— *An Unknown People in an Unknown Land.* London, 1911.

120. —— *A Church in the Wilds.* New York, 1914.

121. Haddon, A. C. *Head-Hunters, Black, White and Brown.* London, 1901.

122. Hardenberg, W. E. *The Putumayo: The Devil's Paradise.* London, 1912.

123. Harrison, C. *Ancient Warriors of the North Pacific.* London, 1925.

124. Hawkes, E. W. "The Labrador Eskimo." *MCDM*, XCI. 1916.

125. Hawkins, B. "A Sketch of Creek County, in the Years 1798 and 1799." *Collections of the Georgia Historical Society*, Vol. III. 1848.

126. Hedin, S. A. *Through Asia*, Vol. I. London, 1889.

127. Herskovits, M. J. *Dahomey: An Ancient West African Kingdom.* New York, 1938. 2 vols.

128. Hitchcock, R. "The Ainos of Yezo, Japan." *Annual Report of the Board of Regents of the Smithsonian Institution, Year Ending June 30, 1890.* Washington, 1891.

129. Hobley, C. W. *A-Kamba and other East African Tribes.* Cambridge, 1910.

130. —— "Further Researches into Kikuyu and Kamba Religious Beliefs and Customs." *JAI*, Vol. XLI. 1911.

131. ——— *Bantu Beliefs and Magic.* London, 1922.

132. Hoernlé, A. W. "Certain Rites of Transition and the Conception of Nau among the Hottentots." *HAS*, Vol. II. 1918.

133. ——— "The Social Organization of the Nama Hottentots of Southwest Africa." *AA*, n.s., Vol. XXVII. 1925.

134. Hoffman, W. J. "The Midewiwin or 'Grand Medicine Society.' " *ARBAE*, Vol. VII. 1885–86.

135. ——— "The Menomini Indians." *ARBAE*, XIV. 1896.

136. Holden, W. C. *The Past and Future of the Kaffir Races.* London, 1871.

137. Holy Bible (Am. Standard Version.) New York, 1901.

138. Horne, G., and Aiston, G. *Savage Life in Central Australia.* London, 1924.

139. Hose, C. "The Relations between Men and Animals in Sarawak." *JAI*, Vol. XXXI. 1901.

140. Hose, C., and McDougall, W. *The Pagan Tribes of Borneo.* London, 1912. 2 vols.

141. Hough, W. *The Hopi Indians.* Cedar Rapids, 1915.

142. Howitt, A. W. "The Dieri and Other Kindred Tribes of Central Australia." *JAI*, Vol. XX. 1891.

143. Howitt, A. W. *Native Tribes of Southeast Australia.* London, 1904.

144. Howitt, A. W., and Seibert, O. "Legends of the Dieri and Kindred Tribes of Central Australia." *JAI*, Vol. XXXIV. 1904.

145. Howorth, H. H. *History of the Mongols*, Pt. I. London, 1876.

146. ——— *History of the Mongols*, Pt. IV, London, 1927.

147. Huntington, E. *The Pulse of Asia.* Boston, 1920.

148. Hutton, J. H. *The Sema Nagas.* London, 1921.

149. Hutton, S. K. *Among the Eskimos of Labrador.* Philadelphia, 1912.

150. ——— *An Eskimo Village.* London, 1929.

151. Im Thurn, E. F. *Among the Indians of Guiana.* London, 1883.

152. James, G. W. *Indians of the Painted Desert Region.* Boston, 1903.

153. Jenks, A. E. "The Bontoc Igorot." *Ethnological Survey Publications*, Vol. I. Manila, 1905.

154. Jochelson, W. "The Yukaghir and the Yukaghirized Tungus." *MAMNH*, Vol. XIII. 1926.

155. ——— "People of Asiatic Russia." *MAMNH*, Vol. XV. 1928.

156. Jones, P. *History of the Ojebway Indians.* London, 1861.

157. Johnston, H. H. *The River Congo.* London, 1884.

158. Karsten, R. "Blood Revenge, War and Victory Feasts among the Jibaro Indians of Eastern Ecuador." *BBAE*, Vol. LXXIX. 1923.

159. Keane, A. H. "The Lapps; Their Original, Ethnical Affinities, Physical and Mental Characteristics, Usages, Present Status and Future Prospects." *JAI*, Vol. XV. 1886.

160. Kennard, E. A. "Hopi Reactions to Death." *AA*, n.s., Vol. XXXIX. 1937.

161. Kidd, D. *The Essential Kaffir*. London, 1904.

162. —— *Savage Childhood*. London, 1906.

163. Kohl, J. G. *Kitchi-Gami*. London, 1860.

164. Kolben, P. "Voyage to the Cape of Good Hope." *Mavor's Voyages*, Vol. IV. London, 1706.

165. Kroeber, A. L. "The Eskimo of Smith Sound." *BAMNH*, Vol. XII. 1899.

166. —— "Handbook of the Indians of California." *BBAE*, Vol. LXXVIII. 1925.

167. La Flesche, F. "Death and Funeral Customs among the Omaha." *JAFL*, Vol. II. 1889.

168. Landor, A. H. S. *Alone with the Hairy Ainu*. London, 1893.

169. Landtman, G. "The Magic of the Kiwai Papuans in Warfare." *JAI*, Vol. XLVI. 1916.

170. —— "The Folk-Tales of the Kiwai Papuans." *Acta Societatis Scientiarum Fennicae*, Vol. XLVII. Helsingfors, 1917.

171. —— *The Kiwai Papuans of British New Guinea*. London, 1927.

172. Latcham, R. E. "Ethnology of the Araucanos." *JAI*, Vol. XXXIX. 1909.

173. Leem, K. "An Account of the Laplanders of Finmark, Their Language, Manners, and Religion. Pinkerton, *Voyages and Travels*, Vol. I. 1908.

174. Lindblom, G. *The Akamba*. Uppsala, 1916.

175. Linderman, F. B. *Red Mother*. New York, 1932.

176. Linton, R. *The Study of Man*. New York, 1936.

177. Lipps, O. H. *The Navajos*. Cedar Rapids, 1909.

178. Locke, L. L. *The Ancient Quipu of Peruvian Knot Record*. New York, 1923.

179. Lockett, H. G. "The Unwritten Literature of the Hopi." *University of Arizona Social Science Bulletin*, No. 2. 1933.

180. Loeb, E. M. "Pomo Folkways." *UCP*, Vol. XIX. 1926.

181. Loskiel, G. H. *History of the Mission of the United Brethren among the Indians in North America*, Vol. I. London, 1794.

182. Lothrop, S. K. *The Indians of Tierra Del Fuego.* New York, 1928.

183. Lowie, R. H. "Military Societies of the Crow Indians." *APAM*, Vol. XI, Pt. III. 1913.

184. ———— "The Sun Dance of the Crow Indians." *APAM*, Vol. XVI. 1915.

185. ———— "Notes on the Social Organization and Custom of the Mandan, Hidatsa and Crow Indians." *APAM*, Vol. XXI, Pt. 1. 1917.

186. ———— "Myths and Traditions of the Crow Indians." *APAM*, Vol. XXV, Pt. I. 1918.

187. MacDonald, J. "Manners, Customs, Superstitions and Religions of South African Tribes." *JAI*, Vol. XIX. 1890.

188. McGee, W. J. "The Seri Indians." *ARBAE*, XVII, Pt. I. 1898.

189. MacLeod, W. C. *The American Indian Frontier.* New York, 1928.

190. Malinowski, B. "Baloma; The Spirits of the Dead in the Trobriand Islands." *JAI*, Vol. XLVI. 1916.

191. ———— *Argonauts of the Western Pacific.* New York, 1922. 2 vols.

192. ———— *The Sexual Life of Savages in Northwestern Melanesia.* New York, 1929. 2 vols.

193. ———— *Coral Gardens and Their Magic.* New York, 1935. 2 vols.

194. Mann, E. H. "On the Aboriginal Inhabitants of the Andaman Islands." *JAI*, Vol. XII. 1883.

195. Markham, C. R. *Royal Commentaries of the Incas.* London, 1869. 2 vols.

196. ———— *The Incas of Peru.* London, 1910.

197. Marquis, T. B. *Memoirs of a White Crow Indian.* New York, 1928.

198. Marshall, W. E. *A Phrenologist amongst the Todas.* London, 1873.

199. Martius, C. F. P. von *Beiträge zur Ethnographie und Sprachenkunde Amerika's,* Vol. I. Leipzig, 1867.

200. Martrou, L. "Les 'Eki' des Fang." *Anthropos*, Vol. I. 1906.

201. Matthews, W. "Some Deities and Demons of the Navajos." *AN*, Vol. XX. 1886.

202. ———— "The Mountain Chant." *ARBAE*, Vol. V. 1887.

203. ———— "The Night Chant, a Navajo Ceremony." *MAMNH*, Vol. VI. 1902.

204. Mead, M. *Coming of Age in Samoa.* New York, 1928.

205. Milne, L. *The Home of an Eastern Clan*. Oxford, 1924.
206. Moffat, R. *Missionary Labors and Scenes in South Africa*. New York, 1843.
207. Morgan, L. H. *League of the Ho-Dé-No-Sau-Nee or Iroquois*. New York, 1901. 2 vols. Ed. by H. M. Lloyd.
208. Murdock, G. P. *Our Primitive Contemporaries*, New York, 1934.
209. ———— "Correlations on Matrilineal and Patrilineal Institutions." In *Studies in the Science of Society*. New Haven, 1937. Ed. by G. P. Murdock.
210. Murdock, J. "Ethnological Results of the Point Barrow Expedition." *ARBAE*, Vol. IX. 1887–88.
211. Müller, H. P. N. *Industrie des Cafres du sud-est de L'Afrique*. Collection recueille sur les lieux et notice ethnographique. Leyde, 1893.
212. Musil, A. *The Manners and Customs of the Rwala Bedouins*. New York, 1928.
213. Niblack, A. P. "The Coast Indians of Southern Alaska and Northern British Columbia." *ARSI*, for the Year 1888. 1890.
214. Orton, J. *Andes and the Amazon*. New York, 1876.
215. Ostermann, L. "The Navajo Indians of New Mexico and Arizona." *Anthropos*, Vol. III. 1908.
216. Overbergh, C. Van. *Les Mangbetu*. Bruxelles, 1909.
217. Oyler, D. S. "The Shilluk's Belief in the Evil Eye." *Sudan Notes and Records*, Vol. II. 1918.
218. Parker, K. L. *The Euahlayi Tribe*. London, 1905.
219. Parsons, E. C. "A Pueblo Indian Journal." *MAAA*, Vol. XXXII. 1925.
220. ———— *Pueblo Indian Religion*. Chicago, 1939. 2 vols.
221. Perham, J. "Sea Dyak Religion." *Journal of the Straits Branch of the Royal Asiatic Society*, Vol. X. 1883.
222. ———— "Sea Dyak Religion." *Journal of the Straits Branch of the Royal Asiatic Society*, Vol. XIV. 1885.
223. Pilsudski, B. "Der Schamans mus bei Ainu—Stämmen von Sachalin," *G*, Vol. XCV, nr. 5. 1909.
224. ————, ed. *Material for the Study of the Ainu Language and Folklore*. Cracow, Imperial Academy of Science, 1912.
225. Portman, M. V. "Notes on the Andamanese." *JAI*, Vol. XXV. 1895.
226. Powers, S. "Tribes of California." *CNAE*, Vol. III. 1877.
227. Prescott, W. H. *History of the Conquest of Peru*. Paris, 1847. 2 vols.

228. Priestly, H. I. *The Mexican Nation: A History*. New York, 1923.

229. Pritchard, W. T. *Polynesian Reminiscences*. London, 1866.

230. Quatrefages, A. De. *The Pygmies*. New York, 1895.

231. Radin, P. "Ethnographical Notes on the Ojibwa of Southeastern Ontario." *AA*, n.s., Vol. XXVI. 1924.

232. —— "Ethnological Notes on the Ojibwa of Southeastern Ontario." *AA*, n.s., XXX. 1928.

233. Rasmussen, K. *The People of the Polar North*. London, 1908.

234. —— *Eskimo Folk-Tales*. London, 1921.

235. —— *Greenland by the Polar Sea*. London, 1921. Trans. by A. and R. Kenney.

236. Rattray, R. S. *Ashanti Proverbs*. Oxford, 1916.

237. —— *Ashanti*. Oxford, 1923.

238. —— *Religion and Art in Ashanti*. Oxford, 1927.

239. —— *Ashanti Law and Constitution*. Oxford, 1929.

240. Ratzel, F. *The History of Mankind*. London, 1897. 3 vols.

241. Ray, P. H. *Report of the International Polar Expedition to Point Barrow, Alaska*. Washington, 1885.

242. Reichard, G. A. "Social Life of the Navajo Indians." *CUCA*, Vol. VII. 1928.

243. Reid, A. P. "Religious Beliefs of the Ojibois or Saulteaux Indians." *JAI*, Vol. III. 1873–74.

244. Ricards, J. D. *The Catholic Church and the Kafirs*. London, 1879.

245. Riley, E. B. *Among the Papuan Head-Hunters*. London, 1925.

246. Rivers, W. H. R. "Toda Prayer." *FL*, Vol. XV. 1904.

247. —— *The Todas*. London, 1906.

248. —— *The History of Melanesian Society*. Cambridge, 1914. 2 vols.

249. Rodd, F. R. *People of the Veil*. London, 1926.

250. Ross, J. *A Voyage of Discovery*. London, 1819.

251. Roth, H. L. *The Aborigines of Tasmania*. London, 1890.

252. —— *The Natives of Sarawak and British North Borneo*. New York, 1896. 2 vols.

253. Roth, W. E. "An Inquiry into the Animism and Folk-Lore of the Guiana Indians." *ARBAE*, Vol. XXX. 1908–9.

254. —— "An Introductory Study of the Arts, Crafts, and Customs of the Guiana Indians." *ARBAE*, Vol. XXXVIII. 1916–17.

255. St. John, S. *Life in the Forests of the Far East*. London, 1862. 2 vols.

256. Sarasin, P., and F. *Die Weddas von Ceylon.* Wiesbaden, 1893.

257. Sarat, C. R. *The Mundas and Their Country.* Calcutta, 1912.

258. Sarmiento d Gamboa, P. *History of the Incas.* Ser. 2, Vol. XXII. Cambridge, 1907.

259. Sauer, M. *An Account of a Geographical and Astronomical Expedition to the Northern Parts of Russia.* London, 1802.

260. Saville, M. H. "The Goldsmith's Art in Ancient Mexico." *INM*, Vol. IV. 1920.

261. ———— "Tizoc, Great Lord of the Aztecs." *CMAI*, Vol. VII. 1929.

262. Schebesta, P. R. *Among the Forest Dwarfs of Malaya.* London, 1926.

263. Scheffer, J. *The History of Lapland.* London, 1704.

264. Schmidt, M. *Die Aruaken.* Leipzig, 1917.

265. Schulze, L. "The Aborigines of the Upper and Middle Finke River." *TPRSSA*, Vol. XIV. 1891.

266. Schuyler, E. *Turkistan.* London, 1876. 2 vols.

267. Seaver, J. E. *Life of Mary Jemison.* New York, 1886.

268. Seligmann, C. G. *Melanesians of British New Guinea.* Cambridge, 1910.

269. Seligmann, C. G., and B. Z. *The Veddas.* Cambridge, 1911.

270. Shooter, J. *The Kaffirs of Natal and the Zulu Country.* London, 1857.

271. Sieroshevski, W. *The Yakut.* St. Petersburg, 1896.

272. Sieroshevski, W. "The Yakuts." *JAI*, XXXI. 1901. Abridged and trans. by W. G. Sumner.

273. Silas, E. *A Primitive Arcadia.* London, 1926.

274. Simmons, L. W. "Statistical Correlations in the Science of Society." In *Studies in the Science of Society.* New Haven, 1937. Ed. by G. P. Murdock.

275. Simmons, L. W., ed. *Sun Chief: The Autobiography of a Hopi Indian.* New Haven, 1942

276. Simson, A. "Notes on the Jivaros and Canelos Indians." *JAI*, Vol. IX. 1880.

277. Skeat, W. W., and Blagden, C. O. *Pagan Races of the Malay Peninsula.* London, 1906. 2 vols.

278. Skinner, A. "Notes on the Eastern Cree and Northern Saulteaux." *APAM*, Vol. IX. 1912.

279. ———— "Medicine Ceremony of the Menomini, Iowa and Wahpeton Dakota, with Notes on the Ceremony among the Ponca, Bungi Ojibwa, and Potawatomi Indians." *INM*, Vol. IV. 1920.

280. —— "Material Culture of the Menomini." *INM*, n.s., Vol. XX. 1921.
281. Smith, E. A. "Myths of the Iroquois." *ARBAE*, Vol. II. 1883.
282. Smith, E. R. *The Araucanians*. New York, 1855.
283. Smyth, R. B. *The Aborigines of Victoria*, Vol. II. London, 1878.
284. Speck, F. G. "The Creek Indians of Taskigi Town." *MAAA*, Vol. II. 1907–15.
285. —— "Myths and Folk-Lore of the Timiskaming Algonquin and the Timagami Ojibwa." MCDM, Vol. LXXI. 1915.
286. —— "Ethnology of the Yuchi Indians." *UPMAP*, Vol. I. 1919.
287. Spence, L. *The Myths of Mexico and Peru*. London, 1914.
288. Spencer, B., and Gillen, F. J. *Native Tribes of Central Australia*, London, 1899.
289. —— *The Arunta*, Vol. I. London, 1927.
290. Spencer, H. *Descriptive Sociology*. London, 1872–96. 8 vols.
291. —— *The Principles of Sociology* (Revised ed.) New York, 1923. 3 vols.
292. Stair, J. B. *Old Samoa*. London, 1897.
293. Steensby, H. P. "Contributions to the Ethnology and Anthropogeography of the Polar Eskimo." *Meddelelser om Gronland*, Vol. XXXIV. Kjobenhavn, 1910.
294. Stephen, A. M. "The Navajo." *AA*, Vol. VI. 1893.
295. —— "Hopi Journal of Alexander Stephen." *CUCA*, Vol. XXXIII. 1936. 2 vols. Ed. by E. C. Parsons.
296. Stevenson, J. "Ceremonial of Hasjelti Dailjis and Mythical Sand Paintings of Navajo Indians. *ARBAE*, Vol. VIII. 1889.
297. Stites, S. H. *Economics of the Iroquois*. Lancaster, 1904.
298. Sumner, W. G. *Folkways. A Study of the Sociological Importance of Usages, Manners, Customs, Mores and Morals*. Boston, 1906.
299. Sumner, W. G., and Keller, A. G. *The Science of Society*. New Haven, 1927. 4 vols.
300. Swanton, J. R. "Haida Texts and Myths." *BBAE*, Vol. XXIX. 1905.
301. —— "Contributions of the Ethnology of the Haida." *MAMNH*, Vol. VIII. 1909.
302. —— "Religious Beliefs and Medical Practices of the Creek Indians." *ARBAE*, Vol. XLII. 1925.
303. Swanton, J. R. "Social Organization and Social Usages of the Indians of the Creek Confederacy." *ARBAE*, Vol. XLII. 1925.

304. Tanner, J. *Thirty Years among the Indians.* New York, 1830.
305. Tate, H. R. "Notes on the Kikuyu and Kamba Tribes of British East Africa." *JAI*, Vol. XXXIV. 1904.
306. Taylor, B. *Northern Travel.* New York, 1865.
307. Theal, G. M. *Kaffir Folk-Lore.* London, 1882.
308. Thurston, E. *Anthropology of the Todas and Kotas of the Nilgiri Hills.* Madras Government Museum, Vol. I, Bulletin, No. 4. 1896.
309. ———— *Ethnographic Notes in Southern India.* Madras, 1906.
310. ———— *Castes and Tribes of Southern India*, Vol. VII. Madras, 1909.
311. ———— *Omens and Superstititions in Southern India.* London, 1912.
312. Titiev, M. "Notes on Hopi Witchcraft." *Papers of the Michigan Academy of Science, Arts, and Letters*, Vol. XXVIII. 1943.
313. Tregear, C. *The Maori Race.* New Zealand, 1904.
314. Trilles, R. P. H. *Le Totemisme Chez Les Fâns.* Münster, 1912.
315. Turner, G. *Samoa. A Hundred Years Ago and Long Before, Together with Notes on the Cults and Customs of Twenty-three Other Islands in the Pacific.* London, 1884.
316. Turner, L. M. "Ethnology of the Ungava District, Hudson Bay Territory." *ARBAE*, Vol. XI. 1894.
317. Tyler, E. B. *Primitive Culture; Researches into the Development of Mythology, Philosophy, Religion, Language, Art, and Custom.* London, 1903.
318. Ubach, E., and Rachow, E. *Sitte und Recht in Nordafrika.* Berlin, 1923.
319. Up de Graff, F. W. *Head-Hunters of the Amazon.* London, 1923.
320. Vámbéry, A. *Sketches of Central Asia.* Philadelphia, 1868.
321. Vanden-Bergh, L. S. *On the Trail of the Pigmies.* New York, 1921.
322. Voth, H. R. "The Oraibi Powamu Ceremony." *FMAS*, Vol. III. 1901.
323. ———— "The Oraibi Oaquol Ceremony." *FMAS*, Vol. VI. 1903.
324. Weeks, J. H. "Notes on Some of the Customs of the Lower Congo People." *FL*, Vol. XIX. 1908.
325. ———— "The Congo Medicine-Man and His Black and White Magic," Vol. XXI. 1910.
326. ———— *Congo Life and Folk-Lore.* London, 1911.
327. ———— *Among the Primitive Bakongo.* London, 1914.
328. Westermann, D. *The Shilluk People.* Philadelphia, 1912.

329. Westermarck, E. *The Origin and Development of the Moral Ideas*. London, 1906. 2 vols.

330. ———— *Ritual and Belief in Morocco*. London, 1926. 2 vols.

331. Whiffen, T. *The Northwest Amazons*. London, 1915.

332. ———— "A Short Account of the Indians of the Issa–Japura District." *FL*, Vol. XXIV. 1923.

333. Williams, M. W. *Social Scandinavia in the Viking Age*. New York, 1920.

334. Williamson, R. W. *The Mafulu Mountain People of British New Guinea*. London, 1912.

335. ———— *The Social and Political Systems of Central Polynesia*. Cambridge, 1924. 3 vols.

336. Woods, J. D. *Native Tribes of South Australia*. Adelaide, 1879.

INDEX OF SUBJECTS

INDEX OF TRIBES

INDEX OF AUTHORS